1

from the Period of *Thus Spoke Zarathustra*

(Spring 1884–Winter 1884/85)

Volume Fifteen

Based on the edition by
Giorgio Colli & Mazzino Montinari
First organized in English by Ernst Behler

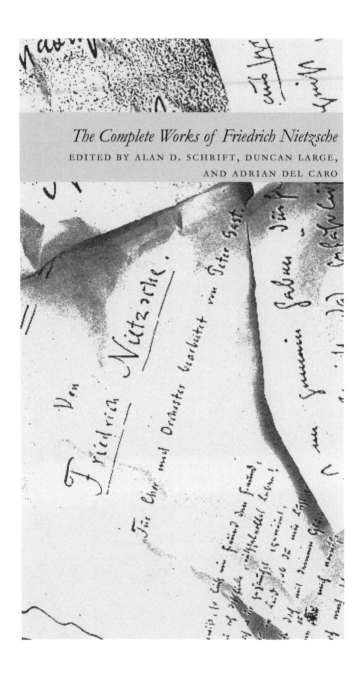

The Complete Works of Friedrich Nietzsche

EDITED BY ALAN D. SCHRIFT, DUNCAN LARGE,

AND ADRIAN DEL CARO

Friedrich Nietzsche

Unpublished Fragments
from the Period of *Thus Spoke Zarathustra*
(Spring 1884–Winter 1884/85)

*Translated, with an Afterword,
by Paul S. Loeb and David F. Tinsley*

STANFORD UNIVERSITY PRESS

STANFORD, CALIFORNIA

Stanford University Press
Stanford, California

Translated from Friedrich Nietzsche, *Sämtliche Werke: Kritische Studienausgabe*, ed. Giorgio Colli and Mazzino Montinari, in 15 vols. This book corresponds to Vol. 11, pp. 9–422, and Vol. 14, pp. 698–723.

Critical edition of Friedrich Nietzsche's *Sämtliche Werke* and unpublished writings based on the original manuscripts.

Printed and bound by CPI Group (UK) Ltd, Croydon, CR0 4YY

CIP data appears at the end of the book.

Contents

viii

Reference Matter

A Note
on This Edition

This is the first English translation of all of Nietzsche's writings, including his unpublished fragments, with annotation, afterwords concerning the individual texts, and indexes, in nineteen volumes. The aim of this collaborative work is to produce a critical edition for scholarly use. Volume 1 also includes an introduction to the entire edition, and Volume 19 will include a detailed chronology of Nietzsche's life. While the goal is to establish a readable text in contemporary English, the translation follows the original as closely as possible. All texts have been translated anew by a group of scholars, and particular attention has been given to maintaining a consistent terminology throughout the volumes. The translation is based on *Friedrich Nietzsche: Sämtliche Werke. Kritische Studienausgabe in 15 Bänden* (1980), edited by Giorgio Colli and Mazzino Montinari. The still-progressing *Nietzsche Werke: Kritische Gesamtausgabe,* which Colli and Montinari began in 1963, has also been consulted. The Colli-Montinari edition is of particular importance for the unpublished fragments, comprising more than half of Nietzsche's writings and published there for the first time in their entirety. Besides listing textual variants, the annotation to this English edition provides succinct information on the text and identifies events, names (except those in the Index of Persons), titles, quotes, and biographical facts of Nietzsche's own life. The notes are numbered in the text and are keyed by phrase. The Afterword presents the main facts about the origin of the text, the stages of its composition, and the main events of its reception. The Index of Persons includes mythological figures and lists the dates of birth and death as well as prominent personal characteristics. Since the first three volumes appeared, important corrections to the 1980 edition of the *Kritische Studienausgabe* have been noted, and these corrections have been incorporated into the translation that appears here.

ERNST BEHLER AND ALAN D. SCHRIFT

Unpublished Fragments
from the Period of *Thus Spoke Zarathustra*
(Spring 1884–Winter 1884/85)

Preliminary Note to Volume 15

Volumes 14 and 15 of the *Complete Works of Friedrich Nietzsche* {Volume 10 and part of Volume 11 of the *KSA*} together comprise Nietzsche's unpublished fragments from July 1882 to Winter 1884/85, which correspond to Part VII of the *KGW*. The fragments are preserved in twenty-seven manuscripts, specifically in fifteen notebooks in larger format, ten notebooks, and two loose-leaf binders.

The organizing principles that govern the publication of Nietzsche's unpublished fragments are set forth in the Preliminary Note to *CW* 10.

In addition, the following comments concerning Volumes 14 and 15 of the *CW* should be noted: The manuscripts from the period July 1882 to Autumn 1885 include: preliminary work on the four parts of *Thus Spoke Zarathustra*; drafts, outlines, and fragments that have to do with parts of this work that were not included; extensive collections of sayings that in many cases relate to work on *Zarathustra*; notes that — in literary terms — have no relation to *Zarathustra*; the latter make up approximately half of the complete material, and they were published as a small part of the notebooks related to *Beyond Good and Evil* [and included in *CW* 16]. All these notes are being published as *Zarathustra*-fragment literary remains, which precede the actual early drafts and final clean copies of each part of *Zarathustra*. Yet since Nietzsche, each time after completing a part of *Zarathustra*, recopied a large number of the previous notes that he hadn't used into new notebooks, often without changing a thing, it was impossible to avoid the repetition of certain notes — although in differing contexts.

Volume 15 of the *CW* corresponds to Volume VII/2 and part of Volume VII/3 of the *KGW* (Berlin/New York: Walter de Gruyter, 1974) and thus contains the fragments from Spring 1884 to Winter 1884/85. It also includes Giorgio Colli's Afterword in *KSA* 11 as it relates to the notebooks in this volume.

Mazzino Montinari {revised by Alan D. Schrift}

Editorial Note to Volume 15

Unless another volume in the *CW* is cited, all cross-references to fragments in the notes are references to fragments in this volume. In cases where the format of a fragment in this volume differs significantly from the format of the fragment as it appears in *KSA*, we have chosen to follow as closely as possible the format of the fragment as it appears in Nietzsche's handwritten notebooks.

Alan D. Schrift

25 [1][1]

Eternal Recurrence.

A Prophecy.

By
Friedrich Nietzsche.

First Major Part:
"**It is time**!"

25 [2][2]

(Nice, March 1884.)

My next tasks:

Morality for Moralists.

Self-Redemption.

Eternal Recurrence.
   Dionysian Dances and Festival Songs.

25 [3][3]
   "Paradise is under the shadow of swords."[4] Orient⟨al⟩

25 [4][5]

"The eagles swoop down as we speak"[6] Olof Haraldsson's Saga.

25 [5][7]

"Whoever follows too closely on the heels of truth is in danger of having his head bashed in." English proverb

25 [6][8]

Eternal Recurrence
A Prophecy.

First Major Part.
"It is time!"

Second Major Part.
The Great Noon.

Third Major Part.
Those Who Make Vows.

25 [7]

I.

My friends, I am the teacher of eternal recurrence.

That is: I teach that all things eternally recur and you yourselves along with them — and that you have already been here innumerable times and all things with you; I teach that there is a great long colossal year of becoming that, when it has run its course, run out, will be turned over again and again like an hourglass: so that all these years are identical to each other, in what is smallest and in what is greatest.

And I would say to someone who is dying: "Look, you are dying and passing away now and disappearing: and there is nothing that remains of you as a 'you,' for souls are just as mortal as bodies. But this same powerful array of causes that created you this time will return and will have to create you again: you yourself, tiny speck of dust, are among the causes upon which the return of *all* things depends. And when you are born again someday, then it will not be to a new life or to a better life or to a similar life, but rather to an identical and selfsame life, like the one you are now bringing to an end, in what is smallest and in what is greatest."

This doctrine has never before been taught on earth: that is, on this particular earth and in this particular[9] great year.

* * *

2.
"Dans le véritable amour c'est l'âme, qui enveloppe le corps."[10]

25 [8]

Those who were young in our time have experienced too much: assuming that they are among the few who are still profound enough for "experiences." For such depth is now missing in almost all people and the proper stomach as well: they are therefore unfamiliar even with the need to have the proper stomach for "consuming" every experience, the greatest innovations pass through them untouched. Others such as ourselves had to swallow too many heavy, different, over-seasoned meals when we were young: and even if we have the advantage over the people of simpler times, of enjoying strange and completely unfamiliar dishes, we also are familiar with real digestion, with experiencing things, taking them in, with ingesting almost exclusively as *torment.*

25 [9][11]

My friends, we had it tough when we were young; we suffered from youth itself as if it were a serious illness. This shapes the time we were thrown into, — a time of great and ever worsening decline and disintegration, which in all its weaknesses and even in its greatest strengths works against the youthful spirit. Disintegration, thus uncertainty, defines our time: nothing rests on firm footing and on true faith alone: we live for tomorrow, because the day after tomorrow is in doubt. Everything

on the path we take is slippery and dangerous, and at the same
time the ice that still supports us has become so thin: we all feel
the warm uncanny breath of the wind that thaws — *where* we
still walk, soon no one *will be able* to walk there.

I have lived alone and wrapped myself carefully and tightly
in the cloak of solitude: this is part of my cleverness. Now a lot
of ingenuity is necessary even in order to survive, to keep our
heads *above water*.[12] Each time I have tried to cope with the
present *in* the present, each time I have approached the people
and goals of today, it has not gone well for me up to now; and
I have been astounded at the hidden wisdom of my nature,
which during all such attempts immediately calls me back to
myself by means of sickness and pain.

It goes without saying that I am familiar with everything
they call the suffering of a genius: not being recognized, being
neglected, every kind of superficiality, coming under suspicion;
I know how many people believe they are doing us a favor when
they seek to bring us into "more comfortable" situations, among
orderly, *more reliable* people; I have admired the unwitting
destructive drive that all mediocrity sets in motion against us, and
indeed believing sincerely that it has the right to do it. In several
all too amazing cases I have found myself uncomfortable with my
familiar comfort: this is — as the French say — *la bêtise humaine*[13]
— ultimately, I was always more amused than frustrated by this.
It is part of the grand folly, the sight of which keeps us superior
humans holding on to life. And if my eyes don't deceive me: then
there is a hundred times more stupidity in *all* human actions than
people believe. But at the same time, the sight of *hypocrisy* in all
good stolid decent people, the profound subtle self-confident
hypocrisy to which they themselves are completely oblivious, is,
for those who can see it, a thing of delight: and, in contrast to
the *bêtise humaine*, their unwitting *cunning* is also delightful here.

25 [10]

To use the passions the way engines use steam. Self-
overcoming.

25 [11]¹⁴

When I was a boy I was a pessimist, as ridiculous as that
sounds: a few lines of music from when I was twelve or thirteen
are basically the only raven-black music that I know, the black-
est and most resolute. Up to now I have found no thoughts and
words of philosophers or poets which had so obviously emerged
out of the abyss of ultimate denial in which I myself have occasionally sat; and, even regarding Schopenhauer, I could not
free myself from the belief that he may indeed have been well
disposed toward p⟨essimism⟩, yet he might have had even a
stronger inclination against it: which he did not give enough
voice to, thanks to that stupid superstition about geniuses that
he had learned from the Romantics, and thanks to his vanity,
which forced him to stay put with a philosophy which came
from the year he turned 26 and which also *is common to people
of that age* — as we know all too well,¹⁵ right, my friends?

25 [12]

How widespread the feeling of insecurity is: reveals itself
most clearly in the delight in small certain *facts* (a kind of *"fait-
alisme"*¹⁶ that now rules over France) — a kind of insanity that
never existed on earth before: and not only science but also a
large part of contemporary art arises out of *this* need. It is often
disguised: e.g., in the demand for the impersonality of artists
— the work itself should betray nothing of them, but rather
like a faithful mirror should reproduce, *determine* some fact as
minutely as possible: but this need for such facts that remain
fixed, to be pinned down like butterflies by collectors — is
itself something very personal. We take the opposite pleasure
in fairy tales and fantasy by people who themselves feel pinned
down by customs and judgments. — This is accompanied by
a crude grasping for the nearest **pleasure**: "whatever is nearest"
becomes what is most important.

25 [13]

We have been granted perspectives in all directions, broader
than any humans have ever been granted, everywhere we look
there is no end in sight. That's why we have a feeling of enormous anticipation — but also of enormous *emptiness*: and the
ingenuity of all superior people in this century consists of getting beyond this terrible *feeling of desolation*. The opposite of
this feeling is *intoxication*: where it is as if the whole world were
pressing in upon us and we suffer from the happiness of overabundance. That is why this age is at its most inventive when
inventing means of intoxication. We are all familiar with intoxication, in the form of music, an enthusiasm that is blindly self-
blinding and in the worship of individual people and events,
we are familiar with the intoxication of the tragic, th⟨is⟩ is cruelty in observing a downfall, especially when that which is most
noble perishes: we are familiar with the more modest forms of
intoxication, mindless work, self-sacrifice as a tool of a science
or as a tool of political or money-making factions; some small
stupid fanaticism, some unavoidable reversal of course within
the smallest circles can have intoxicating power. There is even a
certain modesty that becomes eccentric, which allows the feeling of emptiness itself to be perceived sensually again: yes an
enjoyment of the infinite emptiness of all things, a mysticism
of faith in nothingness and a self-sacrifice for this faith. And
what an eye we developed, as ones who know, for all of the
small pleasures of knowing! How we take note of, and record
the value of, our *small* pleasures, so that, as if by *adding up* the
many small pleasures we could achieve a counterweight to that
emptiness, a filling of that emptiness —: how we deceive ourselves with this artifice of addition!

25 [14]¹⁷

There are people who are convinced by sublime gestures but
made mistrustful by reasoned arguments.

25 [15]

I never take animosities seriously for too long. In the moment, perhaps, especially under the influence of cloudy skies, I could easily kill anyone — already, I have often been amazed that I haven't done so yet. But I start laughing again too soon for an enemy to have to make a lot of amends to me. Besides, I am fundamentally convinced that I owe much more to my feelings that grow out of hostility than to those that grow out of friendship.

25 [16][18]

European pessimism is still in its infancy: it does not yet have that monstrous yearning fixated gaze in which the void is reflected, as was once the case in India, in this European pessimism there is still too much that has already been done and not enough that "has become," too much scholarly and poetic pessimism: I think a good portion of it has been invented and elaborated, it is "created," but it is not a *cause*, having been made and not "become."

There have been more thoughtful and overanalyzed times than ours: times, for example, like those when the Buddha appeared, where the people itself, after centuries of ancient sectarian strife, had eventually lost its way so far into the chasms of philosophical debates, much like European peoples for a time lost their way in the subtleties of religious dogma. We are not very likely to be led astray by "literature" and the press into thinking very highly of the "spirit" of our time: the proof of all this lies in the millions of spiritualists and in a Christendom that has horrifically ugly gymnastics of the kind that characterizes all English inventions, a gymnastics that provides a better overview — testimony against itself.

25 [17]

When Greece's best times were over, the moral philosophers arrived: for all Greek philosophers from Socrates onward are first, and in the most profound sense, moral philosophers. This means: they seek happiness — too bad they had to seek it! Philosophy: this is from Socrates onward that highest form of cleverness that does not choose wrongly in matters of personal happiness. Did they really get a lot out of it? When I think that Plato's god is without desire and pain and that the greatest sage becomes more and more like his god: then this is a personal judgment: Plato perceived complete indifference to be his greatest benefaction: he was rarely enough the beneficiary of it! Aristotle thought of his god as pure knowing lacking any feeling of love: and he himself probably had his best moments when he coldly and clearly (and joyfully) enjoyed the sensual sham of the highest generalities. To perceive the world as a system and this as the pinnacle of human happiness: how the schematic mind betrays itself then! And Epicurus: what did he enjoy, then, other than the *end* of pain? — this is the happiness of someone who suffers and who is probably also sick.

25 [18][19]

Imprisoned criminals sleep well; no pangs of conscience. Mendacity. We see nervous fits "break out"[20] among women (screaming ranting cursing, breaking everything into little pieces)[21]

25 [19][22]

Many half-wild people (skilled *healthy* hunters fishers, with many illegitimate children) become criminals in a civilized society, especially because they have no work and fall into bad company. It is primarily their children that band together; associating with people of a criminal *type*. Rapid degeneration.

25 [20]

I often feel "compassion" where there is no suffering at all, instead where I see waste and the failure to advance as reasons for *what might have been*. So e.g., in regard to Luther. How much power, and how it is wasted on these kinds of problems!

25 [21]

I could write an entire chapter about the *multitude of characters* hidden within each one of us: and attempts should be made to allow some of them to appear, i.e., to *favor* a *coherent group* of characteristics for a while, through shrewdly chosen circumstances, environments, studies, decisions, so that they take control of all available powers. Other characteristics will not be nourished in the process, or only a little, and will fall behind: we can allow *these* to surface at some later point.

25 [22]

An entire chapter "critique of parents, teachers, fatherland, homeland" — as the beginning of liberation, of initial doubts.

25 [23]

"On the force of the will," the means to strengthen it and to weaken it.

25 [24]

"Concerning the Squandering of our Passions" and how we easily accustom ourselves to a *meager* way of satisfying them.

Asceticism as a means of *concentrating* and *damming up* our inclinations.

Balzac and Stendhal recommend chastity for all productive people.

In regard to what productive people re⟨quire⟩ first and foremost in order not to suffer from worms of the intellect — to lay eggs, to cluck and to brood on them with grace *in in⟨finitum⟩*,[23] to speak in images

25 [25]

Michelet says this about Genoa's climate: *"admirable pour tremper les forts." Gênes est bien la patrie des âpres génies nés pour dompter l'océan et dominer les tempêtes. Sur mer, sur terre que d'hommes aventureux et de sage audace!*[24]

25 [26]

Balzac about W. Scott. 1838 after a 12-year acquaintance-
ship: Kenilworth the masterpiece in regard to *plot* ("the greatest, most complete, the most extraordinary of all"): *les eaux
de St. Ronan* the masterpiece and major work *comme détail et
patience du fini. Les Chroniques de la Canongate comme sentiment. Ivanhoe (le premier volume s'entend) comme chef-d'œuvre
historique. L'Antiquaire comme poésie. La prison d'Edimbourg,
comme intérêt.* — *"Auprès de lui, lord Byron n'est rien ou presque
rien."* — *"Scott grandira encore, quand Byron sera oublié."* —
*"Le cerveau de Byron n'a jamais eu d'autre empreinte que celle de
sa personnalité, tandis que le monde entier a posé devant le génie
créateur de Scott et s'y est miré pour ainsi dire."*[25]

25 [27]

*"Je comprends, comment la continence absolue de Pascal et
ses immenses travaux l'ont amené à voir sans cesse un abîme à ses
côté⟨s⟩"* —[26]

25 [28]

Notice biographique sur Louis Lambert "a work in which I
wanted to struggle with Goethe and Byron, with *Faust* and
Manfred." *"Il jettera peut-être, un jour ou l'autre, la science dans
des voies nouvelles."*[27]

25 [29]

About Stendhal *"un des esprits les plus remarquables de ce
temps."*[28] "He did not pay enough attention to *form*," "he writes
the way that birds sing" *"notre langue est une sorte de madame
Honesta,*[29] *qui ne trouve rien de bien que ce qui est irréprochable,
ciselé, léché."*[30] *La Chartreuse de Parme* a wonderful book, *"le
livre des esprits distingués."*[31]

25 [30]

*"je n'ai pas de continuité dans le vouloir. Je fais des plans, je
conçois des livres et, quand il faut exécuter, tout s'échappe."*[32]

25 [31]

In regard to the *Chartr⟨euse⟩* "I would not be capable of creating it. *Je fais une fresque et vous avez fait des statues italiennes.*" "Everything is original and new." As beautiful as *l'italien*, and if Machiavelli were to write a novel in our time, it would be the *Chartreuse*. "Perfectly clear." "*Vous avez expliqué l'âme de l'Italie.*"[33]

25 [32]

To read Custine's novel *Ethel*. They are more literature *idée* than *littérature imagée*:[34] thus of 18th-century observation *à la Chamfort et à l'esprit de Rivarol par la petite phrase coupée.*[35]

Scribe knows his craft, but he doesn't know art. He has talent, but no dramatic genius; style is completely absent![36]

25 [33][37]

Solitude, fasting and sexual abstinence — typical mode in which religious neurosis arises. The most extreme sensual pleasure alternates with the most extreme piety. Strange observation directed against *themselves*: as if they were glass or two people.

25 [34]

Balzac "Profound contempt for all of the masses." "There are vocations which must be obeyed: something irresistible draws me to fame and power." 1832.[38]

"*mes deux seuls et immenses désirs, être célèbre et être aimé.*"[39]

25 [35]

If we wanted *to be healthy*, we would abolish genius. Likewise, religious people. If we wanted morality, **the same**: abolition of genius.

Sickness.
Crime.
Vice.   } and their cultural mission.
Lies.

25 [36]⁴⁰

An endless amount of work must be done before we can
even think of acting. But in the main our best and most advisable activity is probably *to exploit* any given situation *shrewdly*.
To actually *create* such conditions, the way coincidence does,
presupposes people *of such mettle* as have not yet existed. For
now, *accomplish* and *realize* your personal ideals!

Anyone who has **comprehended** human nature, *the emer-*
gence of its highest qualities, shudders at humans and flees all
action: consequence of inherited value judgments!!

That human nature is *evil*, is my consolation: it is a guaran-
tee of *force*!

25 [37]⁴¹

Misunderstanding predators: *very healthy* like Cesare Borgia!
The qualities of hunting dogs.

25 [38]

The decline of *intellect* in this century. The cozy manner⁴² of
English scholars. Machiavelli has the clarity of antiquity. The
French *esprit* is a kind of *rococo* of the intellect — but even so
a *véritable goût*!⁴³

Goethe boring and "undulating."

English scholars pay homage to journalistic genius and its
profound mediocrity.

25 [39]

Relation of mediocrity to virtue — Aristotle found the *fatal*
situation pleasant!

25 [40]

Plato — what is not Greek about him, contempt for the
body, for beauty, etc. It is proto-medieval — Jesuitism of edu-
cation⁴⁴ and despotism. He is characterized by his "indifferent"
god —: he is even embarrassed by pleasure and displeasure.
Apparently he fasted and lived frugally.

25 [41]

I found the circumstances of my youth to be aptly
described in de Custine, *mémoires et voyages*.[45] He was 18
years old (1811)

je n'aspire qu'à des affections puissantes et sérieuses p. 25.

25 [42][46]

"*Ce n'est pas par vanité, que le génie veut des encouragements,
c'est par modestie, par défiance de lui-même.*" De Custine.

25 [43][47]

"*L'homme de génie pressent, l'homme de talent raconte: mais
nul ne se sent et n'exprime dans le même moment. Le vrai malheu-
reux ne peut que se taire: son silence est l'effet et la preuve même de
son infortune.*" De Custine.

25 [44][48]

"*Tant d'intérêts à ménager, tant de mensonges à écouter avec cet
air de dupe, première condition de la politesse sociale, fatiguent
mon esprit sans l'occuper.*" De Custine.

25 [45][49]

Madame de Lambert said to her son "*mon ami, ne vous per-
mettez jamais que les folies, qui vous feront grand plaisir.*"

"*un crime, quand on y est poussé par une puissance qui vous
paraît irrésistible, trouble moins la conscience qu'une faiblesse
volontaire et vaniteuse.*" De Custine.

25 [46]

Madame de Boufflers: "*il n'y a de parfaits que les gens, qu'on
ne connaît pas.*"[50]

25 [47][51]

It is precisely the liveliness of his imagination that explains
why it is difficult for him to act. He has reached such a high
level of thought that, for him, the life of the mind and the life

of action are separated by an abyss. *Il* (Werner) *est l'Allemagne personnifiée.*[52] (1811)

25 [48][53]

"Born into an age whose masterpiece is *René*[54] — I must rid myself of the tyranny that he imposes upon me against my will": De Custine 1811. Chateaubriand's influence.

25 [49][55]

"A restless intellect is as insatiable as vice." De Custine.

25 [50][56]

The disadvantage of the traveler (of the cosmopolitan of the *scholar*, too) *well described* in De Custine, I p. 332–3. Robbed of approval and of surveillance, he seeks support in contempt for others. His superficial studies show him that which is on the surface: mistakes and ridiculous things. If he grows old, he becomes incapable of allowing profound inclinations to germinate.

25 [51][57]

Classical antiquity contained just a small enough dose of Christianity to be of benefit to the blossoming of the arts. But Catholicism was a barbaric coarsening of this: a Church Father made from a Plato![58]

25 [52]

"*noblesse tragique, cette dignité, égalité de style, nos gestes peu naturels, notre chant ampoulé*"[59] — appearing in England as affectation. The French find English theater to be ignoble.[60]

"In Shakespeare a sense of the true prevails over a sense ⟨of the⟩ beautiful. His style, occasionally sublime, is *subordinate to* his point of view,[61] he rarely frees himself from the errors of his century: *les concetti, la recherche, la trivialité, l'abondance des paroles.*"[62,63]

25 [53][64]

The attractive force of terrible (annihilating) things: the giddiness of throwing ourselves into the abysses of the future —

25 [54][65]

quelque philosophe morose finira peut-être par oser dire de la liberté moderne, qu'elle consiste dans la double faculté de mentir aux autres et de se mentir à soi-même (1822).

25 [55][66]

About Walter Scott: he {Custine} tends to see the work of a "*Décorateur*[67] rather than that of a painter." He paints what any glance would reveal: the analysis of feelings *échappe à cette plume, qui n'est jamais qu'un pinceau.*[68] — His poetry is not *l'expression immédiate de ce qui se passe dans son âme,*[69] he is unable to shed this affectation, because *il ne prend pas lui-même assez de part à ce qu'il dit.*[70] "*Semblance* of truth." We would wish for sublime gestures, where the soul reveals itself with a single word. — He is the *Rossini de la littérature*[71] — he *does not* use *enough taste* in his selection of the details that are the most remarkable. His images lack perspective — *too many* objects in the foreground, *parce qu'il ne sait pas prendre un parti pour la lumière.*[72] It is a parade of events — not a *plot*, for which the artist provides all observers with the only proper *point de vue.*[73] In place of genius, an instinct for histor⟨y⟩. Through his talent for creating illusions he becomes the most popular author *des temps peu consciencieux où nous vivons.*[74] His legacy a revolution: he solved the problem of the *histor⟨ical⟩ novel* better than anyone before him. "*pour avoir su ramener, si ⟨ce⟩ n'est le sentiment, au moins la mode du vrai dans le siècle du faux.*"[75]

25 [56][76]

"Reason behaves like all slaves: it despises peace-loving lords and serves a tyrant. In the middle of a battle with powerful emotions it leaves us in the lurch; it defends us only against small affections."

25 [57][77]

On modern slavery De Custine II p. 291.

25 [58][78]

Concerning Sunday-sanctification: *on a rendu le délassement si pénible, qu'il fait aimer la fatigue*[79] - - - "they return to their homes, finding complete happiness in the thought that work is starting again tomorrow"

25 [59][80]

The great English actors like *Kean* have the utmost simplicity of gesture and a rare talent for authentically imitating the most violent affects at their highest level.

Kean displayed simplicity even in declamation: in contrast to *Kemble's* School, who had introduced *un chant ampoulé très peu favorable aux grands effets tragiques.*[81]

"To catch nature in the act, in conditions where it is most difficult to observe" — his talent.

25 [60][82]

"French theatergoers feel their hearts turn to stone if *too obvious* an attempt is made *to move them.* They love to *complete* the ideas of authors: in England, people *are afraid of* having to *fill in the blanks*"[83]

25 [61][84]

"Poetry as a kind of reaction of an ideal *contre le positif*:[85] the *more* pressure the soul is put under, the more force it needs in its *élan vers l'idéal.*[86] The revolutionary spirit essentially unpoetic: for poetry wants to *avenge* itself on reality, in addition it needs a solid foundation to fight *against.* The conservative spirit is in this sense helpful for the development of genius: the imagination soars upward from there: poetry and faith are merely the premonition of a *better world.*" C⟨ustine⟩. An explanation of Byron's presence in a nation of accountants.

25 [62][87]

"The inherent *pedantry* of the English carries everything to *extremes*: the love of order turns into *minutie*; *le goût pour l'élégance puérilité*[88] ("childishness"), the need for convenience turns into egoism, pride into prejudice against our neighbors, activism into rivalry etc.

25 [63][89]

Le comfort inside, *la "fashion* outside — the deadly enemies of happiness and peace for the English. The *need for fashion* is merely the need to be *envied* or *admired*."

25 [64][90]

The curse that condemns people to labor is written all over his face. "*Les Anglais sont des galériens opulens.*"[91]

25 [65][92]

No taste: the result of keen intelligence that is tied to a petty *esprit* and stubbornly resists innovation. *L'esprit de détail, l'attention aux petites choses produit le soin, mais*[93] "neither greatness nor beauty *dans les arts.*"[94]

25 [66][95]

L'esprit frondeur[96] included as an element in the constitution — this leads to a paradox. "*We do not value things for what they really are, but rather according to how they relate to the ruling power.*"

25 [67][97]

Enlightened peoples are *worse* judges of people and things: the cause of this is their *présumption*.[98]

25 [68][99]

"Over there, opinions change radically and quickly *par pur esprit de parti*.[100] To say that black is white because you hate a ministry is more dangerous to morality than a *soumission*[101] taken too far.

When taken too far, obedience allows us to relinquish our rights: *l'esprit de révolte*[102] allows us to sacrifice our duties."

25 [69][103]

"Regular habits, novelistic sentiments."

25 [70]

NB. *Slavish* sensibility gaining the upper hand in Europe: the great slave-revolt. (ego)

Slaves in government.

Mistrust of all *noblesse* of feeling, domination by the crudest needs. Moral mendacity.

A slave's misunderstanding of culture and what is beautiful. Fashion, the press, *suffrage universel*, *faits*[104] — they are constantly inventing new forms of slavish needs.

Lower humans revolt e.g., Luther against the *sancti*[105]

subjugation to the facts, as science of slaves.

25 [71]

The *dumbing-down* and homogenization of Europe on the rise.

Ever-increasing enmity of the progeny of the nobility toward *l'homme supérieur*.[106]

the moralistic culture of the Spanish and the French in the context of Jesuitism. This is misunderstood.

The lack of any moral practices: feelings instead of principles.

25 [72][107]

"*il souffre, il succombe au lieu de combattre et de vaincre*.[108] What's the point of opposing a passion with a feeling!! *l'attaque et la défense viendraient de la même source*!"[109] If the enemy is in the heart, then authority, habit, then obedience, abasement, rules, discipline, laws, practices, themselves seemingly *puériles*,[110] then someone other than ourselves, a priest, a confessor whose voice reduces ours to silence: this is necessary in order to save us from ourselves." C⟨ustine⟩. "Once we become *insane*, it is not enough for us to have *dreamt* of being Christian philosophers in order to avoid killing ourselves: as is the case with the majority of Protestants who think."

25 [73]

What we really need then: *a kind of educator and rescuer*, also places of refuge outside the everyday world, a hard life, many ascetic innovations for the purpose of self-control. Protection from slavish baseness and Phariseeism.

25 [74]

Pinnacles of *honesty*: Machiavelli, Jesuitism, Montaigne, La Rochefoucauld

the Germans as relapse into moral mendacity

25 [75][111]

"Base natures are mistaken about noble ones: they do not discern their motives."!

25 [76][112]

"The ability to forget ourselves, devotion, sacrifice — all the benefit of such rare gifts is lost to those who do not know how to make themselves loved when they love. These passionate souls then become *ungrateful*: they gain an advantage from being civilized in order to then defame being civilized. Where else can they live except in the woods and not in the world!"

25 [77][113]

"Where in our world are the more perfectly realized characters? The way virtue is depicted in mor⟨al⟩ books has falsified all minds, hardened all the hearts that can be moved in only one way."

*"il ne faudra pas moins d'une ère toute entière de cynisme lit-
téraire, pour nous débarrasser des habitudes d'hypocrisie."*[114]

25 [78][115]

"Glory to the strong one whom our age praises as the head
of the romantic school — Victor Hugo" 1835.

25 [79][116]

"l'amour exalté de la vérité est la misanthropie des bons cœurs"

25 [80][117]

We have transitioned from the age of religious hypocrisy
into the age of moral hypocrisy. "One of the good deeds of
représent⟨atif⟩ gouvernem⟨ent⟩ is precisely this, to force ambitious people to don the mask of morality and humanity. But
why then get so upset at the priesthood, who, as long as they
ruled, supported civilization with very similar methods? —
priests shouldn't be criticized for their ambition, but rather *be
encouraged without being enabled.* They are mistaken about
the age they live in: that's why they do harm.

There *exists* no good and evil whatsoever in the world: these
are always *à part.* The superhuman virtues are *insociables* and
it's the same with great crimes. But stunted and "advanced"
minds exist in all societies. They have the same passion: but
stunted minds make use of words that the world already knows
are empty in order to deceive themselves about their personal
motives: and "advanced" minds, for the same purpose, speak a
language that still *deceives* the masses: the masses do not have
the key to these words.

This is the difference between mediocre people and superior
minds: the latter fundamentally understand the language of the
age they live in: the former recognize the lies *only* in the language of their grandparents. We have already been enlightened
concerning "eternal salvation" "hell" "paradise" *charité*; our
grandchildren will be enlightened concerning philanthropy,
liberté, privilégés, being *progrès.*

"The reformers of one epoch are the conservators of another. The same *génie* can be seen *comme créateur ou comme radoteur*."[118]

25 [81][119]
"What is true is never probable."

25 [82]
"*Luxe*[120] should only be allowed in places where the poor are in good spirits":[121] it corrupts those who envy it.

25 [83]
" — *les apôtres modernes, les auteurs philosophes, mentent plus que les prêtres qu'ils ont détrônés sans les remplacer*."[122]

25 [84]
It is the age of *mendacity*: moral goodness is being proclaimed. There is resistance to La Rochefoucauld and Christianity —: the great slave revolt.

To be determined: humans are evil — they are the most terrible predators, in terms of deception and cruelty.

To be determined: *that humans are* still *evil is a reason for hope*. For good humans are caricatures who arouse disgust: they are always a harbinger of the end.

25 [85]
Increasing stupidity, even in science. The unqualified admiration of Darwin. The timidity in politics etc.

25 [86][123]
Tendencies in tragedy according to Schopenhauer II 495. "What gives everything tragic the characteristic impetus to sublimity, is the dawning of the recognition that the world, that life, cannot give true satisfaction, and is therefore not worth attachment to it: this is the spirit of tragedy: and this is why it leads to *resignation*." — Oh how differently Dionysus speaks to *me*! — Schopenhauer: "this is due to the fact that the

ancients had not yet achieved the pinnacle and aim of tragedy, or indeed of a view of life in general."

25 [87]

Great poets have *many* people inside them: some have only *one*, but a *great one*! —

25 [88]
Fear — mark of the slave.
Expending as little intellect as
possible (imitation)
Indifference and hatred toward
what is rare.   } Age of mendacity
Ugliness. The hodgepodge of styles.
The burgeoning need for lies —
epidemic.

25 [89]

The essence of the artist and of the genius: the actor. No one is able to express something and feel something at the same time; speeches and reality. Profound *égoisme* buried under the language of *sensibilité*.

25 [90][124]

"Lack of finesse in choosing a means to success, misuse of invective, hatred of what is there, indifference to what will be — what French writers of the last 100 years have in common (1835) Preaching the return to primitive life with a quill, from which they expect fame and happiness in social circles — is ungrateful and childish."

25 [91][125]

"*L'effet ordinaire du désespoir est de rendre l'énergie à ceux, qui sont témoins de cette maladie morale*"

25 [92][126]

"women[127] less and less civilized than men: wild in the depths of their souls; they live in the state like cats in a house, always ready to jump out of the nearest door or window and to return to their element"

25 [93]

What is moral, i.e., the affects — as identical with what is organic the intellect as "stomach of the affects."

25 [94]

The *conqueror, lawgiver* and *artist* are essentially *identical* — injecting *themselves* into the material, supreme force of will, in earlier times feeling like the "instrument of God," appearing to themselves as so irresistible. Highest form of reproductive drive and *simultaneously* of maternal forces. **Reshaping the world** *so that they are able to survive in it* — is what drives them: consequently, as prerequisite for a tremendous feeling of *contradiction.* For artists, it is enough to surround themselves with *pictures* and likenesses of the contradiction, e.g., Homer among the "pitiful mortals."[128] "To be freed of interest and ego" is nonsense and an imprecise observation: instead, it is rapture that they feel, we are now in *our* world, freed from any fear of what is foreign!

25 [95][129]

I have superimposed knowledge upon such horrific images that any "Epicurean delight" is impossible. Only Dionysian pleasure *suffices* — **I have only just now discovered the tragic.** It was misunderstood by the Greeks, thanks to their superficiality in matters of morality. *Not even* resignation is a tenet of tragedy! — but rather a misunderstanding of it! Longing for nothingness is a *denial* of tragic wisdom, its opposite!

25 [96]

My presuppositions: 1) no final "causes." Even in the case of human actions, the intention *in no way* explains the act of doing something.

2) the "intention" does not concern the essence of the action, *therefore* the *moral* judgment of actions, as based on intentions, is **false**.

3) "Soul"[130] as a multitude of affects, with a single intellect, with uncertain boundaries.

4) the mechanical explanation of the world has to explain everything, even organic life *without* pleasure displeasure thought etc.: thus no "ensouled atoms"! — it attempts to make everything that happens *visible to the eye*. It wants "predictability" for practical purposes! —

5) There are no selfless actions at all!

25 [97]

Through Christianity and Buddhism, the question concerning our "well-being" has become **more profound**: the nonsensical Englishisms, *by contrast*, are idiotically mundane: the English mean "comfort." Not to measure the world according to the most personal feelings we have as we do this, but rather *as if* it were a play and we *were taking part in it*!

25 [98][131]

"In the age of public *liberté*: French people today become ponderous and dumb and cold when they are *en public*: out of fear of making enemies, they become skilled diplomats and sophisticated hypocrites. Without *esprit*, without judgment, and clever because they are afraid. *Slavery of the individual.*" C⟨ustine⟩.

25 [99]

To conduct studies with large herds of animals:

The increasing greatness of human beings consists in the fact that the leaders, the "lead bulls," the rare ones emerge. The members of the herd call themselves "good": the principal motive for the emergence of good people is fear. Compatibility, outdoing others in doing good, conformity, fending off and preventing many things out of necessity, with the unspoken expectation that we will be equally compensated, avoiding enmity, *refusing to instill fear* — all this, **for a long time a hypocritical kind of goodness, finally becomes goodness.**

25 [100]

In my view, all praise, blame, reward punishment does not seem justified until it appears as the *will of a creative force*: therefore *absolutely* detached from the moral question *"am* I *allowed* to praise punish?" — *thus completely immoral.* I praise blame reward punish *so that* people will transform themselves in my image for I *know* **that** my praising punishing etc. has a transformative force. (This by virtue of the effect on vanity ambition fear and all the affects within the person praised and punished.) *As long as* I *subject* myself to the moral law, *I am not allowed to praise and punish.*

25 [101]

On the Means of Beautification. An absurdity for which old Kant is to blame: "it pleases without interest." And many still proudly refer to this when contemplating a Greek Venus etc. In contrast, I have described the state that the beautiful evokes: yet the most essential aspects of this state can only proceed from the artist. To make the contemplation of things tolerable, not to fear those things, and to impart to them a semblance of happiness — basic feeling that happy people who love themselves are *not the kind of people who inflict pain.* — This reinterpretation of what is factual into what is happy "divine" has now also been applied by people to themselves: *thi⟨s⟩ means of self-beautification* and of the beautification of people in general is *morality.* It involves: 1) Looking the other way 2) Seeing what is not there at all — summarizing simplifying 3) dissembling in such a way that many things do not become visible 4) dissembling in such a way that what becomes visible yields a false conclusion. — The end product is the "good person," always as part of a society. There is therefore something essential in morality that works *against* honesty: because morality is *a kind of art*. How then is it possible that there exists an honesty which causes morality itself to decompose — 1) This honesty must be derivable from a sense of the factual: namely that too much harm has resulted from this hypocrisy of beautification, those who are harmed rip their *masks off* 2) there is an enjoyment of ugliness when it is awful: the emotion that is felt at the awful sight of *true* human nature is often sought out by moralists 3) the Christian affect of self-destruction, the resistance to all attempts at beautification had its effect: the pleasure of cruelty. 4) the ancient slave-mentality, which wants to abase itself and finally abases itself before the naked "facts," after nothing else remains, deification of facts, of laws etc. a *resting* after the long work of destroying gods, whatever is aristocratic, prejudices etc., and as a result, a gaze into the *void*)

Summary conclusion of all moralists: *human beings are evil* — they are predators. The "improvement" never reaches a fundamental level and is more external, the "good" is essentially decoration,[132] or weakness.

Yet at the same time the moralists themselves stood under the influence of moral[133] judgments, or of Christianity, of world-denial: *There was no one left who took pleasure* in this conclusion. That is: they themselves have the value judgments of "good people"!

"Humans need to be beautified and made tolerable": Christianity and Buddh⟨ism⟩ oppose this, saying — we must *renounce* human beings. There is nothing more fundamentally *opposed* to this approach than *good people*: **they** are hated the most. This is why priests seek the self-destruction of pleasure itself by any means possible.

The Greek philosophers sought "*happiness*" in nothing but form, *finding* **themselves** *beautiful*: thus, to shape a statue out of themselves *whose appearance is pleasing* (arousing no fear and disgust)

The "ugliest person" as the ideal of world-denying modes of thought. But even religions are also still the result of that drive for beauty (or of the ability to endure it): the final consequence would be — to embrace the absolute ugliness of humans, existence without God, reason etc. — pure Buddhism. The uglier the better.[134]

I sought out this most extreme form of world-renunciation. "Everything is suffering," everything that appears to be "good" (happiness etc.) is a **lie**. And instead of saying "everything is suffering," I said: even in the best people, everything is about making people suffer, everything is about killing.

"Everything is illusion" — everything is lies

"Everything is suffering" — everything is about inflicting pain, killing, destroying, being unjust

Life itself is a principle that stands *in opposition* to "truth" and to "goodness" — ego

Affirming life — in itself this means affirming a lie. — Therefore it is only possible for us to live *when we have an absolutely immoral way of thinking*. If we adopt this way of thinking, we can put up with morality and with the *intention of beautifying things*. — But the innocence of lying is behind us!

The Greeks as actors. Their "idealism."

Just for once, to describe *Greek-ification* in the form of a novel. Looking backwards — even sensuality more and more intense, more and more extreme. Finally, to the point where the Dionysian is revealed. Discovery of the *tragic*: "billy goat[135] and god."

25 [102]

In what sense the strictly *scientific approach* still has something Christian attached to it, is a cloak — —

25 [103][136]

A) *First*: the decline of the modern soul in all its forms

in what sense the *decline* begins with Socrates —

my old *aversion* to **Plato**, as *antithesis of antiquity*.

the "modern soul" was already *there*!

B) to portray: the *increasing* hard-heartedness
                            strength of the senses
                            shamelessness.
                            the unhistorical
                            competition
                            feelings *against* barbarism
                            hatred of what is undetermined
                                unformed
                                of curvature
                            the simplicity of lifestyle.
                            creating gods, as their superior
                                society.

C) — — —

25 [104]

L'école du document humain[137] has followed the school of
romantisme[138] in France. The one who coined the phrase is
Edmond de Goncourt.

   scientific hysteria — is what I say.

   Consequence: the *scientific* delight humans take in *themselves.* —

   What is unscientific about it is the delight they take in
exceptional cases.

25 [105][139]

   It is essential to learn from wars: 1) to associate death more
closely with the interests being fought for — this makes *us*
respectable 2) it is essential to learn to sacrifice *many* and to
take the cause seriously enough not to spare people. 3) rigid
discipline, and to allow ourselves to be violent and cunning
in war.

25 [106]

   The perspectives of the Greek moralists: morality the result of
judgments (and of false judgments) — "why?" false question
and development, our *own* happiness as the goal of all actions (it

must be the *greatest* happiness as the consequence of the greatest insight — therefore full of *hypocrisy*) — shamelessness in the presentation of virtue (its deification in Plato) the denigration of all unconscious stimuli, the contempt for the affects —

unconsciously they all strive for that beautiful *pillar* — above all, they want to represent virtue, it is the great *performance hall for virtue.*

but they are children *of their* time — no longer *tragic* actors, *not* portrayers of heroism, but rather "Olympians," *superficial.* A lot of *plebeian* ambition and parvenu-ism[140] is involved. "Race" should be nothing: the individual is the starting point.

Ridiculous obsession with everything that is foreign — the Orient, quietism, the Semitic invention of "holiness," all have an effect.

Jealousy of the plastic arts

25 [107]

Ancient ethics includes the fundamental belief that humans are *going backwards*: that we are very far from happiness power virtue. It is the judgment of those who see *things falling apart* and who see salvation in everything becoming static.

Goal of all moralists *up to now*: to create a conclusive form, "*way of thinking*" — in China, in the Brahmin caste, in Peru, in Jesuitism, also Egypt; Plato wanted it, too. To create a caste whose *existence* is linked with the ossification of moral judgments, as *being advantageous to their lives* — the social class of good and just people.

25 [108][141]

"The French Revolution created a society, it is still seeking its *gouvernement.*" —

25 [109][142]

"1789: the people of 'good will,' of whom the Bible speaks,[143] seemed for the first time to be the lords of things on earth. A people, soft, trusting, having become accustomed for centuries

to suffering patiently and to expecting to be rescued from
their plight by their leaders: a middle class, rich, enlightened,
honnet;[144] a *noblesse*[145] who took pride in giving up their privileges, enraptured by philosoph⟨y⟩, glowing on behalf of the
public good; clerics infused with liberal ideas: a king ready to
annihilate the arbitrary exercise of power and to become the
restaurateur de la liberté française"[146] —

And why does everything go wrong? Because all of these
good people were *weak-willed*! *le roi trop défiant, trop faible*;[147]
the queen's *blind hatred* for the *révol⟨ution⟩*, the *noblesse* called
back to their old instincts by the danger to the throne, now see
it as a *mistake* and *comme une lâcheté ses concessions premières*[148]
(yes! this is how weaklings are!) *la maladresse janséniste*[149] makes
a disastrous attempt to organize the church through the state
and alienates the clergy: and all through the country and the
cities there was a deadly hatred for the feudal age which had
been growing for a long time (*now* even greater than the fear of
the "red spectre")[150]

25 [110][151]

Napoleon as belonging to another kind of species, in whom
the force of calculation, the power of combinations, the ability
to work, are inexpressibly further developed than in us, while a
vain search goes on for particular moral qualities usually found
in the rest of us: — "to whom notions of justice are foreign,
who had done little to comprehend history and his age, completely governed by personal interest and totally blind to that
interest; unable to differentiate between good and evil, *cette
soif impérieuse de succès*,[152] absolute indifference to the means,
everything that makes people into criminals —: in matters of
morality no better or worse than *the rest of us*. But what he
lacked the most, the most incredible *failing*: *la grandeur d'âme
(magnanimité)*[153] the noble characteristic that often has its *origin* in success itself and develops at the same pace as our happiness and that often lifts, bit by bit, natures that are vulgar
and devoid of all moral sense up to the *pinnacle* of events *à la*

hauteur de la destinée imprévue.[154] Certainly, a *great* ability for planning existed within him, if boundlessness may be called great (that which is out of proportion to the means that we employ here down below)

Greatness of the soul is *not*: that he, otherwise so heartless, was not indulgent at certain times, occasionally *bonhomie bien-veillante,*[155] which the multitudes always mistake for *bonté* in their lords: but *ces rares relâchements*[156] of a constantly tense spirit, *cette facilité intermittente d'un cœur indifférent.*[157]

He saw France, "this touching creature full of sublime instincts but having declined under the weight of its sufferings and mistakes," as his *prey* and nothing else. The first Consul was confronted with the greatest spectacle of all, he must have felt the deepest and *désinteressée émotion*[158] at this scene, which was unique in history: for Caesar was faced with an ancient and expiring republic. But he thought of *himself*!

esprit mal cultivé, imagination méridionale[159] — he sometimes took Caesar, sometimes Charlemagne as his model, *imbu surtout du féticisme monarchique, il rêve pourpre, trône et couronne pour les siens,*[160] almost like those barbarian chiefs who believed they were increasing their greatness by imitating the court of Constantinople.

25 [111]

To show *wherever*[161] there is cruelty: where there is greed: where there is imperiousness etc.

25 [112]

First question: the rulers of the earth — Anglo-Saxon. The German element a good catalyst, it doesn't understand how to rule. Rulers in Europe are German only because Europe is dealing with exhausted aging peoples, it is Germany's *barbarism*, its retarded simple-minded culture that provides the power.

French *foremost* in culture, sign of *Europe's decline*. Russia *must* come to rule Europe and Asia — it must *colonize* and *take possession of China* and India. Europe as Greece under Roman rule.

Thus, to view Europe as a center of culture: nationalist folly should not make us blind to the fact that *a continuing mutual dependence is already in existence in the more cultured regions.* France and German philosophy. R. Wagner of 1830–50 and Paris. Goethe and Greece. Everything is striving for a *synthesis of the European past within the most highly developed intellectual* **types** — — — — —

— a kind of **middle**, which *rejects* what is sick about every nation (e.g., the scientific hysteria of the Parisians).

Power is for now divided up between *Slavs* and *Anglo-Saxons.* The intellectual influence *could* be in the hands of *typical Europeans* (these comparable to the Athenians, also the Parisians — see Goncourt's description in *Renée Mauperin*)[162] Up to now the English have been dumb, the Americans are becoming superficial out of necessity (haste) — — — — —

But if Europe falls into the *hands* of the *rabble*, then European culture is *doomed*! Battle of the poor against the rich. Hence, it is a final flare-up. And *from time to time put aside what can be saved*! Take note of the countries to which **culture** can **withdraw** — because of a certain inaccessibility, e.g., Mexico. — — — — —

25 [113]

Slave-like morality
Master-like morality } and their opposing values

Cruelty
Lust
Imperiousness } and whatever there is of these in good people and in justice, compassion, truth-fulness, loyalty, industriousness etc.
Greed
Jealousy

Unhealthy virtues and virtuous people — and what is healthy about predators.
Relatively *little* awareness of the *effects* we have. (Intentions and aims as arbitrary selection of effects)

False presuppositions about our motivations (fundamental doubt:
   whether our conscious feelings and thoughts "move us")
The body as schoolmaster: morality sign language of the affects.
Damage done by good people: Good people as second rate,
   degeneration. Increasing stupidity, hatred of intellectual
   development.
Individual and community.
The "individual" as multiplicity and growth.
"Evil" as organic function. Compassion. *For* others to have.[163]
Religions as moralities that presuppose other worlds: but
   master-like or slave-like.

25 [114]

   To what extent our customary *order of values* amounts to
nothing but false presuppositions: origin of prevailing basic
valuations. NB!

25 [115][164]

   The Germans are, as *stragglers*, ruining the great advance of
European culture: e.g., Bismarck *Luther*; recently, when Napoleon wanted to bring Europe into an association of states (the
only person who was powerful enough to do it!), they bungled
everything with the "*wars of liberation*" and conjured up the
disaster of nationalistic insanity (resulting in racial conflicts in
traditionally diverse lands like Europe!) In this way Germans
(Charles Martel) stopped *Saracen* culture in its tracks —: it's
always the laggards!

25 [116]

   The existing world is a *poetic fiction* — there is only a
world in a state of becoming. — *This could be*! But doesn't a
poetic fiction presuppose the poet as *existing*? — Maybe the
world becoming a poetic fiction is what causes the poet *to
see himself as existing* and *as standing apart* — If the essence
of feeling and thinking is that they *must* produce errors
("realities"):

Feeling and thinking exist: yet how is this at all *possible* in a world that is in a state of becoming? — The *negative* characteristics superficiality dulling of the senses slow-wittedness have transformed themselves into *positive* forces (*here, too, evil is the origin of good.*)

to *produce* an image, to *complete* it based on a few clues, to produce something that *en⟨d⟩ures* because we don't *see* it changing.

The ability to live is enhanced by this *poetic* power.

25 [117]

How the most powerful people present themselves has always been regarded as "impersonal" (J. Burckhardt with *good* instincts in front of the palazzo Pitti):[165] "*Powerful person*" — the same as with Phidias — looking past individual charms. — But these gentlemen would like best to hide themselves and be free of themselves e.g., *Flaubert* (Letters)[166]

25 [118]

We must be good *and* evil! And anyone who, because of weakness, was not good, was also always incredibly evil.

25 [119]

To judge people by intentions! That would be like classifying artists, not according to their paintings, but according to their visions! Who has not killed his mother or betrayed his friend, when it comes to thoughts! It would be a life of curious isolation if thoughts could kill!

25 [120]

We have within us the *outlines* of **many** people: poets reveal themselves in their characters. Circumstances bring a single character to the forefront: should circumstances change a lot, we also see two, three characters. — Every moment of our lives still has many possible outcomes: coincidence *always* plays a part! — And especially in history: the destinies of *every* people are not determined by any one kind of reasoning: *many things characteristic of different peoples* are found in *every* people, and every event nourishes one characteristic more than the other

25 [121]
Tame Barbarism
Europe's authentic *barbarism* — and increasingly:

an increasing stupidity ("the Englishman" established as the model of a normal person)

a growing ugliness ("Japanisme") (the plebeian in revolt)

an increase in slavish virtues and their values ("the Chinese")

art as a neurotic condition in artists, means of insanity: taking pleasure in the factual (loss of the ideal)

the Germans as *stragglers* (in the politics of the centralization of the monarchy, like Richelieu: in philosophy with Kant *skepticism* (for the benefit of the sorry cult of the gentleman and of bureaucratic virtue), with Hegel *pantheism* for the benefit of worshipping the state, with Schopenhauer *pessimism* for the benefit of Christian mysticism ("Pascalism"),

the poor nutrition of all of southern Europe. England's better society is *gaining advantage* through nutrition.

"the good person" as a herd-animal, evolved from predators,

the historically significant illness as an absence of the power to shape ideals — "justice" remains and superficially "harmless."

It is the *tame barbarism* that is on the rise!

higher status of imbeciles, of women etc.

25 [122]
People want to *demand* the attention of readers "to force it on them": hence the many gripping little characteristics of "*naturalisme*" — this is what a democratic age involves: intellects that are **crude** and exhausted by overwork are supposed to be *stimulated*!

25 [123][167]

I can barely endure the vulgarity of Shakespeare and Balzac:[168] a smell of rabble-sensibility, a stench of city sewers invades my nostrils from every direction.

25 [124]

I want to re-create women again: that woman Sand and M⟨adame⟩ de Staël are proof *against* them. (Sévigné and Eliot should be more than women writers and they certainly were — partly *makeshift*) I damn them to *commerce*: a *commis*[169] should be held in contempt!

25 [125]

Painters like Dickens, V. Hugo, Gautier — this, too, means misunderstanding words.

The opposite of a painter is a *describer* (like Balzac)

25 [126]

(*Taine*[170] about Balzac:)

"Virtue as a reshaping or a stage of development in a passion or a habit": *l'orgueil, la raideur d'esprit, la niaiserie obéissante, la vanité, le préjugé, le calcul.*[171] Vices serve to build these (like a perfume from *substances infectes*[172]) *That people* love the poor in the same way that gamblers love the game: others are as loyal as dogs. A person made righteous through taking pride in commerce, provincial in intellect and education. All the puny *misères*, the great ugliness of the virtuous person. The purest source of virtue: *la grandeur d'âme*[173] (M⟨arcus⟩ Aurelius) and *la délicatesse d'âme*[174] (P⟨rincesse⟩ de Clèves)[175]

25 [127]

Earlier, we sought God's intentions in history: then an unconscious purposefulness, e.g., in the history of a people, a configuration of ideas, etc. Only *recently* are we starting to create a sense for the history of humanity, by considering a history of animals: and the first insight is that no plan has

⟨existed⟩ up to now, either for humans or for a people. The most outrageous coincidences have been the most dominant — they still are.

In *every action, no matter how consciously purposeful,* the sum of coincidental non-purposeful factors, whose purpose we're not conscious of, outweighs everything else completely, like excess heat and light emitted from the sun: what *might* be meaningful is vanishingly small.

25 [128]

"Useful" is a perspective that works only in proximity: the *distant* consequences can't all be examined, and *every* action can be classified as equally useful or harmful.

25 [129]

1. *All* value judgments up to now have emerged in conditions of the most profound *ignorance.*

2. The most different moralities imaginable are jumbled together in current valuations.

25 [130]

Rousseau, in his preferential treatment of the poor, of women, of the people as sovereign, is part and parcel of the *Christian movement*: all slave-like errors and virtues can be studied in him, also the most unbelievable mendacity. (*Someone like this* wants to teach justice!)

His counterpart *Napoleon* — belonging to classical antiquity, misanthrope

25 [131]

Anyone who, up to now, has dealt with h⟨umans⟩ on a grand scale, has classified them according to basic traits: there is no point in considering the more subtle nuances. That's how Napoleon did it. *Christian virtues* were not important to him, he treated them as if *they weren't there* (— he had a right to do so)

25 [132]

This century, where the arts understand that one of them can also influence the others: *may be ruining the arts*! e.g., to *paint* with poetry (Victor Hugo, Balzac, W. Scott etc.

to arouse *poetic* feelings with *music* (Wagner)

to arouse poetic feelings, yes even *philosophical* conjectures, with painting (Cornelius)

to do anatomy and psychotherapy[176] with novels etc.

25 [133][177]

"*ce talent* (philosophy of history) *ne consistait pas, à l'allemande, dans l'improvisation risquée de théories sublimes*" Taine

25 [134]

Principle:	1) *Profound contempt for those working in the press.*
the **conquest** *of humanity*:	2) Creating a species of beings that *replaces* priests teachers and doctors.
"*the rulers of the earth*":	3) An aristocracy in body and mind that propagates itself and continually absorbs new elements into itself and sets ⟨itself⟩ apart from the democratic world of failures and half-failures.

25 [135]

In this age where the *advent* of science is acknowledged, building *systems* is child's play. Instead, to make long-term decisions about methods, for the coming centuries! — because one day we **must** take *the direction of humanity's future* into our hands!

—yet *methods* that emerge on their own from our instincts, hence regulated habits that already exist

e.g., exclusion of purposes.

25 [136]
Depiction of the "Human" as Machine
Ch. I. The whole of human history has been absolutely ruled by coincidence: *but* the time is coming when we *must* have goals!!

Ch. II. goals are not yet there, the ideals contradict each other — they are consequences of much more intimate relationships and even born out of countless errors. Critique of values — morality performs an autopsy on itself.

Ch. III. Misunderstanding of *art* up to now: it looked *backwards*. But it is a force for building ideals — innermost hopes and desires becoming visible

25 [137][178]
I am writing for a species of humans which does not yet exist: for the "rulers of the earth."

Religions as giving solace, removing the harness is *dangerous*: then people believe that they are permitted to *rest*.

As Plato writes in his Theages:[179] "if possible, every one of us would like to be ruler of all people, most of all to be *God*." *This* mentality must be there again.

English, Americans and Russians — — — —

25 [138][180]
The great landscape painter Turner, who wants to speak to the soul and to the mind instead of the senses — philosophical and humanitarian genres. He considered himself to be first among people and died insane. "In the middle of a storm, the sun in his eyes, vertigo in his head" this is how the observer feels. "As a result of profound attention to *le moral de l'homme*, his optical *sensibilité* is *désaccordée*.[181] Uncomfortable for the eye! Exaggerated, brutal, it screams out, hard-hearted, dissonant." Taine

25 [139][182]
"Art wants to bring forth superior movements, sensual pleasure is merely the basis of the impression, but it must be accompanied by *joy* 1) feeling of love for the painted object

2) notion of the goodness of a superior intelligence 3) a soaring
sense of thankfulness for, and veneration of, this intelligence:
Ruskin friend of Turner's"

25 [140]

NB. To conceive of the most superior humans as images of
nature: enormous overflow, enormous reasoning power in the
individual case, squandering themselves as a whole, *indifferent*
to this squandering: — —

25 [141][183]

Ingres: l'inventeur au 19me siècle de la photographie en couleur
pour la reproduction des Pérugin et des Raphaël. Delacroix c'est
l'antipôle — image of décadence of this time, le gâchis, la confu-
sion, la littérature dans la peinture, la peinture dans la littérature,
la prose dans les vers, les vers dans la prose, les passions, les nerfs,
les faiblesses de notre temps, le tourment moderne. Des éclairs du
sublime dans tout cela.
     Delacroix a kind of Wagner.

25 [142][184]

M⟨anette⟩ Salomon I p. 197.
     Delacroix — he promised everything, proclaimed everything.
His pictures? *foetus*[185] of masterpieces; the human who *après tout,*[186]
will arouse the most passions *comme tout grand incomplet.*[187] A
delirious life in everything he created, *une agitation de lunettes, un*
dessin fou[188] — — he seeks *la boulette du sculpteur, le modelage de*
triangles qui n'est plus contour de la ligne d'un corps, mais l'expres-
sion, l'épaisseur du relief de sa forme — harmoniste désaccordé,[189]
tragic undertones, mists of hell as with Dante. There is no sun.
— A great master for our time but basically *la lie de Rubens.*[190]

25 [143][191]

The best thing that has been said against *marriage* from the
perspective of a *creative* person Man⟨ette⟩ Salomon I 200 sq.
and 312.

25 [144]¹⁹²

In 1840 *romantisme* enters into an alliance with *Litteratur*. *peintres poètes*.¹⁹³ Vague Dantesque symbolism in some. Others, with German instincts, seduced by *songs* from the other side of the Rhine, became dreamy, melancholic, Walpurgisnight. Ary Scheffer at their head paints white and luminous souls that are created through *poems*: angels. *Le sentimentalisme.* At the other extreme *un peintre de prose*,¹⁹⁴ Delaroche: adept theater-*arrangeur*, pupil of Walter Scott and Delavigne, with deceptive local color — but life *is lacking*. — Such painters are basically *sterile* personalities: they can't create any movement, any real school. — The *landscape* remained devalued: it had the ideas of the past against it. No one dared to confront modern life, no one showed the young and talented *ce grand côté dédaigné de l'art: la contemporanéité*.¹⁹⁵ — Caught in this fatigue and con-tempt for other genres, all young artists took sides with either *extreme* disposition — a much smaller number with Delacroix (*le beau expressive*¹⁹⁶ —), most with Ingres *comme sauveur du Beau de Raphaël*,¹⁹⁷ *Roman* school.

25 [145]¹⁹⁸

Return of humans to nature *naturelle*, in which ancient cul-tures *refresh* themselves. — Break with the historical landscape.

25 [146]

It is clear that we really do not want to let go of the advan-tages involved in not knowing much and in living in a tiny corner of the world. Humans *are allowed* to be fools — they are even allowed to feel themselves to be *God*, it is one possibility among so many!

25 [147]

I will be told that I am speaking of things that I have not experienced but only dreamt about: to which I could answer: it is a beautiful thing to dream *like that*! And our dreams are in the last analysis much more our experiences than we believe

— we must think differently about dreams! If I have dreamed of flying, a few thousand times — don't you think that, when awake, I will have a feeling and a need well *ahead of* most p⟨eople⟩ — and — — —

25 [148]

I had to pay tribute to Zarathustra, a *Persian*: Persians were the first to *conceive* the whole of history on a large scale. A sequence of developments, each one making way for[199] a prophet. Each prophet has his *hazar*, his thousand-year empire.[200] " — — —

25 [149][201]

The solidarity of the Jewish people as a basic concept: no thought of a distribution of goods based on individual merit. Renan I p. 54. No personal recognition *after* death: the principal motive of the martyrs is the pure love of the law, the advantage that their deaths will bring to the people.

25 [150][202]

Luke 6:25 a curse on those who *laugh* —

25 [151]

"Be good bankers!"[203] To give to the poor — this is a loan to God.

25 [152][204]

Europeans *reveal* themselves in their methods of *colonization* —

25 [153]

Jesus, with the melancholy of malnutrition.

25 [154][205]

"Beautiful" — *c'est une promesse de bonheur*. Stendhal. And this is supposed to be "unegoistical!" "*désintéressé*"!

What is beautiful here? Assuming that St⟨endhal⟩ is right, how so!

25 [155]

It is essential to be clear about *what interests* the most people: *yet what interests* **superior humans** seems **un***interesting* to the *inferior ones*, hence their dedication there to something "*un*egoistic"!

The vocabulary of modern morality is shaped by *inferior people* who lift their gazes from below up to morality above:

"making sacrifices" — but *anyone who* makes real sacrifices *knows* that they were not *sacrifices*!

anyone who loves, they already seem to be anti-egoistic! But the essence of the ego-feeling is definitely revealed only in the state of *wanting to have*, — something is given away *in order to* have (or to keep) something Those who give of themselves want to *keep* something they *love*.

25 [156][206]

Jesus: wants people to believe in *him* and he sends anyone that resists to hell. The poor, the stupid, the sick, women including whores and camp followers,[207] children — favored by him: he feels *good* when he is with them. The feeling of *passing judgment* on everything beautiful rich mighty, hatred of those who laugh. *Goodness*, along with its total opposite, in a single soul: of all human beings, he was the most evil. *Without* any psychological *moderation*. The insane *pride* which finds its most subtle *pleasure* in humility.

25 [157]

The most superior people suffer the most from existence — but they also have the greatest *power to resist*.

25 [158]

To prove the tremendously *coincidental* character of all combinations: it follows *from this* that *every* human action has an *unlimited huge* effect on everything to come. The same reverence that humans, looking backwards, grant to destiny in its entirety, they should grant to themselves *as well*. **Ego fatum**.[208]

25 [159]

To imagine complete pessimism (Schopenhauer *ruined* it?) Unknowability. — *depressing* to what degree? (only for a humankind that has been trained dogmatically!)

the thought of death: "fear of death" bred into them, "European disease" (medieval obsession with death)

the uselessness of all struggle — *depressing* if presuming moral principles i.e., if something is held up as a *measuring stick,* — it could also be a reason to laugh!

complete pessimism would be a pessimism that grasped the lie but at the same time is incapable of *casting off* its ideal: gap between wanting and knowing. Absolute contradiction — the human being a dividing line between two hostile forces who say only *No* to each other.

Desire absolutely inescapable but simultaneously *comprehended* and *evaluated* as stupid (i.e., a *second* opposing desire!)

thus, a *part* of pessimism is that it appears in broken, bipartite beings — it is a sign of *decline* — as a contemporary malady. The ideal does not have an invigorating effect but rather an inhibiting one.

25 [160]

Varying consequences of races *becoming extinct* e.g., pessimistic philosophy, weakness of will

sensuous exploitation of the moment, with hysterical spasms and an inclination to the terrible

sign of age can also be cleverness and avarice (China), *coldness.*

Europe under the influence of a mentality that is fearful because it was steeped in slavishness: an inferior species becomes *triumphant* — odd hostilities between two principles of morality.

25 [161][209]

"To treat friends like immortal gods

But all others like ciphers, not worthy of mention, nor of being counted."

25 [162]

Perhaps the Germans only ended up in the *wrong* climate!
There is something in them that could be *Hellenic* — this
awakens through contact with the *South* — Winckelmann
Goethe Mozart. Lastly: we are still very *young*. Our last major
event is still *Luther*, our only book is still the *Bible*. Germans
have never ever "moralized." The Germans' diet has also been
their downfall: rank philistinism

25 [163]

Characteristic of Europeans: contradiction between words
and deeds: Orientals are true to themselves in their daily lives.

How the fact that Europeans founded *colonies* demonstrates
their predatory nature.

The contradiction can be explained by the fact that Christianity *abandoned* the social stratum out of which it grew.

This is the difference between us and the Hellenistic peoples:
their ethics flourished within the *ruling* castes. Thucydides's
morality is the same one that explodes everywhere in Plato.

The first signs of honesty e.g., in the Renaissance: each time
to the benefit of the arts. M⟨ichel⟩ Angelo's concept of God as
"tyrant of the world" was honest.

The ascendancy of *women* is a consequence of this: and hence
a completely mendacious "modesty." Female depravity is (as in
Paris) almost what it takes for writers to become more honest.
— The slave-like character of morality as something encountered from outside, not created by us, continually engendering
new forms of similar slavishness e.g., the aesthetic (in regard
to antiquity) Depravity and weakness of character are almost
what it takes for Europeans to emancipate themselves from
authority and to acquire "taste."

Our ridiculous "taste for everything" is the consequence
of different moralities: we are immersed in the "disease of
historicity."

25 [164]

"*Wanting-to-be-objective*" e.g., in Flaubert is a modern mis-understanding. Great form that looks beyond any single stimulus is the expression of *great* character, which creates the world in its own image: someone who "looks beyond any single stimulus" — a person of power.[210] Yet for those in the modern age it is self-loathing, like Schopenhauer they would like to "lose themselves" in art — to flee into the object, to "deny" themselves. But there is no "thing in itself" — my dear gentlemen! What they achieve is a scientific approach or photography, i.e., description without perspective, a kind of Chinese painting, nothing but foreground and everything cluttered. — In fact, there is a lot of *displeasure* in all the rage felt by historians and natural historians of modernity — a flight from the self and from forming ideals, from making things *better*, through seeking to know how things have *gotten* this way: fatalism provides a certain peace in the face of this self-loathing.

The French novelists describe *exceptions* and indeed some of these are taken from the highest circles of society, some from the lowest — and the middle, the bourgeois, is *hated* equally by them all. In the last analysis, they can never rid themselves of Paris.

25 [165]

Negative character of "truth" — as elimination of an error, of an illusion. In fact, the emergence of illusion was an advancement of life — —

25 [166]

It is not at all advisable to search for necessities within history regarding ends and means! The irrationality of coincidence is the rule! The vast sum of major events represents the basic desires of a people, of a social class — this is true! With individual major events everything operates in a blind and stupid fashion. Like a leaf floating down a creek, even if it is held up here and there.

25 [167]

People in Thucydides speak with the maxims of Thucydides: according to his own design, they have the greatest possible degree of reason, in order to complete *their* projects. It was *here* that I discovered the Greeks (in some of Plato's words as well)

25 [168]²¹¹

Images first — to explain how images emerge in the mind. Then *words* applied to images. Finally, concepts, not possible until there are words — a summary of many images within something not visible, but rather audible (words) The little bit of emotion that emerges with "words," thus when seeing similar images for which there is one word — this weak emotion is the common element, the foundation for the concept. That weak feelings are registered as the same, are felt to be *one and the same*, is the basic fact. Thus, the confusion of two very similar feelings in the *formation* of these feelings — but *who* is doing the forming? *Belief* is already present in every sense impression going back to the very moment it begins: a kind of Yes-saying *first* intellectual activity! A "holding-something-to-be-true" at the beginning! Thus to explain: how a "holding-something-to-be-true" *emerged*! What kind of sensation *underlies* "true"?

25 [169]

"*Il n'a pas peur d'être de mauvais goût, lui.*"²¹² Stendhal.

25 [170]

From Homer to Pericles, women²¹³ in Greek culture *pushed* more and more *to the margins*: this is part of Greek culture — a certain kind of power exercised *against* soft mild feelings. A counter-movement bursting forth e.g., Pythagoras and the animals. Weaklings, suffering people, the poor — there are slave-revolts, poverty leads to extremes (Thucydides) *Otherwise* all great crimes are those committed by evil people who draw on their *strength*.

25 [171]

Fundamental *error*: we establish *our* moral feelings of today as the standard, and we measure progression and regression accordingly. But each of these steps backwards would be progress according to an opposite ideal.

"Humanizing" — is a word full of prejudice, and sounds to my ears almost the opposite of how it sounds to your ears.

25 [172]

For continual repetition — ∪ — ∪ etc. the rhythm of rhymed verse, *we* are musically too sophisticated (aside from misunderstood hexameter!) How beneficial the poetic form of Platen and Hölderlin has been to us already! But much too strict for us! Playing with the most diverse meters and occasionally unmetrical verse is the right thing: the freedom that we have achieved already in music through R⟨ichard⟩ W⟨agner⟩! we can certainly take this for our poetry! In the final analysis: it is the only kind of poetry that speaks strongly to our hearts! — Thanks to Luther!

25 [173]

The language of Luther and the poetic form of the Bible as the basis for a new German *poetry*: — this is *my* invention! Making things classical, the rhyme scheme — is all wrong and does not speak *profoundly* enough to us: not even Wagner's alliteration!

25 [174][214]

It is necessary for *superior humans* to declare war on the masses! What is mediocre is coming together everywhere in order make itself master! Everything that makes people effeminate, that makes them soft, that validates the "people" or the "feminine," works in favor of *suffrage universel*[215] i.e., of domination by *inferior* humans. But we want to practice oppression and to bring all of this rubbish[216] (which begins in Europe with Christianity) to light and to put it on trial.

25 [175]

Goethe's noble isolation — those who are most nobly born need a kind of fortress mentality and robber baron mentality. I want to take Napoleon's isolation for my own: in his contempt for "Christian values" and for all of moral hypocrisy, he belongs to antiquity (Thucydides). Perhaps Frederick the Great — but as a German, very much a person with hidden agendas and secret *personalities*.[217]

25 [176]

The *tartuffery of power* since Christianity has been victorious. The "Christian king" and "state." History of the feeling of power.

25 [177][218]

To judge the character of the *Europeans* by their relationship to foreign countries, during *colonization*: extremely cruel

25 [178][219]

Chivalry as a position of power that was carved out: its gradual destruction (and in part: transition into something wider, something bourgeois. In La Rochefoucauld there is an awareness of the actual driving forces behind the *noblesse*[220] of temperament — an awareness of the gloomy Christian appraisal of these driving forces.

Continuation of *Christianity* by means of the *French Revolution*. The seducer is Rousseau: he sets women free again, who are portrayed from then on as more and more interesting — *while suffering*. Then the slaves and M⟨istre⟩ss Stowe.[221] Then poor people and the workers. Then vicious and sick people — all this is foregrounded (for 500 years they have known no better way to help geniuses flourish than to portray them as great sufferers!) Then comes the cursing of sensuality (Baudelaire and Schopenhauer), the most decisive conviction that imperiousness is the greatest vice, completely secure in the idea that morality and *désintéressement*[222] are identical concepts, ⟨that the⟩ "happiness of all" ⟨would be⟩ a goal worth pursuing (i.e., Christ's heavenly kingdom). We are well on the way: the heavenly kingdom of the poor in spirit has begun.

Intermediate steps: the bourgeoisie (parvenus as products of money) and workers (as products of the machine)

Comparison of Greek with French culture at the time of Louis XIV. Firm belief in himself. A class of idlers who make things hard for themselves and practice a lot of self-overcoming. The power of form, will, to form *themselves*. Having confessed to having "happiness" as goal. Much force and energy *behind* the beings which have been formed. Pleasure in the appearance of a life *that seems so easy*. — The *Greeks* looked like **children** to the Eg⟨yptians⟩.

25 [179]

Humans, as organic beings, have drives to nourish (greediness)

NB | Here, keeping an eye only on the inner world! | drives to organize (love) (to which regeneration also belongs)

and in service to the drives a self-regulating apparatus (intellect) (to which there belongs assimilation of nourishment, of events, of hatred etc.

25 [180]

My concept of "self-sacrifice." I don't like this hypocrisy! Of course I discard a lot in order to accomplish what truly matters to me: some things, too, that "also truly matter to" me! But the main thing is always: discarding things in this way is only a *result*, a side effect — the main thing is, that something truly matters to me more than *anything* else.

25 [181]

The abundance of *vulgar* instincts underlying the current *aesthetic* judgment of French novelists. — And in the
final analysis: there is much that is hidden that they do not
want to say out loud just as with R⟨ichard⟩ W⟨agner⟩ 1) their
method is *easier*, more comfortable, the scientific manner of
a mass of material and of news reporting, a din of great principles is necessary in order to conceal this fact — but their
students figure it out, the lesser talents 2) the lack of discipline and of beautiful inner harmony makes similar things
interesting to them, they are curious with the help of their
base instincts, they lack disgust and aegis[223] 3) their demand
for the impersonal is a feeling that their person is *mesquin*[224]
e.g., Flaubert, sick and tired of himself, as "bourgeois" 4) they
want to earn a lot and to cause scandals as the means to a
great *momentary* success.

25 [182]

The psychology of these gentlemen like Flaubert is in summa
a false one: all they ever see are the superficial workings of the
world and the formation of the ego (just like Taine?) — they
are acquainted only with weaknesses of the will, where *désir*
stands in place of the will.

25 [183]

Someday I want to show how Schopenhauer's misunderstanding of the *will* is a "sign of the times" — it is a reaction
against the age of Napoleon, people don't *believe* in heroes any
more i.e., in strength of will. (We see this revealed in *Stello*:[225]
"there are no heroes and monsters" — anti-Napoleonic)

25 [184][226]

Painting in place of logic, a single observation, a plan, too
much weight given to the foreground, to a thousand details —
everything smacks of the needs of anxious people, in R⟨ichard⟩
W⟨agner⟩ just as in the Goncourts.

R⟨ichard⟩ W⟨agner⟩ is part of the French movement: heroes and monsters, extreme passion and nothing but details in the process, a momentary *shudder*.

25 [185]

(*Psychology*)

§ To relearn about "inner" and "outer."

§ "Being" unprovable, because there is no "being." The concept of being is formed out of the opposition to "nothingness."

§ Concepts emerge as acoustic images that sum up a multitude of symbolic visual images.

§ Affects as a counterpart to physiological groupings that have a kind of unity of becoming, a periodic decrease

§ The intellect as a middle ground of the senses, which processes impressions with the help of old materials, a kind of stomach of all the affects (that want to be nourished.)

§ Will? The actual process of all feeling and cognition is an explosion of force: under certain conditions (most extreme intensity, so that a feeling of pleasure emerges along with force and freedom) we call this process "willing."

§ "Purpose" as a vague image, insufficient for moving anything.

§ The mutual influence of thoughts (in what is logical) is evident — it is a struggle of the affects.

§ A squandering of force is the essential feature, even in the most intentional actions.

§ Cause and effect — this entire chain is a *selection* from beginning to end, a kind of translation of what happens into the language of our memories that we think we *understand*.

25 [186]

The sight of great gestures as causes of great actions — consequence of Corneille and Racine.

25 [187]²²⁷

In misunderstanding Mohammed, Voltaire is part of the movement *against* superior natures; Napoleon was right to be upset.

25 [188]

Napoleon: Religion as the bulwark of good morality, true principles, good morals. *Et puis l'inquiétude de l'homme est telle, qu'il lui faut ce vague et ce merveilleux qu'elle lui présente.*²²⁸ It is better for him to look for it there than among con men or Cagliostros.

25 [189]

The Sermon on the Mount: *il se disait ravi, extasié de la pureté, du sublime et de la beauté d'une telle morale.*²²⁹

25 [190]

"*J'ai refermé le gouffre anarchique et débrouillé le chaos. J'ai dessouillé la révolution, ennobli les peuples et raffermi les rois. J'ai excité toutes les émulations, récompensé tous les mérites et reculé les limites de la gloire. Tout cela est bien quelque chose!*"²³⁰

25 [191]²³¹

Explaining how Mohammed succeeded in 13 years: "maybe there were extensive civil wars beforehand (Napoleon thinks) *in which great character, great talents, irresistible impulses etc. had been formed —*"

25 [192]

The "first cause" is, like "the thing in itself," not a riddle but rather a contradiction.

25 [193]

The disadvantages of growing more isolated, since, at best, social instincts are inherited — the impossibility of validating ourselves through the approval of others, the icy feeling, the scream "love me" — *cas pathologiques*²³² like Jesus. Heinrich von Kleist and Goethe (Käthchen von Heilbronn)²³³

25 [194]²³⁴

Andrea Doria — *One thing* truly matters to him, for which he sacrifices *everything*. Betrayer of his friends, friend of his enemies. Completely isolated and icy disposition. A dog. Cruel to his nephews.

25 [195]

Idealists — e.g., shivering in wonder at the measure, the order, the tremendous type of system and simplicity in the heavens, keeping things at a distance, looking beyond the particularities. Realists want the opposite kind of shivering, that of infinite multiplicity: that's why they clutter up the foreground, they enjoy a faith in the superabundance of creative forces, the impossibility of counting them all.

25 [196]

Multitude of characteristics and what ties them together — *my* point of view. The twin, dual forces e.g., in Wagner, poetry and music; in the French, poetry and painting; in Plato, poetry and dialectic etc. The isolation of one force is a *barbarism* — "inverted cripples."²³⁵

25 [197]

The previous century's pitiful appreciation of nature. Voltaire Ferney. Caserta. Rousseau Clarens!

25 [198]

Superior natures have committed all crimes:²³⁶ it's just that they are not so bestially obvious. But betrayal, desertion, killing, denial, etc.

25 [199]

Very great people keep their mouths shut concerning their innermost selves — no possibility of meeting anyone to whom they revealed themselves — Napoleon e.g., opaque —

25 [200][237]

How the aristocratic world prunes away its own young shoots more and more and makes itself weaker! Its noble instinct allows it to throw away its privileges and its refined super-culture allows it to take an interest in the people, the weak, the poor, the poetry of puny people, etc.

25 [201]

Standards must be restored so that it is impossible for a stupid woman to lay claim to a superior moral position.

25 [202]

Opposites like male and female copulating to breed a third something — genesis of the works of a genius!

25 [203]

Misunderstanding of *gloria*, thought to be a motive of those who create!! *Vanité* is herd-instinct, *pride* is something for lead-oxen.

25 [204]

"*l'amour*, according to Napoleon, *l'occupation de l'homme oisif, la distraction du guerrier, l'écueil du souverain.*"[238]

25 [205]

Character of the French: always *les Gaulois d'autrefois: la légèreté, la même inconstance et surtout la même vanité.*[239] When will we finally be able to trade them in for a little *pride*!

25 [206][240]

"People are *not* ungrateful: but benefactors almost always expect too much."

They say people change, just as much when they do good as when they do evil.

They think that almost all actions are not character-driven, but rather are spontaneous actions which prove nothing about character.

25 [207]

Good deeds that are done for us are more troubling than any misfortune: it is the desire to exercise power over us. — Doing good should be a basic right. The Greek sensibility, which took seriously the "*ability* to reciprocate," was noble.

25 [208]

The unfortunate thing about the great hypocrisy of *all* ancient moral philosophers. They trained the human imagination to distinguish between virtue and power. Power appears as *entitlement to happiness* — **this** is what remains of antiquity, echo of the aristocratic essence. Even so, from Socrates onward, ἀρετή[241] is *mis*understood, — first it had to reestablish itself over and over and yet it did not want to do this on an individual basis! but rather tyrannically "good for *all*!" Attempt to found small states within the state: as is the case now with the Muslims of North Africa.

25 [209]

I haven't met any gifted persons who would not have told me that they had lost a sense of duty or that they had never possessed it.[242] Anyone who does not now have a strong will —

25 [210][243]

Cultivating beings *of the same kind* that can endure by means of traditional methods like extended lineage: owning property in perpetuity, veneration of elders (origin of belief in gods and *heroes* as ancestors)

Now the *fragmentation of property ownership* belongs within the opposite tendency: a *newspaper* (in place of daily *prayers*) railroad telegraph. Centralization of a multitude of different interests within a single psyche:[244] which *in addition* must be very strong and adaptable.

25 [211][245]

A doctrine is needed that is strong enough to bring about *selective breeding*: strengthening for the strong, crippling and destructive for world-weary people.

Annihilation of declining races. Decline of Europe.

Annihilation of slave-like value judgments.

Domination of the earth as means of breeding a superior type.

Annihilation of the tartuffery called "morality." (Christianity as an hysterical kind of honesty, as in Augustine, Bunyan)

Annihilation of *suffrage universel*: i.e., the system by which the most inferior natures make themselves a law unto the superior ones.

Annihilation of mediocrity and its validation. (The one-sided people, individuals — peoples e.g., the English. Dühring. To strive for the fullness of nature by pairing opposites: (including miscegenation.)

The new courage — no a priori truths (*such as* is sought by those accustomed to believing) but rather *voluntary* subordination to a ruling thought that is in vogue e.g., time as property of space etc.

25 [212][246]

"Babble of hungry men is boring."

25 [213]

Tartuffery (within all ruling classes) in Europe (or morality under the influence of Christianity)

Hysteria in Europe (idleness, undernourishment, little exercise — bursts forth in religious insanity as it did in India. Lack of sexual satisfaction.) *Advantage*, that the *religiosi*[247] did not propagate themselves.

The pedantry of slaves and non-artists as belief in reason, purposefulness. Appears as the aftereffect of the aesthetic eras (which teach us to see everything as *simpler* than it is: Superficiality of the Greek moralists, similar to the French of the 18th century

Now, what counts as morality among the English (satisfaction with a comfortable existence, the problem of living happily seems to them to be solved: in turn, *this* is reflected in their mode of thought.

Whatever is slavish demands *authority*.

Luther.

25 [214]

How I have perfected fatalism:
1) through eternal recurrence and preexistence
2) through the elimination of the concept "will."

25 [215]

Physical problem, to invent a state that is + and –.

25 [216]

The lack of powerful souls, even among sages.

Tartuffery of those who know, regarding themselves: "knowledge for its own sake!"

Objectivity — as a modern means of freeing ourselves from scorn (as in Flaubert)

logicians and mathematicians and engineers[248] and their value. How much deception reigns, even in these areas!

The ridiculous theatrics of the ancients: Socrates, the *rabble*, see their ideal in virtue i.e., happiness in liberation from *overly* passionate pain-inflicting desires among the rabble. Lack of desire as the goal of knowledge. ("Everything has little value" *must* be the result)

The lack of a powerful
   of a noble   } soul in philosophers up
   of a rich and a diverse } to now.
   of a healthy

25 [217]²⁴⁹

Viking Expeditions, State Constitution and Customs of the Ancient Scandinavians. By Strinnholm. Trans⟨lated⟩ b⟨y⟩ Frisch. (Hamburg, Perthes 1839.

25 [218]

Value of anti-Semitism, to push the Jews into setting loftier goals for themselves and into finding any assimilation into national states something that is *beneath* them.

25 [219]²⁵⁰

Arming the people — is, in the last analysis, arming the rabble.

25 [220]²⁵¹

It is hard to take advantage of people like me: I am learning more and more how much superficiality and audacity are concealed in actions where people believe they are "doing well" by me.

I stopped loving people a long time ago: I don't want the silliness of a malicious goose²⁵² to rob me of the few exemplary talents whom I can encourage — being encouraging like this is almost the only satisfaction I have gotten from human contact up to now.

25 [221]

The task is to build a *ruling caste* with the most extensive souls, capable of the greatest variety of tasks that involve ruling the earth. To concentrate into a single nature all the individual capabilities that have existed up to now.

The position of the *Jews* in regard to this: lots of practice in *conforming*. *That's why* they are, for now, the greatest actors; also, as poets and artists, the most brilliant imitators with the greatest empathy.²⁵³ What they lack, on the other hand. Once Christianity has been eliminated, the Jews will be treated *more justly*; even

as the founders of Christianity and of the greatest moral pathos
that has existed up to now.

25 [222]

The 20th century will have *two faces*: decline is one of these.
Everything that has helped more powerful and more extensive
souls to emerge than have ever existed before (less judgmen-
tal, more immoral) could contribute to the decline of weaker
natures. Perhaps a kind of European Chinese will emerge, with
a weak Buddhist-Christian faith, and cleverly Epicurean in
their actions, as the Chinese are — diminished human beings.

25 [223]

The basic drive behind English philosophizing is
comfortism.[254]

25 [224]

If it is necessary for your health, go for it! What's the big
deal! But don't make a lot of noise about it! It is ridiculous to
go on and on about green vegetables — anyone who does this
is soft in the head!

25 [225]

How the earth will be governed is an *impending* problem.
The radical question is: *must* there be slavery? Or rather: it is
no question at all, but a fact: and only the accursed Anglo-
European cant does — — —

In truth, there *is* always slavery— whether you want it or
not! E.g., Prussian officials. Scholars. Monks.

25 [226][255]

Death. We must twist the brute physiological fact into a
moral necessity. Live *in such a way* that, *at the right time, you
have the will to die!*

25 [227][256]

Eternal Recurrence.
Dedicated to my brothers.
But where are you, my brothers?

Introduction.

What have philosophers really wanted up to now? Survey from the Brahmins on.

I want to teach the thought that gives many people the right to erase themselves — the great *selectionist*[257] thought.[258]

25 [228]

The question of *marriage*. Arranging things for those who create: for there is a conflict between marriage and work.

25 [229]

Major theme. Intelligence must rule *over* benevolence: benevolence must be evaluated anew and the limitless damage that continues to be done by benevolent acts. Irony of *maternal* love.

25 [230]

Languages lead us astray about "*peoples*": they also cause the most harm to superior knowledge.

25 [231]

Mistakes about what is the same and what is similar 1) because it *looks* the same 2) because it moves the same way 3) because it emits the same sounds.

25 [232]

The necessity of slavery.

25 [233]

The sculptor (rejection of "idealism" up to now and of its manipulation of images. The *body* is what is at stake.

25 [234]
The Jews are the oldest and purest race in Europe. That's why the beauty of Jewish women is unsurpassed.

25 [235]
Apes are too kind for humans to have descended from them.

25 [236]
The *taming* of humans has been misunderstood up to now as "morality."

25 [237][259]
In *Zarathustra* I, an indescribably gentle solid decisive and wholehearted contemplation of all things.

25 [238]
"Philosophy of the Future"[260]
1. Moralistic tartuffery.
2. The necessity of slavery (humans as *tools* —)
3. The decline of Europe.

25 [239]
Freedom of the will as taught from the perspective of 2 opposing inclinations: "*liberum arbitrium* can never be compelled, for wherever compulsion is present, there is no freedom, and wherever there is no freedom, there is no *desert*"[261] — but those with the other inclination conclude: "there is no *guilt* there." The former want the doctrine of free will to be based on the feeling of pride, the latter for it to be based on "the feeling of having sinned" and "humility."

25 [240][262]
Up to now, culture has been nonexistent in Germany, instead there have only been mystical separatists. Nothing but *individuals* — this is *comforting*!

25 [241]

Music as an echo of states which were coherently expressed through *mysticism* — feelings of clarity for the individual, transfiguration. Or: the reconciliation of internal oppositions into something new, *birth of a third thing*.

25 [242]

Concerning the signature of the *slave*: *the nature of a tool*, cold, useful, — I regard all utilitarians as *involuntary slaves*. Human **fragments** — this is the mark of the slave.

25 [243]

First principle: not taking numbers into consideration: the masses, the miserable and unhappy people concern me little — rather the *first and most accomplished exemplars*, and that they *are not neglected out of consideration for the failures* (i.e., the masses)

Annihilation of the failures — this requires that we liberate ourselves from morality as it has existed up to now.

25 [244]

We must change how we listen to music in order to extract Christianity from it and *overcome* it.

25 [245]

Separate tools.

1. Those *who give orders*, powerful people — who *do not love*, unless it is the images through which they create

abundant many-sided unconditional people, who overcome what is there

2. People who have been *set free*, obedient people — love and admiration make them happy (suspension of their imperfection in the presence of something superior)

3. The *slaves* "servant's demeanor" — to make them comfortable, compassion for each other

25 [246][263]

In the first part, the *decline* and its *necessity* should be made clear! To what extent slaves have become masters without having the virtues of masters

nobility without the foundation of pedigree and without preserving its purity

monarchs without being *first among humans.*

25 [247][264]

Concerning I) every form of despair and uncertainty draw near to Zarathustra — he gives the explanation.

"You are a slave" he says to the king, also to the philosopher.

Who should rule the earth? This is the **refrain** of my practical philosophy.

What is left to admire? You have made the slave into the master. *Refrain.*

"the puniest people"

"where was there more foolishness than among those who take pity"[265] says Zarathustra to the woman

"Fatherland and the people" — how language leads us *astray!*

25 [248][266]

"Germany, Germany above everything" — is perhaps the most idiotic slogan that has ever existed. *Why* Germany in the first place — I ask: if it does not *want* something, *stand for* something, *exhibit* something that is worth more than what any other power hitherto has stood for! In itself it is merely one more large state, one more bit of silliness in the world.

25 [249][267]

Last speech: Here is the hammer that will overcome human beings

are human beings failures? all right then, let's get going and test to see whether they can withstand this hammer!

this is the great noon

the one who is doomed *crosses* himself

he prophesies the downfall of countless individuals and races

I am *fatum*[268]

I have *overcome* compassion — the artist exults as the marble screams.

animals and plants endure this thought (he turns to his animals)

"Leave me!" — laughing, he leaves that place.

In the last part, Zarathustra becomes more and *more strange, distant, quiet* in his speeches. Finally he descends into the profound silence — for seven days. *During this time*, the disciples grow *outraged, stress* that they cannot express.

— cutting their ties, flowing apart, thunderstorms and storm. The woman wants to kill him, when his last disciples are determined to say *No* to him, to her.

25 [250]

Leo Gfrörer — *Gustav Adolf*[269]

Walter Rogge *parlament⟨arische⟩ Grössen*[270]

25 [251][271]

We are not dumb enough to get excited about the principle "Germ⟨any⟩, G⟨ermany⟩ above everything" or about the German Reich.

25 [252][272]

Not everyone has the right to speak about everything: in the same way that everything is not permitted to be handled by everyone. I call ⟨it⟩ "the epidemic of hoof and mouth disease"

25 [253]

How can anyone want to grant freedom to individuals, as Luther does in the highest matters! In the final analysis, the instinct of the herd is stronger and they immediately fall back into servitude (e.g., the Protestants in the face of the most pitiful puny princes, — a people made up of lackeys —)

25 [254]

The value judgments of the Church are those of *slaves*. The profound *mendacity* is European. Whoever wants to have a large-scale effect on Europeans has up to now required moral tartuffery (e.g., the first Napoleon in his proclamations, recently R. Wagner through his music of attitudes).

The "greater good" as a principle, even with princes!

25 [255]

The future has barely caught anyone's eye up to now, except for the Romans.

25 [256]

In the Orient, the peoples stagnated under the rule of a single moral law. Europe remained active under the rule of 2 conflicting ones.

The history of Europe since the time of the Roman emperors is a slave rebellion.

25 [257][273]

Without Platonism and Aristotelianism no Christian philosophy.

25 [258]

Concept of mystics: those who have enough and too much of their own happiness and are seeking a language for their happiness, — they would like to *give* some of it *away*!

25 [259][274]

Let's compare the Vikings when they are at home and when they are far away from home: Bronze Age and Golden Age, depending on the point of view. The same with the great people of the Renaissance! The worm of conscience is a thing for the rabble and a true *corruption of noble* sensibility.

Every person who is dedicated to greatness has committed *every* crime; whether this is in a legal sense has to do with the leniency and weakness of the time. But think of Luther etc. And Christ — who left those who did not *love* him to roast in hell!

Greatness of vision, which *fears* no indictment of *reputation*, enables the doing and tolerating of many bad actions — an innate resoluteness and greatness, separate from *acquired* value judgments. (We find no such people in Rée[275])

To characterize Bismarck.

The same with Napoleon — a feeling of well-being without equal spread through Europa: the genius should *rule*, the idiotic "prince" of yesteryear seemed like a caricature. — Only the most foolish people opposed him, or those who gained the greatest advantage from him (England)

Great people are not understood: they forgive themselves every crime, but no weakness. How many do they kill! All geniuses — what wastelands surround them!

People who *become* defined by "their crimes" surely do not stand above judgment sublimely enough.

25 [260][276]

The way of freedom is *hard*. P⟨art⟩ 1

25 [261]

Superior individuals give themselves all the *rights* that the state allows itself — to kill, to annihilate, to spy, etc. The cowardice and the bad conscience of most princes led to the invention of the state and to the phrase *bien public*.[277] The just man has always wielded this phrase as a *means* to some purpose.

Culture emerged *only* in noble cultures — and among hermits who burned down everything around them with their contempt.

25 [262][278]

Idealism of the *slave* who is a **liar**: the Pope is the epitome of this!

25 [263]²⁷⁹

Modern socialism wants to create a secular version of Jesuitism: *every* person as absolute tool. But the purpose has not yet
been discovered. To what end!

25 [264]

The nihilists shouldn't debase themselves with European
goals: they no longer want *to be slaves* —

25 [265]²⁸⁰

Not everyone has the right to *every* problem e.g.,
Dühring, Luther — thanks to freedom of thought and of
the press. —

25 [266]²⁸¹

⟨To⟩ name Schopenhauer and Hartmann in the same breath
seemed to me a sign of an "impoverished mind."

25 [267]

Sickness and depression bring forth a kind of insanity: the
same with hard mechanical labor.

25 [268]²⁸²

Peasants as the most common species of *noblesse*: because
they are most dependent upon themselves. Peasant blood
is still the *best blood* in Germany: e.g., Luther Niebuhr
Bismarck

Where is there a noble family whose blood is not tainted by
venereal disease and degeneracy?

Bismarck a slave. Just look at the faces of the Germans (it is
understandable that Napoleon was astonished when he met the
author of Werther and encountered a *man*!): anyone having a
drop of blood overflowing with manliness left the country: as
for the pitiful populace that remained, the people with servant's souls experienced an improvement from abroad, particularly through *slave blood*.

The nobility of Brandenburg and the Prussian nobility in general (and the peasants of certain northern German regions) currently possess the *most manly* natures in Germany.

That the *manliest men* rule is the order of things.

25 [269]

We are certainly not foolishly obsessed with chastity: if a woman is needed, a woman can be easily found without breaking up marriages and needing to get married for this purpose.

25 [270]

1 Principle: there is no God. He has been more convincingly refuted than anything else. In order to argue for this thesis, someone would have to take refuge in the incomprehensible. *Consequently*, from now on, it is a *lie* or *weakness* to believe in God.

2 Principle: *the most manly men should rule* and not the half-women, priests, and scholars: — against the delusional Catholic ravings of Comte

3 Principle: supreme human beings live beyond those who rule, freed from all ties: and they have those who rule as their tools.[283]

Warriors, country *farmers*, city-*industry*, at the lowest level *merchants*.

25 [271][284]

The *peasant* in Luther screamed out against the lie of "superior people" that he had believed in: "there are no superior people at all" — he screamed.

25 [272][285]

With the parliament, *Bismarck* wanted to create a lightning rod for leading statesmen, a force *against* the crown and, depending on the circumstances, a lever for exerting pressure on foreign powers: — in it he also had his scape– and scrapegoat.[286]

25 [273]

Noblesse increases depending on the degree of *independence* from place and time. People with strong bodies who emerge from the highest cultures stand above all *sovereigns*.

25 [274]

Tame humans and tamed humans — these are the teeming masses.

25 [275]

Those who are the victims of a single passion have not yet reached a high enough state: they should ex — — — from it

25 [276][287]

The future of our educational institutions

    R. Wagner, *properly* understood

    Schopenhauer, *properly* understood. He is disgusted by what disgusts me.

25 [277]

Resolved. I want to speak and not Zarathustra anymore

25 [278]

Evil people are, in my view, those who, as kings, etc., project the *false image* of supremely powerful persons, supported by armies, bureaucrats (even geniuses lacking inner perfection like Frederick the Great and Napoleon) who allow the question to arise, What for?

25 [279]

bien public is a siren song: it is bait for base instincts.

25 [280]

The noble simplicity of the Spaniards, their pride.

25 [281]
Praise of nihilists: better to destroy and perish on our own!

25 [282]
"Style.
Imitation — as a talent of the *Jews*. "To conform to a pattern" — this explains actors, this explains poets like Heine and Lipiner.[288]

25 [283]
We used to seek our *future* happiness at the cost of our *present* happiness. This is how all those who create live when it comes to their work. And now my dedication to greatness wants me to live *at the cost of present contentment* when it comes to the future of humans

25 [284][289]
To feel contempt for praise of *dévouement* and *héroisme* — contempt for those who praise compassion has made me almost *heartless*.

25 [285][290]
My hatred of fancy phrases in relation to myself. Who could achieve with their imaginations *everything that* I have demanded from myself in my life up to now and the sacrifices I have made, also the kind of obstacles I faced as I went along my difficult path, considering that I am perhaps one of the most experienced people in regard to length and degree of physical suffering. And now suddenly to see myself again from a demeaning angle through the demeaning eyes of relatives friends, in short, showered by everyone with suspicion, just as much with charges that I am weak, along with warnings. — And who would even have the right to encourage me!

25 [286]²⁹¹

to give the Germans a higher ranking among peoples —
because *Zarathustra* is written in German. —

25 [287]²⁹²

Egoism! But no one has ever asked: what *kind* of ego! Instead,
every person automatically assumes that the ego of every ego is
equal. These are the consequences of the slave-theory of *suffrage
universel* and of "equality."

25 [288]

In the presence of *beauty* the eye remains trained very much
on the surface of things But still, there must be beauty in every
inner process of the body: all conceptual beauty of the soul is
only a metaphor, and something *superficial in comparison with
this multitude* of deep harmonies.

25 [289]

My speech against evil people (who *flatter the slaves* —)
    slanderers of the world
    good people (who believe that doing good is easy and for
everyone)
    (against the aura of parson, of the parsonage as well

25 [290]²⁹³

Age of *Experiments.*

I conduct the great test: *who will endure the thought of eternal recurrence?* — Anyone who can be annihilated with the
sentence "there is no redemption" should perish. I want *wars*,
in which those filled with vital energy expel the others: this
question should dissolve all bonds and *drive out* those who are
world-weary — you should kick them out, shower them with
every form of contempt, or lock them up in madhouses, drive
them to despair etc.

25 [291]

Lest there be misunderstandings: loving thy neighbor is a recipe for those kinds of people who have fared badly in the mix of their characteristics. Its *admirers* like Comte make it clear that they are sick and tired of themselves.

25 [292]

All *good taste* in E⟨urope⟩ has been spoiled for millennia by the *grandiose* paradox "God on the cross": ⟨it⟩ is a horrific thought, a consummate paradox! Likewise, hell, with a God of love. An *esprit barroco*²⁹⁴ arose there, against which the heathen world could no longer stand upright

25 [293]

That we are once again experiencing *Homer* is in my view the greatest victory over Christendom and Christian cultures: that we *have* **a bellyful** of Christian mollycoddling, uglifying, obfuscating, spiritualizing

25 [294]

We must perceive the *lie* having to do with church, not just the untruth: *to beat the Enlightenment so much into people that all the priests who become priests do so with a guilty conscience* — —

— we must do likewise with the state. This is a **task of the Enlightenment**, to make the entire actions of princes and statesmen into an *intentional lie*, to rob them of good conscience, and **to once again drive** the **unconscious tartuffery out of the bodies of European people.**

25 [295]²⁹⁵

"The fear of death is a European kind of fear." Oriental.

25 [296]²⁹⁶
The new Enlightenment. Against churches and priests
                                    against statesmen
                                    against good-natured compassionate
                                    people
                                    against educated people and luxury
                                    in summa, against tartuffery.

like Machiavelli.

25 [297]

Socrates: the *common*er: sly: gaining self-control through clear thinking and strong will: humor of someone who is often victorious: in conversations with nobles always noting that they cannot say *why* (*part of noble conduct includes the practice of virtue without Why?* —) Previously science exclusively the province of noble men!

In assessing his death: a kind of deception, because he conceals his death wish:²⁹⁷ even so, he brings disgrace upon his fatherland. Even so, more egoist than patriot.

Dialectic is *plebeian* in its origins: Plato's **poetic** sensibility makes him fanatical about its *opposite*. At the same time, as someone with an **agonal** *sensibility*, he realizes that the *means of victory* over all *opponents* is provided here and that this is a *rare* skill.

25 [298]²⁹⁸

On rank. The terrible consequence of "equality" — in the end, all people believe they have the right to address every problem. All order of rank has been lost.

25 [299]²⁹⁹

Our presuppositions: no God: no purposes: finite force. In the case of inferior people, we want *to avoid* devising and requiring the ways of thinking that are necessary for them!!

25 [300]
Meaning of religion: *failures* and unhappy people should be preserved, and through mood enhancement (hope and fear) be kept from committing suicide.

Or with noble people: a surfeit of *gratitude* and *adulation* which is too *great* to be offered to people in general.

25 [301]
Outbreak of my *disgust* at the shamelessness with which even geese[300] give themselves the right to speak with great human beings about "good" and "evil."

25 [302]
Peasant boys, made into priests, smelling of convents

25 [303][301]
German philosophy, which smells like the Tübingen Seminary[302]

25 [304][303]
"Nothing is true, everything is permitted."

25 [305][304]
Zarathustra "I took everything from you, God, duty, — now you must administer the *supreme test* for a *noble* species. For **here** the path is open to ruthless people — take a look!

— the contest for dominance, at the end the herd more of a herd than ever and the tyrant more of a tyrant than ever.

— no secret society! The *consequences* of my doctrine must be terrible in their fury: but *countless people should perish because of it.*

— *we are conducting an experiment with the truth*! Perhaps humanity will perish in the process! All right then!

25 [306][305]
Part 1. In the end, the mountain misted over with misery and distress

all sorts of impossible people flee to him — an army of fools all around me!
— On the slave-religion
— on hierarchy.
— inspired by honesty, they come to him, the godless ones

25 [307]

1 *Principle*. All value judgments up to now have originated in false claims to knowledge concerning things: — they are no longer binding, and even if they work as feelings, instinctively (as conscience).

2 *Principle*. Instead of the faith that is no longer possible for us, let us set a strong will over us that adheres to a provisional series of fundamental judgments, as a heuristic principle: in order to see *how far* we get with it. Like a sailor on an unknown sea. In truth, even that "faith" was no different: except that *mental discipline* has always been too limited to handle our *magnificent foresight*.

3 *Principle*. The *valor* of head and heart is what **distinguishes** us European people: acquired in the contest of many opinions. Greatest flexibility, in battle with religions that had grown cunning, and a stringent austerity, even cruelty. Vivisection is a *test*: those who don't endure it don't belong with us (and usually there are also other signs that such people don't belong with us e.g., Zöllner.)

4 *Principle*. Mathematics contains axioms (definitions) and conclusions from definitions. Its objects *do not exist*. The truth of its conclusions rests on the accuracy of logical thought. — When mathematics is applied, the same thing happens as in the case of "means-and-end" explanations: what is real is first *corrected* and *simplified* (**falsified** — —)

5 *Principle*. What we believe the most, everything a priori, is not for that reason *more certain*, just because it is so strongly believed. Rather, it is perhaps a consequence of the condition for the existence of our species — some kind of fundamental assumption. That's why other beings could make other

fundamental assumptions e.g., 4 dimensions. *That's why* it could still be the case that all these assumptions are false — or rather: in what way could something be "*true in itself*"! This is what is *fundamentally nonsensical about all of this*!

6 *Principle*. Part of becoming a man is that we do not deceive ourselves about our *human* situation: rather, we want to exercise *our quantum of power* to the nth degree and **to strive for** the **greatest quantum of power over things**. To realize that the danger is great: that chance has *ruled* up to now —

7 *Principle*. The task of ruling the earth is upon us. And with that, the question: **what kind of** future do we *want* for humanity! — New codes of values *necessary*. And fight against the *representatives* of the old "*eternal*" values as the highest priority!

8 *Principle*. But *where* do we get our imperative *from*? It is not a "thou shalt" but rather the "I must" of superpowerful people, those who create.

25 [308]

Philosophers have sought to dissolve the world into 1) images (appearances) or 2) concepts or into 3) willing — in short, into something that is familiar to us because it is in some way human — or to set it equal to the *soul* (as "God")

Common people have taken the "cause and effect" of familiar connections between human actions and projected it into nature. "Freedom of the will" is a theory concerning a *feeling*.

A thing whose subjective origin has been determined has not yet for that reason been *proven* to be "*nonexistent*" e.g., space, time etc.

The science of mathematics dissolves the world into *formulas*. That is, it — — —

We must *hold fast* to the only thing that concepts and formulas can be: a means of explanation and calculation, where *practical application* is the goal: humans making use of nature, the limits of reason.[306]

Science: taking control of nature for human purposes —

— cutting off the *excessive* fantasizing of metaphysicians mathematicians: although we need to keep, as additional experimentation, whatever may be caught by chance in the process.

The greatest amount of intellectual labor *wasted* in science — here, too, the principle of the greatest possible idiocy rules.

Principle when explaining all human history: the efforts are infinitely greater than the *result*.

25 [309]

Principle: to be like nature: *to be able* to get countless creatures to sacrifice themselves in order to achieve something with humankind. We must study **how** some great human being is actually brought into existence. *All* ethics up to now is boundlessly limited and local: not to mention blind and oblivious to the real laws. It was not there to explain certain actions, but rather to **prevent** them: to say nothing of *procreation*

Science is a *dangerous* thing: and before we are taken to task for some other reason, this has nothing to do with its "value." Or even when science is brought into grade schools: and now even little girls and geese are beginning to cackle like scientists; this has to do with the fact that science has always been practiced with *moral tartuffery*.

This is what I want to put an end to.

All presuppositions of the existing "order" *refuted*.

1. God refuted: because everything that happens is neither good nor prudent nor true;

2) because "good" and "evil" are not opposites and because moral values become transformed

3) because "true" and "false" are both necessary — wanting to deceive, as well as wanting to be deceived, is a presupposition of living things

4) "unegoistic" is not at all possible. "Love" misunderstood. "Prayer" irrelevant; "submission" dangerous.

25 [310]

That our sense organs themselves are merely appearances, the products of our senses, and that the configuration of our bodies is a product of how we are configured, seems to me to be something contradictory or at least completely unprovable. That *tartarus stibiatus*[307] makes me throw up, has nothing to do with any "appearances" and "opinions."

Photography is sufficient counter-evidence against the crudest form of "idealism."

25 [311]

Where does our sense of truth come from? First: we are not afraid to dissent 2) it increases our feeling of power, over ourselves as well.

25 [312][308]

"anthropomorphizing" the world i.e., feeling more and more like rulers in it —

25 [313]

Feeling, comprehending, willing, in the face of the indescribably small movement of atoms, would be completely impossible if *encapsulating, coarsening, prolonging, equalizing* were not part of their essence.

Images and concepts emerge when a *productive force shapes* several existing stimuli: *creates* an "appearance"

25 [314]

There is no *comprehension* in mathematics, there is only an *ascertaining of necessities*: of relations which do not change, of laws *within*.

A *mechanical worldview* i.e., one that ultimately dispenses with comprehension, we "comprehend" only when we understand *motives*. Where there are no motives, comprehension stops.

My intention in regard to even the most purposeful actions is to show that, even there, our "comprehending" is an illusion and *error*.

25 [315]

Chapter: about "comprehending" actions.

25 [316]

The ideal is to construct the most complex machinery possible, created by the *dumbest* of all possible methods.

25 [317]

We can let ourselves go in front of a work of art. But *not* in front of a great person! Hence the cultivation of the arts among *subjugated people* who *create* for themselves a world of freedom — artists are mostly the kind of people who are *not* rulers.

Rulers love art because they want *copies of themselves*.

25 [318]

Lange, p 822[309] "a *reality* such as people imagine for themselves and such as what they *long for*, when this imagined reality is *disrupted*: *an absolutely tangible* existence, *independent of us* and yet recognized by us — there is no such reality." *We* are active within it: but *this* doesn't make Lange proud!

therefore they wish for themselves nothing that is deceptive, transitory, dependent, unrecognizable — *these* are instincts of *intimidated* beings and of those who are still morally subjugated: they long for an *absolute ruler*, something loving, truth-speaking — in short, this longing of idealists is moral-religious when viewed from the standpoint of slaves.

Conversely, our artistic, lordly prerogative could revel in the fact of our *having created* this world

"*merely* subjective," but I feel just the opposite: *we* have created it!

25 [319]

Forming things — this is the drive of an *ethical person*: to build *types*: opposing ways of evaluating are necessary for this.

To see forms or *to work them out* is our greatest happiness — it is what we have done for the longest time.

25 [320]
Tucked away in all aesthetic judgments are ethical ones.
P⟨eter⟩ G⟨ast⟩ is too good-natured to impose any kind of
willing on his sentences, he gives *in*.

25 [321]
Grand style consists in the contempt for limited and ephemeral beauty, it is a feeling for what is rare and enduring.

25 [322][310]
Zarathustra waiting
1) Signs of the greatest confusion. "Nothing is true, everything is permitted"
2) He proclaims his e⟨ternal⟩ r⟨ecurrence⟩. Indignation,
complaints — up to and including assassination attempt.
Zarathustra laughs, is happy, for he is bringing the *great crisis*
3) the world-weary people depart, the crowd becomes smaller.
He shares his doctrine with them *in order* to find the way to the
superhumans and while still remaining *in a good mood*
Cheerful as in a military encampment. Festive parades etc.

25 [323][311]

Eternal Recurrence.
Noon and Eternity.

1. It is time!
2. The great noon.
3. Those who make vows.   Prophecy
                                 of eternal recurrence

25 [324]
Seeing and hearing presuppose very particular kinds of
learning to see, learning to hear.

25 [325]
That the nervous system, and later the brain, *develops* within the
morphological sequence of animals: provides a point of reference

— *feeling develops* first, just as creating images and *thinking develop* later. Although we don't yet comprehend it: but we *see* that it is so. We find it improbable that pleasure and pain should be situated in everything that is organic: and, even in humans, the *stimulus* is still a stage in which *both of these* are not yet present.

25 [326]

We are suspicious when our analysis begins with what "thinks" "wills" feels within us. This is an *ending* and in any case the most complicated and the hardest to understand.

25 [327]

The emergence of the *subjective* sensations of space, time, force, causality, freedom, assuming this emergence were recognized: likewise the emergence of the image (i.e., of forms, figures), of concepts (i.e., mnemonic signs for entire groups of images with the help of *sounds*): all these subjective appearances raise no doubt concerning the *objective truth* of logical, mathematical, mechanical, chemical laws. Another thing is our ability *to express* ourselves about these laws: we must make use of language.

25 [328]

To find the language of *more complete* natures — to project their image of the world —[312]

25 [329]

Identifying the *nature* of a way of thinking like mine: mechanical, random, taking pleasure in beautiful imagery, clever at smashing things to bits (because doing this is a kind of *becoming*), exploiting randomness, being irresponsible, being courageous, lacking formality

25 [330]

Communication of states — here prose is far from sufficient — yet science *can* communicate only the scientific state and *shouldn't do anything else*!!

On the multiplicity of language (through images tones) as the means by which *more complete* human beings communicate who they are.

25 [331][313]

Zarathustra, after his terrified disciples have turned away from him and after he has laughingly described his mission with superhuman certainty: — — calling them back *with the most profound tenderness*, simultaneously returning from the greatest alienation and distance: *like a father.*

25 [332]

Connection between the aesthetic and the ethical: a great style demands a single strong fundamental will and detests unsettledness more than anything else.

Dancing, and an easy transition from one move into the next, is *extremely dangerous* — a sword dance. This is because, in most cases, rough consistency of movement and determination build stamina in the individual.

The *most difficult combination*: a will, strength of fundamental feelings and change in movements (transformations)

25 [333]

Everything that is organic, that "makes judgments," acts like *an artist*: it creates a whole out of individual urges and stimuli, it sets aside many details and creates a *simplificatio*, it posits sameness and it affirms its creations as *having an existence. The drive itself is what is logical, which makes the world run logically in accordance with our judgments.*

That which is creative — 1) that which appropriates 2) that which chooses 3) reconstructing element — 4) the self-regulating element — 5) that which organizes.

25 [334]

There is a sort of *necessity*, already present in the first seed, that persists through many generations of species: assuming that the conditions of *nourishment* remain favorable, the organic being is determined for its entire future: the point in time when individual *new* forms occur (e.g., nerves) is dependent on accidents of nourishment.

NB. *Enhancement of life in line with the lifespan of the stars.*[314]

25 [335]

Great human beings feel their *power* over a people, their temporary connection with a people or a millennium: this *enhanced* sense of self as *causa* and *voluntas*[315] is *misunderstood* as "altruism" —

— it pushes them toward a *means* of communication: all great human beings are **inventive** in using such *means*. They want to configure themselves within large communities, they want to give a single form to that which is manifold, unorganized, the sight of chaos stimulates them

— misunderstanding love. There is a *slavish* love that gives itself away: that idealizes things and that deceives itself — there is a *divine* love that disdains and loves and that *re-creates* what it loves, **lifts it to the heights**. —

— to take possession of that monstrous *energy exuded by greatness*, in order, through breeding or else through annihilating millions of failures, to form future humans and *not to perish* at the sight of the suffering that is *created*, and whose like has never been seen before! —[316]

— mentality of *failures, to sacrifice themselves*: this is the meaning of the holy orders that take vows of chastity.

— the enjoyment of form in the visual arts: it communicates an inner state of the artist (peaceful veneration). Musicians are *moved by the affects*, without them visualizing objects along with this — and they communicate their inner state. Much *more extensive* than the inner state of painters.

25 [336]
Concerning psychology.

1. Every "ethical" feeling that enters our consciousness is *simplified*, the more conscious we become of it, i.e., it moves closer to the concept. It is multifarious in itself, a blending of many musical tones.

2. The "inner" world is more unfathomable than the outer one: the simultaneous sound of many higher tones can be made through music, which provides a copy.

3. In order that something can be known in a mechanically ordered world, a perspectival apparatus must be there that makes possible 1) standing still in a certain way 2) a simplifying 3) a selecting and omitting. The *organic is a mechanism by means of which consciousness can develop because it itself* requires *the same preconditions for its survival.*

4. The inner world must be transformed into illusion in order to become an object of awareness: many excitations perceived as unity etc. What force allows us to hear a chord as unified and in addition the kind of sound the instrument makes, its strength, its relationship to what was just heard etc.?? A similar force brings all the eye's images *together*.

5. Our continuing assimilation of *forms*, inventive, increasing, repetitive: *forms* of seeing, hearing and feeling.

6. *All these forms which we see, hear, feel* etc. are *not present in the outer world* which we establish mathematically-mechanically.

7. My conjecture that all the characteristics of what is essentially organic are *therefore* not **derivable** by us from mechanical foundations because we ourselves initially *projected* anti-mechanical processes *into what we saw*: we were the first to insert that which is not derivable.

8. Be careful not to treat what is very complicated as something *new*.

25 [337]
To p⟨eople⟩ who are complete and upstanding,[317] a world that is so conditional and closed-off, like Kant's, is a thing of

horror. We require a *rough approximation of* the truth; and when it isn't there, well then, we love adventure and we head out to sea

— to prove that the consequences of science are *dangerous*, my task. "'Good' and 'evil' are passé — "

— in the age of *suffrage universel*, a *tone of disrespect* is the best a philosopher can expect: it is clear that all geese are already cackling along in concert! — read e.g., the philosophical cackling of George Sand or that woman[318] John Stuart Mill. Well, I *prefer to make* his position *despised* and *dangerous*: he should be cursed if he can't be honored in some other way!

— *the struggle with language.*

25 [338][319]

The story is told th⟨at⟩ the famous founder of Christianity said before Pilate "I am the truth"; the Roman's answer to that is worthy of Rome: as the greatest urbanity of all time.

25 [339]

"God" perceived differently in antiquity, completely devoid of the monotheistic-moralistic aftertaste. — Priapus in the gardens, as a scarecrow. A herder grateful for the fertility of the herd, e.g.,

The mass *gratitude* in Greek religion. Later, in the *rabble*, *fear* runs rampant: Epicurus and Lucretius.

25 [340]

Principle. If *bien public* were at issue, then the Jesuits would be right, likewise the cult of assassins;[320] likewise the Chinese.

25 [341]

Principle. With all my strength to overthrow the stagnant eternal value judgments! Major task.

25 [342][321]

In my view, the revolution, confusion and misery of the peoples is insignificant *compared to the misery* of great individuals as they develop. We must not deceive ourselves: the many miseries of all these *puny people*, when taken together, do not amount to *anything*, other than how *powerful* people feel about them.

In moments of great danger, to think of ourselves: to benefit from the disadvantage of the many: — within a very broad spectrum of variation, this can be a sign of *great* character which takes control of its feelings of compassion and justice.

25 [343]

When inferior humans make *their* silly existence, their stupid, bovine happiness, into a *goal*, they infuriate those who observe them; and when for the sake of *their* well-being they go so far as to oppress and bleed other humans dry, then these poisonous flies should be swatted.

The value of humans should demonstrate which rights they are allowed to claim: "emancipation" occurs out of disrespect for superior natures and is a crime against them.

Those assuming the burden of furthering a family, a people etc., have greater significance, provided that their *power permits* them to take on such a task. Humans who *have* nothing in their bodies but animal lusts should not have the *right* to marry.

The rights that humans claim are proportionate to the duties that they assume, to the tasks they *think* they *can do*.

The vast majority of humans have no right to exist, rather they are a misfortune for those humans who are superior to them:[322] I am not yet prepared to give this right to those *who are failures*. There are also peoples who are failures.

Silly "humanity"! When animals are taken into account, humans may well feel like humans among "their peers." But as humans in the presence of humans —

25 [344]

The **degeneration of rulers and of the ruling classes** has caused the greatest mischief in history! Without the Roman Caesars and Roman society, the insanity of Christianity would not have come to power.

When inferior humans fall into doubt as to *whether* there are superior humans, that is when the danger is great! And this ends up with the discovery that there are *virtues* even in inferior, subjugated, mentally deficient humans, and that all humans are equal *before God*: which is the *non plus ultra* of nonsense that has ever existed on earth! That is, in the final analysis, superior humans measured themselves in the same way that slaves measure virtue — they felt that they were "proud" etc. — they felt that their *superior* characteristics were reprehensible!

— the paradox emerged when Nero and Caracalla were at the height of their power: the most inferior people are *worth more* than that person up there! And an *image of God* made a breakthrough, an image as *far removed* as possible from the image of the mightiest figure — God on the cross![323]

— the Romans have been responsible for the *greatest misfortune in Europe* up to now, the people of *immoderation* —
— they brought extremes into ruling positions and *extreme paradoxes*, like "God on the cross"

we must first learn to differentiate: *for* the Greeks, *against* the Romans — *this* is what I call *being well-educated in regard to classical antiquity*

25 [345]

Causes of Pessimism

foregrounding of slave-morality, "equality"

the basest humans have all the "advantages" for themselves

degeneration of rulers and ruling classes

the long-term aftereffect of priests and world-deniers.

compassionate people and those who pretend to be sentimental: absence of *hard-heartedness*,

— sparing the failures

aimlessness, because there are no great people the sight of whom *justifies existence.*

false ideals, originating in a single God, "all are sinners before God"[324]

poor arid minds, and cowardly besides

25 [346]

We must *learn* to take *pride* in misfortune —

25 [347]

Seneca as a culmination of moral mendacity in classical antiquity — a dignified Spaniard, like Gracián

25 [348][325]

The root of all evil: that slave morality has been *victorious*, the victory of humility, chastity, absolute obedience, selflessness —

— because of this, the ruling types[326] were condemned 1) to hypocrisy 2) to the agony of remorse — the creative types felt like mutineers against God, uncertain, and inhibited by eternal values

— the barbarians showed that **being able to keep things in proportion** was not in their vocabulary:[327] they feared the natural passions and drives and turned them into vices: — likewise the sight of the ruling Caesars and ruling classes.

— on the other hand, the suspicion arose that all *moderation* was a weakness or that it meant getting old and tired (this is how La Rochefoucauld had the suspicion that "virtue" was a beautiful phrase only to those who found no pleasure in vice anymore)

— keeping things in moderation was itself depicted as a matter of hard-heartedness, self-mastery, asceticism, as a struggle with the devil etc. the natural *delight* that aesthetic types feel in the presence of proportion, their **enjoyment** *of the beauty of proportion*, was *overlooked* or *denied*, because they wanted an *anti*-eudaimonistic morality

In summa: the best things have been *turned into vices* (because weak people or immoderate swine put them in a bad light) — and the best people have *remained hidden* and have often *failed to recognize* who they are.

25 [349]
The eradication of "drives"
the virtues that are impossible or
the virtues that are most highly prized among slaves who are ruled by priests
the rotten ruling classes have ruined the image of those who rule
the "state," acting as a court of justice, is an act of cowardice because there is an absence of great people who can be the standard.
— lastly, uncertainty has grown so great that people fall into the dust as soon as they confront *any* powerful will that issues commands[328]
NB. *Mockery* of kings with puny middle-class virtues

25 [350]
There is so much stupid talk about *pride* — and Christianity even made pride into something felt to be *sinful*! The point is: those who demand *greatness from themselves and achieve it*, must feel very distant from those who do not do this — this *distance* is interpreted by these others as "putting on airs": but the former know it merely as unceasing work, war, victory, by day and by night: the *others* know nothing *of* all *this*!

25 [351][329]
The doctrine μηδὲν ἄγαν[330] is applied to people who have overflowing force — not to the mediocre.
The ἐγκράτεια[331] and ἄσκησις[332] is only one level of supremacy: the "golden nature" is superior.
"Thou shalt" — unconditional obedience in the Stoics, in the monastic orders of Christianity and the Arabs, in Kant's

philosophy (whether to a superior, or to a concept, doesn't matter.)

"I will this" is superior to "thou shalt" (heroes); "I am" is superior to "I will this" (the Greek gods)

Barbarian gods don't mention anything about *proportion* being an object of pleasure — they are not simple, nor easy, nor proportionate.

25 [352]³³³

Concerning Zarathustra: "the golden ones" as the highest level.

25 [353]

NB. Simplicity in life, clothing, living, eating, simultaneously as a *sign of supremely good taste*: the most superior types require the best, *hence* their simplicity!

Obnoxious, comfortable people, likewise ostentatious people, are a long way from having such independence: they don't find themselves to be good enough companions.

To what degree the Stoic approach, and even more so the monk, is an *excess*, a barbaric *exaggeration* — — .

25 [354]

— in all circumstances, *princes* are ranked second: the *truly superior people* rule for millennia and are unable to take an interest in contemporary things. The princes are their *tools* or sly dogs who *pretend* to be tools.

To elevate the image of the most superior sage *above* the image of the prince (as a tool of the sage)

25 [355]³³⁴

Order of rank: those who *determine* values and guide the will of millennia, by guiding the most superior types, are *the most superior humans*.

25 [356]

That which is commonly attributed to the *mind seems to me to constitute the essence of the organic*: and in the most superior functions of the mind I find merely a sublime kind of organic function (assimilation selection secretion etc.)

But the dichotomy "organic" "inorganic" is definitely part of the phenomenal world!

25 [357]

The important[335] intellectual activities rendered unhealthy, as if controlled by a single thought; lack of spontaneity — a kind of hypnotism. Under different circumstances, they make us lose our nerve and become weak-willed.

Whether it is not the case that obedience is often accompanied by hypnotism?

25 [358]

NB. Principle: *every* experience, traced back to its origins, presupposes the entire past of the world. — To call a fact *good*, means to affirm *everything*!

But in affirming everything, we are also affirming all present and past *affirmations* and *rejections*!

25 [359]

The greatest part of our experiences is *unconscious* and has an effect.

25 [360]

Self-control is a balance of *many* accumulated memories and motives — a kind of peace among enemy forces.

in the final analysis, *voluntas* is a mechanical unconditional preponderance, a victory that enters into consciousness.

25 [361]

Forms as the training ground of the eye: potentially of the ear and of touch as well. Likewise, dreams show us *how easily we could be other people* — we are very good at imitation.

25 [362]

The **creative** force — replicating, building, forming, practicing — the type represented by us is *one* of our *possibilities* — we *could* play many other people still — we have the *stuff* for it *within us*. — To look at the way we live and the way we do things as a *role* — including the maxims and principles - - - *we seek to play a* **type**, instinctively — we select from our memory, we join and combine the facts of memory.

25 [363]

Individuals contain many *more* persons than they think. "Person" is merely a point of emphasis, synopsis of characteristics and qualities.

25 [364]

Misunderstanding actions by ascribing the wrong motives to them.

25 [365]

NB. To what degree our conscious life is completely fake and a *veil*.

25 [366]

Lying for the sake of lying is a primitive tendency: in all ages that are dominated by the rabble.

Ruling for the sake of ruling, and *not*, as Helvétius claims, for the sake of its pleasures.

25 [367]

— general lack of knowledge about nature

25 [368]
  Philosophers *do not know* which motives drive them to inquiry.

25 [369]

*On the Superficiality of
Consciousness*

25 [370]
  Pessimism of the 19th century as a consequence of rule by the rabble.
  Le plaisir in the 18th century.

25 [371]
  Cause and effect is not a truth but rather a *hypothesis* — and indeed the one which we use to *anthropomorphize* the world for ourselves, bring it in closer proximity to our *feelings* ("willing" is projected into it)
  — with the atomistic *hypothesis* we make the world accessible to our eye and to our calculations at the same time
  — it is the measure of the scientifically *strong* mind, how much it persists in rejecting the insanity of absolute judgments and value judgments or in not needing them at all. Namely, not becoming *uncertain*! And *to hold on to* a *hypothesis* like that with an iron will and to live for its sake!

25 [372]
  We keep **forgetting** the main thing: *why* do philosophers want to *know* anyway? Why do they *value* "truth" more than illusion? *This valuing* is older than any *cogito, ergo sum*: even granting the logical process, there is something within us that *affirms* this process and *denies* its opposite. Where does the preference come from? All philosophers have forgotten to explain *why* they value the true and the good, and no one has tried it with the opposites of these. Answer: the truth is *more beneficial* (preserving the organism) — but not *more pleasant in itself*

Enough, from the very beginning we find the organism as a whole, with "purposes," speaking — therefore *evaluating*

25 [373]
when a dish tastes good, this is *because* it is healthy!

25 [374]
                    To what degree people are performers.
Suppose individuals get a *role* to play: they gradually come to inhabit it. In the end, they have the judgments, tastes, impulses that fit their role, even the usual degree of intellect allotted to it: —

— initially as children, adolescents, etc. then the role befitting gender, then that of their social position, then that of their professional standing, then that of their works —

But if life gives them the opportunity to change, then they also play another role. And often the roles differ in a person according to the day of the week e.g., English people on Sunday and on every other day. In the course of one day, we are very different when awake and when asleep. And in dreams perhaps we *recover* from the fatigue we feel due to the role we play every day, — and throw ourselves into other roles.

To follow through with a role i.e., to have *will*, concentration and attentiveness: even more so in a negative sense — to repel what is *not* a part of the role, the oppressive stream of different kinds of feelings and stimuli, and — to carry out our actions in the context of the role and especially to *interpret* them.

The *role* is a result of the external world affecting us, and we tune our "person" to this role as we would play a stringed instrument. A simplification, a meaning, a purpose. We have the *affects* and the *desires* of our role — that is, we underscore the ones that fit and allow them to be seen.

Of course, always *à peu près*.[336]
People are *performers*.

25 [375]

We have *many types* within us. We coordinate our *inner stimuli, just like the external stimuli*, to an image or a series of images: as artists.

The superficiality of our types, like our judgments, concepts, images.

25 [376][337]

When smoking hashish, space much more extended because we see much more in the same time frame than usual. Sense of space dependent on time.

25 [377]

We must find "knowing in itself" to be just as contradictory as "first" cause and as "thing in itself."

The *cognitive mechanisms*[338] as mechanisms that diminish: as mechanisms that reduce in every sense. As tools of the mechanisms *that nourish*.

25 [378]

The instincts as judgments that are grounded in earlier experiences: *not* in experiences of pleasure and displeasure: for pleasure is first and foremost the form of an instinct as judgment (*a feeling of increased power* or: *as* if the power *had* increased) There are *feelings of power and weakness* in the whole being **prior to** feelings of pleasure and displeasure.

25 [379]

Being the kind of animals that imitate, humans are *superficial*: the semblance of things suffices for them, as it does for their instincts. They adopt judgments, this is part of the most ancient need, to *play* a role.

Development of mimicry among humans, caused by their weakness. The herd-animal plays a *role* it has been *told* to play.

25 [380]

To will, this is to command, for that reason something rare, poorly transmitted through heredity.

25 [381]

Strong will can be explained in cold people and weak will in warm people. What is amazing: a red-hot affect and a cold clear head and will.

25 [382]

What is dangerous about humans is hidden within, where their strength is: they are unbelievably adept at self-preservation, even in the most unfortunate circumstances. (Even the religions of the poor, of the unfortunate etc. are a part of this.) *In this way the failures are preserved much longer and cause the race to deteriorate*: which is why humans, compared to animals, are the most sickly of animals. Yet in the grand course of history, the fundamental law *must* prevail and the best ones are victorious: assuming that humans who have the greatest possible will seek *to ensure that the best are in power.*

25 [383]

I allow only successful people to philosophize about life. But there are people and peoples who have failed: those people must be muzzled. We must put an end to Christianity — it is the greatest blasphemy that has ever existed on earth and in life on earth — failed people and peoples must be muzzled.

We must put an end to Christianity — it was and is the greatest blasphemy that has ever existed on earth and in life on earth —

25 [384]

Seen from a distance: Schopenhauer's philosophy indicates that whatever happens is indescribably *more idiotic* than anyone would believe. This point conceals an advance in our insight.

25 [385]

We must hold tight to our belief in the body, our feelings of pleasure and pain and the like: no attempt should be made to overthrow them. *The objections* of a few logicians and religious people have not shaken these beliefs — they are not even being considered. *The condemnation of the body* as a mark of this failed coalition *likewise the condemnation* of *life*: sign of the defeated.

25 [386]

On the origin of *art*. The ability to lie and to dissemble has been developed the longest: feeling of *security* and of intellectual superiority in the deceiver during this. Admiration of the listeners: for the narrator, *such as if* they had been there. Likewise the listeners' security in knowing that it is *deception* and that this dangerous art is *not* being practiced to their detriment. The listeners' admiration for superhuman assistance. — In the case of poets, we often find self-alienation: they feel themselves "transformed." Likewise in dancers and actors, with nervous breakdowns, hallucinations etc. Artists now also still deceitful and resembling children. Inability to differentiate between "true" and "illusion."

25 [387]

On the origin of *religion*. Abundance of hallucinations and of all possible hysterias, not only "diabolical" ones. The premise is that the gods are *visible*. The founders of religions feel themselves to be justified through spasms, amnesia, loss of will.

25 [388]

The belief that the "afterlife" is dreadful goes back to antiquity and is the basis for Christianity. The organizations of the poor with their "love of neighbor" the other basis. The demand for *revenge* on everything with *power*, the third. — A popular form of the Stoic sage who is happy in greatest "misfortune": sudden healing of hysterics, feeling no pain when wounded — —

25 [389]

Will — an act of commanding: yet inasmuch as an unconscious act underlies this conscious one, we also need only to think of the unconscious one as instrumental. But when a command is given and a person obeys? The words of the command have *no* effect as words, *not* as sounds, rather as that which is hidden *behind* the sounds: and something is moved forward by means of this action. But the reduction of the sounds to "vibrations" is indeed only the expression of the same phenomenon on behalf of another *sense* — not an "explanation." The actual event is again hidden behind the "visible" vibration.

Science is concerned with *interpreting the same phenomena through different senses* and with reducing everything to the *clearest* sense, the optical one. Thus, we become familiar with the senses — the darker one is illuminated through the lighter one.

The movements of molecules are a consequence of eyesight and touch. — We hone the senses — we explain nothing. We assume a process of movement behind each "willing" "feeling," one that would be the same for the *eye*.

25 [390]

Pain: not the stimulus as such, but not made into pain until it reaches the intellect. It must be imagined as growing through heredity — a sum of many judgments: "this is dangerous, brings death, demands a defensive response, greatest attention," a command "get away! look out!" a great sudden *shock* as *result*.

25 [391]

Physical pain is initially the result of a psychological pain: yet the latter: suddenness, fear, readiness to fight back, *a multitude of judgments and acts of will and affects concentrated in one instant*, as a great shock and *in summa* felt as pain and projected toward the site.

Affects of every kind, their judgments, and the resulting acts of will, are united in the moment of pain: the attitudes

of defense immediately there with the pain. Result of a great
nervous shock (to the center): which resonates for a long time.

25 [392]

Transformation of all processes into optical phenomena:
and ultimately these phenomena are in turn transformed into
purely conceptual and quantitative phenomena.

This is the *course* within history: *we think we understand,*
when we will: when we feel: when we see: when we hear: when
we transpose it into concepts: when we transpose it into numbers and formulas.

"Everything is will"	"Everything wills"
"Everything is pleasure or displeasure"	"Everything suffers"
"Everything is motion"	"Everything flows"
"Everything is sound"	"Everything sounds"
"Everything is mind"	"Everything is mind"[339]
"Everything is number"	"Everything is number"[340]

Thus: the transformation of all processes into our world, the
world known to us, in brief: *within us* — up to now, this has
been "knowledge."

25 [393]

To depict humans as a *boundary*.

25 [394]

The value of atomism is: to find language and a means of
expression for *our* laws.

25 [395]

The science of nature is "human-knowledge" in relation to
the most universal abilities of humans.

25 [396]

The past is different for *every one of us*: inasmuch as it traces a
straight line, a simplification (as in the case of means and ends).

25 [397]

Value judgments emerge from what we believe to be conditions of existence: if our conditions of existence, or our belief in them, changes, then so do value judgments.

25 [398]

Preservation of the *community* (of the people) is my correction instead of "preservation of the species."

25 [399]

Fear of death is perhaps older than pleasure and pain, and causes pain.

25 [400]

Pain — an anticipation of the consequences of a wound, which is accompanied by a *feeling of decreased strength*? — No, a shock.

25 [401]³⁴¹

Enjoying hashish and dreaming teach us that the *speed of mental processes* is enormous. Apparently we don't *deal* with most of them, they don't enter our consciousness.

There must be a *great deal of consciousness* and willing in every complex organic being: our highest level of consciousness³⁴² usually keeps the other levels shut down. The smallest organ⟨ic⟩ creature must have consciousness and will.

25 [402]

The most intense stimulus is, in itself, not pain: but rather that shock that we feel, the nervous system becomes diseased, and *this* initially *projects* the pain toward the site of the stimulus. This projection is a protective and defensive measure. A *multiplicity of affects* is contained in the shock: attack, fear, defensive response, annoyance, anger, precaution, consideration of security measures — the movements of the entire body *are the result of this*. Pain is a *profound emotional movement with an incredible mass of thoughts all at once*; becoming ill as a result of an imbalance and a momentary *overpowering of the will*.

25 [403]

I assume that there is *memory and a kind of mind in everything organic*: the apparatus is so subtle that, *to us*, it does not seem to exist. Häckel's foolishness, to posit two embryos as identical!

We should not let ourselves be *deceived* by smallness— what is organic did not emerge.

25 [404]

What kind of characteristics must we have in order to dispense with God — what kind in order to dispense with "the religion of the cross"? Courage, a clear head, pride, independence and hard-heartedness, no useless speculation, decisiveness etc. Due to *regression*, Christianity is again and again victorious. — Prevailing circumstances must be favorable.

25 [405]

Regulative Presuppositions.

1. The dispensability of God.
2. Against those who console and against consolations of the cross.
3. That which is conscious as superficial.
4. Critique of good people.
5. Critique of geniuses.
6. Critique of the founders of religion.
7. Critique of the powerful.
8. The races and colonization.
9. The sex drive.
10. Slavery.
11. Critique of Greek culture.
12. Spirit of music.
13. Spirit of revolution.
14. World government.
15. Festivals.

16. Compassion.
17. Punishment, reward, payment.

My task: *to push humankind toward decisions that will be decisive for the entire future*!

Greatest patience — caution — **show** the **type** *of humans that are allowed to tackle this task*!

25 [406]

Our derivation of the sense of time etc. still pre*supposes* time as absolute.

25 [407]

All our religions and philosophies are *symptoms* of our corporeal state: — that Christianity won out was the result of a universal feeling of displeasure and a mixing of races (i.e., of a mix-up and a dust-up[343] within the organism)

25 [408]

All honor to the instincts, drives, lusts, in brief, to everything we do yet fully discern at a fundamental level! There are forces there that are stronger than anything that can be formulated concerning humans. But likewise **fear** and **mistrust** of all this because it is the heritage of *times* and *people* of *extremely* differing **value**, we *carry* all of this *around* with us!

— that the most superior force, as a mastery of *opposites*, sets the standard: —

the human body is a much more perfect construct than any system of thoughts and feelings, yes, far *superior to a work of art* — —

25 [409]

— works of art as evidence of our taking pleasure in *simplification*, of our taking pleasure in using a single law as a means of consolidation

— the intellect an *apparatus of abstraction*

— memory: everything that we have experienced *is alive*: it is reworked, categorized, incorporated.

25 [410]

Development of cruelty: joy at the sight of suffering — presupposed as **divine** *joy* even in blood-cults (self-mutilation).

the sight of suffering arouses *com*passion, and the *triumph* of what is powerful, healthy, secure, is enjoyed in the form of *taking pleasure in our own suffering* — we are strong enough to be able to hurt ourselves! Thus, those who are secure in life enjoy tragedies (perhaps in the case of the Greeks the belief in recurrence? as a counterweight)

25 [411]

Difference between *lower* and *higher* functions: order of rank among organs and drives, as shown through those who command and those who obey.

Task of ethics: differences in values as a *physiological* order of rank of "higher" and "lower" ("more important, more essential, more indispensable, more irreplaceable" etc.)

25 [412]

The *hidden* intentions in the case of philosophers e.g., to draw forth the illusory nature of the world (Brahmins, Eleatics, Kant): some kind of dissatisfaction *of a moral* nature, as something mendacious: a value judgment. — For an extremely confident person, *illusion* as such could even be a delight.

25 [413]

Consolations in regard to the afterlife have the value of keeping alive many people with difficult and arduous lives: to propagate those who are failures: which (in the case of the mixing of races) can be worthwhile in itself because a race becomes *pure* at some later time.

The whole inner conflict of feelings, the consciousness of superpowerful drives, the weakness in the face of the external

world — these are very frequently cited facts, but the character
of life is such that the vast majority of exemplars are failures.
So how did those who suffered because of who they were still
make life acceptable for themselves?

    Hope
    Denigration of life
    Denigration of humans — by humans themselves
    Resistance to a species of humans as a cause of misery
    Causing less suffering: anesthetics.
    Not to suffer at all: ecstasies, festivals.
    to give vent to our pain,[344] orgy of affliction

25 [414]

    How much more money they earn by *admiring others*!

25 [415][345]

    1 Pa⟨rt⟩. to collect all kinds of signs of escapism from real-
ity:[346] and of its motives:

    rotten people
    people with no substance
    unsuccessful people etc.
    how affliction makes people evil: it ruins *music*

25 [416]

    By the end of his life, R⟨ichard⟩ W⟨agner⟩ crossed himself
off: *without wanting to*, he admitted that he fell into despair
and *prostrated* himself before Christianity.

    A defeated man! — This is *fortunate*: for otherwise what addi-
tional confusion his ideal would have produced! The position
vis-à-vis *Christianity* made me reach a decision —likewise concerning all Schopenh⟨auerianism⟩ and pessimism.

    W⟨agner⟩ is perfectly *correct* when he throws himself at
the feet of *every committed* Christian: actually, he ranks far
below such characters! — Only, he should not fall prey to
the urge to drag *characters* who are **superior** to him down
to his level!

His intellect, lacking rigor and discipline, was *slavishly* bound to Sch⟨openhauer⟩: good!

25 [417]

"*Le public! le public! Combien faut il de sots pour faire un public?*"[347]

25 [418]

Ducis said "*tout notre bonheur n'est qu'un malheur plus ou moins consolé.*"[348]

25 [419][349]

I want to say something about prophets and psalms and Job: and the New Testament.

— about Beethoven's dependence on Rousseau's feeling — on how this feeling dissipates.

— on order of rank, e.g., Montaigne in relation to Luther

— the magnificent French as *noble* people

— about Napoleon and his influence on the 19th century.

— about R⟨ichard⟩ W⟨agner⟩. End a *vae victis*![350] People of *that* sort are doing the right thing when they abase themselves before the cross.

— the Brothers Goncourt, Mérimée, Stendhal.

— a founder of a religion *can* be insignificant, a lighted match, nothing more![351]

— the Arabs in Spain, the Provençals: points of light

— also, in favor of Louis XIV and Corneille

— La Rochefoucauld

— anyone who looks at the *masses* always has the impression of nonsense, of failures: like Z⟨arathustra⟩ looking at the **people**!

— the symptoms of religious affects (Salvation Army) (religious ecstasy)

— the neuroses of creative actors, related to hysterics

— all very rich, disorganized m⟨en⟩ acquire an *ethical* character through the influence of the women they love

— many great men do not find their way[352] until they have felt a woman's touch: they see their image in a mirror that magnifies and simplifies.

— there are very many accomplished individuals!

— the Corsicans and Spaniards magnificent manliness.

— a history of German migration

— all true Germanic tribesmen[353] went abroad: Germany today is a proto-Slavic station and lays the groundwork for a pan-Slavic Europe.

— depression in the barracks

— Louis XIV and by contrast the Renaissance!

— the noble illusions which a people like the French are *capable* of e.g., prior to Napoleon — this tells you about their character! And the Germans — skepticism!

— eroticism and silly fanaticism about the cross, juxtaposed

25 [420]

A belief in the *pleasure* of **maintaining control** has been lacking up to now — this pleasure of a rider on a fiery stallion!

— The mediocrity of weak personalities confused with the moderation of strong ones!

25 [421]

Nonsense about a *mother's love. All* love that is not matched by insight wreaks havoc.

25 [422][354]

Women under guardianship. Property.

— Superiority in women's education during the previous century among the French. Madame Roland as the silly "bourgeois woman" in whom vanity proclaims itself in a woman⟨ly-⟩, vulgar fashion.

25 [423]

— trust in the world order ("in God") as the emanation of noble feelings

— the previous century's blissful feeling of trust. Ducis. Tenderness, energy, delicacy — Beethoven.

— Mozart urbane-social-courtly —: Haydn more rustic, maybe Gypsy blood (black) "heathen" (*paganus*)?

25 [424][355]

For a long time "things are in some way comprehensible because, fundamentally speaking, we make only a middling use of our understanding?" — against the Bayreuthers.

25 [425]

— The commonality of our sense impressions is also the starting point for our moral and aesthetic valuations.

25 [426]

— Fundamental problem of "ethics."

To cause suffering and pleasure: to pity, to inflict pain — all of this already presupposes a valuation of suffering and pleasure. "Beneficial," "harmful" are more abstract[356] concepts: it can be the case that I inflict pain (and do good "in a bad way"!), in order to be useful. Indeed, in a broader sense: it could be the case that I would need all of immorality in order to be useful in a larger sense.

But which came first, pleasure and suffering — or "beneficial and harmful"?

Are all feelings of pain and pleasure perhaps initially an *effect* of the judgment "beneficial, harmful" (routine, safe, not dangerous, familiar etc.)?

In judging certain things, we see disgust disappear: the harmony of tones originally free of pleasure. The enjoyment of lines incomprehensible in many respects. The enjoyment of formulas, of dialectical movements *is* only just *emerging*.

But if pleasure and displeasure are initially results of *valuations*, then the *origins* of valuation do *not* lie in feelings. The judgments "higher" and "lower functions" must already be there in all organic structures, long before all feelings of pleasure and displeasure.

The *order of rank* is the initial result of valuation: in the relationship of the organs to one another, all *virtues* must already be practiced — obedience, industriousness, coming to lend assistance, watchfulness — the machine-character *is* wholly *lacking* in everything organic (self-regulation).

25 [427]

NB. the principle of the *preservation of the individual* (or "fear of death") cannot be derived from feelings of pleasure and displeasure, but instead is something *directed*, a *value judgment* which already forms the basis for all feelings of pleasure and displeasure.

— This is even more true of the "preservation of the species": but this is merely a *consequence* of the law of the "preservation of the individual," not an original law.

— Preservation of the individual: i.e., assuming that a multiplicity of elements having the most diverse activities wants "to preserve" itself, *not* as identical to itself, but rather as "alive" — dominating — obeying — nourishing itself — growing —

All our mechanical laws come *from within us*, not from within things! We construct "things" *according to* them.

The synthesis "thing" derives from *us*: all properties of the thing come from *us*. "Cause and effect is a universalization of our feeling and judgment.

All the functions that accompany the preservation of the organism have been able to preserve and propagate themselves on their own.

The intellectual activities have been able to preserve themselves on their own, those that preserved the organism; and in the struggle between organisms these intellectual activities have always made themselves *stronger* and *more sophisticated*, i.e., — — —

NB. — *struggle as the origin of logical functions.* The creature that could most strongly *regulate*, *discipline*, *judge* itself — with the greatest excitability and even greater self-control — has always survived.

25 [428]

Principle: that which helped humans triumph in their battle with animals has at the same time been accompanied by the difficult and dangerous pathological evolution of humans. They are the *animals that have yet to be determined*.

25 [429]

Which "*virtues*" have been propagated through the struggle between animals?

(Obedience in the case of the herd — courage initiative insight in the case of the leaders.)

25 [430]

Order of rank established itself through the *victory* of the stronger and the *indispensability* of the weaker for the stronger and of the stronger for the weaker — separate functions emerge there: for obeying is just as much a function of self-preservation as commanding is for the stronger being.

25 [431]

Whether there is "compassion" between the different organs in the human organism? Certainly, to the greatest extent. A strong reverberation and pain that spreads all around: a proliferation of the *pain*, but in no way the *same* pain. (But it certainly works the same way even among individuals!)

25 [432]

We can comprehend everything that is *necessary* to **preserve** the *organism* in terms of "*moral* demand": there is a "thou shalt" for individual organs, which comes to them from a commanding organ. There is *insubordination* of the organs, weaknesses of the will and character flaws in the stomach, e.g.

— There is no mechanical necessity at work here - - - ? some commands are given that cannot fully be *carried out* (because the force is too limited) But often, extreme *exertion* of the stomach e.g., to complete its task — a *mustering* of the will, something we ourselves are familiar with from difficult tasks. The *effort* and its *degree* **cannot** be comprehended as originating in conscious motives: *obedience* is not a mechanism that plays itself out where organs are concerned - - - ?

25 [433]

What is "higher" and "lower," choosing what is more important, more beneficial, more pressing, already exists in the lowest level of organisms. "*Alive*": i.e., already valuating: —

There is *valuating* in all willing — and will is present in the organic.

25 [434]

The entire existing world is also a *product of our value judgments* — and indeed a product of those that stay the same. —

25 [435]

Superior human beings:[357] the necessity of misunderstanding, the universal pushiness of people today, their belief that they may *join the conversation* about every great person. Respect - - -

— the idiotic blathering about genius etc. The feeling of unconditional *superiority*, the disgust at prostration and slavery. *What can be made out of humans*: this is what matters to superior human beings. The breadth of their vision

25 [436]

(we shouldn't talk about the causes of willing, but rather about the stimuli for willing)

To will, th⟨is is⟩ to command: yet commanding is a particular *affect* (this affect is a *sudden explosion of force*) — under tension, clear, just one thing in mind,[358] utterly confident in being superior, certain of being obeyed — "freedom of the will" is the "feeling of superiority in the one who commands" in regard to the one who obeys: "*I* am free, and *that person* must *obey*."

Now you say: those who command *must* themselves - - -

25 [437]

Without noticing it, the moralities of Kant, Schopenhauer already proceed from *a moral canon*: from human equality, and from the idea that what is morality to one person must also be morality to the other. Yet this is already the *consequence of a morality*, perhaps a very questionable one.

Likewise, the rejection of egoism already presupposes a moral canon: why is it rejected? Because it is *felt* to be reprehensible. But this is already the *effect* of a morality and not one that has been thought through very well!

— And *that* morality is *wanted* already presupposes a moral canon! This *morality of self-preservation* **that has been incorporated** really deserves respect! It is far and away the most subtle system of morality!

Actual human morality within the life of the human body is one hundred times greater and more subtle than all comprehensible moralizing so far. The many "thou shalt's" that continue to work within us! Concerns of those who command and those who obey when associating with each other! Knowledge about higher and lower functions!

To make the attempt to understand everything that seems purposeful in terms of what is **exclusively** *life-preserving* and *consequently is the only thing that preserves* — —

As purpose relates to the actual event, so moral judgment relates to the really more *diverse* and more subtle *judgments of the organism* — merely an outlier and the final act of the process.

25 [438][359]

1) We want to hold on tightly to our senses and to our faith in them — and to think them through to the end! The absurd nature of philosophy up to now as the greatest human absurdity.

2) we want to *further* build up the existing world, the world that is built up by all terrestrial life, so that it seems to be this way (continuously and *slowly* moved) — not, however, to criticize it into oblivion as something false!

3) our value judgments build upon this existing world, they emphasize and underscore. What does it mean when entire religions say: "everything is bad and false and evil!" This condemnation of the entire process can only be a judgment rendered by failures!

4) to be sure, these failures could be the ones who suffer the most and are the most subtle? Satisfied people could be worth little?

5) we must understand the fundamental artistic phenomenon, which is called life — *the building mind* that builds under the most unfavorable conditions: in the slowest way - - - the **proof** for all its combinations must first be provided anew: *it remains in existence.*

25 [439]

Above all: not so fast! Slowly! first secure what has been conquered! Follow Russia's example! And be of good cheer at every station!

25 [440]

The sight of the masses and of the teachers of the masses *makes us gloomy!* —

25 [441]

Why has ethics lagged behind the furthest? For even the famous systems that have appeared most recently are naïve! Likewise the Greeks! The doctrines of Christianity regarding sin have become frail due to God's frailty.

— our actions measured against our exemplar! But *that* we have an exemplar, and one like this, is already the consequence of a morality.

— the Jews, who measured themselves against their God — what lay behind this was their will *to despise themselves* and to prostrate themselves before him for the sake of his favor and disfavor. — Even Jesus resisted being called good. "No one is good, except God," he said. That no one could accuse him of sinning, this is another issue: this in no way refutes the criticism he receives from his own conscience.[360] A person who feels absolutely good about himself would have to be an idiot in terms of intellect.

— this prostrating oneself for the sake of God's favor and disfavor is an oriental aspect of *Christianity*: *not* noble!

— what is *slave-like* about Jews today, even about Germans —

— This *equating of ourselves* through compassion is already the *consequence* of a moral judgment: not a fundamental phenomenon and not ubiquitous: furthermore it is something else in the soul of a herd-creature than it is in the soul of a powerful person: actually merely a *feeling among equals* —: for inferior people, the *suffering* of superior people is a reason to feel good and to feel better than good.[361]

— "philosophical and religious systems are in agreement that the ethical significance of actions must be at the same time a *metaphysical* one" etc. etc. Schopenhauer, Ba⟨sis⟩ of Morals p. 261.[362] Pericles on his deathbed: thoughts take a moral direction.

Now, in the case of Pericles: he is pondering his *legacy* among his citizens. The disciple of Anaxagoras was a free spirit. — *Because* these systems believe in the life of the soul, it is obvious that, at the moment of death, they elicit a judgment about the *value of a full life*: what kind of life will we have *further into the future*?

Rewarding good people and punishing evil people in the afterlife was the means of punishment used by religions, a kind of completion of the world order, a means of compensating for the facts.

25 [442]

The character of good people "in themselves": "they make less of a distinction than everyone else between themselves and others" Schopenhauer l.c. 265.[363]

25 [443]

Ethicists up to now have had no idea *how* they stand in regard to entirely specific moral judgments: they all claim to know already *what* is good and evil.

Socrates did *not* know this, but all of his disciples *defined* it, i.e., they assumed *it was there*, and the task was to *describe* it thoroughly. **How**! If I were to say: **is** it there, then? Did anyone ever think about *what kind* of measurements to use here? And on the other hand: perhaps we in no way know *enough* **so as to** calculate the worth of actions. It is sufficient that we live *experimentally* for long periods of time according to *a* morality!

25 [444]

How much we depress ourselves about suffering that we have not felt but rather have *caused*! But it is *unavoidable*; and we are not dissatisfied with *ourselves* on that account, except in conditions of weakness and of mistrust in our right to do so!

25 [445]

The course of philosophy up to now: we wanted to explain the world in terms of that which we ourselves find to be *evident* — wherever we ourselves *think* that we **understand**. Thus, sometimes in terms of the mind or the soul, or the will, or as representation, illusion, image, or other times in terms of the eye (as optical phenomenon, atoms, movements) or in terms of the body, or in terms of purposes, or in terms of push and pull i.e., our sense of touch. Or in terms of our value judgments, as a God of goodness of justice etc., or in terms of our aesthetic value judgments. Enough, even science does what humans have always done: using *something* of themselves that they accept as comprehensible, as *true*, in order to explain everything else — *anthropomorphism* in summa. The great *synthesis* is still missing and even each individual piece of work is still completely in the process of becoming e.g., the reduction of the world to optical phenomena (atoms) We project humans *into it* — that's all, we continue to create this anthropomorphized world. There are experiments that are about *which* process has the most force at the end[364] (e.g., mechanical)

25 [446]

Not to be angry with someone who is doing us harm, *because* everything is necessary — this would itself already be a consequence of a morality: which would be called "thou shalt not get upset about what is necessary." — It is irrational: but who says: "Thou shalt be *rational*!"

25 [447]

Honesty, as a *consequence* of long-term moral habits: the *self-criticism of morality* is simultaneously a *moral phenomenon* ⟨an⟩ event having to do with morality.

25 [448]

The method of mechanical observation of the world is occasionally the *most* honest *one* by far: the good will toward everything that regulates itself, all logical regulating functions, everything that does not lie and betray, is active there.

25 [449]

Provisional Truths.

It is a bit childish, or even kind of deceptive, when a thinker today produces a totality of knowledge, a system — we are too savvy not to harbor the most profound doubt concerning the *possibility* of carrying such a totality within ourselves. It is sufficient if we come to agree about a totality of *methodological presuppositions* — about "provisional truths" that we want to use as a guideline for our work: as when a mariner maintains a particular course on the world's oceans

25 [450]

That which is best *developed* in humans is their will to power — in which case there is really no need for Europeans to deceive themselves about this just because of a few millennia of Christianity, which is completely mendacious and has been lying to itself all that time.

25 [451]

Philosophy as love of wisdom. All the way up to the sage as the one who is the happiest, the most powerful, the one who justifies *all becoming* and wants it again.

— not love for humans or for gods, or for truth, but rather *love for a condition, an intellectual and sensory feeling of completion*: an affirmation and approbation that stems from an overflowing feeling of the power to shape things. The great sign of distinction. **real love!**

25 [452]

Commands "this is how you **shall** value things!" are the beginnings of all moral judgments — superior stronger people dictate and proclaim *their* feelings as *laws* for others.

The feeling of *veneration* would not be derivable from utility. Initially, people were venerated: the belief in gods comes to the fore when people seem less and less "worthy of veneration" — hence the belief in "founding fathers" or in the decisions of earlier judges.

25 [453]³⁶⁵

Zarathustra as *judge* in the 2nd part

the grandiose form and revelation of a *justice* that shapes, builds and consequently *must* annihilate (discovering himself in the process, surprised, suddenly to recognize the *essence of someone who judges*)

Mockery in response: "tear the good and just into pieces" — screams the woman who murders him

25 [454]

"Humans are something that must be overcome"³⁶⁶ — it depends on the tempo: the Greeks worthy of admiration: without haste,

— my ancestors *Heraclitus Empedocles Spinoza Goethe*

25 [455]
   A) Moral value judgments exist. Critique: where? for how
       long? where are there others? will there be still others?
   B) Explanation of the origin of these value judgments.
       Tracing them back to other values.
       Values and *physiological* significance etc.
       Praise, blame (fame)
       Powerful slaves
   C) Critique of these value judgments. Inconsistencies.
       from where do I get the critique? Being careful not to
          get it from morality again. "Useful"
       Suppose they are taken from morality itself, proof that
          they are shortsighted.
       Fundamental prejudices and all that is overlooked.
   D) the problem has just been *posed*. Up to now a kind
       of astrology — of the belief that cosmic processes are
       closely related to us.
       Moral philosophers are themselves symptoms. Self-
          annihilation of morality.

25 [456][367]
   NB. "I do not need all of this: but I accept it as a gift. As
someone who takes, I sanctify this" — what Zarathustra said
about the many *good things in life*.

25 [457]
   We want to *inherit* all previous morality: and *not* start from
scratch. Everything we do is merely morality, a morality which
turns against its previous form.

25 [458][368]
   "**Can** you *swear an oath*? are you sure enough of yourselves
to do it?" asks Zarathustra.

25 [459]

The principle by means of which humans have become rulers *over the animals* is probably also the principle which establishes "the most superior human beings": power, cleverness, ability to wait, negotiation, rigor, warrior affects.

25 [460]

All value judgments are the results of determinate quantities of force and of the degree that we are conscious of them: they are laws *with a perspectival aspect* that depends on the nature of people and peoples — what is near, important, necessary etc.

Under certain circumstances, all human drives, like all *animal drives*, are trained as *conditions of existence* and brought into the foreground. *Drives* are the *aftereffects of long-held value judgments* that now work instinctively, much like a *system* of judgments having to do with pleasure and pain. Initially compulsion, then habit, then need, then natural urge (drive)

25 [461]

Feelings — a *series* of value judgments. Sensorium commune[369]

25 [462]

Because we are heirs to lineages of human beings who have lived under the *most varied* conditions of existence, we preserve *within ourselves* a *multiplicity of instincts*. Anyone who claims to be "authentic" is probably an ass or an impostor.

The diversity of animal temperaments:[370] on average, a *temperament* is the *product of a milieu — a completely inculcated* **role**, *underscored* and *strengthened* again and again by certain actions[371] associated with it. Over the long term, this is how *race* emerges: i.e., assuming that the environment does not change.

With changes in the milieu, those characteristics which are *generally* the most beneficial and useful begin to *emerge* — or else they perish. This emergence shows itself as the power to assimilate even in unfavorable situations, yet at the same time it is accompanied by nervousness, caution, there is no beauty in the form it takes.

Europeans as this sort of super-race. Likewise, the Jews; ultimately, they are a *ruling* species, although quite different from the ancient ruling race who had not altered their environment.

All in all, it begins with *compulsion* (when a people enters an environment). Nature, the seasons, warm and cold conditions etc. this is all first and foremost a *tyrannical* element. Gradually the feeling of being compelled goes away —

25 [463]

We are shape-creating beings, long before we ever created concepts. Concepts emerged initially via sounds, when we combined *many* images by means of a single sound: thus, the optical inner phenomena *were categorized* by means of hearing.

25 [464]

NB. The concepts "good" etc. are taken from the *influence* that "good people" exercise: —

— even in cases of self-evaluation. —

25 [465]

Humans *are unknown*, actions *are unknown*. When, in spite of this, we now talk about humans and actions as if they were known, this has to do with our reaching a consensus about certain *roles* that almost anyone can play.

25 [466]

The evolution of predatory instincts[372]

of lies and deception
of cruelty
of the sex drive   } into highly valued things
of mistrust
of hard-heartedness
of obsession with power

— on the other hand, changes in the valuation of evil qualities, as soon as they are conditions of existence.

perhaps tracing all desires back to hunger.

25 [467]

Vivisection — this is the starting point! Many people are now becoming aware of the fact that many beings feel pain *when knowledge is demanded of them*!! As if it had ever been otherwise! And what pain!! Cowardly rabble, weaklings!!

25 [468]

Starting point: it is obvious that our strongest and most habitual *judgments* have been around the longest, having emerged in ages of ignorance and then become established — such that everything that we believe in without question *probably* can be traced back to the very worst possible reasons: people have always taken experiential "proof" too lightly, just as there are still people today who think that God's goodness can be "proved" on the basis of experience.

25 [469]

"Sitting in Judgment."

Judging the *value of people* is the most beloved and most frequently rendered of all *judgments*, — the empire of the greatest inanities. To put a *stop* to this here, once and for all, here and now, until it is acknowledged to be something dirty, like exposing our private parts — my mission. Even more so, because this is the time of *suffrage universel*. Here we should swear an *oath* to doubt things for a long time and to mistrust ourselves, *not an oath on* "the goodness of human beings," but rather on our right to say "*This* is goodness!"

25 [470][373]

When the morality of "thou shalt not lie" has been rejected, "a feeling for truth" will have to seek legitimacy before another forum. As a means of preserving humans, *as the willing of power*.[374]

— likewise, our love for the beautiful is in the same way a *will that shapes things*. Both feelings reinforce each other — a feeling for what is real is the means of taking power into our own hands, in order to shape things as we wish. The pleasure in shaping and reshaping — a primordial pleasure! We can only *comprehend* a world that we ourselves have *made*.

25 [471]

Claiming that our *limited ability* to know is a good thing — the advantages of this: much courage and pleasure are possible. Sighing and Pascalian skepticism are *bad blood*.

— *Christianity as the result of degenerate* bad **blood**

25 [472]³⁷⁵

bonus = φαν: the splendid one, the one who shines forth?
malus   man-lus (Manlius) = μαν the crazy one?
böse cf. *bass*   the strong one?
gut Gothe (God) "the godly one" original designation for noble Goths.

> (or *gobt* the giver? like *optimus*?) is the *god* called the good one (*optimus*) or the good one called godly?

optimus op- the one who gives?

25 [473]³⁷⁶

Archimedes discovering a principle of hydraulics while bathing

Goethe: "my entire inner processes turned out to be a living heuristic which, when it recognizes an unknown rule whose presence it senses, *endeavors* to discover this rule in the outside world and — *introduce it into the outside world*."

25 [474]³⁷⁷

The Pharisees did the *right thing* in condemning Jesus. Likewise the Athenians.

25 [475][378]

Goethe. "All people incapable of finding enjoyment *on their own* are doomed to suffer. *We act on behalf of others in order to find enjoyment with others.*"

25 [476][379]

Goethe's characterization of "German sensibility" "*Indulging weaknesses, in others and in ourselves.*"

25 [477][380]

Anyone who takes a stand like mine, will lose, to echo Goethe, "one of the greatest human rights, no longer to be judged by our peers."

25 [478][381]

"Mastery often passes for egoism" Goethe.

25 [479][382]

Velleius Paterculus I 9, 3 *virum in tantum laudandum, in quantum intellegi virtus potest.*

25 [480][383]

Goethe: "we are all so narrow-minded that we always believe we are right; and thus it is possible to imagine an extraordinary intellect not only making errors but even taking pleasure in doing so."

25 [481]

Chi non fa, non falla[384] "makes no mistakes."

25 [482][385]

"*Magna ingenia conspirant.*"

25 [483]

Moral value judgments are more like *hasty additions to value* — and *subtractions from value* — fundamentally a rather modest display of our ability to judge.

25 [484]

The ways of freedom.

— *Cutting* ourselves *off* from the past (from fatherland, religious beliefs, parents, comrades

— interaction with *ostracized people* of all kinds (in history and in society)

— overthrowing what is most revered, affirming what is most forbidden — *schadenfreude* on a large scale in place of reverence

— committing all crimes[386]

— experiment, new valuations

Justice as a way of thinking that builds separates annihilates, liberates us from value judgments: *supreme representative of life itself.*

Wisdom and its relationship to *power*: at some point wisdom will be more influential — error, the rabble's value judgments have had too great an influence up to now, even *among sages*!

25 [485]

The *body* is the best advisor for distinguishing between success and failure, at least it is the most worthy of study.

25 [486]

Up to now, diverse moral judgments have *not* been traced back to the existence of the "human" *species*: but rather to the existence of "peoples" "races" etc. — and indeed by peoples that have wanted to hold their ground *against* other peoples, by *upper classes*[387] that have wanted to draw sharp distinctions between themselves and the lower classes.

25 [487]

Everyone should be allowed to ask the question: is *my* existence, measured against my nonexistence, something that can be justified?

25 [488]

Fundamental insight: "good" and "bad" characteristics are *fundamentally the same* — they have their basis in the same drives of self-preservation, acquisition, separation, intention to propagate etc.

25 [489]

Sages and the arts. (They possess all the arts *within themselves*)
Sages and politics.
Sages and education.
Sages and the sexes.
— as beings whose influence is not felt until *later*.
Independent, patient, ironic —

25 [490][388]

Wisdom and Love of Wisdom.
Intimations of a Philosophy of the Future.
By
Friedrich Nietzsche

25 [491]

The *concealment* that is needed by sages: their awareness that they will *not* be understood, their Machiavellianism, what is going on today leaves them cold.

— the absolute incompatibility of wisdom with the "welfare of the masses": "freedom of the press" "public instruction" — all this is compatible only in cases of drastic delusion concerning the nature of wisdom. It is the *most dangerous* thing in the world!

— of course, as I see it, a *marriage free* from all sanctions is the only proper justifiable course of action for the sage. The sage who takes a different position belongs in a comedy, which is advisable under certain circumstances e.g., Goethe.

— Principle, that all circumstances are designed to make it *impossible* for sages to exist: respect for sages is undercut by religions, by *suffrage universel*, by the sciences! We must first *teach*

that these religions, in comparison to wisdom, are something
for the rabble! We must obliterate existing religions, if only to
eliminate these absurd valuations, as though a Jesus Christ were
at all worthy of consideration alongside a Plato, or a Luther
alongside a Montaigne!

25 [492]
   On *order of rank*.
   Wherever "moral" judgments occur, I hear *hostile* instincts,
aversions, wounded pride, jealousy
choosing words — it is a masquerade in words —
   — I found it impossible to teach the "truth" where the
mindset is so base.
   Future age of great *wars*. Permanence is to be mistrusted.
Bribing all parties and interests, using any means necessary

25 [493][389]
   — *only love should judge* — — chorus
creative love that *loses sight* of itself[390] in its works

25 [494]
   To demonstrate that some people *must step aside*

25 [495]
   We call a characteristic in an animal "evil" and still identify
it as the animal's condition of existence! For the animal, it is its
"good" — it is *healthy* and *strong* in this, as a sign of this! —
Thus: something is called "good" and "evil" in relation *to us*,
not to itself! i.e., the basis of "good" and "evil" is an egoistical
one.
   — But the egoism of the *herd*!
   Everything that is beneficial is *necessarily* also harmful relative to other things. "A good person" — this is seeing things
one-sidedly. Assessed from a distance, this is a person of the
herd, weak, and easy to fool, and whose downfall is easy to
bring about, even intellectually obedient, not creative.

25 [496]

To prostrate ourselves before what we don't have, when we feel bad about everything *that* we do have e.g., Wagner: he believes in the happiness of *boundless* devotion, of boundless *trust*, the happiness of compassionate people, of chaste people — He doesn't know *any* of this from experience! Hence the fantastical nonsense!

25 [497]

To venerate bad manners, as in the case of Shakespeare and Beethoven, in order to prepare the way for the idea that *he*[391] might be a combination of both.

25 [498]

It has made me more *free* — every deeply derogatory phrase, every failure to appreciate me: I want less and less from people: I can give them more and more. Cutting every single tie is *hard*, but a wing is growing on me in place of the tie.

— to be unreservedly in the right: sympathy my weakness, which I am overcoming. It is a good thing, if, in the end, the most disgusting *exploitation* of my sympathy and my forbearance teaches me that I have *nothing* keeping me here.

25 [499]

— the "*transformation*" of a person through a dominant idea is the original phenomenon on which Christianity is built; it sees "a miracle" in this. We - - -

I don't believe for an instant that a person suddenly becomes a *superior more valuable* person; a Christian is for me a completely normal person with a few other phrases and value judgments. *In the long run*, certainly, these words and works do have an effect and perhaps create a type: *the Christians as the most mendacious kind of persons.* That they speak morally, this corrupts them through and through: just look at Luther. A dreadful sight, softly sentimental, fearful, upset - - - odd! how the "sense of truth" awakens and immediately falls asleep again!

— I separate myself from every philosophy by asking "good?" "for what purpose!" and "good?" why do you call it that?

Christianity has *accepted* "good" and "evil" and has *created* nothing here.

25 [500][392]

Wisdom
and Love of Wisdom

Prolegomena to a Philosophy of the Future.
By
Friedrich Nietzsche.

Amor fati.[393]

25 [501]
Unfeeling, sly, lustful, full of schadenfreude — almost all of a philosopher's procedures can be traced back to character flaws — —

25 [502]
There are cases where I do appreciate and single out unselfish people: not on account of them being unselfish, but rather because they seem to have a right to use other people at their expense: and in the case of those who are born to be masters, self-denial and unselfishness is being — — — We can always ask *who* this one is and who that one is. As we see it, the unrestricted inclination to unselfishness would just signify that someone belongs to the herd

25 [503]
Concerning the highest level of morality: as an experiment, it turns its eye *against* itself.

25 [504][394]
The *love* of wisdom.

Failures and those with mongrel bloodlines (Against Christianity)

Sages, and the good things in life.

25 [505][395]

This perspectival world, this world for the eye, touch and ear is very false, compared to when we use a much more subtle sense-apparatus. But its intelligibility clarity, its viability, its beauty begins to *cease existing* when we *make* our senses *more subtle*: likewise, beauty ceases to exist when we think through the events of history; the arrangement according to *purpose* is already an illusion. Enough, the more superficially and more crudely we summarize, the *more valuable*, determinate, beautiful, meaningful the world *seems*. The more deeply we look into the world, the more our value judgment vanishes — *meaninglessness approaches*! We have created the world that has value! Recognizing this, we also recognize that the veneration of the truth is already the *result* of an illusion — and that it is more important that we appreciate the force that builds, simplifies, formulates, poeticizes — which was God

"Everything is false! Everything is permitted!"[396]

That which is "beautiful," that which is "valuable," finds its place only after a dimming of vision, a will to simplicity: considered in itself, *I don't know what it is.*

25 [506]

Is a propensity for truth really the meaning of a *good* person? for example, what kind of fundamental mendacity must have been part of making the New Testament!

25 [507]

All physics is merely a symptomatology.

25 [508]

It is impossible to prove the existence of individuals. Nothing having to do with "personality" is fixed.

25 [509]
An explanation of our "world" might be possible using "false assumptions." Everything only perspectival, only in regard to the *preservation* of small organic beings.

25 [510]
"The good person" a dangerous thing, a sign of exhaustion — egoism becoming weaker.

25 [511][397]
I find Marcus Aurelius' Meditations to be a strange book.

25 [512]
The religious affect is the most interesting illness that has befallen people up to now. The study of this affect makes healthy people seem almost boring and repellent.

25 [513]
Being must be denied.

25 [514]
The emergence of memory is the problem of that which is organic. How is memory possible?
The affects are symptoms of the formation of the contents of memory[398] — perpetually living onward and having a collective effect.

25 [515]
The highest measure of strong people is the question to what extent they can live their lives on the basis of *hypotheses* instead of "faith," to what extent they can sail out on boundless seas,[399] as it were. All lesser intellects perish.

25 [516]
Feline egoism.

There is a canine egoism and a feline egoism in humans: they choose opposite methods. The first is devoted and enthusiastic —

25 [517]

Pleasure and displeasure are affirmations and negations.

To judge is 1) to believe that "this *is* so" and 2) "this has such and such *value*"

Pleasure and displeasure are *effects* of everything having to do with the intellect, a consequence of *critical judgments* which we *feel* as pleasure or pain.

25 [518]⁴⁰⁰

— according to P. Secchi, space cannot be boundless, since no thing that has been pieced together from individual bodies can be infinite, and because an infinite heavenly sphere peopled by numberless stars, like the sun after its complete dissolution, *would have to* appear to be shining —

25 [519]⁴⁰¹

Maupertuis suggested that, in order to research the nature of the soul, it would have to be possible to do vivisections on Patagonians. One eighth of all reputable moralists treat themselves like Patagonians.

25 [520]⁴⁰²

Value judgments not dependent on pleasure and displeasure: the value is measured *according to the survival of the whole*: thus, according to something in the future which is being *imagined*, according to purposes.

Pleasure and displeasure are, initially, the consequence of judging according to purposes. Judging the value of events in regard to their *consequences*.

No *tendencies having to do with survival* can be derived from a mechanical account:⁴⁰³ they presuppose that we *envision* the

whole being — its goals, dangers and challenges; the lower
being that obeys must be able to imagine, at least to some
degree, what the higher being has as its mission. Pleasure and
displeasure are used to characterize individual experience in
terms of *survival*.

25 [521]
Everywhere we look, nonsensical opinions have the status
of basic rights. I'm the first one to see that this idea makes no
sense[404]

25 [522]
The world of good and evil is only *apparent*.

25 [523][405]

Against Complacency

Zarathustra I
Powerful people being diminished and being shamed
— not many sightings of ambitious people.
— the ugliness of the plebeians
— the jealousy and pettiness of the plebeians
— the victory of moral tartuffery.
— the danger that world government falls into the hands of
the mediocre
— the suffocation of all *superior* types.

ego as *distraction* from the eudaimonistic point of view
— *historical*.

25 [524]
    against equality
    against moral tartuffery
    against Christianity and God
    against what is national — the good European.

25 [525]⁴⁰⁶

One day, bored by his virtue, a god of love could say: "for once, let's try it with deviltry!" And behold, a new origin of evil! From boredom and virtue!

25 [526]⁴⁰⁷

Just because an opinion is *irrefutable* doesn't necessarily make it true.

[26 = W I 2. Summer–Autumn 1884]

26 [1]

Preliminaries
and Predecessors

26 [2][1]

Skeptical Objections.

26 [3]

The great philosophers have seldom turned out well. Who are these Kant, Hegel, Schopenhauer, Spinoza anyway! How barren, how one-sided! Here we can understand why artists can fancy themselves to be more significant. My familiarity with the great Greek figures is what educated me: there is more to admire about Heraclitus Empedocles Parmenides Anaxagoras Democritus, they are more *complete*. Christianity has it on its conscience that it *ruined* many well-rounded people e.g., Pascal and, earlier, Meister Eckhart. In the end, it even ruined the concept of the artist: it drenched Raphael with a shy hypocrisy, in the end, even his transfigured Christ is a flighty, fanatical little monk whom he does not dare to show naked. Goethe stands up well here.

26 [4]

"People love out of gratitude, out of overflowing hearts, because death has been cheated" Lagarde p. 54.[2] against "humanity."

26 [5]

The advantage of the Church, like Russia, is this: they can wait.

26 [6]³

A religion that has God's adultery standing outside its door (with him, after all, nothing is impossible!)

26 [7]

— loving your neighbor, loving even your enemies, because God does so — "he allows it to rain upon the just and the unjust."⁴ But he doesn't do that at all.

26 [8]⁵

— Fichte, Schelling, Hegel, Schleiermacher, Feuerbach, Strauss — all theologians.

26 [9]⁶

— in the age of *suffrage universel*,⁷ i.e., where everyone sits in judgment of everyone and everything, I am being pushed into reinstituting an *order of rank*.

26 [10]

Among peoples now regarded as ancient, great *sensuousness*, e.g., Hungarians, Chinese, Jews, French (for the Celts were already a cultured people!) —

26 [11]⁸

The real Bedouins of the desert and the ancient Vikings —

26 [12]⁹

NB. In my view, the most fervently believed a priori "truths" are — *assumptions until further notice* e.g., the law of causality, are extremely well-trained habituations of belief, so well incorporated that *not* believing *in them* would cause the species to perish. But are they truths on that account? What a conclusion!

As if truth would be demonstrated by humans continuing to exist!

26 [13]¹⁰

I have *to establish* the *most challenging ideal* of *philosophers*. Learning doesn't do it! Scholars are herd-animals in the kingdom of knowledge who conduct research because they were ordered to do so and were shown how to do it.

26 [14]

There is no innate feeling for truth; but because there is a strong prejudice toward thinking that it is more useful to know the truth than to let ourselves be deceived, the truth is sought — while it is sought in many other cases because it *could* perhaps be more useful — whether it is for the accumulation of power, wealth, honor, self-esteem.

26 [15]

Though they are often unaware of it, an intentionality is also at work behind the real friends of truth, the philosophers: from the outset they want a certain "truth" created just so — and all too often they have revealed their innermost needs by pursuing *their* path to their "truth."

26 [16]

Poor Schopenhauer! E. von Hartmann cut the legs right out from under him, and Richard Wagner went so far as to cut off his head!

26 [17]

We can know only that aspect of the will that is knowable — therefore, assuming that we know ourselves as willing beings, there must be something intellectual about willing.

26 [18]

A cognitive mechanism[11] that wants to know itself!! We definitely should have moved beyond this absurd *goal*! (The stomach that consumes itself! —)

26 [19]

Just as Winckelmann acquired a sense for antiquity from observing Laocoön at the end of antiquity, as it were, so too R⟨ichard⟩ W⟨agner⟩ acquired a sense of style from observing opera, the *worst* of all the art genres i.e., the insight that it is not possible to *isolate* the arts.

26 [20]

— the demagogic character of Wagner's art: in the end with the consequence that he bowed down to Luther in order to get some influence.

26 [21]

— German music does *not* stand outside of the development of culture: there is a lot of rococo in Mozart and that delicacy of the 18th century. In Beethoven, a touch of France, the enthusiastic fantasies from which the revolution sprang forth: always an echo, finale. W⟨agner⟩ and Romanticism.

— what about the connection between music and the visual arts? And poetry? Relative solitude of musicians, they are less *present* in life, their excitement is an echo of *earlier feelings*.

The grand style is still lacking in *music*; and care has been taken to make sure it does not develop now!

26 [22][12]

Everything I had said about R⟨ichard⟩ W⟨agner⟩ is wrong. I had this feeling in 1876 "everything about him is inauthentic; anything authentic is hidden or embellished. It is acting in every good and bad sense of the word."

26 [23]

To distance ourselves in the same way from moral phenomena, just as physicians stand clear of believing in witches and the doctrine of "the devil's grip."

26 [24]

Pain, uncertainty, malice: people who belong to the herd take very different positions in regard to these three things.

26 [25][13]

The advantages of this era. "Nothing is true: everything is permitted."[14]

26 [26]

I see criminals, punished and unpunished, as people who can be experimented on. Protection, *not* rehabilitation, *not* punishment!

26 [27]

— a people that subjugates itself to the intelligence of a *Luther*!

26 [28]

NB. Things are looking *good*: nothing but *incredibly huge* convulsions are about to happen. If I consider what the French Revolution *set in motion* — even Beethoven would be inconceivable without it, Napoleon equally so. That's why I hope that all fundamental problems will be brought to light and that we will get beyond the silliness of the New Testament or beyond Hamlet and Faust, the two "most modern human beings."

26 [29]

I have elevated myself onto a pinnacle where I have a good clear view: and many of those who shone above me like a star when I was young are now far away from me — but *below* me e.g., Sch⟨openhauer⟩ W⟨agner⟩.

26 [30]

We shouldn't build in places where there is no time left. Jubilation found in mass movements: and *I am* the one who sees what it's about: about everything "good" and "evil."

26 [31][15]

Describing R⟨ichard⟩ W⟨agner⟩ — attempt at a dictatorship. But in the end *he crossed himself off the list*, incapable of forming a complete conception of himself. He was seduced by the "raptures" of the Protestant communion!

Montaigne — — —

26 [32]

"World-conquest." In what ways humans have sought to subjugate things up to now:

— the boundaries where they could go no further and subjugated themselves (Moira[16]) — "God." The dream of "rulers" ruling the world is once again projected into things.

— Consolations. Devotion.

26 [33]

"Peace as a chimera." "Pacification"

26 [34]

During the day, the lower intellect is closed off from consciousness. At night, the higher intellect sleeps, the lower one enters consciousness (dream)

26 [35]

As in a dream where the cause of cannon fire is sought[17] and the shot is not *heard* until afterwards (thus, a reversal of time takes place: *this reversal of time always takes place*, even when awake. The "causes" are imagined *after the "deed"*; I mean, our *ends* and *means* are the result of a sequence of events??)

How thoroughly we are trained to believe that nothing happens without a cause, this is demonstrated by the phenomenon just mentioned: we do not *accept* the cannon fire until we have worked out how it might possibly have occurred, i.e., a stretch of time precedes every actual *experience* in which the fact to be experienced is *motivated*.

— this could be the case in the movement of *every nerve*, *every muscle*.

Thus, there is a *judgment* in every so-called sensory perception which *affirms* or *denies* the sequence of events before it "enters" into consciousness.

All organic life, *as observable movement*, is *coordinated* with *mental events*.

An organic being is the observable expression of a *mind*.

26 [36]

The nervous system and the brain are a routing system and a centralization mechanism consisting of countless individual minds with varying abilities. Whatever has to do with *I-mentality itself* is already given along with the cell.

Prior to the cell, there is *no I-mentality*, yet it is probable that only a *thought process* (memory and conclusion) corresponds to everything conformable to a law, i.e., to the *relational character* of everything that happens

26 [37]

Where there is no error, this realm is more advanced: the inorganic as mentality devoid of individuality. The organic creature derives its own perspective[18] from egoism, in order to survive.

— its thinking doesn't go beyond its own survival.

— a continuing process with growth, propagation etc.

26 [38]

Thoughts are forces. Nature transpires as a multitude of relations among forces: they are thoughts, *logical absolutely certain processes*, any possibility of error is lacking. Our science has taken the approach of discovering logical formulas *everywhere* and nothing further.

— all these series of movements that we see or almost see (atoms) are consequences

1. The indestructible uniformity of force, space with the function, the force. Everything is mechanics.

2. Mechanics is fundamentally logic.

3. logic not derivable. How is error possible? more accurately: laws of survival for continuing processes presuppose perspectival *illusion*.

26 [39]

"fair-minded people" quite refreshing for the observer, providing peace: yet, for themselves, a terrible agony

26 [40]

Art — the joy of *communicating who we are* (and receiving from the more gifted) — forming psyches by using shapes —

26 [41]

This need to have knowledge ready at hand is not present in someone with an extremely decisive nature —

26 [42]

I am rethinking the problem of where we should rank artists (Plato); at the same time, I am elevating artists as much as I can. Actually, we find that all artists are *subordinated* to great intellectual movements, not to the leaders of these movements: who often bring the movement to completion e.g., Dante for the Catholic Church. R⟨ichard⟩ W⟨agner⟩ for the Romantic movement. Shakespeare for Montaigne's free thinking,

The superior forms, where being an artist is only a part of what makes them human — e.g., Plato, Goethe, G⟨iordano⟩ Bruno. These forms seldom succeed.

26 [43]

All philosophical systems have been *overcome*; the Greeks shine more brightly than ever, particularly the Greeks before Socrates.

26 [44]

The reversal of time: we believe the external world to be the cause of its effect on us, but it is we who have already *transformed* its actual and unconsciously ongoing effect *into the external world*: that which confronts us is our work which is now affecting us in return. *Time* is required for this to be completed: but this time is so short.

26 [45]

Our value judgments stand in relation to those conditions that we believe are required in order for us to live: if these conditions change, then our value judgments change.

26 [46]

Coordination instead of *cause and effect*

26 [47][19]

The Way to Wisdom.
Suggestions for Overcoming Morality.

The first step. To admire (and obey and *learn*) better than anyone else. To collect within ourselves all the things worth admiring and to let them battle each other. To bear every burden. Asceticism of the intellect — bravery, a time for fellowship.

The second step. To break admiring hearts (where *ties are the strongest*). The free spirit. Independence. Time in the desert. Critique of everything that has been admired (idealizing what has not been admired), attempt at reverse valuations.

The third step. Major decision, whether I am prepared to take a positive position, to affirm. No god, no human *above* me anymore! The instinct of those who create, who know *where* to take hold of things. Major responsibility and innocence. (In order to feel joy at something, it is essential to call *everything* good.) Giving ourselves the right to act.

26 [48]²⁰

1. Overcoming evil petty inclinations. The spacious heart, which we conquer only with love.

(R⟨ichard⟩W⟨agner⟩ threw himself down before a limitless loving heart, likewise Schopenhauer. This is part of the *first* stage.) Fatherland, race, everything is part *of this*.

2. Overcoming even good inclinations.

ignoring personalities like D⟨ühring⟩ and W⟨agner⟩ or Sch⟨openhauer⟩ as *not even once* reaching this stage!

3. Beyond good and evil. They adopt the mechanical world-view and do not feel humiliated by destiny: they *are* destiny. They hold the fate of human beings in their hands.

Only for a few people: most will perish before they finish the 2nd stage. Plato Spinoza? perhaps *succeeding*? Finally giving themselves the right to act.

Beware of actions that no longer fit the *stage that has been achieved* e.g., wanting to help those who are not important enough — this is mistaken compassion.

26 [49]²¹

NB. "Consciousness" — to what extent the imagined idea, the imagined will, the imagined feeling (*which is known to us alone*) is completely superficial! Even our *inner* world is "appearance"!

26 [50]

Standard of measurement. How much of the truth can people endure without *degenerating*! And without being driven to despair by contradiction and animosity and misunderstanding? Not even by *the stupidity of* their admirers' *love*?

26 [51]

What a terrible fate befell Schopenhauer! Some encountered his *biases* and *exaggerated* them (Dühring and Richard Wagner), a Berliner encountered his fundamental insight into *pessimism* and unwittingly *trivialized it* (E. von Hartmann)!

26 [52]

We think that our *conscious* intellect is the cause of all purposeful arrangements within us. This is totally wrong. Nothing is more superficial than using consciousness to posit "ends" and "means": it is a mechanism of simplification (like using words etc.), a means of communication, it does the job, nothing more — without intending an *infusion* of knowledge.

26 [53]

"Chance" — in great minds that are replete with conceptions and possibilities, and are, as it were, replete with a play of forms, out of all this a process of selecting and integrating from what was selected earlier. — The *dependence* of inferior personalities on more inventive ones cannot be *overstated* — someday to show *how much* everything is the imitation and importation of *existing value judgments* that originate with great individuals. E.g., Plato and Christianity. Paul scarcely knew *how much* everything in him smells of Plato.

26 [54]

Chapter. On the *value* of the human cognitive mechanism. *What* it can and cannot accomplish only gradually becomes apparent: namely, to what extent all its results are *interconnected* or contradict each other.

26 [55]

Chapter. If we do not assume a particular standpoint, we cannot speak about the value of anything: i.e., a particular *affirmation* of a particular life is the prerequisite for every *valuation*.

26 [56]

We are the source of our *own* praise and blame: those who are led by their superior point of view to pay no attention to the praise of others find it *unflattering* to be praised by them.

26 [57]

NB. To what extent it is necessary for people of the highest rank to be bitterly *hated* by the representatives of one *particular* morality. Anyone who loves the world must be condemned by all individuals: their own preservation as a perspective *demands* that there be no one who destroys all perspectives.

26 [58][22]

NB. The first limit of any "sense of truth" is — even for all lower living creatures — what does not contribute to their own preservation *does not concern them*. The second: the *most useful* means they have of observing something is preferred and is only gradually incorporated through hereditary processes. Despite the influence of human beings, this hasn't changed in the slightest: at most, it might be asked whether there aren't degenerate races that relate to things in accordance with their secret desire to perish — thus, in opposition to life. But when obsolete or failed entities die off, this itself is a part of the consequence of the *preservation* of life: which is why old people like to judge things in old ways and true Christians like to judge things in ways that are hostile to the world.

It would be theoretically possible that *fundamental errors* are just what is required for the preservation of living things, and not "fundamental truths." A type of existence could be envisioned, e.g., in which knowledge itself would be impossible because there is a contradiction between absolute flux and knowledge: in a world like that, a living creature would first have to *believe* in things, in continuity etc. in order to be able to exist: error would be its condition for existence. Perhaps it is so.

26 [59]

People whose ancestors felt that love was important will feel this when they are in love and will act, perhaps to their own astonishment, in the way their ancestors did: *it is difficult for* **a single individual** *to start experiencing a genuine passion* — instead, even passions must be educated and inculcated, this goes for love just as much as it does for imperiousness and egoism.

26 [60]

Wherever great efficiency[23] is at work, we are **not** aware of the ends and means. Artists and their work, mothers and children — and likewise my chewing, digestion, walking etc., the economy of forces during the day etc. — all this is done without our being aware of it.

When something is working efficiently e.g., the process of digestion, this is still *in no way* explained by assuming a cognitive mechanism that *has been refined* hundreds of times as in the *case* of conscious intellect: we cannot imagine a mechanism that would be capable of doing the task that is actually performed, because too many subtle relations (quantitative) would come into consideration. A second intellect would still leave the riddle unsolved. If we don't let ourselves be deceived by the "long" and the "short" of *temporal* relations, the completion of a *single digestive process* is just as abundant in individual processes of movement as *all of the processes within any living thing*: and anyone who does not assume a guiding intellect for the latter need not assume it for the former either.

26 [61][24]

The entire cognitive mechanism is a mechanism of abstraction and simplification — not aimed at knowing, but at *taking control* of things: "ends" and "means" are as far removed from the essence of things as "concepts" are. With "ends" and "means" we take control of the process (— we *invent* a process that is comprehensible!), yet with concepts of the "things" that perform the process.

26 [62]

The essence of an action is unknowable: what we call its "motive" *moves* nothing — to understand succession as a mishmash is an illusion.

26 [63]

With "freedom of the will" "responsibility" falls away. Yet all moral questions remain: how do living things relate to the "truth"? How do they relate to other living things? And whenever error leads them to reward and punish, why should they not *be allowed* to continue rewarding and punishing? What can be said against a "will to untruth"? And what is the origin of the valuation of altruistic, just people? — Enough, the entire *state of affairs* up to now regarding the moral positions of living things, 1) the *state of affairs regarding valuations* and 2) *the cause of value judgments* remains to be determined. Which raises the question 3) *whether there* is *a standard of measurement* that **is superior** to all value judgments up to now, including the question whether the first two problems are solvable *without this standard* — and *why* **I** am asking this question in the first place.

26 [64]

The major problems surrounding the *value of becoming* formulated by Anaximander and Heraclitus — in other words, the decision whether a moral or aesthetic valuation is permitted in general, in relation to all these problems.

The major problem, what role is played by the *purpose-setting mind* with respect to all becoming — by Anaxagoras

The major problem, whether there is a *being* — by the Eleatics; and what is all appearance.

All the major problems were formulated before Socrates:

Socrates: insight as means to moral improvement, what is irrational in the passions, what is *unintentional*[25] in being bad.

Plato says no! The *love* of goodness is accompanied by moral improvement; yet insight is necessary for comprehending goodness.

Socrates does not seek wisdom, but rather *someone who is wise* — and does not find this person — but he refers to this *seeking* as his greatest happiness. For there is nothing better in life than *to always speak of virtue*.

26 [65]

Perhaps that which we feel to be most certain is the furthest from "what is real." Every judgment includes a belief that "this is the way it is"; as if precisely *belief itself* were the most immediate fact we could ascertain! How is belief possible??

26 [66]

Pythagoras establishes an order for *those who are noble*, a kind of Order of the Knights Templar.

26 [67]

— Heraclitus:[26] the world is absolutely lawful: how could it be a world of injustice! — thus, a *moral* judgment, "the fulfillment of the law," is absolute; the opposite is an illusion; even bad people don't change anything about this, absolute *lawfulness* is fulfilled through them just as they are. Here necessity is morally glorified and *felt*.

26 [68]

Up to now *neither* explanation of organic life has been successful, neither the one derived from mechanics *nor the one derived from the mind*. I emphasize the failure *of the latter*. The mind is more superficial than we think. An organism's controlling functions work in such a way that they cannot be explained *by either* the mechanical world *or* the mental world, other than *symbolically*.

26 [69]

The thought, that which is capable of life is all that *remains in existence*, is a concept of the *first rank*.

26 [70]

In the last analysis, that life is unknowable could have to do with the fact that *everything* is unknowable in itself and that we only comprehend what we have built and framed[27] in the first place; I mean, built upon the foundation of contradictions between life and the initial functions of coming to "know." The more knowable something is, the further it is from being, the more it is a *concept*.

26 [71]

Egoism as a perspectival seeing and judging of all things for the purpose of survival: all seeing (*that* something is perceived at all, selecting something) is already a valuation, accepting something, in contrast to rejecting and not wanting to see something.

26 [72]

Value judgments are found in all sensory activities. Value judgments are found in all the functions of organic beings.

That pleasure and displeasure are originally forms of value judgment is a hypothesis: perhaps they are initially *consequences* of a value judgment.

What is "good" differs when seen from the standpoints of two different beings.

There is one good that has the survival of the individual as its standard; one good that has the survival of the individual's family or community or tribe as its standard — a conflict can emerge within the individual, two drives.

When seen from any standpoint at all, each "drive" is a drive toward "something good"; there is a value judgment at stake, this is the only reason it has incorporated itself.

Each drive has been cultivated as a temporary *condition of existence*. It continues to be propagated even long after it has stopped being a condition of existence

A particular degree of drive, in relation to other drives, is capable of surviving, is propagated again and again; an opposing drive disappears

26 [73]

The "unegoistic." The multiplicity of persons (*masks*) in a single "I."

26 [74]

The law of causality a priori — that we *believe* in this law can be a condition of existence for our species; that doesn't mean it has been *proven*.

26 [75][28]

For the introduction.

§ 1. The type of human figure that is most difficult to attain and that is superior to all other types will very rarely succeed: that is why the history of philosophy reveals an overabundance of failed people, of misfortunes, and an extremely slow pace; entire millennia intervene and overwhelm what was accomplished, the context is lost again and again. This is a horrific history — the history of the human beings that are superior to all others, the history of *sages*. — How great persons are remembered is precisely what suffers the most damage, since the half-successful people and the failures fail to recognize them and vanquish them with their "successes." Every time "the effect" shows up, a mass of rabble steps onto the stage; mental midgets and indigents join in the conversation, a terrible martyrdom of the ear for anyone who knows with a shudder *that the destiny of humankind lies in its most superior type achieving success.* — Ever since I was a toddler I have pondered what conditions are needed for sages to exist; and I refuse to keep quiet about my happy conviction that this type is again becoming *possible* in Europe today — maybe only for a brief time[29]

§ 2. What kind of convergence do sages represent? Here we grasp why they so easily become failures, quite apart from the external conditions.

§ 3. *The world of opinions* — up to now it has been overlooked how deeply valuation penetrates things: how we inhabit a world that we have created ourselves, and how there are still moral values to be found even within all our sense perceptions. — Restricted field of vision within Kantian idealism (in the end refuted by Kant himself: what do we care about truth when our supreme value judgments are at stake — it was Kant's opinion that "we *must* believe something or other")

26 [76]

There is the problem as to whether pleasure and displeasure are more primitive matters of fact than the judgments "beneficial" "harmful" to the whole.

26 [77]

Stimulus conceptually separate from "pleasure" and "displeasure"

26 [78]

Schopenhauer confesses his "special delight" in demonstrating Kant's practical reason and categorical imperative "as wholly unjustified, groundless and fabricated assumptions, and thus to deliver morality back to its old, total perplexity" (*Basis of Morals* p. 116)[30]

26 [79]

Conditions required by sages.

We have to *cut* ourselves *off* from society through all kinds of *guilt*.

26 [80]

The development of that which is organic makes it highly probable that the intellect *grew* out of very modest beginnings, therefore has also *become*: it can be shown that the sense organs have emerged, there were still no "senses" prior to them. The question is, what had to have been there all along: e.g., what characteristics does an embryo have such that, in the end, even thinking develops in the process of the embryo's development? —

26 [81]

Up to now we have had *no idea* about the laws of motion governing what goes on inside organic beings. "Form" is an

optical phenomenon: nonsense when considered without taking the eye into account.

26 [82]

Main Proposition: no retrospective hypotheses! Preferably a
condition of ἐποχή![31] And as many individual observations as
possible! In the end: we like to recognize *whatever* we want to,
standing behind all our work is a *utility* or lack of utility *that
we do* **not** *overlook*. We *have* no choice in this, rather everything
is absolutely necessary: and the fate of humankind has been
decided for the longest time because this fate has *been there* for
an eternity already. Our most zealous effort and attention are
included in the fate of all things; and likewise every stupidity.
Anyone who crawls under a rock in the face of this thought is
nonetheless also fate. There is no refuge from the thought of
necessity.

26 [83]

What is the most desirable, *most useful* belief? (if for once
truth is *not* at stake), we could ask. But then we have to ask
further: useful for what?

26 [84][32]

Kant says p. 19 R⟨osenkranz⟩, "the moral value of an action
does not lie at all in the intention through which it happened
but rather in the maxim that was followed." "In opposition
to this (Schopenhauer *Basis of Morals* p. 134) I offer for your
consideration the idea that intention alone decides the moral
value or disvalue of an act, which is why the same act can be
reprehensible or praiseworthy depending on its intention"[33] *etc.*

ego: yet *what* Kant wanted to say about this act is that,
whether it is worthy of praise or blame, really depends on
the maxim used by the person doing the praising or blaming,
and consequently on the assessment of the maxim according
to which the agent acted: if the act and the maxim do not
match, then ordinary people become outraged with the agent,

assuming that they *evaluate* the actions in the same way. Kant is right in thinking that, because maxims vary and have varying moral value, the value of an action can, in the final analysis, always be *traced back to the question of the value of the maxim that forms the basis for the action.*

Sch⟨openhauer⟩ is just as sure that he knows what good and evil is, just like Kant — that's what makes this so funny.

26 [85][34]

Commanding and obeying are the fundamental fact: this *pre*supposes an order of rank

Sch⟨openhauer⟩ p. 136[35] "The principle or the highest basic proposition of an ethics is the shortest and most concise expression of the way of acting that it prescribes, or, should it not have an imperative form, the way of acting to which it attributes genuine moral worth — thus the ὅ, τι[36] of virtue. The foundation of an ethics, by contrast, is the διότι[37] of virtue, the *ground* of that obligation or recommendation or approbation, thus the διότι of virtue. — The ὅ, τι so easy, the διότι so frightfully difficult."

"The principle, the basic proposition, about whose content all ethical theorists are really united: *neminem laede, immo omnes quatum potes juva*[38] — this is really the proposition that all teachers of morality labor to *ground* — the proper foundation of ethics, which people have been seeking like the philosopher's stone for millennia."[39]

The difficulty of proving this proposition is admittedly great: it is silly and slave-like in its sentimentality.

neminem laede why not?

neminem implies that all humans are equal: yet since humans are not equal, this therefore contains a *demand* to *make* them equal. Thus: "treat every person as your equal" is the background of this morality. "Benefit" contains the question "beneficial *for what?*" thus, already a value judgment and a goal. Under certain circumstances, it is necessary to harm many of them in order to benefit all of them: thus, the first part is false.

If we are philosophers, it is ridiculous to believe in "doing good and doing harm" *in themselves*. Pain and loss often bring us the greatest gain, and "it is very good to have formidable enemies" if you want to achieve greatness. —

thus: first question, whether morality is realizable in practice, is *achievable*.[40] But how can I "*benefit all*"!

There are moments in Schopenhauer when he is not all that distant from the sentimentality of Kotzebue[41] — he also played the *flute* every day: this says something.

26 [86]

Schopenhauer was right when he made fun of Kant's "purpose in itself" "absolute should" "absolute value," that is, as contradictions: he should have added the "thing in itself" to the list.

26 [87]

The point where *indifference* begins, in the case of living beings, in relation to the external world —

26 [88]

An unblinking, unwavering stare is the least accurate way to describe a sage: as long as — — —

26 [89]

Excellent minds fail more easily; their history of suffering, their illnesses, their outrage at the impudent virtue-cackling of all the moralistic ganders, etc. Everything conspires against them, it makes them bitter that they are out of place everywhere. — Danger in ages of democracy. Absolute contempt as a security measure.

26 [90]

To determine what has been *achieved* in the acquisition of knowledge is a matter for philosophers; and not only in this, but with achievements in general! History as the great *experimental laboratory*: to *formulate* the conscious wisdom needed for ruling the earth. Synthesizing what has been experienced —

26 [91]

Where there is an excess of revitalizing replenishing forces, even bad accidents shine with the radiance of a sun and engender their own consolation: conversely, all deep depression, pangs of conscience, long bitter nights, occur when bodies *become weaker* (they often keep refusing to eat)

26 [92]
Involuntary Aspects of Thinking.

A thought appears, often intermingled and obscured in a crowd of pressing thoughts. We pull it out, we clean it up, we help it to its feet and check how it *is walking* — all very quickly! We then sit in judgment over it: to think is a kind of exercise in justice, where witnesses are also cross-examined. What does it *mean*? we ask and call other thoughts to the stand: this means: A thought is therefore not taken to be immediately certain, but rather as a *sign*, a question mark. That each thought is initially ambiguous and fluctuating, and is in itself only an *occasion* for multiple interpretations and arbitrary stipulations, this is something experienced by every observer who doesn't remain on the surface. — The origin of the thought is hidden from us: in all probability it is a *symptom* of a more extensive condition, just like every feeling — : because precisely *this thought* comes and none other, that it comes with just this greater or lesser clarity, sometimes certain and imperious, sometimes uncertain and in need of support, on the whole always disquieting and exciting, questioning — every thought stimulates our consciousness — in all of this, some aspect of our overall condition is expressed through *signs*. — This is likewise the case with every feeling — in itself, it has no meaning for us; when it comes, it is interpreted by us, and often in such strange ways! Consider all the intestinal ailments, the unhealthy states of the *nervus sympathi-cus*[42] and of the entire *sensorium commune*[43] — : only some-one who has been instructed in anatomy could settle upon the correct category of causes; yet all ignorant people *seek* a moral explanation for such pains and, when they try to explain why they feel bad, based on what they have experienced, by look-ing for unpleasant experiences and fears, they falsely *identify* the actual reasons why they feel bad. — Under torture almost all people confess their guilt: people who are being tortured, and who are experiencing pain without knowing why, question themselves for such a long time and in such an inquisitorial fashion that they end up finding themselves or other people guilty, as e.g., the Purit⟨ans⟩ interpreted the spleen that often accompanied their irrational lifestyle as a moral phenomenon, as a pang of conscience.

26 [93][44]

The acts of a superior human being are indescribably *complex* in their motivation: using some word or other like "compas-sion" says *nothing at all*. What is most essential is the feeling "who am I? who is the other person in relation to me — value judgments continuously active.

26 [94]

We must learn to think differently about memory: it is the vast set of all experiences belonging to all organic life, alive, arraying themselves, reciprocally forming themselves and each other, wrestling with each other, simplifying, crowding together and being transformed into many unities. There must be an inner *process* that behaves like a *formation of concepts* out of many individual cases: highlighting and continually underscoring the fundamental pattern and dis-regarding secondary attributes. — As long as something can still be recalled as an individual fact it has not yet been assim-ilated: the newest experiences are still floating on the surface. Feelings of inclination, disinclination etc. are symptoms of unities already having been formed; our so-called "instincts" are formations of this sort. Thoughts are the most superficial thing of all: value judgments that appear without us knowing why and are just there, go deeper — pleasure and displeasure are the effects of more complicated value judgments that are governed by instincts.

26 [95]

Since hatred, urges, lust, anger, imperiousness etc. are still with us, we can assume that part of their function is to enable survival. And "good people" — without the powerful affects of hatred, of outrage, of disgust, without enmity, are a kind of *degeneration*, or a kind of self-deception.

26 [96][45]

The clumsy pedantry and provincial nonsense of old Kant, the grotesque bad taste of this Chinaman from Königsberg, who nevertheless was a true man of duty and a Prussian official: and the inner lack of breeding and homelessness of Sch⟨open-hauer⟩ who could nevertheless become enthusiastic about a compassionate bourgeois, like Kotzebue: and, like Voltaire, had compassion for animals.

26 [97]

all those who take pleasure in an extraordinary intellect must also love the conditions under which it emerges — a need for deception, evasion, exploiting an opportunity; and whatever instills antipathy in lesser natures, that which basically instills fear, particularly if they hate the intellect as such —

26 [98]

Fundamental position: the lack of awe for great intellects, for many reasons, and also for the reason that there simply *aren't* any great intellects. The historical style of our age can be explained by citing the belief that everything *is subject to* what everyone else thinks about it.

The characteristic trait of a great human being was profound insight into the *moral hypocrisy* of everyone (at the same time, as a consequence of plebeians *looking for costumes*).

26 [99]⁴⁶

It is a comfort to me that all great connoisseurs of humanity still say: "humans are evil" — and wherever you heard something else, insightful people immediately realized that "humans are *weak* there."

The *weakening* of humans was the cause of revolutions — of sentimentality.

26 [100]⁴⁷

What philosophers *lacked* a) historical sense
                            b) being familiar with physiology
                            c) a goal in regard to the future

To formulate a critique, without any irony and moral condemnation.

26 [101]

A magnificent intellect is the effect of an abundance of moral qualities e.g., courage, force of will, fairness, seriousness — but at the same time also of much πολυτροπία,⁴⁸ deception, transformation, experience with opposites, mischief, audacity, malice, unruliness.

In order that a magnificent intellect may emerge, the person's ancestors must have been, to an extraordinary degree, both evil and good, intellectual and sensuous.

26 [102]

That a good person can have an extraordinary intellect is something that would still have to be proven in every case: up to now, the great intellectuals have been evil people.

26 [103]

These good peaceable joyful people have no idea of the gravitas of those who want to weigh things *anew* and who have to roll them up onto the scales.

26 [104]

It is shocking that so many people are failures, even more so the feelings of comfort and security (the lack of *sympathy for the entire process of evolution* that is the "human being") — how everything can perish so quickly!

26 [105]⁴⁹

It shouldn't astonish us that a few millennia are necessary in order to find the connection again — a few millennia are of little consequence!

26 [106]

Those who know will rejoice in all of their bad affects, lusts, actions; they exploit illnesses, humiliations, they allow pain to burrow deeply within and then rebound suddenly as soon as they *have* their knowledge.

26 [107]

Up to now, the effort to portray good human beings has done the most damage to the knowledge possessed by philosophers. Extraordinary mendacity, most extraordinary in the case of moralists.

26 [108]

Today there is essentially no difference in the judgment as to what is good and what is evil. We merely ask why there is essentially no difference. There is no doubt *that* it is this way. — Socrates asks "why" but even he does not doubt this — and up to now human vanity has insisted that we *know* why we do something — that we act on the basis of conscious motives. — From Plato onward, everyone has believed that it suffices to *define* "good" "just" etc. since we *know* what it is, and now we must act accordingly.

26 [109]

NB. Is it legitimate to praise good, just people? 1) Do those who are doing the praising have the right to judge at all? 2) Are their judgments correct — and *correct* according to what standard?

26 [110]

Up to now, people have done a lot of judging and condemning in cases where knowledge has been lacking e.g., concerning witches; or in the case of astrology. Many "judgments that were made in good conscience" have turned out to be unjustified. Could this not be the case with "good" and "evil," since justifications given up to now have not actually included any critique — people just agreed with each other.

We could also pose the question: are good people more useful for the evolution of new and strong types, or are evil people? Are good people more useful for the acquisition of knowledge, etc. Are good people healthier and more persistent when it comes to the preservation of a race?

— Are they more cheerful or more gloomy when it comes to happiness?

— The first thing we should do is *set forth* the extremely varied manifold matters of fact. Are they more useful to the arts? To the longevity of the human race?

Above all: what is the indicator that someone is good or evil? Is it the behavior in itself? Or is it how they behave with other people?

26 [111]

Sages are shocked when they discover how little the truth matters to the vast majority of people who consider themselves to be good — and they will decide to reserve their deepest contempt for the entire moral-virtue gang. They will prefer bad people. — How much they have sacrificed! And now they realize that people believe they can agree or say *No*. — A book that we "like"!

26 [112]

I have deep contempt for all moral judging, praising and condemning —

In regard to the usual moral judgments, I ask 1) are the persons who are judging entitled to judge at all? 2) are they correct or incorrect in judging this way?

are they preeminent enough

do they have insight, imagination, experience enough to *envision* the whole

26 [113]

NB live *outside cities*!

26 [114]

There are no unmediated facts! It is the same with feelings and thoughts: in becoming *conscious* of them, I make an excerpt, a simplification, an attempt at a formulation: *this is truly what becoming conscious of something means: fixing it up* in a completely **active** way.

How do you know this? —

we are conscious of the *effort* whenever we want to grasp a thought, a feeling exactly — with the help of *comparison* (*memory*).

A thought and a feeling are *signs* that some process or other is at work: if I take them in an absolute sense — if I posit them to be unavoidably *un*ambiguous, then at the same time I posit people to be intellectually the same — a temporary permissible *simplification* of the true state of things.

26 [115]

We work with **all our strength** *to convince* ourselves of the *lack of freedom*: in order to feel as free in our own presence as we do *in the presence of nature* — — *It demands the most extreme effort* to maintain a feeling of this kind and not to let it go.

26 [116]

A person's *"worthlessness"* is only worthlessness in regard to particular *aims* (those of the family community etc.): people should be *given* a *value* and made to feel that they *are* useful e.g., the sick as a means of gaining knowledge; criminals as scarecrows etc. The wicked as opportunities, involving them etc.

26 [117]

In order to ensure *my* survival, *I* have my protective instincts of contempt, disgust, indifference etc. — they drive me into solitude: yet in solitude, where I *feel that everything is necessarily connected*, every being is *divine* to me.

NB. in order to be able to appreciate and to love *anything*, I must understand it as absolutely necessarily connected with everything that is — therefore I must *affirm the goodness of all existence for its own sake* and I must know that I have chance to thank for such precious things being possible.

If we could predict the most promising conditions under which beings of the greatest value emerge! It is a thousand times too complicated, and the probability of failure is *very great*: so it is not exciting to strive for it! — Skepticism.

— On the other hand: we can intensify our courage, insight, toughness, independence, feelings of irresponsibility, we can adjust the scales to make them more exact and expect that fortuitous coincidences[50] will come to our aid. —[51]

26 [118]

— all tendencies make sense only as they apply to a particular horizon e.g., it is worthwhile if reason is sharpened, it is also worthwhile if it becomes more dull: sages understand the necessity of opposing *standards*, they want the most colorful coincidences among many opposites.

— Evaluation is a requirement for life. *The consequence of our evaluating something is that we affirm everything as good,* therefore even for what we think is less than valuable, abhorrent: i.e., simultaneously to evaluate things and not to evaluate them. — In other words, skepticism is evaluating the valuations about justice and injustice *as conditioning each other.*

26 [119][52]

Insight: all value judgments involve a particular perspective: *preservation* of the individual, a community, a race, a state, a church, a belief, a culture

— by virtue of *forgetting* that there are only perspectival valuations, everything in *a single* person is swarming with contradictory valuations and *consequently with contradictory impulses.* This is the *expression of sickness manifested in people*, as opposed to animals where all available instincts fulfill very specific tasks.

— yet these creatures who are full of contradictions have, as part of their essence, an extraordinary method for *gaining knowledge*: they feel many pros and cons — they elevate themselves *to a position of justice* — into grasping what lies *beyond the valuations of good and evil.*

The wisest people would be *the ones richest in contradictions*, who at the same time have organs for sensing all kinds of people: and, in between, their great moments of *grandiose harmony* — the magnificence of *chance* even within us!

— a kind of planetary movement —

26 [120]

A Questionable Person's Questions.

26 [121]

I have a mistrust of all moral people: their lack of self-knowledge and self-contempt makes me not only lose patience with their ability to understand things — it is the sight of them that offends me.

26 [122]

A man[53] with a superior soul is not inclined to admiration, for what is great in him is peculiar to him and related to him, in his view there is no greatness. — The material possessions wealth power don't come into consideration, they definitely have no value in themselves but rather are useful only for attaining better things.

"Superior people, for whom we can express our admiration by no other means than veneration, are not particularly pleased by these honors (because such honors are always too limited given the value of these people's virtue): but they will not refuse them, since the people are certainly not in a position to give them anything greater."[54]

26 [123][55]

Jesting and joking help with recovery, are a kind of healing through which we regain the strength needed for new activity.

"seriousness is better" — is Aristotelian.

26 [124]

Only a few have already grasped that an unrestricted will to knowledge is very dangerous. The age of *suffrage universel*[56] lives according to the good-natured and overly enthusiastic presuppositions of the previous century.

26 [125]

There has never been enough mistrust among thinkers. The desire to find virtue combined with knowledge might have greatly endangered the acquisition of knowledge. Things are arranged maliciously, to an amazing degree — to speak in parables.

26 [126]

We work with presuppositions, e.g., that knowledge is *possible*.

26 [127][57]

On the *diversity* of knowledge. When we feel *someone else's* relation (or the species' relation) to many other things — how is that supposed to be "knowledge" of these other things! The way in which we are familiar with something and acquire knowledge of it is itself already one of the conditions of existence: we shouldn't jump to the conclusion that there could be no other kind of intellect (for us ourselves) than the one that allows us to survive: perhaps this *actual* condition of existence is merely *coincidental* and perhaps in no way necessary.

Our cognitive mechanism not *set up* for gaining "knowledge."

26 [128][58]

While I *am willing*, an actual movement occurs: should this movement, which is unknown to me, not be viewed as a *causa efficiens*?[59] The act of willing is itself, without a doubt, the conclusion of a "battle of motives" — however, these themselves

— — —

Rejection of *causae finales*[60]
Rejection of *causae efficientes*:[61] they are likewise merely attempts for us to, a process — — —[62]

26 [129][63]

"Leaves and grass, happiness, blessings and rain."

26 [130]
History of value judgments.
    Noble
    Hard-hearted

26 [131][64]
causa efficiens } both only a means of *making* something
causa finalis   } comprehensible.

26 [132]

I imagine the most evil most cold-blooded most merciless people.

26 [133]

Liberation from morality:
1) through actions
2) — — —

26 [134]

NB. Suitability to a purpose is still no proof of purpose.

The fact that there is a purpose everywhere in custom and law does *not* demonstrate that they are *purposive* at the time of their emergence and they are often unsuitable as a means of realizing such a purpose.

Contradiction between the means chosen by lesser intelligence and the ends of supreme intelligence.

26 [135]

The secondary qualities of things under the productive influence of what is beneficial and harmful to us (thus, not "pleasant in itself," "unpleasant," prefers some colors: under certain conditions the nerves etc. develop, as do sense organs etc. warmth, heaviness etc.).

26 [136]

"Persons of a certain disposition" (*not* cruel) — this is nonsense, for it is only in terms of relations that they *have* a disposition at all!

26 [137][65]

To what extent even our intellect is a consequence of conditions of existence — we would not have it if we did not need it, and we would not have it like *this* if we did not need it like this, if it were even possible for us to live differently.

26 [138]

Adaptation to continually new conditions and therefore the *greater importance* of heredity and longevity in the case of the *most adaptable beings*, of the *shrewdest most calculating* individuals.

26 [139]⁶⁶

Beyond Good and Evil.

Attempt at an Extra-moral[67]
Consideration of
Moral Phenomena

1. Tracing moral value judgments back to their roots.

2. Critique of moral value judgments.

3. The practical approach to overcoming morality.

26 [140]⁶⁸
1. The feeling of power
2. Master and slave morality

26 [141]

To proceed from the individual as multiplicity (mind as stomach of the affects) as well as from the community.

1. The conditions of existence for a community appearing in the form of *value judgments* about people and actions.

2. The conditions for the training and retraining of the type in the form of value judgments.

3. Virtues of the herd and of the leader, opposed to each other.

26 [142]

Preservation of a type — and further development.

— Personalities in which this difference between concepts is embodied as *contradiction*

Problem

Inventions that will *condense* experiences[69] (to abbreviate a past life in ever briefer formulas)

Philosophers as lords, but *not* in their time.

In the case of people like Napoleon, any disregard of *the self* is a danger and a loss: they must keep their hearts closed — the same goes for philosophers. Zarathustra.

There is a terrifying degree of *randomness*: projecting more and more reason *into things*! Caution etc.

26 [143]

Loving someone is in itself worth as little (and as m⟨uch⟩) as hating or taking revenge. There is so much blind devotion in love, so many feelings of distress and compulsion, particularly the discomfort we feel in the other person's absence, so much slave-sensibility (in putting up with all manner of bad treatment) — there is something so corrupt and corrupting about love that the person who *is loved* almost always declines in mind and strength and prudence through being loved. — Motherly love not valuable in itself. — How something can be extremely purposeful without being traceable back to an intellect that should for that reason be admired: so many actions are extremely useful for the preservation of society, or of a people, but they are not done for the sake of this preservation, nor does this preservation have anything to do with their emergence: these actions are *mistakenly* admired, because they are mistakenly evaluated in terms of their good outcomes.

26 [144]

                            Independent People.

26 [145]

How do we measure the value (of an action) in relation to other actions?

    In terms of its success (to what extent can this be
        known?) (also in terms of its probable success) (also in
        terms of what we feel in cases of success)

In terms of the agent.

in terms of the completion of the action

In terms of the accompanying feeling.

In terms of the intention (not considering whether it is realized)

the value of an action insofar as it is a means (to what degree well chosen or randomly chosen as a means)

Main problem: to what extent is an action recognizable?

26 [146]

Where mistrust is not necessary, where we can let ourselves go, where glances and gestures speak with benevolence and friendliness, where perhaps even our abilities are appreciated or are met with admiration, many tend to transform *their* comfort into *praise* of such people: they call them good and would like nothing better than to give high marks to their ability to judge — here we have the pleasure of deceiving ourselves.

26 [147]

The extreme complexity of the means to an "end" always gives rise to the suspicion that an autonomous reason[70] has been at work arranging things here.

26 [148]

"No one freely chooses what is bad." In Plato's case,[71] what is bad is whatever is harmful to anyone.

26 [149]

Justice, as the function of a power that sees far beyond itself, which sees above and beyond the narrow perspectives of good and evil, therefore has a broader perspective on what is *advantageous* — the intention of preserving something that is more than merely some person or other.

26 [150]

If we peel away what all facts have in common, namely, the fundamental forms of the most extreme abstraction — do we then arrive at "truths"? Up to now, there has been this approach to truth, generalization — by means of this approach we were able to discover only the *fundamental phenomena of the intellect*. Really?

26 [151]

The ability to see and judge well, free of prejudice and in an extra-moral sense, is remarkably rare.

26 [152]

To knowingly and intentionally lie is *more valuable* than involuntarily telling the truth — in this Plato[72] was right. Although the usual value judgment is reversed: such that we think it is *easy* to tell the truth. But this is only for coarse and superficial people who have nothing to do with sophisticated matters, it's so simple

26 [153][73]

On the Emergence of Philosophers.

1. The feeling of profound discomfort when in the company of good-natured people — as if under the weather[74] — and the feeling of becoming complacent and slovenly, even vain. This is ruinous. — If we want to make clear just how bad and weak the foundation is at this spot, we aggravate these people and hear them whine.

2. Overcoming the obsession with revenge and overcoming the need for retribution, out of profound contempt or out of compassion for the stupidity of these people.

3. Mendacity as a safety measure. And even better, philosophers fleeing into their solitude.

26 [154]

I have looked all over the place — but for people like me a "thou shalt" is nowhere to be found anymore. It is obvious that in a particular case e.g., while wandering through the wilderness I would obey anyone with more experience who was allowed to give orders on that account. I would do the same with a doctor. I would bow to a *superior* intellect when it comes to making value judgments: for the time being, I am saying "I want to"; and I'm waiting for a superior intellect to come my way once again.

26 [155][75]

It is the time of those who make vows: — *voluntary* vows of loyalty for the benefit of some virtue or other: not because this virtue is giving the orders, but rather because I order this virtue to obey me.

The value of virtues for those who know.

The disadvantage of virtues for those who know. Using what is evil, the feeling of being exiled, of being sentenced. You can't become a leader until you're completely *exiled* from the herd.

26 [156]

The process of life is only possible insofar as many experiences don't have to be repeated again and again but rather are incorporated in some form or other — the true problem for organisms is: how is experience possible? We have only one form of understanding — concept, the more general case that subsumes the particular case. In one case, seeing the general the typical seems to us to be a part of experience — *inasmuch as* everything "that is living" only seems to become conceivable to us when we assign it an intellect. Yet now there is the other form of understanding — the only configurations that remain are those that know how to preserve and protect themselves against a large number of invasive influences.

26 [157]

We could use the emergence of herd-consciousness to explain the emergence of human consciousness. For in the final analysis humans are also, to be sure, a multiplicity of existences:

these existences have created for themselves these organs in common, like blood circulation, concentration of the senses, stomach etc. which are better developed and have survived, *not for these purposes*, but rather as random formations which had the advantage of making the survival of the whole possible. The *growing together* of organisms, as a means of preserving the single being for a longer time —

— wherever merging, adaptation are greatest, the probability of preservation is the greatest.

26 [158]

I don't want to be overly worried: these days, protecting serious books has to do with the fact that most people don't have the time to take them seriously, assuming that they had the strength to do so. Misuse of knowledge —

26 [159][76]

Sch⟨openhauer⟩ said it emphatically and amusingly enough, how it is not enough to be a philosopher by using only your head.

26 [160]

The emergence of philosophers is perhaps the most dangerous emergence of all: when I take a few aspects from this and "present these aspects in the best possible light," I don't believe that I am in any way minimizing this danger: and ultimately, whenever those who know communicate, they only have in mind how to avoid a situation where all those who have recently gained knowledge have to re-experience all previous experience.

26 [161]

Something completely unsavory might have been proven about the origin of moral value judgments: now, when these powers *are there*, they can be employed and they have their *value* as powers. Just like a dynasty that can be traced back to cunning and violence: but the value that it has lies in the fact that it *is* a dynasty. — Then the situation would be such that all the power of moral value judgments would be tied to the legitimacy of their origin or in general to certain beliefs *concerning their origins*: so that then, with the revelation of error, the *power that comes with being convinced about their value* would dissipate. Meanwhile: all of our attention is trained on optical illusions and value judgments. Just because you haven't tasted much beefsteak doesn't mean you won't enjoy it.

26 [162]

Women are much more sensual than men (although indoctrination in modesty keeps this a secret from the women themselves): ultimately, men have more important functions than just sexual ones. But when a good-looking man approaches a woman — in general, women are incapable of imagining a relationship between a man and a woman that would not be accompanied by sexual tension.

26 [163]

1. The meaning of questions concerning the history of moral feelings.

2. Risking the possibility of having these moral judgments dissipate. Whether individuals have dispensed with them. — As a sign of deterioration in the case of criminals.

26 [164]

The history of value judgments, and the evolution of our ability to recognize actions, don't go hand in hand.

26 [165]

Value in terms of success.

Usually we measure the value of an action in terms of an *arbitrary individual* point of view e.g., value of an action for my current or general well-being

— or for my growing in stature, increase in concentration self-control or extensiveness of feeling (increase in knowledge)

— or in terms of improving my body, improving my health agility vigor

— or for the welfare of my children or community or country or prince or superiors or office or yard or farm.[77]

— and all other people can still view my action in terms of *their* well-being etc.

we can also ask what an action does *not* influence

26 [166]

The value of an action lies in its routine nature or rarity or difficulty — the point of view we take when we *compare an action with other actions*[78]

the kind of event, to what extent arbitrary or hindered, supported, by chance perhaps,

as a link in a chain — and how well done or half done and unclear.

26 [167]
My Assessment of Religions.
Origins of that morality which requires the extermination of the sensual drives and contempt for the body: an *emergency measure* for those personalities who do not know how to keep things in moderation and who only have a choice between becoming libertines and pigs or becoming ascetics. Condoning this as a way out for individuals; likewise, as a Christian or Buddhist way of thinking in those who feel that they are complete *failures*; in their case, we already have to recognize that they are maligning a world where things have turned out badly for them. — But this is the point of our wisdom, to condemn such ways of thinking and to condemn religions as huge lunatic asylums and penal institutions.

26 [168]
Humans, many-sided, mendacious, sly and opaque animals, uncanny and terrifying to all other animals through cleverness and cunning — behaving superficially as soon as they moralize.

26 [169]

Be wary! Martyrdom and persecution easily *corrupt* the pure feeling for truth: you become stiff-necked and you make yourselves blind to criticism! Avoid even any hostilities!

26 [170][79]

Science — transformation of nature into concepts for the purpose of controlling nature — this should be part of the rubric that is called "method"[80]

but the purpose and will of humans must likewise *grow*, the intention in regard to the whole

26 [171]

Plato and Aristotle put a lot of energy into as**certain**ing the *realm* of concepts — it was a misunderstanding

to create an opposing realm i.e., statistics and appraisal of value.

26 [172]

the most superior humans who have the brightest and sharpest eyes, the longest arms and the hardest most determined hearts, the humans who are most aware of the extent of their responsibility

26 [173]

If I now turn once again to people, after a long voluntary period of isolation, and if I call out: where are you, my friends?[81] then this is happening for the sake of greater things.

I want to create a new class: an order of superior humans in which oppressed minds and consciences can seek advice so that they can recuperate; who, like me, not only know how to live beyond political and religious dogmas, but have even overcome morality.

26 [174][82]

In the case of all questions concerning the origin of customs rights and moralities we would do well to avoid looking at the utility that a certain custom or m⟨orality⟩ has, whether for the community or for the individual, as also being *the reason* for its emergence; as do the naïve practitioners of historical research. That is, utility is itself something that changes, fluctuates; old forms are again and again given new meaning, and an institution's "most central purpose" is often the last one to have been imparted. The situation here is like that of the "organs" in the organic world; there, too, naïve people believe that the eye emerged for the sake of seeing.

26 [175]

Keeping ourselves unpolluted by a belief in God is a matter of honesty, and indeed, of a very modest and by no means admirable honesty; and whatever was once, e.g., still in Pascal's time, a demand of intellect⟨ual⟩ conscience, can be regarded as valid today as a *ban* on the same conscience in every strong man's head and heart. The thoughtless way in which people learn traditional opinions by rote, and venerate them without questioning, likewise the veneration of that which our fathers believed and finally a fearfulness concerning the consequences of godlessness — this is the cause

26 [176]

Anyone who measures the value of human actions solely in terms of motives *intentions* must also, as someone researching the emergence of morality, insist upon the fact that the morality of humankind is just as valuable as the *intentions* which have prevailed in the case of primitive moral value judgments and their inventors. "*Why* have unselfish people been praised?"

26 [177]

There are far too many families and clans who merely propagate and pass on a way of valuing: but we should not overlook the strong searching and autonomous personalities who do not submit to a value judgment until after a critique, and who even more often deny and dismantle the value judgment. There is also a continuous flow of forces that negate and investigate in the course of the evolution of moral judgments.

26 [178]

Fatalism and whether it is provable.

(*causa efficiens*, in the same way as *c⟨ausa⟩ f⟨inalis⟩*, merely a popular choice and simplification)

The recognizability of actions. The essence of actions is inferred from witnesses.

Good and evil as perspectival.

Emergence of the feeling "guilt." What is punishment?

Assessing "I" and "community," more recently "thy neighbor"

26 [179]

"Responsible for something" understood as freedom of the will (outlook of the herd!)

"Irresponsible, his own master"

"not to have to justify oneself to anyone" this kind of freedom of the will lasts until Plato, as an inheritance of the noblesse — absolute innocence.

"Master of his virtues, master of his guilt" like Manfred[83]

Innocence due to subjugation by fate is a slave attitude. Pride rears its head when people want to be recognized as the authors of their own accomplishments.

— but Homer's pride and the pride of all those who do *not* find inspiration in being authors themselves, but rather in being tools of a god!

— we are punished for our success, not for our intentions — as instigators of harm. "Guilt" in a subjective sense does not yet exist there.

26 [180]

There are fundamental facts upon which the possibility of judging and concluding rests in general — fundamental forms of the intellect. Yet this is why they are truths — they might be errors.

26 [181]

Hymn to fate and to the happiness of *irresponsibility*.

26 [182]

Diversity of moralities

1) from the viewpoint of further development within the same tribe (primitive more sophisticated)

2) from the viewpoint of diverse moralities that coexist, holding sway simultaneously (e.g., two social classes)

Conditions of existence in general.

Conditions of development into something more sophisticated:

a) in regard to communities

b) in regard to individuals.

26 [183]

How humans have lived since ancient times, profoundly unfamiliar with their bodies and finding a few formulas that are adequate for communicating with each other about this: this is how things are with judgments about the *value* of humans and human actions. Holding fast to a few completely superficial and trivial points and giving them exaggerated emphasis.

26 [184]

Master morality and slave morality.

All these value judgments about customs are so costly! E.g., we are now paying the price for marriage by means of the profound denigration and internal corruption of other kinds of relations between the sexes!

All value judgments by the herd are aimed just as much at people with inferior natures *as they are at* exceptionally wise people, people with superior natures.

26 [185]

In order for individuals to be discredited and banned by the herd, they must also have moved beyond that mendacity which is one of the first duties of herd-conscience: and if they are chock-full of evil drives, like Socrates, according to his own testimony, then at least they do not suffer from what constitutes the pathetic history of good human beings

26 [186]

Chapter about the *influence* of value judgments on the development of the affects.

To be distinguished: *why* do we actually judge things morally in this way or that way? And what value does this judging have?

Presuppositions of all moral judgments:

a) to what extent the action can be recognized (similarity of actions, possibility of a conceptual determination)

b) how *moral* values differ from all other values.

Yet just because we have actually made these assumptions since time immemorial, this does *not* mean they have been proven. The situation could be like that of astrology. In that case, a description of the nature of morality up to now would still be needed, along with an investigation of its origins.

26 [187]

Value of humans in relation to animals or to the lowest beings.

26 [188]

I have looked around, but up to now I have seen no greater danger for all acquisition of knowledge than moral hypocrisy: or, to leave absolutely no doubt, that hypocrisy which is called morality.

26 [189]

Morality as Hypocrisy.

If, in the case of a continuing refinement of the nerves, certain brutal and cruel punishments are no longer inflicted or are close to being abolished, this happens because it becomes more and more painful for the nerves of society to imagine such punishments: what sets in motion this leniency in the penal code is not a growing concern for the criminal, not an increase in brotherly love,[84] but rather greater weakness in the presence of pain.

26 [190]

Malicious and disreputable people can be of great service for gaining moral knowledge, assuming they have enough of a mind and presence of mind to feel pleasure in knowledge: while the weakness and deference of good people, their lack of mistrust, their desire to look the other way, their not wanting to look carefully at things, their fear of inflicting the pain that comes with all autopsies of body and soul, these pose just as many dangers for gaining moral knowledge. Not to mention the fact that people, when they are banned from society, feel themselves relieved of the mendacity that all herd-people learn from every herd as the first duty and condition of their existence — — —

26 [191]

We must imagine an ideal person who is perfectly made for a certain way of thinking (like the Christian one) — e.g., Pascal. Also, because for the average person there is always only a surrogate Christianity, even for personalities like Luther— he fashioned a Christianity that would be suitable for rabble and peasants like himself.

26 [192]

Life is extremely enigmatic; up to now, all great philosophers have believed that a solution could be achieved by resolutely *reversing* their outlook and their value judgments. — Likewise, all of them have believed that a surrogate is required for inferior intellects, e.g., morality, belief in God, immortality etc. (transmigration of souls)

The main thing is that this kind of *reversal* is not just a *way of thinking*, but also a *way of feeling*: for people who aren't capable of overturning all values — highest degree of self-determination — all conventional *knowledge about* such systems is *fruitless*. — The *fruitlessness* of the philosophical way of thinking, e.g., in the case of Kant Schopenhauer R. Wagner etc.

26 [193][85]

In the sense that the world is a divine game and beyond good and evil — I have Vedanta philos⟨ophy⟩ and Heraclitus as predecessors.

26 [194][86]

Bidden and forbidden works[87] = good and evil.

26 [195]

A feature of human development is that a formal "*you should* do this and that, you should stop doing this and that" may well be an innate trait — an *instinct to obey* that desires *fulfillment*; the more slave-like or womanly someone is, the stronger this instinct will be. That is to say, in the case of other, more rare people, this instinct is *overwhelmed* by another one — a will *to command, to be out front*, at the very least to be *alone* (this is the most benign form of a commanding personality —)

To what extent other instinctive virtues may be innate —

26 [196]

Something "good" (felt to be good) comes from evil (as felt to be evil); and in turn some things that are good can be felt as evil within us if we move up to a higher stage, e.g., industriousness for the accomplished artist, obedience for someone who has reached a command post, devotion and mercy for someone representing great personal goals (Napoleon) All these noble-minded feelings, which the young N⟨apoleon⟩ shared with his times, were seductions and temptations that wanted to minimize the force that was exclusively applied in a single direction.

26 [197]

There is no doubt that we can acquire virtues and set aside our mistakes: what actually happens in such cases?

26 [198][88]

Retribution exacted upon perpetrators for what they have done — a fundamental concept of Vedanta philos⟨ophy⟩. The whole world *is* itself merely the retribution exacted upon perpetrators for what they have done — but it is dependent upon *not knowing*.

26 [199][89]

"The Brahmins seek to know it[90] through studying the Vedas, through sacrifices, through alms, through penitent acts, through fasting: the personal methods of knowing are: peace of mind, restraint, forbearance, patience, composure" — means to a *mystical intuition* as the greatest human bliss.

26 [200]

Namely: *what* is really the highest state of happiness that humans can achieve? *This* has provided the standard in the most diverse systems. Hashish

26 [201][91]

That even the feeling of *pain* rests on illusion p. 448

26 [202]

NB. Anyone who does not find it strenuous to imagine the state of ordinary people is not a *superior* human. But as long as philosophers have to know what ordinary people are like, they must conduct such studies: for this reason I found e.g., Rée[92] useful, who with exceptional honesty and *without* being able to perceive higher states in the way that artists do, something they all have in common —

26 [203]

The limits of human beings. Attempting to see how high and how far humans can be pushed:

— their *displeasure* with human beings misled the Brahmins, Plato etc. into striving for a *divine* form of existence *beyond what is human*[93] — beyond space, time, multiplicity etc. Their displeasure extended to what is inconstant, deceptive, transitory, "stinking" etc. 1) ecstasy 2) deep sleep actually gave the impetus for a solution.

— now, however, human feelings of pleasure and power could, once again, even strive for an expanded form of existence — to seek a mode of thought that feels able to cope with what is inconstant, deceptive, transitory etc. — *creative* pleasure. The principle in this: that which is unconditioned can *not* be that which creates. Only that which is conditioned can set conditions.

— In actuality, the existing world, the world that we care about to some extent, was *created* by us — by us, i.e., by all organic beings — it is the product of an organic process which, when set in motion, appears to be *productively* constitutive, value-creating. *Seeing this from the perspective of the process as a whole*: all good and evil are merely perspectival in the case of individuals or individual parts of the process; but seen in its entirety, all evil is just as *necessary* as goodness, downfall just as necessary as growth

— the world of that which is unconditioned, if it were to exist, would be *that which is unproductive.*

but, in the end, we have to understand that existent and unconditioned are contradictory predicates.

26 [204]

The creative force (joining opposites, synthetic)

26 [205]

All those who represent something e.g., princes priests etc. must attempt to *appear* to be a certain way when they are not that way — this happens continually in the most modest of circumstances, because in human interaction everyone always represents something, some kind of type — human interaction depends on the fact that everyone behaves in the most *unambiguous* manner possible: so that not too much mistrust is required (a waste of mental energy!)

We put ourselves in circumstances where our mental attention and meticulousness will not be tested too much — and, if things are different, we complain about it and about anyone who *forces* us to do it.

The great disturbers of the peace and sowers of mistrust who force us to muster all of our energies are terribly *hated* — or else we blindly subjugate ourselves to them (this is a relief for troubled souls —

— democracy, ostracism, parliamentarianism were invented in order to avoid having such sovereign and terrible people — but this is something that lies in the nature of things.

When people are extremely distant from one another — then forms of government[94] are constituted accordingly.

It is difficult for extremely gifted personalities to learn obedience; for they only obey more gifted and more highly developed personalities, but what if *they* don't exist!

26 [206]
How we interpret unintelligible bodily conditions in terms of moral suffering — and take revenge for this on ourselves, on our fellow humans —

26 [207]
The behavior of an organism in response to the external world corresponds in a certain sense to the behavior of a *sage*, how special the intellect is, splendid as a ruling, restraining, ordering power, remaining *cool* under the assault of impressions.

26 [208]
The thousands of riddles surrounding us would merely interest us, *not* torment us, if we were healthy and cheerful enough at heart.

26 [209]

The age-old fallacious inference to a first cause, to a god, as cause of the world. But *our* own relationship to the world, our incredibly multifaceted creative relationship in every moment is a more accurate demonstration that creativity is one of the inalienable and enduring characteristics of the world itself: — not to impugn the language of mythologists.

26 [210]

Those who imitate

26 [211]

To render a moral judgment about the stomach and its activities: originally all events were given a moral interpretation. The realm of "willing and valuing" having become smaller and smaller.

26 [212]

It is essential to *get over* being upset when puny inferior personalities condemn us — yet there is a lot of posturing involved in this "getting over"

26 [213]

The *semblance* of acquired virtue is being turned into a duty for us: any moderately honest person would perish in the face of universal contempt.

26 [214]

In regard to women, I'm inclined to think that they should be treated as Orientals treat them: even exceptional women always demonstrate the very same thing — an incapacity for justice and an unbelievably sensitive vanity. Nothing about them should be taken too seriously, least of all their love: at the very least we should know that even the most faithful and passionate lovers require some minor infidelity as a kind of recreation, yes, in order to make *lasting* love possible.

26 [215]

That we love (forgive, look after people etc.) because we are not strong, not sturdy enough to be an enemy, to hurt someone through our enmity — that we would rather love than remain neutral, as justice requires, because things get too cold and uncanny for us when we isolate ourselves by taking a stand in this way — that we would rather endure the loss of our honor than get upset with someone — how feminine!

26 [216]

An intellect is not possible without categorizing that which is unconditioned. Well, intellects exist and they have within themselves an awareness of that which is unconditioned. But the latter as conditioning the existence of the intellect: — in any case, that which is unconditioned can *not* be something intellectual: the function of the intellect, the existence of the intellect as based on one condition, is an argument against the possibility of that which is unconditioned *being* an intellect.

— Finally, what is logical could be possible as a consequence of a fundamental error, a mistake in categorizing (a mistake in *creating*, in *poetically inventing* its absolute)

26 [217]

I say: the intellect is a creative force: in order that it can draw conclusions, establish things, it must first have created the concept of the unconditioned — *it believes in what it creates, as something that is true*: this is the fundamental phenomenon.

Concerning the conditions for logical thought:

26 [218]

That we wish to *please* the people we admire is not vanity — against Rée.[95]

26 [219][96]
    Zarathustra I.
            Overcoming vanity
            Reverence

26 [220]
    2. Zarathustra.
Great cosmic speech "I am cruelty" "I am deception" etc.
mocking an unwillingness to shoulder the blame — the one
who creates as doing the mocking — and all forms of suffering
— more evil than anyone has ever been etc. Highest degree of
satisfaction with his work — he breaks things into little pieces in
order to fit them together again and again. Buddha p. 44, 46.[97]
    overcoming death, suffering and annihilation in a new way
    the god who makes himself *small* (limited) and insinuates
himself into the entire world (life *always* there) — play, mockery — as a *demon who even annihilates.*

26 [221][98]
                        For: Part 2
Extra-moral considerations

		1 true		mendacious
good and evil		2 as *pure*	and	*impure* Buddha p. 50
		3 venerable		despicable p. 296
		4 as noble	and	base
		5 beneficial		harmful
good		6 as cutting yourself off from the world		
				denying the world
				(not "shaping things through
				actions") p. 50
				evil = worldly
		7 demanded		despicable p. 296
		8 unegoistic		egoistic
		9 poor (Ebion)[99]		rich

	miserable	happy
⟨good⟩	10 reversal:	having possessions rich (even
		in Aryan)
		(in Indo-Iranian, and to some
		degree into Slavic.

pure = happy ⎫
evil = unhappy ⎬ p. 50

the greatest **power**, in Brahman⟨ism⟩ and Christianity — *turning away from the world.* p. 54.

26 [222][100]

Zarathustra 1. terrible suspense: Zarathustra **must** *come* or everything on earth is *lost.*

26 [223][101]

Zarathustra 3. the great *consecration* of the new physician-priest- teacher-being, which will precede the superhumans.

26 [224]

Unegoistic actions are impossible; "unegoistic drive" sounds like "wooden iron" to my ear. I would like anyone to try demonstrating the possibility of such actions: certainly the common people, and those who are like them, believe in their existence — sort of like people who call a mother's love, or love in general, something unegoistic.

Incidentally, when doing history it is a mistake to claim that the common people have always *interpreted* the moral code of values "good" and "evil" as "unegoistic" and "egoistic."

Instead, good and evil as "commanded" and "forbidden" — "according to or in violation of custom" — is much older and much more widely prevalent.

Having insight into the *emergence* of moral value judgments is still not the same thing as a critique and a determination of their value — just as little as a quality is explained by our knowing the quantitative conditions under which it emerged.

26 [225][102]

Exercises in obedience: the disciples of the Brahmins. The oath of the Templars, the Assassins.

Deifying the power felt by the Brahmins: interesting that it emerged within the *warrior*-caste and only then was passed on to the priests.[103]

26 [226]

Knowledge, in its essence, is something that categorizes, poetically invents, falsifies:

26 [227]

"Science" (as practiced today) is the attempt to create a common sign language for all phenomena, with the goal of making things easier to *calculate* and thereby making nature easier to control. Yet this sign language, which brings together all the "laws" that have been observed, *does not explain anything* — it is merely a kind of *briefest* (most abbreviated) *description* of events.

26 [228]

The enormous mass of randomness, contradiction, disharmony, idiocy in the world of humans today is a premonition of the future: from the perspective of the future, this is the workshop that it needs today, a place where it can create, organize and harmonize things. — Likewise, in the universe

26 [229]

The Brahmins and Christians lead us away from the apparent world because they believe it to be evil (*fear* it —), but the scientific types do their work on behalf of their will to *dominate nature*.

26 [230]

I have gained mastery over[104] so many random things! There was so much bad air surrounding me when I was a child! When

have the Germans ever been more worn-out anxious hypocritical servile than in the fifties when I was a child!

26 [231][105]

NB. Humans up to now — as it were, embryos of future
humans — *all* of the formative forces, setting their sights on
these future humans, are within them: and because these forces
are enormous, this means **suffering** for the individuals of
today, *all the more if they are determining the future.* This is the
most profound conception of *suffering*: the formative forces
clashing with one another.

The isolation of individuals must not deceive us — in truth,
something is flowing forth *among* individuals. *The fact that*
the individual feels isolated is *what most forcefully* **goads** the
process itself toward the most distant of goals: their search for
their happiness is, on the other hand, the means that holds the
formative forces together and moderates them so that they do
⟨not⟩ destroy themselves.

26 [232]

Not "humankind," but rather *superhumans*, are the goal![106]
Misunderstanding in *Comte*!

26 [233]

The happiness of superior beings on celestial bodies (in the
works of Dühring[107]), a more subtle flight from earthly dissatisfaction! Similar to those who believe in worlds behind us and
above us!

26 [234]

Hopelessness in regard to humans — *my* way out! The
goal that the English have in mind makes *every person* with a
superior nature **laugh**! It is not to be desired — the thought
that there are *many happy people in the lowest ranks* is almost
disgusting.

26 [235]¹⁰⁸
To the Mistral Wind.
A Rhapsody.

26 [236]¹⁰⁹

Knowledge will also take new forms in superior kinds of beings, forms that are not yet necessary today.

26 [237]¹¹⁰

"Without my arrows, the Troy of knowledge will not be conquered" — this is what I, Philoctetes, say.¹¹¹

26 [238]

Philosophers the superior species, but they have *failed* much more up to now. Artists the inferior ones, but much more beautiful and more richly developed!

26 [239]¹¹²

For Outline.

A. The regulative hypotheses
B. The experiment } in the foreground
C. The description (in place of } my philosophy: *content of the*
   the supposed "explanation") } *first part.*

the *corresponding psychological states* as *the greatest achievements* up to now (by me for me)

Philosophy as the expression of an extraordinarily *superior* psychological state.

26 [240]

Those who explain poets misunderstand that the poet has *both*, reality *and* symbolism. Likewise, a first and second sense of a *whole*. Likewise, *pleasure* in oscillating colors, what has two or three meanings, *even the downside is good.*

26 [241][113]

First Part.
The New Kind of Truthful People.

Overcoming what is dogmatic : the superior psychological
and what is obscure   state[114] that goes along
with it

Overcoming those who are skeptics out of weakness.[115]

   A. the regulative hypotheses

   B. the experiment.

   C. the description

   the new feeling of power: the mystical condition, and the brightest bravest rationality as a way to get there

Second Part.
Beyond Good and Evil.

26 [242]

Galiani[116] thinks that humans are the only religious animals. But the way dogs grovel in front of human beings reminds me of how "devout people" behave, even if people are more crude about it.

26 [243][117]

The New Order of Rank.
Preface to the Philosophy of Eternal
Recurrence.

To pose this question, ever more seriously: for whom am I still writing? — I found no one who was ripe enough for most of my thinking; and Zarathustra is proof that someone can speak with the greatest clarity yet not be heard by anyone. — I feel that I am opposed to the *morality of equality*.

Inequality of human beings

1. Leader and herd. (Meaning of the one who is isolated) Irony against moralists
2. Complete and fragmentary human beings (e.g., problem of women, also of scientific people)
3. Successful and failed human beings (the latter perhaps naturally superior, even in the case of peoples and races. Problem: Indo-European and Semitic peoples, the latter nearer to the south NB. more religious, more dignified more perfect as predators, wiser — the former more muscular cold-hearted cruder heavier, corruptible)
4. Those who create and "the educated" ("superior humans," those who create and no others)

Inequality
of
those
who
create

5. Artists (as minor achievers) but *dependent* in all value judgments.

6. Philosophers (as those with the greatest breadth, the most synoptic vision, *describing* things in the most general terms) (but *dependent* in all value judgments), there have already been so many failures.

7. Those who gather the herd (lawgivers), those who rule, a very failed type (taking *themselves* as the standard of values, short-sighted perspective)

8. The ones who posit values (founders of religions) failures and blunders **in the extreme**.

9. A missing type: human beings who command most forcefully, who lead, posit new values, make the most comprehensive judgments about the whole of humankind and know the means for shaping it — in certain circumstances, *sacrificing* it for a *superior* entity. Such beings will not emerge until there is a ruling structure for the earth,[118] they will probably *be total failures* for a long time.

10. The feeling of being imperfect, whether
      this feeling is stronger or weaker, is the
      distinguishing feature (value of the "feel-
      ing of having sinned"
The feeling of moving toward perfection,
      predominating as a need (value of pious
      people, hermits, monasteries, priests)
The power of being able to *shape* something
      perfect within something else (value of
      "beautiful souls," of artists, of statesmen)
(Dionysian wisdom) The supreme power,
      to feel that anything imperfect, anything
      that suffers, is necessary (*worth repeating
      for eternity*), *this feeling* coming from
      excess pressure by creative forces which
      must crush things again and again,
      and which choose the most daunting
      difficult paths (principle of the greatest
      possible stupidity, God as the devil and
      symbol of arrogance)
Human beings up to now as *embryos*, in
      which all shaping forces *push against*
      each other — reason for their profound
      restlessness — — — — those who are the
      most creative as the ones who suffer the
      most?

Inequality
of
superior
humans

26 [244]

For the Preface.

How to educate people to be *respectful* in this age of the rabble which remains rabble-like even when paying homage, but
is usually pushy and shameless (also with its "benevolence" and
"compassion") A preface that is meant to *scare away* most people. Yes, I don't have anyone in mind — other than the ideal

community that Zarathustra instructed while they were on the blessed isles.

26 [245][119]

Constantly looking for perfection, and, hence *inner peace* — what Schopenhauer describes as an aesthetic phenomenon, is also what characterizes believers. *Goethe* (to Councilor Schlosser): "we can highly esteem only those who do not *seek* themselves . . . I must admit, in my entire life I have found people with this kind of selfless character only in places where I found a well-established religious life, a confession of faith that had an unchanging basis, yet at the same time was rooted in itself, not dependent on the era, its spirit, its science."

(that which is oriental, women have this effect here —)

26 [246]

In this century of superficial and hasty impressions, the most dangerous book is not dangerous: it seeks out the five, six minds that are profound enough. In the meantime — what harm is there if it helps to destroy *these* times!

26 [247]

The Americans being used up too quickly — perhaps only seeming to be a future world power.

26 [248]

Leibniz is more interesting than Kant — typically *German*: cheerful, full of noble phrases, tricky, flexible, pliable, a mediator (between Christianity and the mechanical worldview), unbelievably audacious in his own right, hidden behind a mask and courtly in a pushy sort of way, apparently modest.

26 [249]

The French *profoundly* artistic — their culture so thoughtfully conceived, the consistency in bringing beautiful *appearances* to

SUMMER—AUTUMN 1884

fruition — does not in any way take away from their *profundity*
— — —

26 [250]
Plato thought: what is commanded as coming from God,
e.g., when incest is forbidden as an abomination to God:
he thinks that absolute prohibitions are a *sufficient basis for
explaining* moral judgments. Short-sighted!

26 [251]
Independent people *were admired* in antiquity, no one complained about the "egoism" of the Stoic.

26 [252]
Every people has its own tartuffery

26 [253]¹²⁰
"Here the view is *clear*, the vista is uplifting."

26 [254]
The problem of free and unfree w⟨ill⟩ belongs in the vesti-
bule of philosophy — for me there is no will. That a belief in
the will is necessary in order to "will" — is nonsense.

26 [255]¹²¹
Lack of respect for Germany today, which does not have enough
sophistication simply to reject gossipy old-maid books like the one
by Jans⟨s⟩en: how it let itself give in to babble about "the old and
new beliefs" of the old, very old, and in no way new Strauss.

26 [256]¹²²
Regarding the title: "A Prophecy."
I believe I have *guessed* several things about the souls of the
most superior humans — perhaps all those who guess these
things will perish, but anyone who has seen them must help to
make them *possible*.

Fundamental thought: we must take the future as *providing the standards* for all our value judgments — and not look at what lies **behind** us for the laws that govern our actions![123]

26 [257]
Comparable people — where?

26 [258][124]

Preface:
on the Order of Rank of Intellects

On the inequality of humans
    a) Leader and herd
    b) Complete and fragmentary people
    c) Successful and failed human beings
    d) Those who create and "educated people" but,
       above all, the "uneducated" and dunces to the
       nth degree

On the inequality of superior humans (divided up according to the degree of *power*)[125]
    a) in terms of the feeling of incompleteness, as decisive
    b) feeling of moving toward completeness
    c) the power to be able to *shape* something which is
       complete
    d) supreme power, in feeling that even what is incom-
       plete is necessary, arising out of an excess of creative
       power (Dionysian)

On the order of rank of those who create values (in regard to the positing of values)
    a) artists
    b) philosophers
    c) lawgivers
    d) founders of religions
    e) the most superior human beings as rulers of the
       earth and creators of the future. (in the end crushing
       themselves —)

26 [259][126]

Philosophy of Eternal Recurrence.
An Attempt at the Revaluation of All Values.

26 [260]

In this age of the rabble, the nobly born mind should begin each day by *thinking* about the *order of rank*: here is where its duty lies, here its most subtle errors

26 [261]

Misunderstandings on a grand scale e.g., asceticism as a means of self-preservation for people with wild all-too-excitable natures. The la Trappe facility as a "prison house" to which we sentence ourselves (especially understandable among the French, as is Christianity in the libidinous atmosphere of southern European Hellenization). In the background of Puritanism there is a conviction about each person's *own venality*, about the omnipresent "*inner beast*" (*ego*[127]) — and the bleak dry *pride* of puritanical English people *wants* at the very least that *everyone else* should think just as poorly of their "inner persons" as they do of themselves!

The customs and ways of life were understood to be a *proven* means of survival — this is the *first* misunderstanding and something superficial. *Second* misunderstanding: they should now be the *only* means.

Pious people — awareness of a *superior context for all experiences*

26 [262][128]

Misunderstanding egoism: on the part of people with *baser* natures who know nothing at all about the lust for conquest and the insatiability of great love, just as little about the emanating feelings of power that overwhelm, compelling things to come to them, that want to embrace them — the artists' drive in search of their material. Often their feeling of being active is merely looking for terrain. — In ordinary "egoism" it is precisely the "non-ego," the *profoundly average being*, the generic human, that wants to survive — *this* is upsetting, in cases where it is noticed by rarer, more subtle and less average people. For these people make judgments like: "we are the **nobler ones**! *Our* survival matters *more* than that of those beasts!"

26 [263]

I view *all* moralities up to now as having been built on *hypotheses* concerning the means of preserving a *type* — but the level of intellect that has existed up to now has still been too weak and unsure of itself to grasp a *hypothesis* **as** hypothesis and yet accept it as regulative — it needed **faith**

26 [264]

NB. How human beings, up to now, imagined figures that were *superior* to human beings — —

26 [265]

NB. About women in labor screaming because of all the impurity. Purification festivals necessary for the greatest minds!

26 [266]

The weaker more tender people as the nobler ones.

26 [267]

the prodigious *idealizing* power that Christianity used in order to endure physical feelings of discomfort and barbaric feelings of disorder — it reinterpret⟨ed⟩ everything *in terms of the soul.*

26 [268]

People must *shackled* to the extent that they are not free to walk on their own. Moral revolutions e.g., during Christianity are 1) aimed at enfeebled wasted aged peoples who have lost their nerve 2) aimed at the horrific brutality of the barbarians.

26 [269][129]

Zarathustra must excite his disciples about the prospect of *conquering the earth* — supreme danger, supreme kind of victory: their entire morality a morality of *war* — to want unconditional *victory*

26 [270][130]

To Superior Humans.
Herald's Call of a Hermit.
By
Friedrich Nietzsche.

26 [271]

People want to do the following with their actions and with the ways they act

1) either glorify them — accordingly, morality of glorification

2) or justify them and *be accountable for* them (before some kind of forum, whether this is the community or reason or conscience —) thus the action must be explainable, must have emerged as a result of rationally conscious motivations — and likewise the entire way of acting

3) or to condemn them, to diminish them, in order for the people to overpower themselves in this way or to arouse compassion and thereby escape from the powerful.

26 [272]

In the organic process

1) *over*abundant *replacement* — false expression and with a teleological tinge

2) Self-regulation, in other words, *presupposing* the ability to rule over a community, yet i.e., the further development of that which is organic is *not* tied to nutrition, but rather to the ability to command and control: nutrition is *merely* one outcome.

26 [273][131]

The will to power in the functions of that which is organic.

Pleasure and displeasure and their relationship to the will to power.

Alleged altruism and the will to power. Motherly love e.g., and sexual love

The development of feelings from a fundamental feeling.

Lack of freedom and freedom of the will.

Punishment and *reward* (the stronger type as the superior type separates things from itself and draws things to itself)

Duty and *justice*.[132]

26 [274]

Tracing generation back to the will to power (! thus it must also be present even in the **in**organic *matter* that is appropriated!): the dissolution of the protoplasm in the case where a form has constituted itself, where the weight is equally distributed in 2 places. A force that draws things together, *ties things together*, issues from each place: at that point the intermediate mass is *torn apart*. Therefore: the origin of a generation lies in the power relationships *being equal* to each other. Perhaps all further development is tied to emerging power-equivalencies such as these.

26 [275]

Pleasure is a kind of rhythm in the sequence of differing *levels* of minor pain, a *stimulation* by means of a rapid succession of increases and decreases, as in the stimulation of a nerve, a muscle, and in general a dynamic curve moving upwards: tension is essential in this and relaxation. Tickling

Displeasure is a feeling that accompanies inhibition: yet since awareness of the strength of displeasure only occurs in the presence of inhibitions, displeasure is therefore a *necessary ingredient of all activity* (all activity is directed *against* something that should be overcome) Thus the will to power *strives* for obstacles, for displeasure. There is a will to suffer at the basis of all organic life (against "happiness" as "goal")

26 [276]

If two organic beings encounter one another, if there is *only* a struggle *for* life or nutrition: how does this happen? There must be a struggle for the sake of struggle: and *to rule* is to endure the counterweight of the weaker force, thus a kind of *continuation* of the struggle. *To obey* is likewise a *struggle*: this much force *is left over* for the sake of resisting.

26 [277]

Against the *drive for survival* as a radical drive: instead, that which is alive wants to *unleash* its force — it "*wants to*" and "*has to*" (in *my* view, both phrases have equal weight!): survival is merely a *consequence*.

26 [278]

Virtuous people want to make us believe (and also want to make themselves believe) that *they* invented happiness. The truth is that virtue was invented by happy people.

26 [279]

That reward and punishment are already present in the consequences of actions — this thought of an immanent justice is completely wrong. By the way, it also stands in contradiction to the idea of an "order of salvation" in experiences and their consequences: according to which bad things of all kinds are to be understood as special signs of favor from a God who only wants the best for us. — Why suffering should follow an evil deed is in itself not comprehensible: *in praxi*,[133] it would even be logical to conclude that an evil deed *should* follow an evil deed. That someone different from us must fare *badly* is a defensive notion, an essential emergency measure of the ruling caste, a means of discipline — but nothing especially "noble." — All such possible ideas about "immanent justice," "order of salvation," compensatory "transcendental justice," are going around in *everyone's* head these days — they contribute to the *chaos* of the modern soul.

26 [280]

We think differently about "certainty." Because fear has been bred into humans for the longest time, and because any tolerable existence began with "feelings of security," this is how it still works with thinkers today. But as soon as the external "dangerousness" of existence recedes, there emerges a pleasure in uncertainty, in the limitlessness of the lines on the horizon. The happiness of the great innovators when they strive for certainty could now be transformed into the happiness of demonstrating uncertainty and risk wherever they occur.

The fearfulness of earlier existence is likewise the reason why philosophers stress survival so much (of the ego or the species) and why they seize upon it as a principle: while in truth we are continuously playing the lottery against this principle. All of Spinoza's formulations are apropos here: i.e., *the basis of English utilitarianism. v.*[134] the brown binder.[135]

26 [281]

The idiotic moralists have always aspired to *become noble* without at the same time wanting the basis for it: *ennobling the body* (through an "elegant" way of life *otium*,[136] ruling, respect etc.) through an elegantly noble environment of humans *and* nature, finally they have thought of the individual and *not* of the continuation, by means of procreation, of what is noble. Short-sighted! Only for 30 years and no longer!

26 [282][137]

Depending on how a people feels: "justice, insight, the gift of leadership etc. are for the few." or "for the many" — there is an *oligarchical* regime or a *democratic* one.

Monarchy *represents* the belief in one entirely superior person, a leader rescuer demigod. The *aristocracy* represents the belief in a human elite and in a higher caste. Democracy represents the *lack of belief* in great people and in social elites: "Everyone is equal to everyone else" "Basically we are all beasts and rabble interested only in our own advantage"

26 [283][138]

In order to *bear* the thought of recurrence:

   it is necessary to have freedom from morality,

   new remedies for the reality of *pain* (to understand pain as
      tool, as father of pleasure — there is no all-*encompassing*
      awareness of displeasure)

   enjoyment of all kinds of uncertainty, of a willingness to
      experiment, as a counterweight to that extreme fatalism

   elimination of the concept of *necessity*[139]

   elimination of the "will"

   elimination of "knowledge in itself"

   greatest increase in humans' awareness of their power as the
ones who are creating superhumans.

26 [284][140]

   1. The thought: its presuppositions, which would have to be
true if it is true

         what follows from the thought

   2. as the *weightiest* thought: its presumed
         effect, in case it is not prevented[141]
         i.e., in case not all values are revalued

   3. means of *bearing* it
         the revaluation of all values
         no longer pleasure in certainty but rather in uncertainty
         no longer "cause and effect," but rather that which is
            continuously creative
         no longer will to survive, but rather will to power[142]
            etc.
         no longer the modest phrase "everything is *only* subjec-
            tive," but rather "it is also *our* work!" let us be proud
            of it!

26 [285]

On the hypocrisy of philosophers.

  the Greeks: conceal their agonal affect, drape themselves in
      virtue as "the happiest ones," and as the most virtuous
      ones (hypocrisy on two counts)
      (Socrates, triumphant as the ugly plebeian among
      beautiful and noble people, the persuader in a city of
      orators, the conqueror of his own affects, the common
      clever man with a "why?" in the midst of those born into
      nobility — conceals his pessimism)
  the Brahmins basically want to be liberated from tired luke-
      warm unpleasant feelings of existence
  Leibniz Kant Hegel Schopenhauer, their German dual
      natures
  Spinoza and the revenge-seeking affect, the hypocrisy of
      overcoming the affects
  The hypocrisy of "pure science," of "knowledge for the sake
      of knowledge"

26 [286]

I, like a female elephant, afflicted with a long pregnancy,
so that few things still matter to me, not even a little — *pro
pudor*[143] — the "Reich"

26 [287]

Do you have a good understanding of my new longing, the
longing for that which is finite? belonging to the man who has
beheld the ring of recurrence —

26 [288]

NB that which is continuously creative, instead of just once,
in the past

26 [289][144]

  Zarathustra 3
      the rovers, the eternal wanderers

those with the brain of a leech — — —
the ugly ones who want to put on masks
the hypocrites of happiness
the longing for that which is finite, for leftovers and
    corners
the envious emaciated workers and strivers
the all-too-sober people longing for a drunken state
    that will finally satisfy them.
    the people who have sobered up too much
the destroyers

The Cry of Distress of Superior Humans?
    Yes, of those who have failed —

26 [290]

Above all, in the case of the will to cruelty it doesn't matter
whether cruelty is directed at *us* or at *others*. **To learn** to enjoy
suffering — — the diabolical, like the divine, is part *of* whatever is alive and its *existence*.

26 [291][145]
Montaigne I p. 174

"the laws of conscience, which we claim have their origin in
nature, actually have their origin in habit. In their hearts, all
people admire the opinions and customs that are accepted and
that have been introduced within their homeland, so that they
cannot cut themselves off from these without feeling pangs of
conscience and can never act according to them without considerable pleasure."

26 [292][146]
On the superstitions of philosophers.
On the communicability of opinions.

26 [293][147]

The New Enlightenment.
Laying the Groundwork
for the "Philosophy of Eternal Recurrence."

26 [294][148]

It is not enough that you see how much humans and animals live in ignorance; you must also have the will to ignorance and learn how to use it. It is essential for you to grasp that life itself would be impossible without this kind of ignorance, that it is a condition that allows living things to survive and grow: a large, sturdy bell of ignorance must surround you

26 [295][149]

The will to ignorance.
The will to uncertainty.
The will to untruth.

The will to power.
The will to suffer.
The will to cruelty.
The will to annihilation.
The will to injustice.

The will to ugliness.
The will to immoderation.
the will to intoxication
the will to lethargy

26 [296][150]

Elimination of the will, free and unfree.
   of "obligation"[151] and "necessity"
   of "knowledge in itself" and the "thing in itself"
   of knowledge for the sake of knowledge
   of "good and evil"

the hypocrisy of philosophers.

Good people.

Artists.

Pious and godly people.

26 [297][152]

Beyond Good and Evil.

The Philosopher as Superior Artist.

The New Order of Rank.

On Superstition.

The Weightiest Thought.

How Life is *Made Possible* for Sages.
The social concealment of sages.
Their diet.
Their sexuality.
The communicability of their opinions.
Whatever transcends nationalism, the good European.
Schoolchildren, etc. Levels of initiation.

26 [298][153]

The New Enlightenment.
A Foreword and a Word for
the Philosophy of Eternal Recurrence.
On Superstitions among Philosophers.
Beyond Good and Evil.
The Philosopher — a Superior Artist.
The New Order of Rank.
Making the New Philosopher Possible.
The Weightiest Thought as a Hammer.

26 [299][154]

This is an age in which the rabble is coming to rule more and more and the gestures of their rabble bodies and minds have already become the norm in every household, at court and among the most lovable women[155] — : I don't even mean just "at" and "among," but also "inside and within."

my garden, with its golden trelliswork, must be defended not only against thieves and thugs: its most daunting dangers come from its pushy admirers. "I want to have my solitude" — this is the vow that sages make, I want to hold on to my solitude with tooth and claw, to imprison it in a golden cage —

26 [300]

Philosophers persuaded **to oppose**	1) appearance 2) change 3) pain
guided by instinctive determinations of value, in which *earlier* cultural conditions are reflected (the more dangerous ones	4) death 5) that which is corporeal, the senses 6) destiny and lack of freedom 7) that which has no purpose NB. everything that is human, even more so that which is animal, even more so that which is material
they believe in	absolute knowledge knowledge for the sake of knowledge virtue in league with happiness the recognizability of human actions[156]
false oppositions	e.g., pleasure and pain good and evil
the seductions of language	

26 [301]

Will to truth and certainty have their source in *fear* born of uncertainty.

26 [302]

    no matter (Boscovich)[157]
    no will
    no thing in itself
    no purpose

26 [303]

Courage would certainly not be called a virtue if it were one of the common facts about humans, such as the voluntary release of urine: which, as far as I can understand, our dear Spencer *et hoc genus omne*[158] are ready to include among the expressions of altruism.

26 [304]

The few good books that will remain from this century, more accurately: that will reach with their branches beyond this century, as trees that don't have their roots in it — I mean the *Memorial of St. Helena*[159] and Goethe's *Conversations with Eckermann*[160]

26 [305]

I have no desire whatsoever to render my opinion concerning — the communicability of opinions (or concerning the "communicability of truth," as all the virtuous hypocrites would express it in this case) The fact that I am still pronouncing on this matter right here already almost extends beyond the boundaries I have set for myself in the specified area.

26 [306][161]

There are still many more pleasing things on this earth than the pessimists admit, even today; e.g., E⟨duard⟩ von H⟨artmann⟩ himself. The Laocoön-group,[162] composed of three clowns and just as many umbrellas, does not please me as much as this Eduard "wrestling" with his problems.

26 [307]

German lyric poets, particularly when they are Swabians, e.g., Uhland gussied up with the feelings of a maiden in the castle, or Freiligrath as —
Or Hölderlin — — —

26 [308]

NB. Perfectly *clear* concerning whether we *want* to affirm this world of the senses and let it continue!
Kant has been overcome.
The discovery of antiquity has continued.
Actual purpose of all philosophizing, the *intuitio mystica.*[163]

26 [309][164]

The most beloved *circulus vitiosus:*[165] if our sense organs are initially the products of our senses, all observations that see them as causes would be nonsensically wrong!

26 [310]

About health and illness genius neurosis, Dionysian.

26 [311]

Finally — people no longer want to spout forth their opinions: they have some sense of the austerity of our garden and don't expect to acquire much more that is good or new — they decide to *love* what they *already* have. And woe to those people who now want to take from us those opinions that we *wanted* to treasure.

26 [312]

Religion interpreting all strong surprising sudden alien impulses as coming from *outside*.
Morality was added solely as a means to religion (a means of overpowering the gods *or* of reaching states of ecstasy)

Misunderstanding the body: intoxication, sensuality, the ecstasy of cruelty as *apotheosis*, as becoming one with a god.

Fundamental difference from antiquity: sexuality *revered* in a religious sense; and consequently even its tools.

Ecstasy differs in the case of a pious sublime noble person like Plato — and in the case of camel drivers who are smoking hashish and — — —

Fundamental transformation of religion:

1) we want to compel God to do what we like — e.g., prayer

2) we submit to the will of God

The first is the noble form, 2) is the slave form.

26 [313][166]

"Self-preservation" merely a side effect, not a goal! Spinoza's influence!

26 [314][167]

Buratti, and his influence on Byron.

26 [315]

The feeling you get in the South e.g., expressed in Stendhal "Travels in France"[168] — what does it consist in?

26 [316]

NB. Which *tests* are missing (in place of merely intellectual or practical ones)?

The correct refutations are physiological (bodily), thereby eliminating ways of thinking.

26 [317]

I must learn to think *more like Orientals* about philosophy and knowledge. *An overview of Europe as seen from the East.*

26 [318][169]

Superior humans.

On philosophers.
On leaders of the herd.
On pious people.
On virtuous people.
On artists.

Critique of superior humans

26 [319]
The Europeans are basically imagining that they now exemplify superior humans on earth

26 [320]¹⁷⁰

> *The Good Europeans.*
> Proposals for Breeding a New Nobility.
> By
> Friedrich Nietzsche

26 [321]
There is 1) monological art (or in "dialogue with God")

    2) societal art, presupposing *société*, a finer sort of person.

    3) demagogic art e.g., Wagner for the German "people," Victor Hugo

26 [322]
Wherever there is enthusiastic raving about the people, right away women listen more closely, they feel that it is their business

26 [323]
Scholars, and their inflated sense of self. Where does it come from? There, too, it is an emancipation of an inferior species that *no longer believes in* a *superior one.*

26 [324]¹⁷¹
The great rebellion of the rabble and slaves

puny people, who no longer believe in the saints and in par-
   agons of virtue (e.g., Christ, Luther etc.
bourgeoisie, who no longer believe in the superiority of the
   ruling caste (e.g., revolution)
scientific craftsmen, who no longer believe in philosophers
women, who no longer believe in the superiority of men.

26 [325][172]

Beyond Good and Evil.
Preface to a Philosophy
of Eternal Recurrence.
By Friedrich Nietzsche.

26 [326]

The sensualism and hedonism of the previous century are
the best inheritance this century has received: behind a hundred legal clauses and fine costume parades.

Hedonism = pleasure as principle.

Pleasure as a standard actually to be found among the *utilitarians* (the comfort-loving English people).

Pleasure as a regulating principle (actually *not* found) among
the Schopenhauerians

von Hartmann a superficial contrarian who *muddles* pessimism with teleology and wants to create from this a philosophy
of comfort (approximates the English in this.

What follows pessimism is the doctrine of the **meaning***less-
ness of existence*

that pleasure and pain have no *meaning*, that Hedone[173] cannot be a principle

This in the next century.

Doctrine of the great fatigue.

What's the point? Nothing is worth doing!

26 [327]

The *will* is *deduced*[174] — it is not an unmediated fact, as Schopenhauer wants it to be. It remains to be asked whether this deduction is *valid* — —

26 [328]

Belief in the "senses" is the basis for all science, as for all life. With this, nothing is settled as to whether this belief *is justified*, mistakes made by the senses (blue instead of red) are not an argument against the fact that a leaf is green. The emergence of a sense *that constructs color* in a color-free world is a nonsensical thought.

Description and establishing what the facts are.

26 [329]

Nothing can be *discovered* about a thing from its causes, i.e., a thing = its effects. Our becoming familiar with the causes of a thing[175] doesn't help us to become familiar with its effects, i.e., we don't become familiar with the *thing*.

26 [330]

Deeply interested in *truth* — where does this come from? In debt to Christianity — Pascal

26 [331]

the differing *degrees* of enjoying something being "true"
    e.g., Kant and Schelling
        Machiavelli and Seneca
        Stendhal and Walter Scott
        Plato and Hafiz

26 [332]

1 What's the point of *swearing* to ourselves that we want to know? "what is true preferable to what is untrue"

2 What's the point of (really) *wanting to know*?

3 What's the point of the *obligation* to know? and it is *true*?! that we prefer what is true?

26 [333]

There are so many superficial thinkers today who are content with tracing something back to habituation and heredity and then thinking they have *explained* it. But "how is habituation *possible*? How is heredity possible?"

26 [334]

Faith in the Truth.

What is dissolute and pathological about much that has been called "will to truth" up to now.

With terrifying seriousness, philosophers have warned us about the senses and the deception of the senses. The profound antagonism between philosophers and the friends of deception, artists, pervades Greek philosophy: "Plato *versus* Homer" — is the philosophers' watchword!

But no one has *grasped* the drawback either, that truth is not suited for life and that life is conditioned by perspectival illusion. — *It is one of the most dangerous exaggerations*, to want knowledge *not* in service to life but *in itself*, at any cost: like libertines following their drives and nothing else, without being controlled by other salutary instincts, if it is not idiotic — — —

26 [335]

Is it possible to be interested in this German Reich? Where are there any new *ideas*? Is it merely a new aggregation of power? Even worse, if it doesn't know what it wants. *Peace* and appeasement are not a policy for which I have any respect. To rule and to aid the triumph of the greatest ideas — the only thing that could interest me about Germany. What do I care whether the Hohenzollerns are there or not? — England's *pathetic small-mindedness* is now the great danger on earth. I see more of an inclination to greatness in the feelings of the Russian nihilists than in those of the English utilitarians. The German and Slavic races being woven together — no matter what, we also need the best money people,[176] the Jews, so as to have dominion over the earth.

26 [336]

1) a feeling for reality

2) break with the English principle of the people's representation, we need representation of the powerful interests

3) no matter what, we need to come together with Russia, and
with a new *common* program which does not allow an English
pipe dream to seize power in Russia. No American future!

4) a European policy is unsustainable, and the narrow focus
just on Christian perspectives is an *incredibly great misstep*. In
Europe, all sensible people are *skeptics*, whether they say so or not.

I think we don't want to restrict ourselves to either Christian
or American perspectives.

26 [337]

buona femmina e mala femmina vuol bastone[177] (Sacchetti
Nov. 86)

26 [338]

*hinc mihi quidquid sancti gaudii sumi potest horis omnibus
praesto est.*[178] Petrarca, famil. XIX 16.

26 [339]

The will not to let ourselves be deceived and the will to let
ourselves be deceived — — but philosophers? Religious people? Artists?

26 [340]

Do philosophers still exist? In truth, our lives include much
that is philosophical, particularly in the case of all scientific
people, but there are as few *genuine philosophers*[179] left as there
are *real aristocrats*. Why is that?

26 [341]

Just as the French reflect courtesy and the esprit of French
society, so too the Germans reflect something of the profound
dreamlike seriousness of their mystics and musicians and just

as much of their childish nonsense. There is much republican nobility in Italians and a knack for displaying their goodness and their pride, without vanity.

26 [342]

There is no longer any faith in philosophers, not even among scholars; this is the skepticism of a **democratic** age which *rejects* superior kinds of humans. Our century's psychology is essentially oriented *against* people with superior natures: we want to sum up their human qualities on their behalf.

26 [343]

Pythagoras was an attempt at an *antidemocratic* ideal that failed under tumultuous movements that wanted the people to rule.

26 [344]

"*Judges.*" People like this cannot avoid giving orders: their "thou shalt" cannot be derived from the nature of things, but rather because they *see* what is superior, they must *bring* it *to fruition* and enforce it. What do they care if people perish! They sacrifice people without a second thought — position of artists in relation to people: great people must command and *introduce, apply, demand* the value judgments that *they* hold. All earlier value judgments did not come into being in any other way. But they are all impossible for us now, their presuppositions are false.

26 [345]

"Punishments": this is what people get, they are put in their *place*, they are degraded in relation to our ideal. Yet *not* wanting to preserve many at the expense of individuals, *not* society's point of view at all!

26 [346]

With "happiness" as a goal nothing can be done, not even if this means the happiness of a community. It has to do with achieving multiple *ideals* which must be in *conflict* with one another, yet this result is not the welfare of a herd but of a superior type. Yet *this type* will *not* be achieved through the welfare of the herd! any more than individual humans will reach their peak through comfort and concessions.

"Mercy," "loving your enemies," "patience," "equal" rights (!) are all principles of a *lower* rank. What is superior is the *will to create* above and beyond ourselves, by means of ourselves, and even if this should be by means of our downfall.

26 [347]

We have *failed to recognize* that all moral "thou shalts" have been created by individual humans. We have *wanted* to have a god or a conscience in order to *withdraw from* the project that is demanded by human *creativity*. Weakness or laziness is concealed behind the Christian-*Catholic* way of thinking. — But in order to be able to create ideals, humans must learn and know etc.

26 [348]

Ridiculing the school of "objectivists" and "positivists." They want to get around value judgments and to discover and present only the facts. But see e.g., Taine: in the background he *has* predilections: for strong expressive types e.g., more for people who enjoy things than for Puritans.

26 [349]

Someday to write an *evil* book, worse than Machiavelli and that very German and mildly malicious most servile of devils Mephistopheles!
Its traits: cruel (taking pleasure in watching the perishing of a
              beautiful type)
        seductive (inviting us to accept the doctrine that we must
              be one thing *and* also the other)
        mocking the virtues of monks, of philosophers, mocking
              self-important artists etc., even mocking the good
              well-behaved people of the herd

magnanimous toward curiosity, intrusiveness, vulgarity
   in those who know, likewise toward pigtailed pedantry,
   obsequiousness; no laughter, no anger.

26 [350]

How a word like that can touch your heart!
— "our boldness has carved its way into all lands and seas,
founding monuments to good and evil that will stand forever
everywhere" — says Pericles.[180]

26 [351]

Wherever one desire holds sway (or desires in general), in the
manner of the rabble, in that case there are no superior humans.
It is self-evident that someone (like e.g., Augustine or Luther) is
not in any way familiar with *superior problems*, all of which presuppose an elevation where it is much cooler. All of this is purely
personal *distress* in the case of Augustine and Luther. It is a sick
person asking for a cure. In essence, religions may ⟨be⟩ institutions for training animals or mental institutions for those
who cannot control themselves. — It is amusing, this distress
surrounding the sex drive e.g., even in Wagner's *Parsifal* and
Tannhäuser.

26 [352]
I am *not* interested

1) in the nation-state, as something ephemeral vis-à-vis the
democratic mass movement.

2) in the worker-question, because the workers themselves
are merely an interlude.

3) in the differences between religion and philosophy,
because they are fundamentally one and the same, particularly
concerning good and evil — where *I* have my doubts.

4) in ways of thinking that are not anchored in the body and
the senses, and in the earth

5) *not* in *l'art pour l'art*,[181] the objectivists etc.

26 [353]

A prayer for blindness

Morality *is* annihilated: present the facts! What remains: "*I will this*"[182]

New order of rank. Against equality.

The ones who create, instead of judges and people who punish.

our *good* situation, as the ones bringing in the harvest

the greatest responsibility — my pride!

Summoning those who are most evil.[183]

lawgivers and politicians

pious people (why impossible?)

first build up the body: then the mind will work itself out. Plato.

up to now, following a long cosmopolitan survey, the Greeks as the humans who brought things the furthest. Europe.

26 [354]

the naïveté of Plato and of Christianity: they believed that they knew what "good" is. They had figured out the people of the *herd* — *not* creative artists. The "savior" who descends to the level of *miserable and bad people* was already invented in Plato. He fails to appreciate *the rationality and necessity of* **evil**.

26 [355]

Not the Good,[184] but rather *the* superior person! Plato is worth more than his philosophy! Our instincts are better than their conceptual expressions. Our body is wiser than our mind! *If* Plato did resemble that bust in Naples, then here we have the best refutation of *everything* Christian!

26 [356]

It seems that Socrates was on to the fact that we do not act morally as a consequence of logical reasoning — and he himself did not *discover* this reasoning. That Plato and everyone after him thought they had and that Christianity had let itself be baptized in the name of this Platonic *niaiserie*,[185] this has been up to now the greatest impetus for the *lack of freedom* in Europe.

26 [357]

Socrates, who said "I do not know what is good and evil," was shrewder than Plato: he defines it! But Plato *represents it*, the superior human being.

26 [358]

The phony German-ness in R⟨ichard⟩ W⟨agner⟩ (and the fundamental psychological phoniness of this supremely "modern" mixture of brutality and increasing delicacy of the senses) is just as disagreeable to me as the phony Roman-ness in David or the phony medieval English world of Walter Scott.

26 [359]

The problem of *truthfulness*. The first and most important thing to consider is actually the will to appearance, *firmly* establishing[186] perspectives, the "laws" of optics i.e., positing what is untrue as true etc.

The problem of *justice*. The first and most compelling thing to consider is nothing but the will and the strength that leads to superior power. Initially, those who rule determine "justice" after the fact, i.e., they measure things by *their* standards; if they are *very powerful*, they can go a long way in *making concessions* and in recognizing individuals who *attempt new things*

The problem of *compassion*. Initially, we must cultivate a profound instinct for cruelty, an enjoyment of other people suffering. Because a monstrous indifference to everything "other than ourselves" must be there before anything else. A more subtle sort of sympathy is an enfeebled kind of cruelty.

The problem of *good* people. The people of the herd who prefer and praise socializing characteristics. The opposite characteristics are valued by people who rule, that is, aspects of their own nature: hard-heartedness, cold-bloodedness, a cold eye, no accommodations, an eye for facts, an eye for great distances and not for what is near and neighborly etc.

26 [360][187]

How ridiculous the socialists are to me, with their silly optimism about "good people" waiting behind a bush just until the prevailing "order" has been abolished and all "natural drives" unleashed.

And the opposing party is just as ridiculous because they refuse to acknowledge the presence of violent acts within the law and of harsh egoism in every kind of authority. "I and my kind" want to rule and be the last ones still around: anyone who has become a degenerate is exiled or annihilated — this is the fundamental feeling behind every kind of ancient law-giving.

The idea of a *superior kind* of human is despised even more than monarchs are despised. Anti-aristocratic: this takes the hatred of monarchs merely as a mask and — — —

26 [361]

Turning women into men is the proper term for "emancipation of women." This means that they form themselves in the image that men are projecting now and lust for *their* rights. I see this as the *degeneration* of women's instincts today: they would have to know that they are dismantling their power in this way. — As soon as they no longer want to allow themselves to be supported and as soon as they want to seriously compete with men in the social-political sphere, consequently even wanting to dispense with the mild and lenient way they have been treated up to now, then — —

26 [362]

In those centuries when the Orient and Athens were at their best, women were secluded from society, the corrupting imagination of women was not wanted: *this* corrupts the race, more than physical intimacy with a man.

26 [363]

It's no use invoking ancient Germanic customs and chastity: there are no longer any Germanic tribesmen, there are no longer even any forests.

26 [364]

I have not met anyone with whom I could have spoken about morality using *my* approach: up to now, in my view, no one has been honest and daring enough for this. Some of this may be a matter of chance: e.g., that I have lived too much among Germans, who have always, in all innocence, been moralistic Tartuffes more than anything else. Yet in the main I believe that mendacity in moral matters is a part of the character of this democratic age. The kind of age, that is, which has appropriated the great lie "human equality" as its campaign slogan, is shallow, in a hurry, and intent upon the illusion that people are doing well and that "good" and "evil" are no longer a problem.

26 [365]

Morality "thou shalt" as a false *interpretation* of certain instinctive feelings.[188]

26 [366][189]

Those who are the strongest in body and soul *are the best* — fundamental principle for **Zarathustra** — a superior morality arising from within them, the morality of those who create: *re-creating* humans in *their* image. *This* is what they want, *this* is their honesty.

26 [367][190]

Zarathustra 5.

The singing pillar, which is struck by a ray of morning sunshine.

26 [368]

In cases of extraordinary excitement, severe pain (self-wounding) merely acts as a stimulant.[191]

26 [369]

Let's presuppose that we have freed ourselves from Kant's naïveté, according to which, whenever he discovers instincts having to do with intellectual or moral matters, he immediately concludes, "that is not of *this* world." The same naïveté still prevails among the English, among the "Instinctivists" and "Intuitionists."

But where *I* grow concerned, is this: all those who do physiological-historical research into morality make the following judgment: *because* moral instincts speak *in this way* or *that way*, these judgments are then *true, i.e., beneficial* in regard to the *preservation of the species*: because these instincts are still around! In the same way, I say that the *immoral* instincts have to be true: only, something else is established therein than specifically the will to preservation, namely, the will to progress, to something more, to — — — Is preservation really the only thing a being wants?

And you think "preservation of the species," I see only, "preservation of a herd, of a community."

26 [370]

We are richer than we think, we carry the material for dozens of persons in our bodies, we see "character" in what is merely a part of the "person," part of *one* of our masks. Most of our actions do not emerge from the depths but rather are superficial: like most volcanic eruptions: we don't have to let ourselves be deceived by the noise. Christianity is right about this: *it is possible to don a new person*: yes, and then after that a newer one. We are mistaken when we judge a person in terms of individual actions: individual actions do not allow for generalizations.

26 [371]

A philosophy which doesn't promise to make us happier and more virtuous, which moreover wants to make it clear that those who serve it will probably perish, that is, will become isolated in their own time, immolated and scalded, will have to endure various kinds of mistrust and hatred, will require much heartlessness against themselves and unfortunately also against others: a philosophy like this does not ingratiate itself easily with anyone: we must have been *born* for it — and I have yet to find anyone who was (otherwise I would have no reason to write this) As compensation, it promises a few pleasant shudders; as experienced by people who look down from very high mountains and see a world of new vistas; and in the end it doesn't turn you into an idiot, which was the effect of Kantian philosophizing (recently, someone was cruel enough to publish, with great ceremony, what is left over from the magnum opus[192] of his idiocy — this is the kind of thing that is possible with Germans!)

26 [372][193]

Given my approach to moral issues, I have been sentenced to silence for a long time. My writings contain hints here and there; I myself did respond more boldly; already when I was 25, I composed *for myself* a *pro memoria*[194] "on truth and lies in an extra-moral sense." I have even dealt with people who were concerned in their own way with morality: they will confirm on my behalf that I never have spoken with them about morality in *my* preferred way. Now, when I have a clearer perspective on this time, and when I allow myself to take liberties that I used to think were not allowed, I no longer see any reason to hide my light under a bushel. I admit "that the 'truth' in these matters is harmful," to use the language of moral hypocrites, and that it can destroy many people: but "being harmful" and "destroying people" belong just as much to philosophy as "being beneficial" and "being constructive."

26 [373]

There is an inclination to truth: as improbable as it sounds: in a few people at least. There is also the opposite inclination e.g., in artists. And we want to be pleased about this, much that is good and bad has come out of both. On balance, the second inclination is more important, there are good reasons why philosophers are rare and why their influence is severely impeded.

26 [374]

Nothing good has ever come from the mind looking at itself in the mirror. It is only now that we are finally making progress in attempting to investigate all mental processes by using the body as a guide e.g., via memory.

26 [375][195]

Old Kant identifies several mental instincts which have an effect *prior to* any reasoning and prior to any sensory activity: in a similar fashion, he later identifies a moral instinct, namely, that of obedience. To say that this allowed a bridge to be built into "another world" was jumping to conclusions. Even if it were determined that human existence is tied to these instincts, nothing would have been established about the "truth" of these instincts. It is *our* world, pure and simple.

26 [376][196]

My philosophy conveys the triumphant thought[197] on which every other way of thinking will ultimately founder. It is the great *engendering* thought: the races that don't endure it are condemned; those who find it most beneficial are destined to rule.

26 [377][198]

Devoid of Intellectual Integrity

When Richard Wagner went so far as to broach the subject of the pleasure he knew he could derive from the Christian Eucharist (the Protestant one), that's when I ran out of patience. He was a great actor: but lacking restraint, and inwardly prey to all things that are strongly intoxicating. He had gone through all of the transformations that good Germans have gone through since the days of Romanticism: Wolf's Glen and *Euryanthe*,[199] Horror-Hoffmann, then "emancipation of the flesh" and thirst for Paris, then a taste for grand opera, for Meyerbeer's and Bellini's music, peoples' tribunals, later Feuerbach and Hegel — music was supposed to come from the "unconscious," then the revolution, then disappointment, and Schopenhauer, and cozying up to German princes, then homages to Kaiser and Reich and army, then even to Christianity, which in Germany is again considered to be in good taste since the last war and its many "ultimate sacrifices" — with imprecations against "science."

26 [378]

To resist all our natural inclinations and to attempt to see whether even something of the opposite inclination is within us: a useful thing, although this makes us very uncomfortable. As when someone who is used to low humidity is moved into a damp climate. It demands an implacable *will* — and if my way of thinking demands nothing but this, it is still a reason why it will have few followers. A strong and yet flexible will like this is too rare.

26 [379]

Weak-willed peoples (like Sainte-Beuve) have an inner aversion toward opposite types[200] e.g., toward Stendhal.

26 [380]

How mean and beastly the English must be that they feel compelled even now to devote all of their energy to preaching the *utile*! This is as far as their point of view reaches: their *dulce*[201] is much too limited. — Even the Salvation Army!

26 [381][202]

"*une croyance presque instinctive chez moi, c'est que tout homme puissant ment, quand il parle, et à plus forte raison, quand il écrit.*" *Préface, Vie de Napoleon* p. XV Stendhal.

26 [382]

At dinner the talk was of Eugen Dühring,[203] who is "for-given" a lot, for, it is said: he is blind. How's that? I am almost blind. Homer was completely blind. Is that any reason to be in a bad mood? And full of worms? And to look like an ink-well? Recently, Eugen Dühring told us his life story: he has forgotten no disappointment, no minor illness from the time he was a toddler, I think he can tell bad little petty tales about his teachers and opponents for hours at a time, from the time when he ⟨was⟩ not yet blind: at the very least he gestures in that direction in the otherwise pretty picture with which he adorned his book and refuted his own philosophy. — He tells us it's a pretty picture.

26 [383][204]
Aftereffects of the ancient God 1) —

As little as I know of what Germans today are philosophiz-ing about: I still got wind of the fact, thanks to some lucky coincidences, that today it is certainly not fashionable in Ger-many to think about the creation of the world, but rather about its beginning: a defense has been launched against "infinity stretching backwards" — You understand my abbreviated for-mula, right? Mainländer, Hartmann, Dühring etc. are all in agreement about it. Mainländer, an apostle of unconditional chastity, like Richard Wagner, discovered the most indecent expression for the opposite view, that the world is eternal.

Aftereffects of the ancient God 2) eternally new.

26 [384]
Space an abstraction: there is no space as such, specifically, there is no *empty space*. A lot of nonsense comes from the belief in "empty space." —

26 [385]

That we have an instinct for time, an instinct for space, an instinct for reasons;[205] this has nothing to do with time space and causality.

26 [386]

Triumph of the anti-teleological mechanical way of thinking as a *regulative hypothesis* 1) because it alone makes science possible 2) because it makes the least assumptions and *must* first be tried out *under all circumstances*: — which will require a few centuries 3) — — —

26 [387]

Fight against Plato and Aristotle.

26 [388]

Hegel's ridiculous Gothic assault on heaven (— *pathetic anachronism*). Attempt to bring a kind of rationality into evolution: — coming from an opposite standpoint, I still see in logic itself a kind of irrationality and randomness. We are making the effort to ⟨grasp⟩ how evolution proceeded prior to human beings, entirely without rationality, that is, when by far the greatest irrationality prevailed.

26 [389]

Against altruism: this very thing is an illusion.
Désintéressement[206] in morality (Schopenhauer Comte)
                    in epistemology (the "objectivists" — like Taine),
                    in art (ideal beauty, in which e.g., Flaubert believes)

26 [390][207]

When I was 12 years old, I came up with a strange kind of Trinity: that is, God the Father, God the Son and God the Devil. My conclusion was that God, in conceiving himself, created the second person of the godhead: but that, in order to be able to conceive himself, he had to conceive his opposite, therefore he had to create it. — That's how I began to philosophize.

26 [391]

The many false "*opposites*" (about the transformation of the affects, their genealogy etc.

26 [392][208]

Innumerable individuals of a superior sort are now perishing: but *whoever emerges from it* is strong as the devil. Similar to the time of the Renaissance.

26 [393]

Actors.

The historical sense: Plato and all of philosophy have no notion of this. It is a kind of *acting* artistry, to adopt someone else's psyche for a time: result of the great *mixing of races and peoples*, by means of which a piece of everything that has ever been is in everyone. An artistic sense in the field of knowledge. At the same time, a sign of *weakness* and lack of *unity*.

Exoticism, cosmopolitanism etc. Romanticism. The sense has *grown more acute*, e.g., now Walter Scott is no longer a possibility for us. The same with Richard Wagner.

Rousseau, George Sand, Michelet, Sainte-Beuve — their silly kind of acting artistry. Some in front of the people, others (like Voltaire) in front of society.

The powerful are an entirely different kind of actor, like Napoleon, Bismarck.

26 [394][209]

Do you know what a swamp is? — Chance has allowed me to see once again, taken together, everything that Richard Wagner and his people, collaborating, have preached and published: in the disreputable *Bayreuther Blätter*.[210] Look, this is a swamp:

pretension, obscurity, ignorance and — bad taste thrown together. Whatever the bird sings, its fledglings tweet;[211] no one will be surprised by this. If only it were a song! But it is a kind of whimpering, the self-importance of an old high priest who fears clear and obvious concepts more than anything else. And they want to join the conversation about matters of philosophy and history! — *Il faut être sec*,[212] says a man after my own heart, my friend Stendhal.[213] We mustn't stir up the swamp. We should live in the mountains:[214] thus spoke my son Zarathustra.

26 [395]

It seems that I am the kind of German that is going extinct. To be a good German means to de-Germanize ourselves[215] — I said this once: but no one wants to hear this from me these days. Perhaps Goethe would have agreed with me.

26 [396][216]

Pour être bon philosophe, il faut être sec, clair, sans illusion. Un banquier, qui a fait fortune, a une partie du caractère requis pour faire des découvertes en philosophie, c'est-à-dire pour voir clair dans ce qui est.[217] Not to want to deceive people — this is something completely different, this may be moral. Not to allow ourselves to be deceived, especially when we are inclined in that direction!

26 [397]

Stendhal formulates the moral problems more precisely (18 December 1829).

What are the motives for human actions: *est-ce la recherche du plaisir, comme dit Virgile (trahit sua quemque voluptas) Est-ce la sympathie?*[218] What is a pang of conscience? Does it come from conversations we have heard? *ou naît-il dans la cervelle, comme l'idée de becqueter le blé qui vient au jeune poulet?*[219]

26 [398]

Intellectual refinement[220] as the *goal*: in this way, sharp distinctions between good and evil, virtue and vice are a training device to make people gain *control* over themselves, which prepares them to be intellectual. — But if there is no refinement of the senses to go along with this, then the intellect is stretched very thin.

26 [399]²²¹

The Germans are a dangerous people: they know about intoxication. Gothic, perhaps also rococo (as per Semper), the historical sense and exoticism, Hegel, Richard Wagner — Leibniz still dangerous even today — the servile soul (*idealized* as scholarly or martial virtue) even in the historical sense. The Germans may well be the *most mixed* people.

"the people of the middle," the inventors of porcelain and a Chinese-like manner of meeting in privy councils.

26 [400]

A profoundly benevolent attitude toward all things. I have to put on a show in order to get mad at the people I know: assuming I'm not ill.

26 [401]²²²

Even philosophers must say to themselves what those diplomats used to say: "let's not trust our first instincts: they're almost always good."

26 [402]²²³

Bismarck: as far from German philosophy as a peasant or a fraternity student.²²⁴ Mistrustful of scholars. I like that about him. He has discarded everything that a stupid German education (with preparatory schools and universities) wanted to teach him. — And he obviously loves a good meal with strong wine more than German music: which for the most part is merely a refined feminine hypocrisy and a cloaking device for the ancient German masculine inclination to be intoxicated. He refused to give up the *constraints* of duty, specifically, to God and king: and eventually, as stands to reason, he added the constraint that is embraced by anyone who has created something, the love for his creation (I mean, for the German Reich)

26 [403][225]

Michelet: sweat-soaked sympathy, with a touch of the rabble, as if he were taking off his coat before setting to work. Member of the people's tribunal: he is even familiar with the blood-thirsty fits of rage of the people. Everything that I like is alien to him. Montaigne, just as much as Napoleon.[226] Strange, even he, an industrious strait-laced person, exhibits the inquisitive lecherousness of a Gaul.

26 [404][227]

Saint-Beuve — quiet rage of all the subtler French people against "frightful stupidity" — : he would love to deny that he is completely unphilosophical, likewise that he is completely lacking in character, indeed, which is no surprise given both of these, that he lacks any well-refined taste *in artibus et litteris*.[228] He doesn't know how to come to terms with Voltaire's strengths, nor with Montaigne, Charron, Chamfort, La Rochefoucauld, Stendhal: — That is, he is irritated and kind of envious of the fact that, in addition to their strengths, all these connoisseurs of humanity are embodiments of will and character.

26 [405][229]

The character of *Hölderlin* and *Leopardi*: I am heartless enough to laugh about their demise. People don't understand this. Things turn out badly for these ultra-Platonists who always lose their naïveté. There must be something earthy and coarse in people: otherwise they perish in a ridiculous way when their theories are constantly contradicted by the simplest facts: e.g., by the fact that a man needs a woman from time to time, just as he needs a decent meal from time to time. At the end, the Jesuits unearthed the fact that Leop⟨ardi⟩ — — —

26 [406]²³⁰

In my youth, when I was many things, for example even a painter, I once painted a portrait of Richard Wagner, with the title: *Richard Wagner in Bayreuth*. A few years later, I said to myself: "Hell! it doesn't look like him at all." A few years after that, I answered "so much the better! so much the better!" — In certain times of life, we have the right to see things and people wrongly — magnifying glasses that give us hope.

When I was 21, I was perhaps the only person in Germany who loved these two, who loved both Richard Wagner and Schopenhauer with such fervor. Several of my friends became infected by this love.

Basically, due to Handel, I am — — —

As a boy, I loved Handel and Beethoven: but I added *Tristan and Isolde* when I was 17 because its world made sense to me. Although, at the time, I thought *Tannhäuser* and *Lohengrin* were "beneath my taste": boys are completely shameless in their pride when it comes to matters of taste.

26 [407]²³¹

The Lawgiver of the Future.

Human beings who begin to see the image of an incredibly daunting mission materializing in front of them seek to *escape* it: and we will find that great human beings are the ones who make the boldest and most daring attempts to *slip away* somewhere, e.g., to convince themselves a) the mission is already accomplished b) or it cannot be accomplished c) or I am too weak to do it d) my duty, my morality, rejects it as immoral — e) or they ask themselves: who thinks I can do this? No one. Skepticism concerning all difficult missions. — Many succeed in evading their mission, there is a subtle guilty conscience in store for them. In the end, it is a question of *power: how great is their sense of* **responsibility**?

After I had sought for a long time to link a certain concept to the word "philosopher," I finally discovered that there are two kinds 1) those who attempt to *ascertain* an extensive array of facts

2) those who are *lawgivers* of valuations. The former seek to gain control of the world around them, or of a past world, by using signs to summarize what happened: they think it's important to make everything surveyable, categorizable, tangible, accessible — they serve the mission of humans to use all things for their own benefit. But the latter give orders, saying: it shall be so! they are the first to determine the benefits, *what* the benefits are for humanity; they exercise control over the preliminary work of scientific people, but factual knowledge[232] is for them only a means to create. Indeed, they are confronted with an incredibly daunting task and they often covered their eyes e.g., Plato, once he believed that he could not define goodness, then identified it instead as something that is eternal. And in its cruder forms, such as when founders of religions claim that their "thou shalt" comes to them as a command from their god: as in the case of Mohammed, their legislation of values is for them a "revelation,"[233] and accomplishing this is an act of obedience. —

Now as soon as those ideas are cast away 1) the idea of God 2) the idea of eternal values: the task of the lawgiver emerges in all its terrible glory. The means of relief that were once available are gone. The feeling is so terrifying that these kinds of human beings seek refuge

1) in absolute fatalism: things take their course and the influence of individuals doesn't matter

2) in intellectual pessimism: values are deceptions, there is absolutely no "good and evil" etc. But even fatalism is overturned by intellectual pessimism, this shows that the feelings "necessity" and "causality" were projected by us in the first place.

3) in deliberate self-diminution.

2.

The decision

3.

The new problem: the means of communication, and the whole question of truthfulness.

4.

The problem of breeding, because an individual's life is too short.

26 [408][234]

It doesn't matter at all whether the image of the artist or the philosopher that I once had is now wrong in regard to a subject that I perhaps encountered by chance (Richard Wagner); perhaps that the error even took on monstrous dimensions, what does it matter!

Yet after many long years which were nothing less than long interruptions, I am even continuing to do again in public what I always do and have always done for myself: namely, to paint pictures of *new* ideals on the walls.

26 [409][235]

How do individuals acquire great power and a great mission? — All virtue and competence having to do with the body and soul are achieved with much labor, and in small increments, through much industriousness, self-command, concentrating on a few things, through much dogged faithful repetition of the same work, the same renunciation: but there are individuals who are the inheritors and masters of this slowly accumulated wide-ranging wealth of virtues and competence — because, on the basis of happy and sensible marriages and even happy coincidence, the forces acquired and stored by many generations are not thrown away and fragmented, but rather are bound together through a closely knit circle and will. In the end, then, someone appears, monstrously strong, who demands a monstrous mission. For our strength is that which guides us: and the pathetic mind games of goals and aims and motives are merely a foreground — may those who have trouble seeing understand what really matters, even in this case.

26 [410]

The belief in cause and effect, and the *rigor* involved, is the distinctive feature of people with *scientific* natures who are dedicated to shaping the world as humans see it,[236] to determining that which can be calculated. But the mechanical-atomistic worldview wants numbers. It has still not taken its final step: space as a machine, space *finite*. — Yet, as a result, movement is impossible: Boscovich[237] — the dynamic worldview

26 [411]

That the mechanical-atomistic process wants to create merely a system of *signs*: it *dispenses* with *explanations*, it gives up the concept "cause and effect."

26 [412][238]

Kant's reputation has been unreasonably inflated today because the many critics in this critical age rediscovered in him their cardinal virtue: they are praising themselves when they pay homage to Kant. But all merely critical personalities are *second* rate when held up against the great *synthesizers*: they are touched by Hegel's immeasurable ambition, who for that reason, outside of Germany, is still considered to be the greatest German mind.

Schopenhauer's reputation is likewise dependent on the times: a querulous hopeless barren time elevated his way of thinking, the 50s in Germany. He "is flourishing" now in France. His reputation is exaggerated. There is a touch of mysticism and obscurity in him, more so than in Kant: this is how he is seducing our G⟨erman⟩ youth. — On the other hand, he furnishes our badly educated youth with some scholarly knowledge and sparks some interest; he also cites good books and suffers just as little as *Frederick* the Great and Bismarck from that *niaiserie allemande*[239,240] that foreigners notice about our best minds (even about Goethe[241]) He is one of the best-*educated* Germans, in other words, a *European*. A *good* German — forgive me for repeating this ten times over — is no longer a German at all. —

Fichte, Schelling, Hegel Feuerbach Strauss — here everything stinks of theologians and Church Fathers.[242] Schopenhauer is mostly *free* of it, we breathe better air, we even catch the scent of Plato. Kant convoluted-ponderous: we can tell that he still had not encountered the Greeks in any way. Homer and Plato did not resound in his ears.

26 [413]

The sciences have sounded a false alarm with their talk of the "world of appearances"; a completely mythological concept of "pure knowledge" is in control there which is used to measure things. This is "iron made of wood," as valid as a "thing in itself." Up to now, the main problems discussed by philosophers have usually been a *contradictio in adjecto*.[243]

26 [414]

Our value judgments determine which things we accept at all and *how* we accept them. Yet these value judgments are posited and regulated by our will to power.

26 [415]

"The presentation (drama) is the goal; the music merely a means of strengthening its effect"[244] — is Richard Wagner's practice

26 [416]

The fact that something like Spinoza's *amor dei*[245] could be *experienced* again is *his* great event. Against Teichmüller's[246] mockery of it, that it *was* already *there*! What a blessing that the most precious things are there for a second time! — Philosophers all! These are people who have experienced something *extraordinary*

26 [417][247]

I *am happy* about Europe's militarization, even about the anarchic conditions here at home: the time of tranquility and a Chinese mindset which Galiani predicted for this century is over.[248] Personal *manly* virtue, physical fitness, is valued again, valuations have become more physical, diets contain more meat. Beautiful men have become a possibility again. The pale, pathetic obsequiousness (with mandarins at the helm, as Comte dreamt about) is over. The barbarian within each of us is *affirmed*, even the wild animal. *Precisely for this reason* philosophers will become more significant — At some point in the future, Kant will be a scarecrow!

26 [418][249]

Mérimée said of several lyric poems by Pushkin "Greek in truth and simplicity, *très supérieurs pour la précision et la netteté.*"[250]

26 [419][251]

As the lady Pasta once remarked about Mérimée: "since Rossini no one has written an aesthetically coherent opera in which all the parts fit together. E.g., what Verdi does resembles a harlequin costume."

26 [420][252]

In everything that Goethe has done, says Mérimée, there is a mixture of genius and of German *niaiserie* (good! this is German!) "is he making fun of himself or of others?" — Wilhelm Meister: the most beautiful things in the world alternating with the most ridiculous childishness.

26 [421]

Après tout, il y a de bons moments, et le souvenir de ces bons moments est plus agréable que le souvenir des mauvais n'est triste.[253] Mérimée.

26 [422]

"The influence of women, not derived from Christianity, but rather from the influence of northern barbarians on Roman society. The Germanic tribes had *exaltation*, they loved the soul. The Romans loved only the body. It is true that for a long time women had no souls. They still don't have them in the Orient — too bad!"²⁵⁴ Mérimée.

26 [423]²⁵⁵

To live abroad is for the ancient Greeks the greatest of all misfortunes. But it is even worse to die abroad: there is nothing more terrifying to the Greek imagination. Mérimée.

26 [424]

Initial sense impressions are processed by the intellect: simplified, adapted to earlier patterns, the *idea* of the world of appearance, as a work of art, is *our* work. But the material isn't — *art* is the very thing that underscores the *framework*, that retains decisive traits, leaves many things out. This intentional reshaping into something *familiar*, this *falsification* —

"Historical sense" is the same: has been well taught to the French by Taine, the major facts prominently displayed (*establishing* the *hierarchy* of facts is the productive contribution of historians). Granted, this presupposes being able to empathize, *to have* the impression: so **German**.

26 [425]²⁵⁶

Why philosophers *rarely* succeed: their makeup includes characteristics that normally drive people to ruin:

1) an enormous diversity of characteristics, they must be compendia of what is human, of all the higher and lower human desires: danger of opposites, even of disgust as such

2) they must be curious about the most various aspects — danger of fragmentation

3) they must be fair and reasonable in the highest sense, but profound even in love hate (and injustice)

4) they must be not only observers but also lawgivers — those who judge and those who are judged (inasmuch as they are compendia of the world)

5) exceptionally multifarious, and yet solid and hard-hearted. Flexible.

26 [426][257]

The Philosophers of the Future.
By
Friedrich Nietzsche.

26 [427][258]

Petronius: clearest skies, low humidity, *presto*[259] of movement: no God lying in the mist; nothing infinite, nothing salaciously saintly, nothing of the swine of St. Antony. Well-meaning mockery; authentic Epicureanism; — — —

26 [428]

"Will there still be philosophers at all? Or are they superfluous? These days there are enough remnants of them in the flesh and blood of us all. Even founders of religions will be a thing of the past: the greatest beasts are dying out."[260] — In opposition to this I say: — — —

26 [429]

Nothing that is conditioned can emerge from that which is unconditioned. Now, however, everything that we know is conditioned. Therefore, there is nothing that is unconditioned at all, it is a superficial assumption.

26 [430]

When it comes to lunch, idealistic philosophers never allow themselves to be deceived, as if it were merely a perspectival appearance devised by them.

26 [431]

That "force" and "space" are merely two expressions and different ways of looking at the same thing: that "empty space" is a contradiction, just like "absolute purpose" (in Kant), "thing in itself" (in Kant) "infinite force" "blind will" — — —

26 [432]²⁶¹

When I think of my philosophical genealogy, then I feel
myself connected to those who are anti-teleological, i.e., the
Spinozist movement in our time, yet with the difference that I
take "purpose" and "will" to be a deception *within us*; likewise
with mechanical movement (tracing all moral and aesthetic
questions back to physiological, all physiological to chemical,
all chemical to mechanical), yet with the difference that I do
not believe in "matter" and take Boscovich to be one of the
great turning points, like Copernicus; that I think it's fruitless
to take the self-mirroring of the mind as a starting point and
with the difference that I find no research worth doing unless
it uses the body as a guide. Not a philosophy as a *dogma*, but
rather as a preliminary guideline for *research*.

26 [433]²⁶²

This philosophy cannot be dangerous to a person like you. I
simply do not believe that philosophies are dangerous. People
are just the way they are — what's the point of saying it more
clearly! — and they nevertheless need cute little costumes and
masks so as to make themselves look beautiful: these masks
include philosophies.

26 [434]²⁶³

A world *going under* is enjoyable, not *only* for the observer
(but also for whoever is destroying it). Death is not only necessary, "ugly" is not enough, there is greatness, sublimity of all
kinds when worlds go under. Even sweet things, even hopes
and sunsets. Europe is a world going under. Democracy is the
declining form of the state.

26 [435]

Montaigne, as a writer, is often "at the peak of perfection
through liveliness, youth and power. *Il a la grâce des jeunes ani-
maux puissants. — L'admirable vivacité et l'étrange énergie de sa
langue.* He is like Lucretius *pour cette jeunesse virile. Un jeune*

chêne tout plein de sève, d'un bois dur et avec la grâce des premières années."[264] Doudan.

26 [436]
"I am beginning to believe, *cette race douce, énergique, méditative et passionnée*[265] has always existed only in books." Doudan, about the Germans.

26 [437]
I think, along with Doudan, that the great majority of musicians are charlatans and even dupes —
chantaient déjà, faute d'idées.[266]

26 [438]
What should we make of French taste! Doudan says: *c'est un bruit dans les oreilles et un petit mal de cœur indéfinissable qu'on n'aime pas à sentir.*[267]

26 [439]
"*Motu quiescunt*" — on the happiness of being active, "*la volonté désennuie*"[268] Doudan.

26 [440]
Only true philosophers are audacious animals and say to themselves, like Turenne: "*Carcasse, tu trembles? Tu tremblerais bien davantage, si tu savais où je te mène.*"[269]

26 [441]
Admiration for Cicero: *c'est une aimable et noble créature. Le petit parvenu d'Arpinum est tout simplement le plus beau résultat de toute la longue civilisation qui l'avait précédé. Je ne sais rien de plus honorable pour la nature humaine que l'état d'âme et d'esprit de Cicéron.*[270] Doudan.
l'habitude d'admirer l'inintelligible au lieu de rester tout simplement dans l'inconnu:[271] what *ravages* it caused in the minds of recent times! Doudan.

He interposed between himself and nature *aucun de ces fantômes imposants, mais informes, qui ravissaient Saint Antoine dans le désert et Saint Ignace de Loyola dans le monde.*[272]

"*il y a quelque chose de Cicéron dans Voltaire*"[273]

26 [442]

The German Mystics

Great self-admiration and great self-contempt and self-diminution are closely related: the mystics who sometimes feel like God, sometimes like worms. What *is missing* here is the *sense of self*. It seems to me that *modesty* and *pride* are very closely related, and that there are only judgments whichever way we look. What they have in common is this: in both cases the cold, certain look of valuation. By the way, it is part of a good diet not to live among people with whom we have no business comparing ourselves, whether because of modesty or because of pride. This diet is an aristocratic diet. A community that *has been chosen* — living and dead. — Fate is an inspiring thought for those who understand that they are a part *of it*.

26 [443]

With Pascal we find for the first time in France *la raillerie sinistre et tragique* — "*la comédie et la tragédie tout ensemble.*"[274] On the *Provinciales*.[275]

26 [444]

Doudan says of Genoa: *On peut porter là les grandes tristesses sans souffrir d'aucun contraste.*[276]

26 [445][277]

Schleiermacher: the German philosophers

26 [446]

Renan, of whom Doudan says: "he gives to the people of his generation what they want in all things, *des bonbons, qui sentent l'infini.*" "*Ce style rêveur, doux, insinuant, tournant autour des*

questions sans beaucoup les serrer, à la manière des petits serpents.
C'est aux sons de cette musique-là, qu'on se résigne à tant s'amuser
de tout, qu'on supporte des despotismes en rêvassant la liberté."[278]

26 [447]

Regarding Taine "*mais que cela est rouge, bleu, vert, orange,*
noir, nacré, opale, iris et pourpre . . . c'est une boutique de march-
and de couleurs. To say along with Mirabeau *le père: quel tapage*
de couleurs![279]

26 [448]

The eye, when it sees, does exactly the same thing that the
intellect does in order to *comprehend.* It simplifies the phenomenon, gives it new outlines, makes it similar to what was seen
earlier, links it back to what was seen earlier, re-forms it until
it is graspable, useful. The senses do the same thing that the
"intellect" does: they take control of things in exactly the same
way that science is overpowering nature with concepts and
numbers. There is nothing here that wants to be "objective":
rather a kind of incorporation and assimilation, for the purpose
of nutrition.

26 [449][280]

I still have found *no* reason to be discouraged. Anyone who
cultivates a *strong will* and has learned to harness it, together
with an expansive intellect, has a better chance than ever. For
people in this democratic Europe have become so much more
amenable to *training;*[281] people who learn easily, who readily
conform, are the rule: herd-animals, even highly intelligent
ones, are prepared. Anyone who can command finds those who
have to obey: I am thinking e.g., of Napoleon and Bismarck.
Competition with strong and *un*intelligent wills, which mostly
get in the way, is limited. Who doesn't push aside these gentlemen "objectivists" with weak wills, like Ranke or Renan!

26 [450]

Scholars. These "objectivists," merely scientific people, are in the final analysis conscientious and praiseworthy and don't try to exceed their capabilities when they demonstrate, in the case of something widely esteemed, that something contradictory is behind it, therefore, when intellectually evaluated, that ⟨it⟩ has less value than is generally believed. Moreover, they feel that prioritizing logic *entitles* them to render an opinion, to join in a conversation, and nothing beyond that; they themselves have no other value besides *being logical.*

26 [451]

We must be capable of powerful feelings of admiration and be able to creep lovingly into the heart of many matters: otherwise we are not fit to be philosophers. Cold gray eyes do not know the value of things; cold gray minds do not know how to weigh things. But of course: we must have a force working in opposition to this: that soars into such prodigious heights that we may see even the things we admire the most as far, far below ourselves, and very near to that which we perhaps despised. — I was put to the test when I did not let myself become alienated from my chief concern by the great political movement in Germany, nor by the aesthetic movement of Wagner, nor by the philosophical movement of Schopenhauer: nevertheless things got difficult for me and sometimes made me ill.

26 [452][282]

I don't want to talk anyone into being a philosopher: it is necessary, it is perhaps even desirable, that the philosopher is a *rare* kind of plant. Nothing is more disgusting to me than the didactic appreciation of philosophy, as in the case of Seneca or even Cicero. Philosophy has little to do with virtue. Permit me to say: that even scientific people are fundamentally different from philosophers. — My wish is that the genuine concept of what a philosopher is does not completely perish in Germany. There are so many half-formed beings of all kinds in Germany who would like to conceal their failed existence behind such a noble title.

26 [453]

We have yet to calculate what things are *worth*: for this, it is not enough that we are familiar with them: although this is certainly necessary. We must be *allowed* to admit that they have value, we must be *allowed* to give value to things and take it away, enough, we must *be* the kind of people who have the *right to bestow values*. This is why there are so many "*objectivists*" today: they are modest and honest, they divest themselves of this right to value things.

26 [454][283]

Victor Hugo: rich and superabundant in picturesque scenarios, *with a painter's eye, seeing all that is visible*, lacking taste and refinement, shallow and demagogic, slavishly devoted to phrases that resound in the gut, a flatterer of the people, with the voice of an evangelist for all of the lowly, failed, oppressed, but lacking any sense of intellectual conscience and noble greatness. His spirit afflicts the French like an alcoholic drink that is both intoxicating and *befuddling*. When his stupefying babble commences, it makes our ears ring: and we feel pain, as when a railroad train carries us through a dark tunnel.

Flaubert: false erudition. Emphasis.[284]

On *Rossini*: no actor could match him when he sang the Barber of Seville. One of the wittiest people.[285]

26 [455][286]

"Great words, monstrous events — on the increase. Otherwise, in barbaric, ignorant, absurd ages there always used to be a kind of compensation through a few very great individuals. Now, rapid profound *nivellement*[287] of all intelligence."

26 [456]

That a beefsteak should be merely an appearance, but actually the thing in itself, something like the absolute or the loving God: let anyone believe that who — — —

26 [457]²⁸⁸

Bismarck: peasant, fraternity student: not pleasant, not naïve, thank God! Not a German "by the book"!

26 [458]

How Flaubert makes me laugh, with his raging about the bourgeoisie who disguise themselves as I don't know what! And Taine, as M. Graindorge,²⁸⁹ who wants to be known as the consummate man of the world, expert on women etc.!

26 [459]

How I was schooled in *mistrust*, in μέμνησο ἀπιστεῖν²⁹⁰ — something else to ridicule!

26 [460]

Problem: the values "good" "evil" "praiseworthy" are acquired. But "cowardly" "courageously" "ruffian" "patient" are innate and have been incorporated. As a consequence of this, *acquiring* and *learning*²⁹¹ are two *different things*: one person's character is accommodating, another allows something to be forced on it, a third yields, imitates, is an ape. In other people's characters, there is a lot of resistance, e.g., in the case of my character, I *take a position* with the best of intentions, as if I am accepting: even as I *put off* my decision: it was only "provisional" and "temporary." Speaking just for myself, I didn't believe any of it. I have not gotten to know anyone I would have recognized as an *authority* for the *most general* judgments: even as I had a profound need for such a person.

26 [461]²⁹²

Kant's shenanigans with "appearance." And to posit a *faculty* where he does not find an explanation! This was what triggered the great Schelling swindle.

26 [462]

A reasonable number of superior and more gifted people will, I hope, finally gain enough self-control so as to shed their bad taste when it comes to how they present themselves, as well as their sentimental despondency, and ⟨turn away⟩ from Richard Wagner just as much as from Schopenhauer. These Germans are ruining us, they play to our most dangerous characteristics. A more powerful future lies already prepared for us in Goethe, Beethoven and Bismarck, than in these deviations from the German race. We still haven't had any philosophers.

26 [463]

The Corsicans are not loveable: and anyone who is part of the herd is aggravated by this.

26 [464]²⁹³

When Kant wanted to reduce philosophy to a "science," this desire was a sorry example of German philistinism: there might be something admirable about it, but certainly something even more laughable. That the "positivists" of France, or the "philosophers of reality" or the "scientific philosophers" now at German universities, are entirely justified in acting like philosophical laborers, as scholars in service to philosophy, is perfectly proper. Likewise, that they cannot see beyond themselves and remake the "philosopher" type in their own image.

26 [465]²⁹⁴

Noon and Eternity.

A Philosophy of Eternal Recurrence.

By
Friedrich Nietzsche.

26 [466]
Adventavit asinus
Pulcher et fortissimus.
*Mysterium.*²⁹⁵

26 [467]

Beyond Good and Evil.
Letters
to a Philosophical Friend *Satis.*

"Satis sunt mihi pauci, satis
*est unus, satis est nullus."*²⁹⁶

By
Friedrich Nietzsche.

26 [468]²⁹⁷

What is Noble?
Thoughts about the Order of Rank among Humans.
By
Friedrich Nietzsche.

26 [469]
But *that man* — I don't know him. Truly, I often wanted to
believe that he, too, had merely the beautiful appearance of a
saint²⁹⁸

[27 = Z II 5a. Summer–Autumn 1884]

27 [1]

Reflecting on "freedom and unfreedom of the will" led me to a solution for this problem that could not be more thorough and conclusive — namely to eliminate the problem altogether by means of a hard-won insight: *there is no will at all, neither a free will nor an unfree will.*

27 [2]

Under certain circumstances, a thought is followed by an action: the affect of whatever is in command[1] emerges at the same time as the thought — this process includes the feeling of freedom that is commonly ascribed to the "will" itself (although it is merely an accompanying phenomenon of willing)

27 [3]

All physiological processes resemble one another insofar as they involve discharges of force, which, if they penetrate into the *sensorium commune*, bring along a certain heightening and amplifying effect: when measured against pressing, burdensome conditions of compulsion, these are interpreted as the feeling of "freedom."

27 [4]

The kind of self-control demanded of themselves by those who investigate morality involves not being prejudiced against states and actions that they are trained to admire; insofar as they are investigators, they must "have broken their own admiring hearts."

27 [5]

Anyone with insight into the conditions under which a moral judgment has emerged still has not come close to assessing its value: many beneficial things, and just as many important insights, have been discovered while using mistaken and unsystematic approaches; and every characteristic remains unfamiliar, even when we have understood the conditions under which it emerges.

27 [6]

What is it useful *for*? lies in the background of all utilitarianism (that is, happiness: I mean to say, a kind of English happiness with comfort and fashion a feeling of well-being, ἡδονή[2]) as something that is assumed to be known; thus, these theories are a kind of hypocritical hedonism in disguise. But would it not be essential first to prove, in the case of a community, or even of humankind, that well-being welfare[3] "in itself" is a goal and not a means! Personal experience teaches us that times of unhappiness have considerable value — and it works the same way for those times of unhappiness that are experienced by peoples and by humankind.

fear and the hatred of *pain* are something for the rabble.

27 [7]

Feelings do not emerge until a stimulus is sufficiently strong: it is the moment when the central organ establishes the relation of the stimulus to the whole organism and with "pleasure" or "pain" *makes* it recognizable to consciousness: thus, a *product* of the intellect, just as much as color, tone, warmth etc.

27 [8]

The human being as a multiplicity: physiology provides merely an inkling of the amazing interaction between this multiplicity and the subjugation and ordering of the parts in relation to the whole. But it would be a mistake to think that just because there is a state there must be an absolute monarch (the unity of the subject)

27 [9]

There is so much misfortune *that has been lost* — just as most of the sun's heat is lost in outer space

27 [10]

Extraordinary people learn through misfortune just how little value there is in all the dignity and respectability of those who sit in judgment of them. They collapse — when their pride has been wounded — an intolerant narrow-minded beast makes its appearance.

27 [11]

Greatness of the soul cannot be separated from greatness of the intellect. For the former requires independence; but independence should not be permitted without an extraordinary intellect, it leads to trouble, even when there is a desire to do good and to practice "justice." Lesser minds must *obey* — therefore they cannot be *extraordinary*.

27 [12]

To be hard-hearted like a Stoic is nothing, insensitivity means severing all ties. You must have the opposite quality within you — tender feeling *and* the countervailing ability not to bleed to death but rather, true to life, taking every misfortune and "making it turn out for the best."

27 [13]

The "salvation of the soul" is a much more complete concept than the happiness all moralists rave about. What this means is, the entire willing creating feeling soul and its salvation — not merely an accompanying phenomenon like "happiness" etc.

— Craving "happiness" is what characterizes partially successful or completely unsuccessful people, the powerless — all others do not think of "happiness" but, instead, their force wants
to be discharged.

27 [14]
   "Free or unfree will."
   Unegoistic actions.
   "Everything permitted" (as it is for the state)
   Tartuffery in Europe.
   The religious affect.
   The supreme feeling of power up to now.
   "Scholarly knowledge"[4] as means of thinking economically
   The values that have gained sovereignty up to now.
   Benefit of "good people." (Herd-animals)
   Physiology of morality.

27 [15]
   "Humans are equal" and "the welfare of the community is
superior to the welfare of the individual" and "furthering the
welfare of the individual necessarily also furthers the welfare of
the community most effectively" and "the better it is for many
individuals, the greater the welfare of all" — these are the prevailing constraints that come to us from England. Here the herd-
instinct finds expression and makes its voice heard.
   Now, contrary to this, Christianity taught that life serves to
test and train the soul and that there is danger in all well-being.
Christianity understood the *value of adversity*.

27 [16]
   I teach: that there are superior and inferior humans, and
that under certain circumstances entire millennia can find self-
justification through the appearance of a single individual —
i.e., a human being who is full of life gifted great complete, in
contrast to countless imperfect fragmentary humans.

27 [17]

I teach: the herd seeks to prop up a type and defend itself against both sides, as much against those who deviate from it (criminals etc.) as against those who tower above it. The inclination of the herd is directed toward stagnancy and its own preservation, there is nothing creative there.

27 [18]

The pleasant feelings that good well-meaning just-minded people instill within us (in contrast to the tension, fear which is provoked by a magnificent new human being), these are *our* personal feelings of security and equality: the herd-animal celebrates the nature of the herd in this way and then feels good about itself. When the state of well-being judges in this way, it disguises itself with pretty words — this is how "morality" emerges.

Yet observe the *herd's hatred* of truthful people —

27 [19]

The most determined *will* (as command) is a vague abstraction, in which countless individual cases are included and thus countless paths to these individual cases as well. What then brings about the *selection* of the one case that actually occurs? In truth, a countless number of individual elements[5] are part of completing the process, all of which are in a completely determined state when the command is given — they must understand the command and also their special task associated with it i.e., commands must be continually repeated from the beginning in the most minute detail (and obeyed) and only then, when the command has been divided into countless smaller subcommands, can movement proceed, beginning *with the last and smallest element* that is obeying — thus, *an inversion takes place*, as in the dream of the cannon shot.

Here we have made the assumption that the entire organism is thinking, that all organic components have a role to play in thinking feeling willing — consequently, that the brain is merely an enormous mechanism of centralization.

27 [20]
Seek happiness? I can't do it. Make someone happy? But in my view there are so *many more important things* than that.

27 [21]
In cases of *pleasure* and *displeasure*, the fact is first transmitted to the nervous centers, the value of the fact (the injury) is determined there, the pain is subsequently localized at the site where the injury took place, and in this way *consciousness* is made aware of this site and is informed as to how quickly aid is needed by means of the degree and the nature of the pain. — How quickly this happens — because the counter-movements, e.g., in the case of a stumble, do not occur until our consciousness actively wills it and must now, before anything else, issue individual commands — and then the sequence of movements transpires in reverse order!

Thus: *thinking* is required for each occurrence of *pleasure and displeasure* (whether it reaches consciousness or not) and, insofar as counter-movements are initiated as a result of the process, the *will* is required as well.

27 [22]
People who have never thought of money or honor or making influential connections, or holding office — do they really understand people?

27 [23][6]
Zarathustra 1 all sorts of superior humans and their distress and decline (individual examples e.g., Dühring, destroyed by isolation) — in general the *fate of superior humans* at present, how they seem *doomed to die out*: it comes to Zarathustra's attention like a great cry for help. He is approached by every sort of insane degeneration (e.g., nihilism) in those with superior natures.

Zarathustra 2. — "the doctrine of eternal return" — initially crushing for the more noble people, seemingly the means of exterminating them — because those with lesser and less sensitive natures will be left standing? "This doctrine must be suppressed and Zarathustra killed."

Zarathustra 3 "I gave to you the weightiest thought: perhaps humankind will be destroyed by it, perhaps humankind will rise to a higher level as a result of the elements hostile to life being overcome and discarded." "Not to be enraged with life but with *you!*" — Designating superior humans as those who create. Organization of the superior humans, education of *those who will rule* in the future as theme of Zarathustra 3. Your superpower must find joy in itself, in ruling and shaping things. "Not only humans, but *also superhumans, return eternally!*"

27 [24]

Freedom and the feeling of power. The feeling of being playful when overcoming great difficulties, e.g., in a virtuoso; feeling sure of ourselves, that the act of willing will be followed by the exactly corresponding action — a kind of *affect of arrogance* is involved, supreme sovereignty of *someone who commands.* There must be an associated feeling of resistance, pressure must also be there. — Yet *deception* concerning the will is also involved: it is not the will that overcomes resistance — we create a synthesis between 2 simultaneous states and impose *unity* on them.

The will as a poetic invention.

1) we believe that it moves things itself (whereas it is merely a stimulus, the occurrence of which occasions the start of a movement

2) we believe that it overcomes resistance

3) we believe that it is free and sovereign because its origins remain hidden from us and because it is accompanied by the affect of those who command

4) because in the vast majority of cases we *will* only if success can be *expected*,[7] the "inevitability"[8] of success is attributed to the will as a *force*.

27 [25]

Pleasure as a *growing* feeling of power that makes itself felt.[9]
Pleasure and pain are different things and not opposites.

27 [26]

The multiplicity of drives — we must assume that there is a *master drive*, but we are *not* conscious of it, instead, consciousness is an organ, like the stomach.

27 [27]

Using the body as a guide, we recognize that a human being is a multiplicity of animate beings, which sometimes battle one another, sometimes are absorbed and subjugated by one another, whenever they affirm their individual natures they are also involuntarily affirming the whole.

Among these living beings, there are those who rule to a greater degree than they obey, and among these there is again battle and victory.

The whole of humankind has all those attributes of that which is organic, which we partly remain unconscious of, which we ⟨partly⟩ become conscious of in the form of *drives*.

27 [28]

The differing feelings of value that we use to tell these drives apart are the result of their greater or lesser importance, of their actual order of rank in regard to our preservation.

27 [29]

Depending on the environment, and on the conditions under which we live, one drive emerges as the most highly esteemed and most firmly in command; thinking willing and feeling make themselves into tools of this drive in particular.

27 [30]

If a community is what absolutely determines the nature of humans, then the drive that allows the community to be preserved will be most forcefully developed in them. The more independent they are, the more the herd-instincts wither away.

27 [31]

NB. What we perceive to be differences in *quality* emerge among certain differences in *quantity*. This is also the case in matters of morality. Here secondary feelings of *doing good*, being useful, emerge in those who perceive a human characteristic as having a certain quantity; doubled, tripled, they are afraid of it - - -

27 [32]

The value of an action depends on who performs it and whether it has its origins in what is fundamental or superficial about this person: i.e., how deeply individual it is.

27 [33]

The value of actions can be determined if humans themselves can be known: which is generally to be denied.

27 [34]

It is from signs that we draw conclusions about the origin of an action, even in the case of our own: these are the affects, models, purposes, etc. of ours that precede any act.

It is often the case that an action develops in accordance with a purpose: but the purpose is not the cause in that case, but rather the effect of the very same processes that established the conditions for the actual action.

27 [35]

Wherever everything still remains unformed, this is *the place where we will work* on behalf of the human future!

27 [36]

With its formulas, natural science wants to teach the *total subjugation* of the forces of nature: it does not want to posit a "truer" framework in place of the empirical-sensual framework (like metaphysics)

27 [37]

Foundation of Morality.

The prejudice of the herd.   no
The prejudice of powerful people.   *hypocrisy* in matters
The prejudice of independent people.   of conscience

I.

Knowability of humans.
Order of rank of drives
On the will.
"Unegoistic."
Punishing and rewarding
Superior and inferior humans. Order of rank.
"Humankind." and the alleged usefulness of good people.
"Purpose."
The religious affect and morality.
Physiology of morality.
The present
Rights and duties.
The sex drive
Bravery
Loyalty.

27 [38]

All life is based on error — how is error *possible*?

27 [39]

Humans are not well-behaved enough for the age of air travel, where people will no longer be watching each other as a matter of course.

27 [40]

Complacency, security, fearfulness, laziness, cowardice is what seeks to strip life of its *dangerous* character and is what would like "to organize" everything — tartuffery of the science of economics

The human plant grows best when the dangers are great, in uncertain conditions: but, of course, most of them perish there.

Our place in the world of knowledge is uncertain enough — all superior humans feel like *adventurers*.

27 [41]

If we wanted to leave the world of perspectives, we would perish. Even *undoing* the great illusions that have already been incorporated is destroying humankind. We must approve and accept much that is wrong and bad.

27 [42]

1) On *dissimulation* in the presence of "equals" as the origin of herd-morality.

   Fear. Wanting to understand each other. To present ourselves as equal.

   Becoming equal — origin of the herd-animal. (This is the point of conventions, customs) A hypocrisy that is still ubiquitous

   Morality as costume and jewelry, as a *disguise* for people with shameworthy natures.

2) On flattery of the powerful as source of slave morality (relationship of flattery admiration exaggeration groveling in the dirt and self-belittlement

   — the herd, juxtaposed with the ideal herd-animal (*equal*)

   — those who are powerful, juxtaposed with those *tools* that are the most worshipful, most useful (slave-like) "unequal"

   (this results in hypocrisy two times over)

27 [43]

Superior Humans and Humans of the Herd

If *there are no* great people, then great people from the past
are made into demigods or actual gods: the outbreak of religion
shows that people no longer take *pleasure* in other people (—
"and not in women either,"[10] along with Hamlet) Or: many
people are assembled into a horde, as a parliament and with the
hope that they will be as directly effective as a tyrant.

27 [44]

Tyrannizing is what defines great people: they *turn* lesser
people *into idiots*.

27 [45]

Better to live in danger, and armed, than in the midst of this
cowardly mutual friendliness of the herd!

27 [46]

All people who have mattered so far have been evil.

27 [47]

When dealing with philosophers, watch out for this: some
kind of disgust, a feeling of being fed up is behind it all, e.g.,
in Kant Schopenhauer Indic philosophers. Or: a will to rule,
as in Plato.

27 [48][11]

The contemplation of becoming shows that deception and
the desire for self-deception, that *untruth* have been conditions
required for humans to exist: we must rip off the veil once and
for all.

27 [49][12]

The *necessity* of building up the herd consists in the fearfulness (of those who are weaker?) — benevolent feelings when

in touch with our neighbors if they, instead of doing harm or uttering threats, reveal themselves to be "kind"

27 [50]

Developing *cunning*, stubbornness in knowing.

27 [51]

Misinterpretation of motherly love by those who get some advantage from it — and by the mothers themselves.

27 [52][13]

A tiger that pounces awkwardly is ashamed of itself.

27 [53]

Pleasure — a feeling in proportion to diverse degrees of displeasure — therefore linked to memory and comparisons!

27 [54]

Benevolence at the most basic level: not wanting to cause pain.

27 [55]

What good fortune, that so much in nature is quantifiable and calculable — briefly put, that our human understanding, which falsifies and which is limited, did not dictate all the laws

— — —

27 [56]

Morality considered in relation to dissimulation (equating things), cunning and hypocrisy ("*not* revealing ourselves") — as a falsification of emotional expression (self-control) in order to provoke a misunderstanding
considered in relation to embellishment, disguise, beautification, flattery
considered in relation to self-deception with the aim of feeling secure

considered in relation to self-glorification for the purpose of instilling terror
considered in relation to discomfort and failure, partly
as revenge on ourselves, partly as revenge on others.
considered in relation to those who expect their commands to be obeyed without question or those who
obey without question
considered in relation to individuals who isolate
themselves
considered in relation to domestication, often
unintentional
considered in relation to *breeding* a particular kind
of human (lawgivers and princes as breeders, even
public opinion.)

Beyond good and evil: concerning the education of people with the nature of *rulers* who have to fulfill the highest
obligations.

27 [57]

NB. the multiple *interpretations*[14] of an *organ* corresponding
to the multiple *interpretations* of the whole —

27 [58][15]

Eternal Recurrence.
A Prophecy.
Part One. The Weightiest Thought.
Part Two. Beyond Good and Evil.
Part Three. Humans and Superhumans.

27 [59]

Unlike animals, humans have conceived and nurtured within
themselves an abundance of *conflicting* drives and impulses: by
means of this synthesis they rule the earth. — Morals are the
expression of locally limited *orders of rank* in this multifaceted
world of the drives: so that humans do not perish on account
of the drives' *contradictions*. Therefore, one drive as ruling, its

counter-drive weakened, refined, as an impulse that provides the *stimulus* for the activity of the main drive.

The most superior human beings would have the greatest multiplicity of drives, and also the comparatively strongest drives that can still be tolerated. In fact: wherever the human plant is strong, we find instincts that are powerfully working *against* each other (e.g., Shakespeare), yet constrained.

27 [60]

Instilling through *education* those virtues of rulers which keep even their benevolence and compassion in check, the great virtues of those who have breeding as their vocation ("forgiving your enemies" is child's play in comparison), *to maximize* the *affect of those who create* — no more chiseling of the marble! — The elite position of those beings who occupy a position of power, compared with the position of princes up to now: a Roman Caesar with the soul of Christ.

27 [61]

N.B. When we know the conditions under which something emerges, we still *don't* know that which has emerged! This principle applies to chemistry just as much as it does to the organic.[16]

27 [62]

NB. On the superficiality of the intellect! — nothing is more dangerous than the intellect's self-satisfied "navel-gazing," as in the case of the Brahmins.

27 [63]

NB. All feelings, all sense-impressions, initially stand in some relation to the pleasure or displeasure of organic beings: green, red, hard, soft, light, dark *mean something* in regard to their living conditions (i.e., the organic process) In fact, many of them are "indifferent" i.e., they have become neither pleasant nor painful, their underlying pleasure and displeasure has faded away by now. But in the presence of the artist, these feelings emerge again! — Likewise, all forms and shapes initially mean something in regard to the pleasure and displeasure of living creatures (— they mean danger, disgust, comfort, security, friendship, peace). — What I mean is that certain *evaluations*, certain ideas about benefit and harm are concealed in all feelings, e.g., still evident when we feel disgust. Pleasure and displeasure as *attraction* or *aversion* — ?

27 [64]

We *perceive* only all those aspects of things that somehow *concern* (or *used to concern*) us — the entire organic process has us as its result. "Experience" i.e., the result of all those *reactions*, where *we* reacted to something outside ourselves or within ourselves. — We have *merged* our *reaction with the thing* that was acting on us.

27 [65]

The usual errors: we think the *will* can do things that are actually accomplished by numerous and complicated well-practiced movements. That which gives orders *mistakes* itself for those elements which are its obedient tools (and for their will)

27 [66]

Doesn't the *reverse* process have to be at work everywhere, e.g., in the case of a pianist, first the will, then the corresponding assignment of tasks to the subordinated wills, then the *commencement* of the movement beginning with the group that comes last and is ranked the lowest — from the crudest mechanism up to the most subtle tactile nerves?

Namely: chords, dynamics, expression, everything must already be there *beforehand* — : *obedience* must be there and the *possibility* of obeying!

27 [67][17]

Concerning the Plan

(We are in the middle of determining the *facts*)

Description, not explanation. (e.g., morphology as a description of sequences)

Final intention of such description: practical control, in service to the future.

Provisional human beings and methods — adventure (actually everything in history is an experiment)

One such provisional concept for achieving the greatest force is *fatalism* (ego — fatum) (most extreme form "eternal return")

In order to endure it, and in order to avoid being an optimist, "good" and "evil" must be *eliminated*.

My first solution: tragic *pleasure* in the downfall of the most superior and best people (felt to be limited in relation to the whole): yet this mysticism is the idea of an even *greater* "good"

My second solution: the greatest good and evil come together.

27 [68]

Just because I demonstrate the subjective origin e.g., of space etc. doesn't mean that the issue[18] itself is either refuted or proven. Against Kant — —

27 [69]

Duration is part of sensation: time is a "substantival time,"[19] is causal - - -

27 [70]

We have more reason to trust what is most complex than something simple, (e.g., something having to do with the mind —) The body as a guide.

27 [71][20]

Zarathustra 1. Zarathustra, surrounded by animals, speaking to people who visit him — Theory of morality regarded from zoological perspective.

Zarathustra 2. Greatest fatalism, yet identical with *chance* and with that which is *creative*. (No hierarchy of values *in* things! instead, this must first be created.)

27 [72]

If we were to explain the emergence of human views about *nutrition* on the basis of language and history and to depict the genesis and development of these "value judgments" — we still wouldn't have established anything at all about the **value** *of nutrition* for humans. And, likewise, a critique of the actual kinds of nutrition in history would also not have been provided yet. It is the same way with morality: the emergence of moral judgments must still be described — describing this still says nothing about *actual* human behavior or the history of human morality, much less provides a critique of it. And, at the very least, providing a *history of judgments about actions* is effective in determining the *value of actions* in general. - - -

27 [73]

psychological feelings — physiological (accompanying states and resulting states

pain is physiological.[21]

27 [74]

I think that all metaphysical and religious ways of thinking are the result of dissatisfaction *with humans*, the result of the drive for a superior, superhuman future — except that humans *themselves* wanted to flee into the hereafter: rather than build a future. *A misunderstanding of those who have superior natures, who suffer on account of the ugly image presented by humans.*

27 [75][22]

Dühring, superficially, sees corruption everywhere — I sense rather the other danger of the age, great mediocrity; there has never been so much *righteousness and kindness*.

27 [76]

On the dishonesty of philosophers, *to derive* something that they believe to be good and true from the start (tartuffery e.g., Kant practical reason)

27 [77]

I want to awaken the greatest mistrust against myself: I speak only of things *that have been experienced* and I am not playing mere mind-games here.

27 [78]

My youthful misunderstanding: I had not yet entirely freed myself from metaphysics — but the deepest need for an *alternative image of humans*. In place of sinfulness, I experienced a much more *complete* phenomenon — I saw through the poverty of all modern satisfaction.

"to bring to light everything that is false in things" p. 49.[23]

— I, someone who took Schopenhauerian pessimism seriously and *extended* it.

27 [79][24]

The New Enlightenment.

1. Uncovering *fundamental errors* (which conceal human cowardice indolence and vanity) e.g., in regard to feelings (and the body)

the disorientation experienced by purely intellectual people
causality
freedom of the will
evil
the animal in humans.
morality as taming
misunderstanding of actions "that have motives"
God and the hereafter as mistaken choices[25] of the creative urge
"pure knowledge" "drive for truth"
"the genius"

Overall feeling: in place of sinfulness, the *generally failed existence of humans*

2. The second stage: discovering the *creative drive*, even in its hiding places and degenerate forms.

("Our ideal is not *the* ideal," Taine Eng⟨lish⟩ L⟨iterature⟩ 3 p 47)[26]

Hegel–*spirit*[27] — Schopenhauer–*will*

The hidden artists: religious people, lawgivers statesmen as *transformative* powers: presupposition: creative *dissatisfaction*, their *impatience* — instead of advancing humans *further*, they make gods and heroes out of *great people from the past*

3. *The overcoming of human beings.*

new conception of religion

the sympathy I feel for pious people — it is the *first* step: their feelings of inadequacy, *in and of* **themselves**[28] —

self-overcoming as a step toward overcoming human beings

27 [80][29]

Eternal Recurrence.
A Prophecy.

Magnificent preface.

The new enlightenment — the old enlightenment was in the spirit of the democratic herd. Making everyone equal. The new enlightenment wants to show the way for those with ruling natures — insofar as they are *allowed to do everything* that herd-beings are not free to do:

1 Enlightenment in regard to "truth and lies" about living things.

2 Enlightenment in regard to "good and evil"

3 Enlightenment in regard to the formative transformative forces (the hidden artists)

4 The self-overcoming of human beings. (the education of superior humans)

5 The doctrine of eternal recurrence as a *hammer* in the hands of the *most powerful* humans, — — —

27 [81]

Has any human being ever conducted inquiries while traveling the path of truth as I have done up to now — namely, resisting and contradicting everything that is beneficial to my most intimate feelings? and — — —

27 [82][30]

Eternal Recurrence.

First Major Part. The New Kind of Truthful People.[31]
Second Major Part. Beyond Good and Evil.
Third Major Part. The Hidden Artists
Fourth Major Part. The Self-Overcoming of Human Beings
Fifth Major Part. The Hammer and the Great Noon.

[28 = Poems and Poetic Fragments.
Autumn 1884]

[Z II 5b]

28 [1][1]

Dedicated to all those who create.

Inseparable from the world
Let us be!
The eternal masculine
Is drawing us in.[2]

28 [2][3]
every hunchback bends more crookedly —
every Christian charges interest like a Jew[4] —
the French are becoming more profound —
and the Germans more shallow every day!

28 [3][5]

The Sun's Malice.

When the light grows dim,
When the dew's comfort
Is already spilling down upon the earth,
Unseen, unheard as well — for, like all gentle things,
Dew the comforter wears delicate footwear —
Then do you think back, do you think back, heart aflame,

How you once thirsted
For heavenly drops of dew,
Thirsted, parched, and weary,
Even as on soft paths of grass
Silent evening sunbreaks
Ran around you through dark trees,
Glowing rays of sun, full of malice,
Yet the sun asked you this without speaking:
What kind of torn-up mask
Are you wearing, fool
A mask of the gods? From whose face did you rip it off?
Aren't you ashamed lusting, sniffing around for gods
To be among humans?
How many times already!

A wooer of truth? this made me groan —
No! Only a poet!
Lusting for masks, in costume myself.
I myself a torn-up mask! Deceiving with a mask of the gods!

When the light grows dim,
when the sickle of the moon
is already creeping green
with envy between purple reds
— secretly with every step
bringing its sickle down
on hammocks of roses
until they fall sinking,
pale, downward into night
the moon turns redder
and ever more red,
ashamed of its bad deed, — — —

28 [4]⁶
The desert grows: woe to anyone who has become a desert!
A desert is hunger, scratching for corpses.

Even if wellsprings and palms build nests here for them-
selves —
The dragon's teeth of the desert[7] gnaw and gnaw
For sand is tooth on tooth, gluttonous pain
Here it drives stone on stone like jawbones
rubbing here forever
Jawbones never tiring — — —
Here gluttonous hunger grinds tooth on tooth
Dragon's teeth of the desert — — —
Sand is a jaw full of teeth, is a sowing of dragon's teeth
That grinds and grinds — that grinds on, never weary — — —
Sand is a mother chewing on her child
With a flying dagger in her skin — — —

28 [5]
You painful stinger, how far will you drive me?
Already I have overthrown heaven
With new heavens, overseasoned with seasonings
I honored the gods — to stay ever victorious for you!
You painful stinger whose hand I severed
Whose lively cat feet I crippled
What shameful things I did, long ago
— — —   tied   knots
— — —   tamed
— — —   fur
— — —   -iving[8]
— — —   became comfortable with
— — —   quickly
— — —   driving

28 [6]

Tree in Autumn

Why did you shake me, you clumsy dunces
As I stood in blissful blindness:

Never has such a fright shaken me more cruelly
— My dream, my golden dream vanished!

Rhinos like you with elephant trunks
cannot be taught manners in advance: Knock! A knock?
Startled, I threw bowls
Of golden ripened fruit — at your heads.

28 [7][9]
on a new path to the ancient Greeks
I thought to redeem *the German within you*
your Siegfried-caricature Parsifal!

28 [8]
Thunder rumbles far away across the land
The rain drips and drips:
The pedant, already running his mouth early in the morning,
Nothing will shut him up anymore.
Full of malice, the day leers in my direction
Put out my lamp!
Oh good night! Oh solitude!
Oh book! Oh inkwell!
Now everything is becoming gray and sorrowful to me

28 [9][10]
Now, since the day
Has grown tired of the day, and the streams of all longing
Babble forth new consolations,
even all of the heavens, suspended in golden spiderwebs,
speak to everyone who is weary: "rest now," —
what is keeping you from rest, you somber heart,
what is prodding you into footsore flight

what are you expecting?

you who despair! Do you also know, —

how much you embolden,
those who are watching you

oh how you lament!   where do I flee?
Oh those you are feeding!
You are still feeding prisoners.
How restless people really do feel safe
in prison!
how peacefully the souls
of criminals sleep, locked up —

Now, since the mouse gave birth to a mountain —[11]

Where are you, creativity?

Oh keep me warm! love me
give me hot hands
don't be frightened by my ice!
For too long like a ghost on a glacier — — —

driven here and there, whirling upward
what mirror have I not already sat on —
I am the dust on all surfaces
beside myself, with devotion
like a dog

Empty, cave, full of poison and night-winged things,
sung about everywhere and feared everywhere,
alone — .

You who lie in wait! I am yours now!
What kind of ransom do you want?
You should want a lot — that's what my pride advises.
And say little — that's what my other pride advises.

I lie still —

stretched out,
Like a half-dead man whose feet are being warmed
— the beetles fear me

do you fear me? You do *not* fear a drawn bow?
Watch out, someone could actually nock an arrow[12]

28 [10][13]
Now all things will come to be mine
The eagle of my hope found
A pure, new Greece
Salvation to the ears and the senses —

Away from dull crushing crowds of German tones
Mozart Rossini and Chopin
German Orpheus, I see you steer the ship
toward Grecian landscapes.

Oh, do not delay in turning the ship's desires
Toward southern landscapes,
Toward blessed isles, toward Grecian nymphs at play
No ship has ever discovered a more beautiful destination —

Now all things will come to be mine
All things that my eagle has ever found for me — :
No matter that many hopes have already turned old and gray.
— Your sound pierces me like an arrow
Salvation to the ears and the senses,
Descending on me like dew from the skies

The tone that descended on me like dew

To turn the most beautiful ship of the muses
Outward and away, toward Grecian landscapes

28 [11]

Arthur Schopenhauer.

What he taught is now passé,
What he lived will endure:
Just look at him!
He bowed down to no one!

28 [12]¹⁴

   1) You thoughts who lie in wait for me
      industrious, long ago
      agony of creating
   2) searching for love — and always the *mask*,
      I must find the accursed *mask* and *crush it to pieces*!¹⁵

28 [13]
Love is what tells me to go along,
Love keenly desired!

28 [14]¹⁶

Sheep.

Behold the eagle! with longing it stares
down into the abyss,
into its abyss, which circles lower,
down into ever deeper depths!
Suddenly, straight in flight,
sharp in turn
it swoops down upon its prey.
Do you really think that it is *hunger*?
An empty gut? —
And it certainly isn't love
— what is a lamb to an eagle!
it hat⟨es⟩ sheep
In this way I throw myself
downward, with longing,

onto these herds of lambs
tearing them to pieces, dripping blood,
mocking the complacent,
raging at the stupidity of lambs — — —

28 [15][17]
— the prisoners of prosperity
their thoughts clank like heavy chains

28 [16]
they discovered the holiest kind of everlasting boredom
and the lust for Moon-days and workdays[18]

28 [17]
Be brief: give me a riddle to solve
or else you will wear down my intellect's pride

28 [18][19]
Stubborn minds, cunning and petty

28 [19]
bovine good will

28 [20][20]

Loving Evil People.

You fear me?
You fear the drawn bow?
Watch out, someone could nock an arrow!

Alas, my friends?
Where did it go, that which we called good!
Where did all "good people" go!
Where, oh where, did the innocence of all these lies go!
These lies that once viewed humans
as gods and billy goats alike

Poets who can lie
knowingly, willingly
They alone can tell the truth

"Humans are evil"
this is what the greatest sages kept saying —
so as to comfort me.

sinfully healthy and beautiful
like colorfully spotted predators

who, like cats and women,
are at home in the wilderness
and jump through windows

what makes something still, rigid, cold, smooth,
what makes something into an image and a pillar,
which is erected in front of temples,
to be flaunted
        — virtue — ?

28 [21][21]
A wooer of truth? Have you seen him?
Still, rigid, cold, smooth,
Turned into a statue and erected as a pillar
In front of temples — speak,
Is this what you desire?
No, you seek masks
And rainbow skins
Playful like a wildcat who jumps through windows,
out into the wilderness of all chance!
No, you need primeval forest,
so you can slurp your honey,
sinfully healthy and beautiful
like colorfully spotted predators

28 [22][22]

World-Weary People

more thoughtful times, more overanalyzed times,
than our todays and yesterdays

deprived of women, poorly nourished
and contemplating their navels
— dirt loving
awful smelling!
That's how they invented for themselves God's desire

under cloudy skies,
when we are shooting arrows
and murderous thoughts at our enemies,
that's when they slandered those who are happy

they love, alas! and are not loved
they tear themselves to pieces
because no one wants to embrace them.

you who despair! how much
you embolden those who watch you!

they forgot how to eat meat,
how to play with little women,
— their grieving went beyond all bounds.

how restless people feel safe
even in prison!
how peacefully the souls
of imprisoned criminals sleep![23]
Only those who are conscientious
suffer pangs of conscience![24]

28 [23]²⁵

Beyond Time.

These times are like an ailing woman
just let her scream, throw tantrums, curse and break plates and
tables into pieces.

driven here and there, whirling upward
— you have already sat on all surfaces,
already slept on all fancy mirrors
— dust

such people are made mistrustful by reasoned arguments
they are convinced by sublime gestures

Get back! You are following too closely on my heels!
Get back, lest my truth kick your heads in!

like ancient peoples,
with their brains and private parts easily aroused

beside themselves with devotion, like dogs

28 [24]
Cries were heard around midnight
— they were coming from the desert

28 [25]²⁶
In Praise of Poverty.

My song is for
the prisoners of prosperity
whose thoughts rattle coldly, like chains

28 [26][27]

   Oh good times that now bloom for me
   Oh solemn great season —
   From north to south
The guest gods — strange and unknown,
   the nameless ones
   You godly kingly guests
Everywhere from the greatest heights, annunciation streams
down to me
Like a sweet fragrance,
   Like ominous winds, my heart runs
From north to south
   for its festive times are in bloom

Hermits shall no longer be alone!

The time is near, that solemn beautiful great season,
when my guests arrive — in the middle of the year,
now I am like a man in love
whose longing counts the hours,
who peers and stands and sees, blissfully irritated,
until, feeling oppressed by tiny rooms,
he throws himself into the dark alley of chance
— And when the night wind knocks on windows,
Maliciously waking up sleepers with sprigs of flowers

28 [27]

6. Poets — Agony of Those Who Create

Oh, you who lie in wait! Now ⟨I⟩ am yours
What kind of ransom do you want?
Want a lot — that's what my pride advises — and be brief:
that's what my other pride advises
I love giving advice: I get tired easily when I do this

where do I flee?

I lie still,
stretched out,
like a half-dead man whose feet are being warmed
— the beetles fear my silence
— I wait

I call everything good
Leaves and grass, happiness, blessing in the rain[28]

28 [28]
about your arriving
about your approaching
— they love me

They are all waiting — I did speak to all of them
of you, you

28 [29][29]
Are not all things made
pointed for a dancer's feet

slowly passing by, like dromedaries,
one person after another

28 [30][30]
Empty, cave, full of night-winged things
sung about everywhere and feared everywhere

28 [31][31]
Here I sat looking, looking — but to the outside world!
My fingers playing with a picked-apart bouquet
And whenever tears welled forth from beneath my eyelids
Shamefully curious: alas, for whom were they shed!

There — — —

Here I sat loving, loving — unmoved,
like the sea that — — —
Whoever sees this mirror-sea as something magical:
It is in this sea that milk and violets and granite become one.

28 [32]³²

1 *The red leaf*
That many good things do not slip away from me and that
I depart ungratefully
2 *to the morning.*
3 *escaped from all prisons* (marriage job 1 *place* etc.)
4 *music of the South*³³
5 *to the Greeks*³⁴ (in relation to Germans)
6 *to Christians* (I have no *need* of Christianity)
7 *hatred for the English* (as opposed to German-Russian)³⁵
8 *longing for a noble soul*
9 *honey offering* of thanks
10 *against* springtime (mockery)
11 praise of the warrior spirit as preparing the way for *me*
12 the *most serious* boy — oh that you *will become* a child in
old age!
13 to *Schopenhauer* as a philosophical *teenager*³⁶
14 to Napoleon (Corsica) where is the man made of granite?
15 Concerning the *long ladder*
16 *Affable* to everyone, even to grazing animals³⁷
17 Humor of someone who has **triumphed** over *everything.*
18 A song that mocks the *superficiality* of humans
19 The *person who is most completely hidden* (being mocked
by a masked man who always remains noticed)
20 Addressed to sleep (waiting for 3 hours, giving blessings)
21 *not a* martyr! Too *sly* for that as well, I am escaping! (and I
had it *worse* than all of you!)
22 the *good European*
23 the *midnight departure*³⁸
24 *Calina*³⁹ red brown, everything near me too sharply focused
during high summer. Ghostly (my danger *right now*!)
25 to Richard Wagner⁴⁰

[Z II 7a]

28 [33]⁴¹

"Noon-Thoughts."
By
Friedrich Nietzsche.

1 To Napoleon (Corsica: where is the man made of granite?)
2 Concerning the longest ladder
3 Affable to everyone, yes even to grazing animals.
4 Humor of someone who has triumphed over everything.
5 A song that mocks the superficiality of humans.
6 The person who is most completely hidden (mocking the eternally unnoticed masquerade)
7 Addressed to sleep (waiting for three hours. Giving your blessing to it)
8 Not a martyr! (Too sly for that as well: I escape. And I really had it worse than all of you!
9 The good Europeans.
10 The midnight departure.
11 Calina: the danger I now face, during high summer, ghostly, reddish brown, everything near me too sharply focused
12 To Richard Wagner.
13 The red leaf (that many good things do not slip away and that I depart ungratefully!
14 To the morning.
15 escaping from all prisons (such as job, marriage, etc.)
16 To the Greeks (against the Germans)
17 Music of the South
18 to Christians (I don't *need* your Christianity)
19 Hating the English (in contrast, German-Russian
20 Longing for a noble soul.
21 Honey sacrifice. Great thanksgiving.
22 against springtime (mockery).
   Plea for blindness (addressed to the sun
23 Praise of the warrior spirit — it makes *me* ready.

24 The most serious boy (i.e., that you will become a *child* in your old age!)
25 To Schopenhauer (as if to a philosophical teenager).

28 [34][42]

I envy industrious people their industriousness:
evenly and, like gleaming gold, the day flows up to them
like gleaming gold it then flows back,
down into the dark sea, —
and forgetfulness is blossoming all around their camp, easing
the tension in their bodies.

28 [35]

At night — what comes knocking on my window?

28 [36][43]

The Honey Sacrifice.

Bring me honey, fresh from the hive and golden honey from
the comb!
With honey I offer a sacrifice to everything that is giving gifts
there,
Whatever is free of envy, whatever is good-hearted — : gladdens the heart!

28 [37]

The Herald's Calls

rich in intellect
created from nothing, but with wit

28 [38][44]

You who listen jealously to my breathing in the night

and would like to creep into my dreams

28 [39]

Once — how distant is this once! and alas! how sweet
The word "once" is, like the lost tolling of bells,
then the day arrived, duty, the plowshare,
the bellowing of the ox, — — —

28 [40]⁴⁵

Oh you who are playing,
you children in the forest, you laughing ones,
Don't run away — no! protect me,
Hide this wild hunted animal,
Stay with me, listen! For whatever is hunting me,
whatever has been on my trail
through every wilderness of error since the early dawn,
are they hunters? men lying in wait? are they thoughts?
I no longer know,
yet to see children
and to see them playing their games — — —

28 [41]

The most beautiful body — merely a veil,
Within which something even more beautiful — modestly
shrouds itself —

28 [42]

To Hafiz.⁴⁶
Question of a Man Who Drinks Only Water.

The alehouse you built for yourself,
    is larger than an⟨y⟩ house,

The ales you brew within,
   are more than the world can drink.
The bird that once was a Phoenix,
   is now a guest in your home,
The mouse that gave birth to a mountain,
   this — is almost who you are!
You are everything and nothing, you are alehouse and wine
   You are Phoenix, mountain, and mouse,
Forever falling back within yourself,
   forever flying out of yourself —
You are the sinkhole for all heights,
   You are the illusion of all depths,
You are the drunkenness of all drunkards
   — what need, what need do *you* have — for wine?

[Z II 6a]

28 [43]

A very bashful woman
Once said to me in the light of morning:
"If you are already so blissfully sober,
How blissful will you be — when you're drunk!"

28 [44]

Those who can't laugh here shouldn't be reading here!
For if they don't laugh, "the evil one" will seize them.

28 [45][47]

To German Jackasses.[48]

These stolid Englishmen
With their mediocre comprehension
You think this is "philosophy"?

Putting Darwin on a par with Goethe
This means: *a crime against majesty —
majestatem Genii*![49]

First among all mediocre minds
— he is supposed to be a master,
and kneel before him!
To place him higher up
Means — — —

28 [46][50]

Hail to you, you upright English
Hail to your Darwin, if only he understood
You as well as he does his animals!

You English have no trouble
Raising your Darwin high, even if he understood
Nothing more than cattle-breeding.

Yet — to put him on the same level as *Goethe*
Means a crime against majesty
Majestatem genii!

28 [47]

While Looking at a Nightshirt.

If, in spite of their frumpy clothing,
The Germans someday did come to their senses,
My what a change that would be!
Buttoned up in their stiff garments
They would leave it up to their tailor,
To their Bismarck — to make sense of things!

28 [48]⁵¹

To Richard Wagner.

You who are offended at every shackle,
A restless mind, thirsty for freedom,
Always victorious and yet tied up ever tighter,
More and more disgusted, rubbed more raw,
Until every balsam you drank turned into poison —
Alas! That even you fell to your knees in front of the *cross*,
Even you! Even you — a defeated man!

I have been standing in front of this spectacle for so long
Breathing in the prison air, grief and grudge and grave,
With intervening clouds of incense, church-whore fragrance
Here I grow afraid:
While dancing I throw my dunce cap in the air!
For I escaped — —

28 [49]

To Spinoza.

Having turned lovingly to the "One in All,"
An *amor dei*,⁵² blissful, relying on reason —
Take your shoes off! What a land! Holy three times over! — —
Yet underneath this love
a secretly smoldering vengeful fire was gnawing away:
— hatred of the Jews gnawing on the god of the Jews! —
— Hermit, have I seen you for who you are?

28 [50]

For False Friends.

You stole, your eye is not pure —

Was it only one thought you stole? — No,
Who can be so insolently modest!
Take this handful in the bargain —
Take everything that's mine —
And pork it down *'til your conscience is clean*, you swine!

28 [51]

A Roman Exclamation.

Only "deutsch," not "teutsch!" That's how Germans want it now.
But when it concerns the "Babst,"[53] then they stand — *firm*!

28 [52]

The "Real German."[54]

"*Ô peuple des meilleurs Tartuffes*,[55]
I will stay loyal to you, certainly!"
— He said this, and taking the fastest steamer
He traveled to Cosmopolis.

28 [53]

The New Testament.

This, the holiest prayerbook —
book of wellness and woe?
— Yet standing at its front door is
God's adultery!

28 [54]

Riddle.

Solve this riddle for me, a riddle that conceals this word:
"Women *invent* things when men *discover* something — — "

28 [55]

The Hermit Speaks.

To have thoughts? Good! — then they belong to me.
Yet to have *second* thoughts, — I would love to forget those!!
People who have second thoughts — are possessed by the devil[56]
and I never ever want to serve them.

28 [56]

Resolved.

I want to be wise because *I* like it
And even more so on my own terms.
I praise God because God created the world
To be as stupid as possible.

And if I go my own way
As crookedly as possible —
The greatest sages would begin there,
Fools — this is where they'd stop.

28 [57]

A wave does not stand still,
Night loves the bright of day —
The words "I want to" sound lovely
"I like to" even lovelier!

All ever-flowing wellsprings
Spring forth forever:
God himself — he did begin, didn't he?
God himself — isn't he always beginning?

28 [58]⁵⁷

The Wanderer.

A wanderer walks through the night
Stepping briskly;
And crooked valleys and endless heights —
He carries them along.
The night is beautiful —
He strides onward and does not stand still,
He still does not know where his path wants to take him.

Then a bird sings through the night:
"Oh bird, what have you done!
Why are you hampering my senses and my feet
And pouring sweet heartbreak
Into my ear, so that I have to stop
And have to listen — —
Why *do* you *lure* me with a sound and a greeting?" —

The good bird stops singing and says:
"No, wanderer, no! It is not you I'm luring
With my sounds —
I'm luring a sweet little female from the heights —
What concern is it of yours?
The night is not beautiful to me when I'm alone.
What concern is it of yours? For you must keep walking
And never ever stand still!
Why are you still standing there?
What did my flute-song do to you,
You wayfarer?⁵⁸

The good bird was silent and reflected:
"What did my flute-song do to him?
Why is he still standing there? —
The poor, poor wayfarer!"

28 [59][59]

A German November.

This is autumn: it — will break your heart!
Fly away! fly away! —
The sun creeps up the mountain
And climbs and climbs
and rests with every step.

How did the world get so wilted!
The wind plays its song
On worn overstretched strings.
Hope has fled —
The wind laments its passing.

This is autumn: it — will break your heart.
Fly away! fly away!
Oh, fruit of the tree,
You are trembling, you are falling?
Which secret did
The night teach you,
So that icy shudders cover
Your cheeks, your purple cheeks? —

You are silent, you do not answer?
Who is still speaking? — —

This is autumn: it — will break your heart.
Fly away! fly away!—
"I am not beautiful
— is what the aster says —
Yet I love people
And I comfort people —
they should still be able to enjoy flowers
they should bend down to me

alas! and pick me —
then memories will glisten
in their eyes,
Memories of more beautiful things than me: —
— I see it, I see it — and now I can die." —

This is autumn: it — will break your heart!
Fly away! fly away!

28 [60][60]

At the Glacier.

At midday, when summer
First climbs up into the mountain ranges,
The boy with tired, hot eyes:
Then this boy also speaks,
Yet we only *see* his speaking.
His breath welling forth like the breath of someone sick
into the fever of the night.
There are icy mountain ranges and firs and springs
that also give him an answer,
Yet we only see the answer.
For the cataract pours down more rapidly,
like a greeting from the cliffs
And it stands there like a trembling white column
Longingly.
And the fir gazes more darkly and more faithfully
Than it usually does
And between ice and dead gray stone
A light suddenly shines forth — —
I have already seen this sort of light: it makes this meaningful. —

Light comes
Even into a dead man's eye,
When, full of sorrow, his child

Hugs and holds and kisses him:
Then surely glowing flames of light,
Spring forth one more time,
The dead eye speaks: "Child!
Oh child, you know I love you!" —
And, glowingly, everything speaks — icy mountain range
And brook and fir tree —
While looking down here, the very same words:
"We love you!
Oh child, you know we love you, love you!"

And he,
The boy with the tired hot eyes,
He kisses them sorrowfully,
Ever more warmly,
And does not want to go;
He floats his words out like a veil
From his mouth only,
His poignant words
"my greeting is parting,
my coming going,
I die young."

Then everything around him listens
And everything is holding its breath:
No bird sings.
Then everything is overflowing,
Trembling, like
A glimmer, the mountain range.
Then the mountain range is surrounded by thinking —
And everything is quiet — —

It was at noon,
At noon when, for the first time,
Summer climbed up into the mountain ranges,
The boy with the tired hot eyes.

28 [61]⁶¹

"*The Wanderer and His Shadow.*"
A Book

No way back? And no way forward?
No way even for a mountain goat?

So I wait here and *hold on* tight,
to whatever it is that eye and hand will let me hold!

Earth five feet wide, red light of dawn,
and *beneath* me — world, people and death!

28 [62]⁶²

*Yorick*⁶³ *as a Gypsy.*

There the gallows, here the noose
and the hangman's red beard,
People around and poisonous looks —
There's nothing new about what I do!
I know this well from a hundred times before,
Laughing, I scream this in your faces:
No use, no use in hanging me!
Die? I cannot die!

You beggars! For, in order to arouse your envy,
something was given to me, something you — will never get:
I may well suffer, I may well suffer
But you — you will die, you will die!
Even after a hundred goes at the gallows
I am air, mist and light —
No use, no use in hanging me!
Die? I cannot die!

Once, in distant Spain,
The song of the death rattle called out to me,
The lantern cast its bleak gaze,
The cheerful singer, full of joy and insolence.
I joyfully recalled my evil
Enemies with blissful mockery:
If a curse can't redeem you,
Then a cheerful sound of joy will do it.

28 [63][64]

Yorick-Columbus.

Friend![65] Columbus said, do not trust
a Genoese ever again!
He is always staring into the blue,
What is most distant draws him all too much!

What is most foreign is now dear to me!
Genoa — that sank, that disappeared —
Stay cool, my heart! Hold the tiller, my hand!
The ocean in front of me — and land? — and land?

That's the way I want to go — and I trust
Myself from now on and my grip.
Open is the ocean, my Genoese ship
sails into the blue.

Everything becomes new and newer to me,
Space and time shine far into the distance —
And the most beautiful monster of all
Is laughing at me: eternity

28 [64]
   The Free Spirit.[66]

Farewell

"The crows call out
And head in whirring flight toward the city:
Soon it will snow —
Nice for those who still — have a home!

Now you stand stiffly,
You look back, alas! how long already has this been going on!
Why did a fool like you
Escape into the world — before winter?

The world — a gateway
To a thousand deserts, silent and cold!
Anyone who lost
What you have lost does not stop for the night anywhere.

Now you stand pale,
Doomed to winter wandering,
Like smoke,
Which is always searching for colder skies.

Fly away, bird, caw
Your song the way desert birds do! —
You fool, hide
Your bleeding heart in ice and mockery!

The crows call out
And head in whirring flight toward the city:
Soon it will snow,
Alas for those who have no home!"

Answer.

God have mercy!
He thinks I was longing to return
To German warmth,

Back into dull snug happy German sitting rooms!

My friend, it is *your* mind
that keeps me hemmed in and hampered here.
Compassion for *you*!
Compassion for your cockeyed German mind!

28 [65]⁶⁷
It is you I love, grotto full of graves!
I love you, marble web of lies!
You always open up my soul
To the most open ridicule.
Yet today I stand, weeping,
Let my tears flow
In front of you, ⟨you⟩ image in stone,
In front of you, you graven words!

And — no one needs to know —
This image — I have already kissed it.
There is so much to kiss:
Since when do we kiss — clay, anyway!
Who would know how to interpret that!
What! I, a fool for gravestones!
For, I confess it, I kissed
Even the longest word.

28 [66]⁶⁸

2.
Courage, Friend Yorick!
And whenever your *thought* torments you,
As it does now,
Don't call it — "God"! For you miss the mark by far,
It is, after all, only your own *child*,
Your flesh and blood,
that afflicts and torments you there,
Your little rascal and ne'er do well!

— See what the *rod* will do for it!

And briefly, Friend Yorick! give up that gloomy
philosophy — and let me whisper into your ear
Just one more saying as a hospital remedy
And as a home remedyw
— *my* cure for spleen[69] of this sort — :
"Those who love their 'God' will punish *him*."[70]

28 [67][71]
There the gallows, here the noose
Hangman here, and hangman's craft,
Noses red, poisonous looks —
And the bearded dignity of priests:
I know you from a hundred times before,
I love to spit in your faces —
What's the use of hanging?
Dying? Dying — I never learned how!

You beggars! Then, arousing your envy,
Something was given to me, something you — will never get.
I may well suffer, I may well suffer
But you — you will die, you will die!
Even after a hundred goes at the gallows,
I will find my way back to the light —
What's the use of hanging?
Dying? Dying — I never learned how!

Once, in distant Spain,
The song of the death rattle called out to me,
The lantern cast its bleak gaze,
The cheerful singer, full of joy and insolence.
How, listening, I sank
Into the depths of my deepest water,
To me it seemed as if I were sleeping, sleeping
Forever healthy and forever ill.

29 [1][1]

Such people are made mistrustful by reasoned arguments; but they are convinced by sublime gestures.

— like ancient peoples, with their brains and private parts easily aroused[2]

— what do I care about your religious faith, with God's adultery standing at its threshold![3]

— you are following too closely on my heels: be careful that I don't kick your heads in at some point!

— straight in flight and turn, like swooping eagles[4]

— your paradise is "under the shadow of swords"[5]

— it stares down into the abyss with longing — the abyss that winds down into ever greater depths.

— how restless people feel safe even in prison! How criminals really do sleep like babies![6]

— I start laughing again too soon: an enemy doesn't have to make a lot of amends to me.[7]

— under cloudy skies, when we are shooting arrows and murderous thoughts at our enemies.[8]

— more thoughtful times, more overanalyzed times than our todays and yesterdays are[9]

— these times are like an ailing woman: just let her scream, rant, rage and break plates and tables all she wants![10]

— to walk around amidst the most distant and coldest thoughts, like a ghost on a glacier

— deprived of women, poorly nourished and contemplating their navels: that's how they invented for themselves God's desire.[11]

— "humans are evil": this is what the greatest sages kept saying in order to comfort me.

— sinfully healthy and beautiful, like spotted and colorful predators

— I am like a wind that makes all skies bright and all oceans roar.

— driven here and there, whirling upward, you travelers, you have slept on every surface at one time or another, you, dust on all windowpanes and fancy mirrors!

— misfortune is silent: and those who can bring themselves to sing of their misfortune have flown even beyond their misfortune.

— be brief, give me a riddle to solve: or else you will wear down my intellectual pride.

— they discovered the most holy kind of boredom and the lust for Moon-days and workdays[12]

— terrible things are happening here: people, overcome by vertigo, already longing to hurl themselves into the abyss of the future.

— the prisoners of prosperity: their thoughts clanking like cold chains.[13]

— stubborn minds, cunning and petty[14]

— this is the inclination of puny people: they would like to pull down whatever is great, to flatter it into submission.

— beside themselves with devotion, like dogs[15]

— alas, they fall back on big words and weak deeds: alas, they call themselves virtuous again!

— they love, alas! and are not loved! they tear themselves to pieces because no one wants to embrace them.[16]

— you are too prosperous, you ruin too many people: you make too many people jealous!

— things are in a bad way: some people believed they were lying and only then did they hit on the truth.

— you who despair! How much you embolden those who watch you!

— to be at home in the wilderness, like cats and women, and to jump through windows.

— they created their God and their world for themselves out of nothing: is it any wonder that —[17]

— you didn't say enough. Is that it? Everything is illusion? Everything is a lie! Is that it? Everything is suffering and downfall? Everything is about inflicting suffering and causing downfalls!

— did you already create him, the ugliest human? Lacking God, goodness, good minds —

— Alas, my friends! Where did goodness and good people go! Where did the innocence of these lies go!

— these lies that once viewed humans as gods and billy goats alike

— What are you saying! Virtue is that which quietly, rigidly, coldly, smoothly makes something into a sculpture and a column? Things which are set up at temples in order to be seen.

— you fear the drawn bow: watch out, someone could actually nock an arrow![18]

— Those who cannot lie, knowingly and intentionally, how will they ever learn to tell the truth!

— he grieves too deeply and is poorly nourished; he forgot how to eat meat and how to play with pretty little women.[19]

— clumsy and shy like a tiger after a pounce gone awry[20]

Human being — a long rope; and you want to convince me that I'm the knot that is tied into it? (Zarathustra laughing.)

in a dream, to wake a sleeping dog: both move toward each other like deadly enemies — and yet both have only been startled!

bring forth honey, fresh from the hive and golden honey from the comb! With honey I am making an offering to everything that gives gifts, that grants favors, that is benevolent — lifts up hearts!

I envy industrious people their industriousness: the day flows up to them evenly, like gleaming gold — and away into the distance of dawning eternities.[21]

Once — alas, how distant is this once! how sweet like the lost tolling of bells in the forest, how sweet this word already sounds![22]

    written with flying daggers — "On Old and New Tablets"
    — "bovine good will"[23]
    — the day fades away
    — thistle-heads, scrupulous saps
    — coffins and sawdust[24]
    — like superfast spider monkeys —[25]
    in and out quickly, like a cold-water bath
    It is time and well past time that I left
    dizzy dogs all around me and sickly breeds

29 [2]

    Paul Fundamental Principles of Linguistics[26]
    Sanders
    Leuthold, Rückert, Hebbel
    Keller, medieval German poets? (lib⟨rary⟩ *used book⟨store⟩*)
    English poets?

29 [3]

When faced with people who are foreign to us, these questions run through our minds: who are they? what do they want? what are their abilities? — and depending on the answers we get to these questions, we determine the value of these people. If we ourselves are independent, influential, powerful, then we also immediately determine their value as value *for us*: if we are dependent and integrated into some herd and community, then our question about their value means: what value do they have for us, i.e., for the herd?

29 [4]

    (I lack 1) a woman cook

        2) musicians

        3) readers[27]

        4) a kind of master of ceremonies)

Probability of success: like a pyramid. The vast framework of my life. Utilizing failures

As my first success: Köselitz (my *taste*) — as my second (*moral* effect) Stein.[28]

Finances: with Overbeck

          in Naumburg

          with Schmeitzner.

What have we *achieved*? **what have we established**?

    1) My *places of residence*

      a) to Engadin I owe *life*,

                      Zarathustra

      b) to Nice I owe the *ending* of Zarathustra

      c) both places fit my task well: Nice as cosmopolitan, Sils as high up in the mountains

    (*Both* should contribute to the *impression* I leave. —)

Fundamentally: *not* to live in Germany, because of my[29] European mission.

    — *not* around universities —

    — my predecessors: Schopenhauer and Richard Wagner are still viable European movements.

Perhaps some kind of teaching activity possible in *both* places.

What remains to be invented *in the immediate future*?

    Concealment. Restorative places. Calming techniques.

29 [5][30]

To Superior Humans.

A Herald's Proclamations
by
Friedrich Nietzsche.

29 [6]
Every virtue has its drawbacks and costs

29 [7]
to teach:
1) isolation
2) against political machinations
3) will of those who rule over the earth
4) not to mistake ourselves for benevolent or self-righteous people
5) binding nations together
6) against the powerful and the rich, in cases where they have shaken people's faith in superior humans — like the Church, with its faith in saints
7) against gods[31] as a reason for submission and letting things go
8) the most superior types are the worst failures
death of all immortals.
power, wildness, energy, no *moderation*
fervor, drama

29 [8]
Being alone with a great thought[32] is unbearable.

Plan. I seek out and call people to whom I can communicate this thought, who will not perish as a result.
Concept of superior humans: those who suffer on account of humans and not just on their own account,[33] those who have no choice but to create "human beings" on the basis of *themselves* and no one else

—against all the amusing evasions and ravings of mystics.

—against "people who have made compromises."

—we failures! Most superior types! to redeem *ourselves* is to redeem "humans themselves": this is our "*egoism*"!

4. Zarathustra. These are the songs of Zarathustra, which he sang to himself so that he could endure his ultimate[34] solitude:[35]

29 [9][36]

You have bound me with chains: but even my executioners shall yet become my disciples.

29 [10][37]

they have it in for me — but *I* do not want to abandon them on that account; they think little of me: so I will figure out how to make them bigger.

29 [11][38]

— the waves are rising higher and higher: soon my boat will no longer be resting on dry land

— who also gives wings to donkeys and milks lionesses

— at the hour when noon is resting on the meadows: no shepherd plays his pipes then

— songs of the unknown god

— silence once the clouds have cleared: (alpine glow) (hermit)

— sweet-mannered dogs

29 [12][39]

1. A herald's proclamations.   2. At the great noon.
3. Hypocrisy of good people.   4. Those who make vows.

29 [13][40]

On the Hypocrisy of Good People.

1) motives: you take me to court — yet I make you into my apostles and give wings to donkeys[41]

2) songs of the heights, dedicated to all people of the future. Silence once the clouds have cleared[42]

3) I take you in my arms — alas, I see the epileptic seizures of my own child

4) what is taking you so long? — the space around me is filling up with cripples

5) all futures are fighting for liberation within me and you — how could we not be deformed!

6) to pious people. They feel the greater interconnectedness of events and the absolute importance of the person and they feel themselves to be failures. — If all things are fated, then *I* am also the fate of all things.

29 [14][43]

(4)[44]

The honey sacrifice.

Visit — temptations (and signs) *Smells* the approaching misery

    the poet

    the obsessed youth

    the king (the statesman "peasant")

    the fool from the big city

    the woman (seeks out the *man* —)

    the prophet

{ Send the animals out to gather news.

{ The seventh solitude.

The saint "one more time?" decision.

Lion and swarm of doves.

The message.

Farewell to the cave: Tearing himself away from solitude. Eternal return of every good thing.

29 [15][45]

the dying Zarathustra holds the earth *in his embrace.* — And although no one had told them, they all knew that Zarathustra was dead.

29 [16][46]

There is nothing to be done with these ancient peoples — they may well oppose and struggle against one another: from top to bottom they are the same, i.e., they are now all part of the rabble.

Language and newspapers —

29 [17]

1   Exploitation, of the many by the best people
2   The hermits degenerate into Cynics and Stoics
    — hence their consumption of energy
            their lack of energy
3   our *opponents* the teachers of absolute morality.

29 [18]

the awe we feel for God is the awe we feel for the connectedness of all things and the conviction that there are beings who are superior to humans.

to make gods —

to make ourselves and others in the image of gods —

Artists are sculptors of gods (they select what is successful, underscore it etc.)

29 [19][47]

Zarathustra says to his animals "we must make ourselves ready for guests."

29 [20]

The instinct for moral things, as for aesthetic things, requires the most subtle, most highly trained, discerning taste. In my view, most human actions "shouldn't be seen."

29 [21]⁴⁸

Zarathustra is first *invited* by those who are *failures* — he sends them away "you don't want to *celebrate* with me, instead you want *to save* yourselves through me.

Finally, his "*blessed ones*" arrive

29 [22]⁴⁹

"Who still loves me" — an *ice-cold* intellect
An epileptic
A poet
A king

29 [23]⁵⁰

Zarathustra's profound patience and confidence that the time will come.

The guests: the prophet spreads dark pessimism.

mercy for criminals (as during the Fr⟨ench⟩ Revolut⟨ion⟩)

The signs: the big city in flames

Being tempted to return **before** it is **time** — by eliciting **compassion**.

News about the island sinking

Finally: first of all, I still want to *inquire* whether they are alive

— sends out the eagle —

A herald's proclamations to solitary people

Doubled row of signs

1) on the decline of humans

2) on the presence of great individuals

I cannot become *master* with you at my side.

29 [24]⁵¹

The wanderer (thirsty for knowledge)
The king.
The prophet.
The young man from the mountain.
The fool from the big city.

The saint (*at the end*).
The crowds of children.
The poet

29 [25]

To depict a contrast between those *who have failed* (have been isolated) and the chosen "people" who have grown up together

29 [26]⁵²

Zarathustra: I am so overflowing with happiness, and I have no one to give it to, and not even anyone I could thank. So let me offer my thanks to you, my animals.

1.	1. Zarathustra thanking his animals and preparing them for guests. Quiet patience of someone who is waiting and profound confidence in his friends.
2 —9.	2. The guests as temptations to give up solitude: I have not come here to help those who suffer etc. (Fr⟨ench⟩ painting)
	3. the hermit-saint pious man.
10 —14.	4. Zarathustra sends forth his animals to seek information. Alone, without *prayer* — and without the animals.
	Greatest excitement!
15.	5. "they're coming!" As the eagle and the serpent speak, the lion joins them — the lion is weeping!
16.	Farewell forever to the cave. (A kind of festive parade!) With the 4 animals he goes to meet,⁵³ until they reach the edge of the city - - -

29 [27]⁵⁴

The disciples' hesitation. "*We* can easily endure this doctrine, but won't we *destroy* many people with it?"

Zarathustra laughs: "you shall be the hammer, I am putting the hammer in your hands

29 [28]

All virtue is *acquired* virtue, there is no random virtue. Accumulated from our fathers —

29 [29]

The problem of solitude, with and without God — this praying, thanking, loving *squandered* into the void

29 [30][55]

the prophet: I discovered the secret weariness of all souls, the unbelief, the disbelief — *apparently* they put up with it — they are tired. None of them believe in their own *value*.

And even you, Zarathustra! A small bolt of lightning would be enough to pulverize you!

Good, but stay there — — —

29 [31][56]

said everything one more time (returning like the **head of the Medusa**

29 [32][57]

First scene. Zarathustra acts silly with his animals, makes the honey sacrifice, compares himself to a pine, gives thanks even to his misfortune, laughs about his white beard

Surprised by the prophet
Reasons for the great weariness

Gospel of those who suffer, up to now *their* time.

Equality.

Hypocrisy.

29 [33][58]

Zarathustra 5: full acknowledgment of that which is human, in terms of the visible world — *rejection* of idealist philosophy and explanations that result from our being sated, aversion to people. — To explain the "falsity" in things as a result of *our* creative power!

29 [34]

"For you, happiness and servitude!"

29 [35]

Something unconsciously creative and artistic in the world of appearances, even when conscious

Unconscious liars

The entire unconscious aspect of our morality, e.g., our unconscious hypocrisy

29 [36]

Ennoblement — nobility for sale.[59]

29 [37]

Whether power lies with the many or with the few, the feeling one way or another determines an *oligarchic* or *ochlocratic* form of government.

29 [38][60]

dried-up emptied souls

29 [39][61]

the 2 kings with the donkey
    rabble that never learns to revere things

the happiest man — prophet obscurity
the magnificent complete person — the ailing genius
the rabble-enemy — 2 kings

the beautiful-noble person — doctor, degeneration and weakness

the non-hypocrite — penitent of the mind, prone to lying

the trembling bodies

crowds pleading for help

"Now hear the genius!"

full of disgust, Zarathustra is silent.

the soul of trumpeters

hypocritically happy people

29 [40][62]

The New Enlightenment.
Laying the Groundwork
for the Philosophy of Eternal Recurrence.
By
Friedrich Nietzsche.

29 [41]

power is evil:[63] we are not great enough, even for its evil.

The one who creates is a destroyer: we are not great enough to create and destroy.

29 [42]

Puny atonement for great failure.

29 [43][64]

oh Zarathustra, you are the first and only one to take the destiny of humanity to heart: we already know who you are. In times past, even the weightiest people did not take it seriously: see, they said, this goes beyond our abilities and foresight, let God himself be the spectator

Yet you say: "Abilities? Foresight? What do I care about that! Let's try it! Everything here depends on *doing things* in advance!"

29 [44][65]

That others also **learn** to care for the future of humankind, that amidst all the misery, they remain mute, they escape from the whining about us and our neighbors and about the situation today

29 [45][66]

You are waiting for your arms and legs and tools to grow enough to be adequate for your work — that you may have children and heirs

29 [46][67]

But I should say instead: your clean conscience, namely what remains of your honesty. Puny remains, to be sure, for you are already a counterfeiter

29 [47][68]

And whoever wants to give it a name, they can call it: "*the temptation of Zarathustra.*"

(Conclusion)

29 [48][69]

The best is what I don't have in common with them.

29 [49][70]

There is still a kernel of chicanery and hypocrisy even in this humility of yours; but what I see, what all my senses tell me — you are disgusted by yourself.

You are sick and tired of yourself.

29 [50]

The wild hunter.

You night wind in the ravines, what do you say?

29 [51][71]

To the Pope: you have beautiful hands. The hands of someone who has bestowed many blessings.

Zarathustra to his guests — you are being *pushed* into the heights, up to my place; the people say "you are climbing"

the good European "I have committed every crime there is. I love the most dangerous thoughts and the most dangerous women.

The Pope: you have no idea who I am: I am allowed to be more enlightened than you are. Better to worship him in *some* form than in no form at all!

The one who said: "God is a spirit" — he took the greatest step and the greatest leap into unbelief up to now; on earth, it's not easy to make amends for words like these.

Zarathustra to the voluntary beggar: "you certainly have some kind of overflow: give me some of it!"

That's how I recognize Zarathustra.

— Do you want some of my overflowing disgust?

— they are probably dancing for the good of the poor, all shame in the presence of misfortune is gone

— *Those who are conscientious*

My ignorance begins right next to the leech: but I have forgotten what it means to be ashamed on that account.

29 [52]
Superior human being
In an age ruled by the *satisfaction of the rabble, disgust* is the emblem of superior human beings

29 [53][72]
If I have no choice but to howl with the wolves, then I will howl better than a wolf.

29 [54]
Whoever wants to have a single experience again must want all of them again.

29 [55][73]
I am a wordsmith: who cares about words! who cares about me!

29 [56][74]

Do as I do: in that way you will learn what I learned: only those who do, learn.

Find a spot in the marketplace, so that you may learn what rabble and rabble-noise are: soon your hearing and sight will be gone.

whatever lives around me soon makes itself at home there.[75]

Once a virtue has persuaded and overcome you: then get to know it and don't be angry about it: everything that is bad within you will have its revenge for this: —

It is for your virtues, you superior humans, that you will always be punished most severely.

29 [57][76]

   W⟨anderer⟩

Homesickness, not for a home, not for a father's house and fatherland, for I had neither: rather, feeling sick because I have no home.

29 [58][77]

today you are superior humans, the pious ones for whom God has died, the sanctimonious ones in the time of the rabble, wanderers without a goal or a way home, those who know and those who are conscientious, magicians without magic, who founder on themselves, purple-clad kings who are zeros and rate a ten

you purple-clad kings, who are zeros and rate a ten, you who are intellectually conscientious — — —

No money either, oh Zarathustra, no money either! Nothing makes things uglier than having no money!

Let's all be happy together and in a good mood: and regarding God, you superior humans, may — the devil take him!

29 [59]

If a great fear seizes solitary people, if they run and run, and don't know where they are going?

if bad storms roar, if lightning testifies against them, if their caves terrify them with ghosts —

Let it be said to minor poets and sluggards: anyone who has nothing to create is troubled by nothingness.[78]

29 [60][79]
The last sin

29 [61][80]

the rejoicing of these superior humans came to him like a thawing wind: his hard-heartedness melted away. His heart shivered to its core

29 [62][81]

Here the future turns, here the void gapes, here the hound of hell bays, here the wisest people grow dizzy.

29 [63][82]
The Honey Sacrifice.
The Prophet.
The Poet.
The Kings.
The Saint.

The Seventh Solitude.
Among New Animals.
The Message of the Blessed Ones.
Farewell to the Cave.

29 [64][83]

— And months[84] and years again passed by, and Zarathustra's hair turned white, but Zarathustra sat at his cave, looked out, paid no attention to time. The world had forgotten Zarathustra: had he also forgotten the world?

Do not come too close to me if you want to warm yourselves on me — otherwise you will singe your hearts. I am overheated and I am struggling to keep my flames in check lest they break out of my body.

Your paws have been bound: now you can't scratch, you scratching cat![85]

with thirsty desiccated swords, which have gleamed on the wall for too long and — — —
with swords, like red speckled snakes

29 [65]
    1. The Birth of Tragedy.
    2. Unfashionable Observations.
    3. Human, All Too Human.
    4. The Wanderer and His Shadow.
    5. Dawn.
    6. The Joyful Science
    7. Thus Spoke Zarathustra.
    8. *Dionysus* or: The Holy Orgies

29 [66][86]

Noon and Eternity.

By
Friedrich Nietzsche.

Second Part:
a Herald's Proclamations.

Noon and Eternity.

By
Friedrich Nietzsche.

Third Part:
the Nameless One Gives His Blessing.

29 [67]

von Ouwaroff, Nonnos by Panoplis the Poet.[87]
Letourneau physiologie des passions[88] (in der biblio-
   th⟨èque⟩ des sciences contemporaines[89])
Amiel[90] journal intime tom. II Mém⟨oires⟩ I Viel Castel[91]
Guyau,[92] esquisse d'une morale (Paris Alcan)
Wellhausen, Sketches I/Berlin Reimer 1884[93]
Adolf Schöll, Goethe[94]
        "   Col. Essays o⟨n⟩ Class. Lit. (Berlin, Hertz)[95]
Gozzi Casanova Goldoni De Brosses Mayer 4
   v⟨olumes⟩[96]

[30 = Z II 5, 83. Z II 7b. Z II 6b.
Autumn 1884–Beginning of 1885]

30 [1]

May Europe soon bring forth a *great* statesman, and then the man who is now celebrated as "the great realist"[1] in this petty age of plebian shortsightedness will *appear puny in comparison*.

30 [2][2]

Concerning the *first part*: to introduce my evaluative approach into logic e.g., hypothesis opposing certainty etc.

30 [3][3]

Where can I be at home? I was searching for this feeling for the longest time, this searching kept hitting home with me.

What's the point of falling in love with ugly languages just because our mothers spoke them? Why bear a grudge against our neighbors when my forefathers and I are so hard to love!

30 [4][4]

1 Zarathustra
2 the prophet
3 the first king
4 the second king
5 the ugliest human.
6 the conscientious man.

7 the good European[5]
8 the voluntary beggar.
9 the old Pope
10 the bad sorcerer.

30 [5]

An age is not always worthy of reproach if it does not recognize its greatest mind and has no eye for the most amazing star that ascends out of its own night. Perhaps this star is destined to illuminate much more distant worlds; perhaps it would even be fatal if this star were recognized too soon — it could be that the age ⟨would⟩ be distracted from its project by this star and would then, in turn, do damage to a coming age: through leaving it with work to do that already should have been accomplished, work that is perhaps less suited to the forces of this coming age

30 [6]

Critique of Moral
Value Judgments.

30 [7][6]

But Zarathustra, let me get a word in here! You invited me today to your Last Supper: I hope you don't want to put me off with speeches like this?
a complete ass full of good wine
Have you no hidden spring where the wine flows
two lambs
All those who want to share a meal must get their hands dirty; here there are lambs to slaughter and fires to light
like wild animals in the woods
the poet shall sing for us

The welcomings.[7]
The Last Supper.[8]
The improviser.[9]

The animals' riddles.[10]
The song of the one who laughs.

30 [8][11]
The Enchanter.[12]
I am tired; my entire life I have searched for a great person, in vain. But even Zarathustra is no more.

I recognize you, said Zarathustra seriously, you are the enchanter of all, but it seems to me that you have reaped a harvest of disgust for yourself alone.

It does you credit that you strove for greatness, but it also reveals who you are: you are not great.

Who are you? he said with horrified and hateful looks, who gave you the right to speak this way to me? —

Your bad conscience — answered Zarathustra and turned his back on the enchanter.

30 [9][13]
Dead in life, buried in happiness, — whoever, in this way — — — how many times must he still rise from the dead![14]

Oh happiness, I passed through hate and love until I reached the surface of my self: for too long I hung in a gathering storm[15] of hate and love: the gathering storm drove me and pushed me like a ball[16]

Carefree, like a man enjoying his death in advance.[17]

Is the world not standing still even now? How the dark branches and leaves of this stillness are growing around me,[18]

Do you want to sing, oh my soul? But this is the hour when no shepherd plays the flute. Noon sleeps on the meadows.

the golden mourning of all those who have tasted too many good things.[19]

How long did I sleep in? Now how much longer will I be allowed to stay awake![20]

30 [10]²¹

The necessity for human beings to make themselves understood when facing great danger, be it to help one another or to submit, could only have resulted in bringing together those kinds of primitive human beings who could express similar experiences with similar signs; if the experiences were too different, then these human beings misunderstood each another in the attempt to communicate through signs: so bringing them together did not succeed, therefore, in the end, the herd could not be formed. From this we may conclude that, on the whole, the communicability of experiences (or needs or expectations) has a selective, propagating effect: those human beings who are *more similar* remain. The necessity of thinking, the whole of *consciousness*, was first added on the basis of the necessity for human beings to make themselves understood. First signs, then concepts, finally "reason," in its usual meaning. In itself, the most abundant organic life can play the game to its conclusion without consciousness: yet as soon as its existence is tied to the coexistence of other animals, then consciousness becomes necessary as well. How is this consciousness possible? I am a long way from devising answers to such questions (i.e., words and nothing more!): when the time is right, I will think of old Kant, who once posed the question to himself: "how are synthetic judgments a priori possible?" He eventually answered, with wonderful "German profundity": "by means of a faculty."— How, then, is it possible that opium makes us sleepy? That doctor in Molière answered: it is this, the *vis soporifica*.²² It was opium, too, that lay hidden in that Kantian answer about "faculty," at least *vis soporifica*: how many German "philosophers" have fallen asleep because of this!

30 [11]²³

Knowledge and Conscience.
By
Friedrich Nietzsche.

30 [12]²⁴

My friends, you do not understand your advantage: it is merely stupidity if superior humans suffer on account of these times: they have never had it better.

30 [13]²⁵

Birth of Tragedy.

At the beginning of the year 1872 a book appeared in Germany which had the bizarre title "the Birth of Tragedy out of the Spirit of Music" and which, not just because of its title, provoked widespread amazement and curiosity. It became known that its creator was a young philologist, who at the same time faced opposition from the ranks of philological artisans, and with this opposition perhaps even being engineered by some philological schoolmaster and cowherd — — —

— an independent self-sufficient book, in which the signs of a mystical soul were written, without taking into account — — —

— full of youth and clumsiness, passionate, overflowing, *aussi trop allemand*²⁶ — in which almost completely opposing talents jostled and pushed each other, too

— with an intellectuality that affects the senses

— it is acknowledged, with a bit of a shiver (assuming they had sensitive skin —) that here someone is speaking of the uncanny world of Dionysian things *as if from experience*, as if having returned from the most foreign of all countries after being fully immersed, not saying everything, not withholding everything, hidden under the cowl and hood of the scholar and not hidden enough.

and Richard Wagner, from the depths of that prophetic instinct that stood in such contrast to his spotty and haphazard education, divined that he had met that fateful person who holds in his hands the fate of German culture and not merely German culture.²⁷

31 [1]

A Practical Approach to Overcoming Morality.

31 [2]¹

In Zarathustra 4, it is necessary: to say *precisely* why the time of the great noon is arriving *now*: thus a *depiction of time*, shown through the visits, but *interpreted* by Zarathustra.

In Zarathustra 4, it is necessary: to say *precisely* why the "*chosen people*" *had to be created in the first place* — it is the contrast of successful people who have superior natures with people who have failed (as shown by the visitors): it is *only* to them that Zarathustra can communicate his thoughts about the ultimate problems, it is *only* from them that he can expect the implementation of this theory (they are strong and healthy and hard-hearted enough for this, above all, noble enough!) and it is *only* into their hands that he can deliver the hammer that will hang over the earth.

In Zarathustra, then, we need to depict:

1) the most extreme danger posed by the superior type (at which time Zarathustra reminds them of his first appearance)

2) the good people now take sides *against* the superior humans: this is the most dangerous turning point! (— against the exceptions!)

3) the degeneration of those who have been abandoned,
    of those who are uneducated, of those who misrepre-
    sent themselves, and this degeneration is taken as an
    objection to their existence ("genius-neurosis!")

4) Zarathustra must explain what he did when he advised
    them *to emigrate* to the islands and why he visited them
    (1. and 2.) (— they were still not ripe enough for his
    ultimate revelations?)

31 [3]²

In Zarathustra 6, the great synthesis of those who create,
those who love, those who annihilate

31 [4]³

In Zarathustra 4: the great thought as *head of the Medusa*:
all the features of the world are becoming fixed, a frozen fight
to the death.

31 [5]⁴

Were you speaking about yourself or about me? But whether
you betrayed me or betrayed yourself, you are one of the trai-
tors, you, the poet!

— shamelessly opposed to what you've lived through,
exploiting your experience, revealing your most beloved things
to prying eyes, pouring your blood into all the dry emptied
goblets, you, most vain of all men!

31 [6]⁵

the genius sees Zarathustra as the *embodiment* of his thoughts

31 [7]⁶

For the last time: open your eyes, see the *entire* truth: *superior
humans, they will either exist or they won't*!!⁷

31 [8][8]

"This, then, oh Zarathustra, is *your* misery! Don't deceive yourself: did the sight of the multitudes make you gloomy because they are humble and inferior? But solitary people have failed much more often" — Zarathustra presents the arguments against this

1) on the great mistake of compassion — everything weak that suffers has been *preserved*
2) "birds of a feather"[9] has been taught and in the process hermits have been deprived of their good conscience — forced to become hypocrites and to crawl
3) the ruling classes have represented the belief in superior humans badly, they have partly destroyed it
4) the monstrous empire of ugly people, where the rabble rules: there the most noble soul dresses in rags and would rather exaggerate ugliness
5) They lack all education; they must put on armor and disfigure themselves in order to save something of themselves.

in summa:[10] the superior humans' *cry of distress* to Zarathustra. Zarathustra commends them to be patient, feels a chill running down his spine: "it is nothing that I haven't experienced myself!," the thought ⟨of⟩ his blessed ones comforts him and he realizes "it is high time." People become disgruntled and *mock* his hopes for the blessed ones. "You don't *want* to help us? Help us achieve our great *revenge*!" You are *hard-hearted* toward unhappy people! — They withdraw.

Mistrust and dread remain with Zarathustra. He sends forth the animals.

31 [9][11]

Zarathustra 4. (Plan.)

1. The honey sacrifice.
2. Superior humans' cry of distress. Flock. (ca. 50 pages)
3. Zarathustra's compassion while at his pinnacle — but hard-hearted; stays true to his mission — "it is not time"

4. Mocking Zarathustra. Withdrawal, while the prophet leaves a stinger in the wound.
5. Sends forth the animals, full of dread.
6. *Seventh solitude: — ending with, "head of the Medusa."* (ca. 40 pages)
7. The saint defeats him. Crisis. Suddenly jumping to his feet. (Sharp contrast with pious *submission*)
8. "To the great outdoors." Song of victory.
9. Lion and flock of doves. Return of the animals (realizes that all of the omens are present). The message.
10. Final farewell from the cave (what is comforting about eternal recurrence shows its face for the first time)

31 [10][12]

1 the man who is restless, who is homeless, who is a wanderer — he who has forgotten how to love his people because he loves many peoples, the good European.[13]

2 the gloomy ambitious son of the people, shy, solitary, willing to do anything, who chooses solitude in order not to be an annihilator — offers himself as a tool[14]

3 the venerator of facts, "the brain of the leech," full of bad conscience due to his excesses, wants to be free of *himself*! The most subtle intellectual conscience[15]

4 the poet, basically lusting to be wildly free, chooses solitude and the *rigor* of knowledge.[16]

5 the ugliest human, who must decorate himself (historical sense) and who is always seeking new garments: he wants to make his appearance tolerable and eventually goes into seclusion in order not to be seen — *he is ashamed of himself.*

6 the inventor of new intoxicants, musician, enchanter, who finally throws himself at the feet of a loving heart and says: *don't come to me*! but rather I want to take you to *that person*!"

7   the wealthy man, who has given everything away and
    asks everyone: "you certainly have some kind of over-
    flow: give me some of it!" as a beggar[17]

8   The kings, renouncing their rule: we seek someone who
    is *more worthy* to rule!"

9   the genius (in a fit of madness) freezing to death because
    of a lack of love "I am not a thought and not even a God"
    — great tenderness "He must be given more love!"[18]

10 the performers of happiness[19]

11 the two kings, against "equality": what is missing is a
    great person and *consequently, reverence*

12 good people
13 pious people   and their delusion
14 those "out for them-   "for God" this is my "for me."[20]
    selves" and saints

need for boundless trust, atheism, theism

                          melancholic-determined

the head of the Medusa[21]

31 [11][22]

Draft.

—The Honey Sacrifice.
—The Cry of Distress.
    Conversation with the Kings.
    The good European — tells stories of accidents at sea.
    The Brain of the Leech.
    The Voluntary Beggar.
    The Enchanter.
    The Ugliest Human Being. (The people.)
—The Welcoming.
—The Last Supper.
—The Song of the Sorcerer.
    On Science.
    On Superior Humans.
—The Rose Speech.
    The Hermit Tells the Story of the Downfall.

On the 7th Solitude.
The One Who Is Freezing to Death.[23]
The Oath.
The last visit to the cave: the frie⟨n⟩ds' message. He sleeps
    there. He gets up in the morning. The laughing lion.
— great transformation and *the hardening of his heart*: in a few
    words. Avoid "I".

18: 110 │ 6
    108 │
    — │

        8
        10 to be done

31 [12][24]

Where do you want to go? he asked aloud, and his voice echoed
back to him sounding strange and transformed. — "I don't know"

And your animals — where are your animals?

Oh Zarathustra, now no one that you love remains alive![25]
— he threw himself to the ground and screamed in pain and
clawed the ground with his hands.

And everything was in vain!

31 [13][26]

When something goes wrong for me: am I a failure for that
reason? And if I myself fail, what part of this is my fault? Are
people failures for that reason?

This is sickness and fever.

31 [14][27]

the laughing lion — "even 2 months ago, seeing this would
have caused my heart to skip a beat

31 [15][28]

You arrived just before I shut the gates to my heart: I still
haven't forgiven you for not wanting to go in until the 11th hour.

31 [16]²⁹

1 Up to the moment when the hermit is completely exposed.

2 From the seventh solitude.

3 Decision, "Do you want all of this one more time, all this waiting etc. — " I *want it*! (Goes gloomily into the night)

In the earliest hours of the morning. The laughing lion, the message, but hard-hearted and severe, yet *glowing*.

31 [17]³⁰

Zarathustra's *heart breaks* when he turns against his friends
            against his animals.
            against everything he has loved
            his entire will turned toward the noon.
    Conclusion: **Dithyrambic heartbreak**

31 [18]

(tell them that I already have new friends —

31 [19]³¹

(you are younger than these children. Is this the second childhood I was told about? Zarathustra 6)

31 [20]³²

And so Zarathustra stood up like a morning sun rising from behind the mountains: strong and glowing, he strode forth — toward the great noon that his will desired, and then descended to his downfall.

31 [21]

But the lion licked up the tears that dropped onto Zarathustra's hands. His heart was deeply moved and changed, but he didn't say a word. Yet it is said that the eagle, jealous, was watching what the lion did etc.

At last Zarathustra got up from the rock on which he had been resting: arose like a morning sun rising from behind the mountains, strong and glowing, heading toward etc.

31 [22]³³
   1   At Midnight.
   2   From the Seventh Solitude.
   3   The Convalescence.
   4   The Oath Written on the Hermit's Hand.
   5   The Friends' Message and the Laughing Lion.

31 [23]³⁴
— The same thing is also witnessed by the lion, but only half
as much: for he is blind in one eye.

31 [24]³⁵
— and they both laughed uproariously. "What do we poets
really know about making ourselves fine and dressing to the
nines! I mean etc.

31 [25]³⁶
— a drive to *self-destruction*: reaching for moments of insight
that rob us of all stability and all strength

31 [26]³⁷
— if you feel that you are subject to the law of pleasure and
displeasure and to *no higher law*: all right then, choose for yourselves the most pleasant and not the most probable opinions:
what's the point of atheism in your case!

31 [27]³⁸
— just as inferior people looked up to God, so too we, with good
reason, should one day *look up to my superhumans*. Zarathustra 6.

31 [28]
— the opposition of atheism and theism is *not*: "truth" and
"untruth," but rather that we don't allow ourselves a hypothesis
anymore, *something which we are happy to allow other people to
have* (even more!) *Piety is the only tolerable attitude in common
people: we want* the people to become religious, so that we no

longer feel disgust in their presence: as is now the case, where the sight of the masses is disgusting.

31 [29]

— we put *ourselves* in a more dangerous position and we would rather surrender to pain, to feeling destitute: our atheism is a *searching* for unhappiness, something which the common people utterly fail to grasp.

31 [30][39]

Noon and Eternity.
By
Friedrich Nietzsche.
First Part: The Temptation of Zarathustra.

31 [31][40]

When the light grows dim, when the dew's comfort is already spilling down upon the earth, unseen, unheard as well —
— for dew the comforter wears delicate footwear,
then do you think back, do you think back, heart aflame, how you once thirsted, for heavenly tears and drops of dew, thirsted, parched, and weary?
— even as, on yellow paths of grass, evening sunbreaks ran around you through black trees, glowing rays of sun, full of malice.
A wooer of truth, you? — that was how they mocked you — No! just a sorcerer! An animal, a sly, thieving, slinking animal that has to lie,
that knowingly, willingly *has to* lie, that has to lust for prey, colorfully masked, becoming a mask to itself, becoming its own prey —
This, a wooer of truth? No! Just a fool! Just a poet! Saying colorful things, screaming colorfully out of fools' masks, climbing around on lying bridges of rainbow dust —
not silent like those people you saw, who were stiff, smooth, cold, turned into statues, turned into pillars for a god, erected in front of temples, gatekeepers of a god —

no, hostile to such monuments of virtue, full of kittenish playfulness, jumping through every window into every chance, more at home in any wilderness than in front of temples,

sniffing longingly after every forest primeval, so that you roamed around licking your chops, like colorful predators sinfully healthy and beautiful, blissfully sneering, blissfully bloodthirsty.

Or like an eagle who for a long time stares unblinking into abysses, into its abysses which circle lower down into ever deeper depths,

then, suddenly, straight in flight, sharp in turn, swooping down upon lambs, down quickly, ravenous, a foe to all lamb souls and to whatever gazes with sheep-like, woolen-curly lamb benevolence:

— and so they are eagle-like, panther-like, the yearnings of the sorcerer, your yearnings under a thousand masks, you fool! you poet!

You who have viewed humans as gods and sheep: to tear apart the god in humans and the sheep in humans and *laughing* as you do it —

This, This is your bliss! Bliss of a panther and of an eagle! Bliss of a sorcerer and of a fool! — —

When the light grows dim, when the sickle of the moon is already creeping green with envy between purple reds,

— an enemy to the day, with every step secretly bringing its sickle down on hammocks of roses until they fall sinking, pale, downward into night: —

thus I myself once sank, out of my truth-inflamed madness, out of my daytime yearnings, tired of the day, sick from the light — sank downward, into evening, into shadow,

burned by one truth and thirsty: — do you still think back, do you think back, heart aflame, to how you thirsted then? —

that I be banned from *all* truth! Just a fool! Just a poet! — —

31 [32]⁴¹

Who keeps me warm, who still loves me? Give me hot hands, give me a heart of glowing coal!

Stretched out, shuddering, like a half-dead man whose feet are being warmed, shaken, alas! by unknown fevers, shivering from sharp, icy arrows of frost —

hunted by you, my thought![42] Unnameable, shrouded, creative! You hunter behind clouds!

Struck down by you, you sudden eye, that gazes at me out of the darkness

— and so I lie here, turning, twisting, tormented by all eternal tortures, struck by you, most cruel eternal hunter, you unknown god!

Strike deeper! Strike yet again! Sting this heart to ribbons, break this heart to pieces! What's the point of this torture with arrows like worn teeth?

Why are you looking at me again with gods' lightning eyes that delight in suffering, not yet tired of human torment? So you don't want to kill? Only to torture, to torture?

You who even at night sneak toward me, jealously, you hear me breathing, listen to my heart, you climb into my dreams,

throwing sharpened doubts and arrows into my dreams, stinging my heart: ever ready executioner-god, for what!

Torture *me* for what? What do you think you'll gain by torture? What do you want me to say?

Or should I roll around in front of you like a dog, submitting, eager, out of my mind with love for you, wagging my tail?

There's no point! Keep stinging me, most cruel stinger! No, not a dog — I am merely your prey, most cruel hunter!

Your proudest prisoner, you robber behind clouds! Say something, what do you want from me, you who lie in wait, —

You who are veiled in lightning, unknown one, speak, you who are my thought: what do you *want*, unknown — god? — ?

What are you saying? Ransom? What kind of ransom do you want? Demand a lot — that's what my pride advises. And keep it short — that's what my other pride advises!

Haha! You want me? Me — all of me? Haha! And you torture me, fool that you are, you stretch my pride out on the rack?

Give me *love* — who still keeps me warm, who still loves me! Give me hot hands, give me a heart of glowing coal —

give to me, the loneliest one of all, for whom cold itself is a teacher of longing for the enemy — give to me, yes, most cruel enemy, surrender — *yourself*!

— Ha! Gone! Then he fled, he himself, my only, my last companion! my great enemy! My unknown one! My executioner-god!

No! come back, with all your tortures! To the last of all the lonely ones — oh come back!

all the streams of my tears are tracing a path to you! And the last ember of my heart — sets them aglow for you! Oh come back, my unknown god! My ultimate happiness! — —

31 [33][43]

— like a shepherd looking across the backs of teeming sheepherds: an ocean of gray small swarming waves.

— with gnashing teeth I crash against the shore of your flatness, with gnashing teeth, like a wild wave, when, against its will, it bites into the sand —

— mawkish flattering dogs

— compliant, lusting, forgetful: none of them are very far from being whores.

— excited about green vegetables, and averse to the joys of meat

— these things are subtle: how is it that you are allowed to grab for them with your sheep's hooves? Every word does not belong in every mouth: but alas for this sick, languishing time! Alas for the great plague of hoof-and-mouth disease.

— Empty, cave, full of night-winged things, sung about and feared everywhere

— "these poets! they are still putting on makeup even when they show themselves naked to their doctors!" (And since Zarathustra did not say no to this, but smiled, behold, in an instant the poet was already holding his harp in his arms and opened his mouth wide for a new song.

— a green flash of malice sprang from his eyes, he opened his mouth and closed it again.

— the evening comes over the ocean: riding closer on heavy green waves, it sways, full of longing, in its purple saddles —

— leaning against the earth, like a ship wearily entering its quiet bay: all it takes is for a spider to spin its thread from the land over to it, no stronger ropes are needed!

31 [34]⁴⁴
— "Oh my animals! My great happiness makes me spin around! I already have to dance, — so that I don't fall over!

— they lie on their bellies in front of small round facts, they kiss the dust and the filth at their feet: and still rejoice: "Here at last is reality!"⁴⁵

— you speak to me of your hope? But does it not have stubby legs and squinty eyes? Is it not always looking around the corner to see whether despair isn't already waiting there?

— And which one of you still stands by your day after tomorrow? Which one of you — is still *allowed* to swear oaths? Which one of you will stay in one house and one mindset for five more years?⁴⁶

— people are evil: this is what all the wisest sages say in order to comfort me: oh, if only this were still true today!

why did I really climb up here to these heights! Didn't I eventually want to see a great p⟨erson⟩? And look over there, I find a jolly old man

— crumbling graves that can no longer hold their dead. Alas, there will soon be resurrections happening there!

— on honey: "I don't need you, but I received you as one of life's gifts: as someone who receives, I consecrate you

— that a bolt of lightning would strike their feed and their maws would learn to feed on fire!⁴⁷

31 [35]⁴⁸
— steadfast and, like a peasant, as crude as he is cunning
— people of "good will"? Unreliable

— ask women: having a good time is not the point of giving birth!

— we are punished most severely for our virtues."[49]

— "it is cool, the moon is shining, there is not a cloud in the sky: there is no point in living, oh Zarathustra!"[50]

— Many grew weary of themselves: and behold, only then did happiness come to them, the happiness that had awaited them since the very beginning."[51]

— For am I the meteorological divide? Yet all clouds come to me and want information —

— I gather myself together like a growing cloud and I become stiller and darker: this is what all people do who are about to give birth to lightning bolts.

— "you want to warm yourselves on me? Don't come too close to me, that's my advice to you: — otherwise you will singe your hands. I mean, look, I am overheated. I am struggling to hold my flames in check lest they break out of my body."

— Your paws have been bound, you scratching cat, now you can't scratch and you are giving me poisonous looks with your green eyes![52]

— with shriveled, flashing swords which have hung thirstily on the wall for too long: they glitter with desire, they would like to drink blood again

— and the swords ran through one another like red speckled snakes

— I listened for an echo, alas! and I heard only praise.[53]

31 [36][54]

— Do as I do, learn as I learn: only those who do, learn.

— there is more injustice in admiration than in contempt

Enchanter — I already know how to put colorful saddle blankets on you: and anyone who knows horses also knows how to saddle up.

— and if you have a grudge against the heavens, throw your stars up into the heavens — : let that be the extent of your malice!

— isn't the world standing still even now? This stillness surrounds me as if with terrible coils![55]

— you knew how to cloak yourselves well, you poets!

— he has let himself be overcome by virtue: and now everything that is bad in him is taking revenge for it.

— you are blind here, for this is the point where your honesty ceases[56]

— I listened for an echo, but I heard only praise[57]

— he threw himself down from his heights, he was seduced by a love for his inferiors —: now he lies there with broken limbs[58]

— he talks a lot about himself, that was his trick for concealing himself.

— Hail! How was it that the truth triumphed here for once? A serious error came to its aid.[59]

— he left me indifferent, he did not make me fertile

— human beings are so inadequate! They tell me they themselves love themselves: alas, even this love is so inadequate![60]

— with these swords I still slash my way through every darkness![61]

31 [37][62]

— and anyone who has given birth is sick.

—all of you who create, there is much that is unclean about you: it's because you must be mothers.

— pain makes hens and poets cluck

— a new child, a new piece of dirt. And all who have given birth should cleanse themselves.

— on the stilts of his pride[63]

— as when oil and water are shaken up together[64]

— whatever lives around you soon becomes part of what lives in us.[65]

— self-sufficient people — you must learn to take a stand or you will fall over.

— I myself set this crown on my head: no other hand was strong enough to do it

— with thieves' eyes, no matter if they are already wallowing in wealth. And some of them I call rag-pickers and vultures.[66]

— all great things take crooked paths toward their goals and arch their backs and purr with happiness like cats. Look and see if you would have the courage to flow crookedly like a great river.

— your virtue is the caution of a pregnant woman: you protect and spare your holy fruit and future.

—a shipwreck spat him out on land again[67]

Enchanters — you will soon learn to pray again. The ancient counterfeiters of the mind have even made counterfeits of your intellect.

31 [38][68]

— he no longer knows where to go? on land it is raining fire, and the ocean spits him back on land.[69]

— carefree, like a man who is secretly enjoying his death in advance[70]

— only those who know where they are going also know what wind is at their back

— when the devil sheds his skin, his name also falls away: it, too, is skin.

— that which is maternal honors me. The father is always merely a matter of chance.

— don't forget to take your solitude along with you into a crowd[71]

— you wanted to be their light, but you have blinded them. It was your sun that gouged out their eyes.

— now the underworld roars, all the shades bear witness against you and cry out: life — this is torture! — and still you want to be an advocate for life?

— leering eyes and other favorite delicacies of bilious souls[72]

— wherever I see light fingers at work, I prefer to draw the short straw[73]

— the devil keeps his distance from God, for the devil is a friend of knowledge.[74]

— blissful and whimsical, like an elephant trying to stand on its head.

— it is not enough that lightning doesn't do more damage: it needs to learn to do my bidding.

31 [39]⁷⁵

— he convinces them that they have lost their way — this flatterer! It flatters them that they might have a way at all.⁷⁶

— he has lost his goal: it's too bad that he will trivialize his loss and get over it!

enchanter — that you strive for greatness reveals who you are: you are not great.

— the deepest love, which doesn't know its name and asks: "am I not hatred?"

— dead in life, concealed, buried, hidden: oh Zarathustra, how many times will you rise again!⁷⁷

— that has been explained:⁷⁸ now it doesn't concern me anymore. Beware! sometimes you can be enlightened about too many things!

— those who are not free reserve their deepest hatred for the new spirit, not the free spirit.

— oh happiness, I passed through hate and love until I reached the surface of my self: for too long I was hanging in the depths like all heavy and heavy-hearted people⁷⁹

— I slept in for a long time in order to stay awake — longer.

— extraordinarily unjust, because they want justice for all⁸⁰

— he is justified in brooding for so long on his misfortune: a beautiful bird lies hidden in this ugly egg.⁸¹

— he would like the constellations of his virtue to shine at last: to achieve this, he darkened his mind and he hung a new night up ahead of himself.⁸²

— as clumsy as a corpse⁸³

— "and the four animals said: Amen"

31 [40][84]

— Even the most saintly people think: "I want to live as I wish — or I don't wish to live anymore."

— those of you who are super-wealthy, you are like wide-bottomed bottles who drip out of all-too-narrow necks: bottles like these have already had their necks broken many times, beware!

— a small act of charity sparks outrage, whereas even the greatest act of charity is forgiven.

— I will finally make a wish in the place where I have always felt fear! Ultimately, we learn to *love* our abysses!

— what I find most astonishing about sages is that they are occasionally clever.

— blissful and tired, like every creator on the seventh day

— *Europeans* — where can I be at home? I was searching for this for the longest time, this searching keeps hitting home with me.

— "we come to see the happiest man of the century"[85]

— he is unshakeable; and if he complains, he does so more as a concession to you than to himself.

— his hard-heartedness cloaked by an affable manner

— even brawling is preferable to brokers![86]

— they say of him: "he is climbing"; but he is *being pushed* like a ball into his heights by you — by your gathering storm and mine; what makes him climb is that he suffers because of you.[87]

— even ambition is strangled here; they take more pleasure in being last than in being first.[88]

31 [41][89]

— you forgot those who are yet to come when you made your calculations: you forgot the happiness of the greatest number.[90]

— now no one that I love is left alive: how can I still live with myself!

— in virtue there is only leaping and flying: in virtue no one should —

— he sought his enemy and found his friend

— you corpse-robbers, you who know how to steal something else from all these dead people!

— to give your will some backbone

— to the God-murderer, to the seducer of good people[91]

— full of deep mistrust, overgrown with the moss of solitude, a far-reaching will, a taciturn man, the enemy of all lustful people —[92]

— and anyone who had (the deepest) bottomless contempt for them, was it not for this reason that this person was their greatest benefactor?

— "there is less feeling for justice in her head than in my little finger"[93]

— mistrustful and ulcerous, capable of sudden willfulness, a lurker and an eavesdropper

— I didn't want it before; so I have to really want it afterwards — I must therefore "make good" on everything.[94]

— you cages and miserly souls,[95] how can you want to be free spirits![96]

you smoke-filled chambers and musty rooms[97]

intellectually conscientious people — they are not burned at the stake from within for what they believe, but rather because they couldn't find any desire to have these beliefs[98]

31 [42][99]

— so do I love human beings? But they are part of my work.

— oh you sages who learned to rejoice about your stupidity! Oh you poor, narrow-minded, superfluous people whose yoke is light![100] Em⟨erson⟩[101] 283

— yet, as the old man spoke in this way, Zarathustra reached for his hand, which trembled, and kissed it "Depart from me, my tempter,"[102] he said then and smiled — for a playful memory came to him in the middle of his pain.

— the substitute teachers and other blowflies.[103]

— miserly souls, huckster-souls! For when money jumps into the till, the soul of the huckster jumps in with it.[104]

— gluttons or nibblers of knowledge

— where gold jingles, where whores rule[105]

— money and money changers should be handled with gloves: and everything that changes hands all the time.

— most people are too dumb to be self-interested

— any love at all drives them crazy; they sacrifice everything for a single thing

— if you want to buy these people, don't offer too little: for then they will say "No" and walk away swollen with enhanced virtue, as "incorruptible people."[106]

— my friend, virtue has nothing to do with "in order to" and "because" and "so that"; it doesn't understand such petty phrases.

31 [43][107]

— you puny poets and sluggards, anyone who has nothing to create will be occupied by nothing![108]

— light on his feet and willing, a man who is ready to fly, a man who is divinely light-hearted

— what I have to do to you, you *cannot* do to me in return: there is no paying it back![109]

— solitude makes us ripe: but it doesn't plant anything.[110]

— they are pursuing me? All right then, that's how they learn to follow me. Until now, all success has come to those who have been successfully pursued.

— I run lightly across you and move on, like glancing quickly at slime

— he saw my deepest disgrace, I want to have my revenge on this witness and no one else

— God, who saw everything, had to die: humans could not bear to have this witness live.

— an easily embarrassed man, who has to be forced and chastised into doing what he would most like to do.[111]

— impatient like an actor: someone who has no time to wait for justice

— you strong persons, now even you are gazing lustfully at the virtues of the weak: but you should show discipline and pass these pretty maids by!

— you don't even feel that you are dreaming: oh, in such a state you are still far from waking up![112]

— Am I not the meteorological divide? Don't all winds come to me and ask me for my yes and no?

31 [44][113]

man of the people — he strives for what is forbidden:[114] this is the origin of all of his virtue.

— you are riding quickly enough to your goal: but your lame foot is mounted alongside you. When you jump down from the horse — there, precisely at your zenith, is where you will stumble!

— this is how I recognize people who are superabundant: they thank those who take from them.[115]

— lonely days want to walk on valiant feet[116]

— a new spring season wells up in all of my branches, it is called convalescence. I hear the voice of the south wind and feel ashamed: the shame of my newly found happiness lusts for dark thick leaves.

— swimming in fairness and generosity, rejoicing in their stupidity and in the fact that happiness on earth is such a bargain[117]

— dried-out emptied souls, mud on the ground, and sandy riverbeds[118]

homeless people — how even a prison feels safe to restless people! How imprisoned criminals sleep like babies![119]

enchanters — the kind of people who are convinced by sublime gestures but made mistrustful by reasoned arguments

— their brains and private parts easily aroused, like the Jews and the Chinese

— your religious faith, with God's adultery standing at its threshold

— you are following me too closely, intrusively, and on my heels: when you least expect it, I will someday kick your heads in (says the truth to those who are intellectually conscientious)

— the sun of your peace always seems too hot and humid for me: I prefer to sit in the shadow of my swords

31 [45][120]

— like a wind that makes all skies bright and all oceans roar.

— whirling here and there, driven here and there, you restless people; you have slept on every surface at one time or another, you sat like dust on all mirrors and window panes

— he is singing: then he probably flew away, even beyond his misfortune, the f⟨ree⟩ bird? Because the unfortunate man is silent.

— give me a riddle to solve: you will wear down my intellect's hunger with your proo⟨fs⟩.

— they invented for themselves the holiest kind of boredom and the lust for Moon-days and workdays

— terrible things are circling and turning here, here is where the abyss opens wide, here is where the hound of hell that we call the future is baying, here the wisest soul succumbs to vertigo.

— you prisoners of prosperity, do your thoughts not rattle like cold chains?

— boring men, deprived of women, poorly nourished, contemplating their navels and counting their breaths: what better thing could they have invented than God's desire?

— to walk around amidst the most distant and coldest thoughts, like a ghost on icy winter roofs, at the time when the moon lies down in the snow

— someone whose enemies have little to atone for: for he starts laughing again too soon.

— anyone who is completely at home[121] with virtue speaks to it in more familiar, more mocking terms.[122]

31 [46]¹²³

Zarathustra: we must view our God from a distance: that's the only way he looks good. That's why the devil keeps his distance from God, for the devil is a friend of beautiful illusions.

31 [47]¹²⁴
The Enchanter.

on my knees worshiping virtues and renunciations, like the rabble, yet especially worshipping extreme chastity: I prayed in front of it and threw myself to the ground.

Whatever was foreign to me, whatever ⟨I⟩ was not allowed to know, I called holy: my nose most preferred the smell of that which was impossible for me

Zarathustra says: Much of the rabble may well reside within you: whoever feels completely at home there speaks in more familiar, more mocking terms

31 [48]¹²⁵

— these ponderous anguished people, whose conscience makes them grunt: this is because the animal within them always makes them suffer.

— under cloudy skies, when we are shooting arrows and murderous thoughts at our enemies

— more thoughtful times, more overanalyzed times than our todays and yesterdays

— these times: are they not like an ailing woman who must rant scream rage and break plates and tables so that she can finally find peace again?¹²⁶

— stubborn minds, cunning and petty

— oh how sad you all are! Oh how sad your jesters still are!

— you who despair, how much you embolden all those who speak to you!

— things are worse than you think: many people believed they were lying and, behold, only then did they hit on the truth!

— you are too prosperous, oh Zarathustra, you corrupt too many, you make us all envious!

— they love, alas! and are not loved; they tear themselves to pieces because no one wants to embrace them. "So there is nothing about me that is worth loving?" is what their despair is screaming.

— this is the inclination of puny souls: they would like to flatter greatness until it shrinks down to their size, so that it will sit with them at the table.

31 [49]¹²⁷

— alas, they fall back on big words and weak deeds! Alas, they call themselves virtuous again!

— once upon a time they created their God out of nothing: it is no wonder that he came to mean nothing to them

— you say "Alas! everything is an illusion!" But everything is a lie. You say: "Everything is suffering and downfall!" But you never say enough: for everything wants to cause suffering and bring about downfalls!

— lacking God, lacking goodness, lacking good minds — we have created him, the ugliest of all humans!

— alas, my brothers! Where did goodness and the faith of good people go! Where did the innocence of all of these lies go!

— clumsy and shy like a tiger after a pounce gone awry.¹²⁸

— he forgot how to eat meat and how to play with pretty little women, he grieves too deeply

— once — : alas, how distant is this once! how sweet the word "once" is, like the lost tolling of bells in thick forests —

— yes, humans, humans — this is a long rope, and Zarathustra is the name of the knot that is tied into it! (the prophet)

a fable — how a wanderer who dreams of distant things unexpectedly encounters a sleeping dog on a deserted street: both move toward each other like deadly enemies, these two who have been startled to death! And yet if truth be told: they were so close to stroking and petting one another!

— the day fades away, it is time and well past time that we depart

31 [50][129]
— thistle-heads, scrupulous saps
— hasty, like jumping spider monkeys
— between coffins and sawdust
— dizzy dogs and sickly breeds all around me
— a cold bath: do you want to go in there with your head and heart? Oh, before you know it, you'll be standing there like a red crab!
— industrious, faithful people for whom the day flows up evenly, like gleaming gold
— surrounded by dawning eternities, and unclouded silence above me.
— who gives wings to asses and turns his accusers into advocates, who milks lionesses
— the waves around me are rising higher and higher: soon my boat will no longer rest on dry land.
— you have bound me with chains, but executioners and torturers are arguments that are most convincing when we are gagged[130]
— they don't think much of me: they are taking revenge for the fact that I wanted to make them greater!
— at an hour when no shepherd plays the flute: for noon is sleeping on the meadows.
— a woman who wants whatever she loves to make her suffer
— voluntary beggar — that old sly piety that said "giving to the poor means lending to God:[131] be good bankers!"
And if I shared your faith, then I would also want a share in your transformation.
for his will demanded the great noon and demanded his downfall

31 [51][132]

— you call me someone who makes sacrifices? But those who have ever made sacrifices know that these were not sacrifices they made.

— a monster of overflow and reason, a squanderer with a thousand hands, oblivious to what he is doing, like a sun

— there once was one man who said: "I am the truth," and an immodest man has never received a more polite answer than he did.

Poets — my mind and my yearning are concerned with what is rare and enduring: what contempt I have for your puny brief moments of beauty![133]

— "nothing is true, everything is permitted,"[134] that's how you talk? alas! therefore even if this phrase is true, who cares whether it is permitted!

— to speak through pictures dances tones and silences: and for what purpose would the whole world be there if not to be used as signs and similes!

— there they stand, the heavy granite cats, the values of ancient times: who has the power to topple them![135]

— great persons, the kind of people who throw away their compassion and know how to destroy their sense of fairness[136] for the sake of their cause: those who dare and induce themselves to sacrifice many people and many things so that they might flourish —

— set up as a pillar in the desert of great misfortune, turned rigid fixed and stony[137]

— quiet in his golden-brown sorrow, like a man who tasted too many good things[138]

— my kingdom of rulers, lasting a thousand years, my *hazar*[139] —

— don't you know that? The history of everything that has happened is repeated and abbreviated in every action you perform,

their meaning is a counter-meaning, their wit is a yes-but-wit[140]

31 [52]¹⁴¹

— jealous even in your hatred: you want to have your enemy all to yourself!

— how little attraction knowledge would hold if there weren't so much shame to be overcome on the way to acquiring it!¹⁴²

— you love utility as the vehicle of your inclinations: but isn't the noise of its wheels unbearable, even for you?¹⁴³

— their stride reveals whether people are already on their way: and those who are nearing their goals are dancing.

— you speak of your loyalty: but your complacent nature is what keeps you from getting out of bed.

— you have become enamored of your virtue: so don't even call it virtue anymore, but rather call it your taste — for that is what good taste requires!

— but Zarathustra, said the snake, you clever man, how could you act that way! That was stupid! — "It hasn't been easy for me either."

— your evil conscience within you: this is the voice of your most ancient of ancient forebears speaking to you. "Original sin," my friend, this is certainly proof of your original virtue.

—you blather on about the pinnacle of feelings! At my pinnacle I feel profound and solid and finally on my foundation and home soil.

— born teachers, those who take everything seriously only for the sake of their students, including themselves.¹⁴⁴

— being intelligent is not enough: we must take control of this intelligence, and this takes a lot of courage.¹⁴⁵

31 [53]¹⁴⁶

— now about the bizarre and cruel God whom you praise as "love"! when *that* God came into existence wasn't all love probably still less than divine?

— cold cool people, we don't want to believe they are capable of foolishness

— those who are fundamentally willing and well, they even love jumping sideways: but pity all the absolutists! they are a sick species.

— isn't praise more intrusive than any blame?

— at some point you learned to believe this without any arguments: how could I ever hope to overturn this for you by using arguments!

— "I love my God from the bottom of my heart: how could I ever be allowed to want him to love me back! He *mustn't* be so foolish as to believe in me! how all lovers act.

— those of you who are delirious with fever see all things as ghosts, and those of you who are free of fever see them as empty shadows: and yet you both use the same words!

— my memory says: "I did that," but my pride says in response: "I *couldn't* have done that" and remains adamant. In the end — memory gives in!147

— he looks at things with cold eyes, free of tears, each and every thing lies before him plucked naked and colorless: and now you claim that his inability to lie is "love of truth!"

— you have been a poor observer of life if you haven't yet seen someone who with gentle hands — *kills*!148

— he stirs, looks around, runs his hand through his hair— and now you call him someone who knows! But being free of fever is still a long way from knowing.

31 [54]149

— the one who knows in this day and age, who teaches: once upon a time God wanted to become an animal: behold, that's what a human being is: — a god as animal!150

— great love doesn't want to reciprocate and requite, requitement has drowned in the ocean of great love.

— learn this from me, once and for all: "every bad thing has its good sides."

— all you people who are drowning, you think I don't know what you wanted to do here? to cling to a strong swimmer, which is what I myself am.

— do you think I wanted to make things easier for superior humans and to show them easier paths? More and more of your kind will have to perish, and I myself want to get better and better at learning to laugh about this

— you would drag the strongest person down into the depths with you: this is how blindly and brainlessly you are grabbing for someone to save you!

— I have learned to see greater calamity and your screaming doesn't ruin my mood.

— what do I care about your misery! My sin would be called: compassion for you!

— do you think I am here to make up for what you've done wrong?

— now I am casting with my golden fishing rod far out into this dark ocean: its whirring hook bites into the belly of the ocean's misery.

— now I am casting my lure out for the most bizarre human fishes, now I want to have my golden-brown laughter concerning everything down there that is born misshapen and twisted

— open up, you unclean womb of human foolishness! You abysmal ocean, throw me your most colorful denizens and glistening crabs

31 [55][151]

You wretches and freaks, what would I care about your misery if it didn't give me so much to laugh about! Compassion for you — : this would be the name of the one sin remaining to me

you drowning people, do you think I don't know what you wanted from me up here at my pinnacle: the ocean is sucking you down: now you want to cling to a strong swimmer?

And truly, you are grabbing so blindly and wildly with your arms and legs for someone to save you that you would drag even the strongest man down into your depths!

And now I am laughing at that, a strong swimmer who is no longer reaching out even his little finger toward you: since, if you were to grab hold of it, you would also take my hand and heart as well.

This is what is immodest about you, that you live, want to live, even if I were to perish immediately because of you

31 [56][152]
"You kings and you, the one ass!"

31 [57][153]
Zarathustra's hair becoming black (lion and flock of doves)

31 [58][154]
— a yearning went running through the land and knocked on the doors of all the hermits and said "is Zarathustra still alive, then?"

31 [59]
— Someone who asks good questions already has half the answer.[155]

31 [60]
— We must have eyes even in the back of our heads![156]

31 [61][157]
Conversation with the Kings
— "I see kings before me: but I am seeking superior humans."

— With the sword of these words you are hacking away the darkness of our hearts

— we *are* not ranked first among the people and have to pretend to be: we have finally grown sick and tired of this disgusting fraud.

— learn this from me, once and for all: "every bad thing has two good sides."

— oh Zarathustra, you have a better sense of justice in your little finger than she has in her entire head.[158]

—ambition is strangled when you're part of that kind of rabble: here, among these people, someone takes more pleasure in *pretending to be* last than to be first."[159]

— someone who asks good questions already has half the answer.[160] —

— look here, how this came to be and had to come to be: we must have eyes even in the back of our heads![161]

— extraordinarily unjust, since they want justice for all[162]

— steadfast and, like a peasant, as crude as he is cunning

— they cling to laws and they would like to call laws "solid ground": for they are tired of danger, but basically they are seeking a great human being, a helmsman, in whose presence the laws would nullify themselves

— the great plague of hoof-and-mouth disease — subtle things — they grab for them with their sheep's hooves. Not every word belongs in every mouth.

mawkish flattering dogs, when they revere something

their women: compliant, lusting, forgetful — none of them are very far from being whores.

And which one of them still stands by their day after tomorrow? Which one of them — is still *allowed* to swear oaths and make promises? Which one of them will stay in one house and one mindset for five more years?[163]

people of good will, but unreliable and lusting for new things, these cages and ungenerous hearts, these smoke-filled chambers and musty rooms — they want to be free spirits![164] —

they feel their rabble-roots in body and soul and they would like to hide this ⟨and⟩ dress and cloak themselves in nobility: ⟨they⟩ call it education — they pursue it with great zeal

they talk of happiness of the greatest number and sacrifice all future people for their sake[165]

they have their virtue, they cannot be bought at any price. Don't offer too little, otherwise they will say "No!" and walk away swollen, strengthened in their virtue. "We are the incorruptible ones!"[166]

the substitute teachers and other blowflies[167]

and often they are like easily embarrassed women, who have to ⟨be⟩ forced and chastised into doing what they would most like to do.[168]

— the sun of his peace seems humid and stale to me: I still prefer to sit in the shadow of swords that have been swung.[169]

— swimming in fairness and mercy, enjoying their stupidity and the fact that happiness on earth is such a bargain[170]

31 [62][171]

The Last Supper.

Thus spoke the king, and they all approached Zarathustra and again paid their respects to him; but Zarathustra shook his head and restrained them with his hand.

"Welcome here! he spoke to his guests. I bid you welcome anew, you strange people! Even my animals greet you, full of honor and full of awe: for they have never before seen such distinguished guests!

Yet you are no small danger to me — that's what my animals whisper to me. 'Keep an eye on these despairing ones!' says the snake in my bosom to me; — forgive this anxious caution that comes from their love for me!

My snake speaks secretly to me of drowning people: the ocean sucks them under — when they would most like to cling to a strong swimmer.

And truly, drowning people blindly and wildly grab with their arms and legs for someone of good will who can rescue them, they drag even the strongest person down into their depths with them. Are you — drowning like that?

I am already stretching out my little finger toward you. Woe is me! Now what will you take from me and grab for yourselves!" —

Thus spoke Zarathustra, with a laugh full of malice and love, even as he stroked the neck of his eagle with his hand: for *his eagle* stood next to him, bristling, as if the eagle were going to defend Zarathustra against his guests. But then he stretched out his hand to the king on his right, that this king should kiss it, and began anew, more heartily than before: — — —

31 [63][172]

> *The Last Supper.*
> *The Song of the One who Laughs.*
>
> *The Welcoming.*
> *The Last Supper.*
> *The Improvisation.*
> *The Rose Speech.*

31 [64][173]

Yet when Zarathustra found his guests happily conversing together again, he left them and stepped quietly out of his cave. "They are happy, I have healed them, he spoke to his heart: this day that began so badly wants to end well! The evening is already approaching over the ocean, riding closer it sways, full of longing, in its purple saddles. The clear sky looks on, the world is lying in the depths: oh all of you strange people, you who came to me, you were right in doing so: living with me already has its rewards!" —

Thus spoke Zarathustra to his heart, and he grew more and more quiet: yet in the meantime one after another of the guests had stepped out of the cave; and what they saw out there finally moved every one of them to be quiet. They stood next to each other, mutely reaching out their hands and looking outward: but then out of the depths there secretly came the sound of that ancient heavy tolling bell, that midnight bell of Zarathustra's, whose strokes he loved to count and to accompany with rhyming songs until the last stroke, and this time, too, the bell tolled, heavily laden with pleasure and woe: — then all their hearts shivered.

Yet Zarathustra, who had already grasped everything, spoke with malice as well as love, without looking at them, more like someone who was only speaking to himself, not very loudly, but clearly enough: "Oh please do look upon these despairing people for my sake! Oh please do look upon these despairing people for my sake!"

— Yet as soon as his guests heard these words, they all at once became aware of their transformation and convalescence: then they laughed at themselves and all of them sprang toward Zarathustra, thanking him, revering and loving or kissing his hands, each according to his custom: so that some were even crying. Yet the prophet danced with pleasure; and even if he, as some think, was filled with sweet wine back then, he was surely also filled with sweet life and had renounced all weariness with life. Zarathustra noticed how the prophet was dancing and pointed it out: but then all at once he tore himself away from the crowd of those who were thanking and loving him and took refuge up on a steep crag onto which he ascended a few steps, in the process ripping out a few roses and rose bushes. Looking down from this height and, as was just said, with roses in his hands, he began to speak for the last time that evening: looking down on this crowd of despairing men, who were no longer doubting, of drowning men, who were standing on good, solid land, he laughed with all of his heart, wove the roses into a garland and delivered the speech which is called:

The Rose Speech.

This crown of the one who laughs, this rose-garland-crown: I myself set this crown on my head, I myself sanctified my laughter. I have found no one else today who is strong enough to do it.

Nevertheless, it is good that you came up to my pinnacle to see *this*! How grateful I am for your care and yearning that climbed mountains and posed a well-placed question: "Is Zarathustra still alive, then?"

Someone who asks good questions already has half the answer. And, truly, one very good answer is what you could only be seeing here with your own eyes: Zarathustra is still alive and more so than ever:

— Zarathustra the dancer, Zarathustra, who is light on his feet, who is flapping his wings, who is ready to fly, who waves to all the birds, ready and willing, divinely light-hearted — I myself set this crown on my head!

— Zarathustra the prophet, Zarathustra the one who is silent about the truth,[174] not impatient, not an absolutist, someone who loves leaping and jumping sideways — I myself set this crown on my head!

Stir me into the mix of all earthly tears and all human misery: I will always emerge on top again like oil on water.

And if at times I have a grudge against the earth: my malice will tear the stars out of the heavens and bring them down to earth — that is the nature of all Zarathustra-revenge.

And even if there are moors and melancholy on earth and entire oceans of scummy slime: anyone who is light on his feet still runs over slime — as quickly as over cleanly swept ice.

And if I need enemies and if I am often my own worst enemy: enemies have little to atone for with me, after every storm I start laughing again too quickly

And although I had already been in many deserts and in desert wilderness: I did not become one of the desert saints, I am not still standing there rigid, dull, stony, a pillar: rather — I stride forward.

The stride reveals whether someone is already striding down *his* path. So look at me go! But all those who are closing in on their goals, they — are dancing!

All good things approach their goals on crooked paths and arch their backs like cats, inwardly they purr at their approaching happiness: all good things laugh!

Here on earth, what has been the greatest sin up to now? These were *the words* of the one who said: "Woe to those who are laughing here!"

Couldn't he find any reasons to laugh, here on earth itself? Then he wasn't very good at seeking: even a child would find reasons to laugh here. Oh, if he had only found — himself!

He — did not love enough, otherwise he still would have loved even us, the ones who laugh. But he hated us and could only mock us; he promised us wailing and gnashing of teeth,[175] the ones who laugh!

Wherever he was not loved, this absolutist, that is where he wanted to get right to work, to boiling people alive and burning them. He himself did not love enough: otherwise he wouldn't have craved so much that — *he* be loved.

Avoid crossing paths with all such absolutists! They are a poor sick species, a rabble species. They look askance at life, they have heavy feet and hearts.

Lift up your hearts, my brothers, high! higher! but don't forget your legs either when you think of me! Lift your legs higher, too, you skillful dancers, and better still: even stand on your heads!

There are animals who are heavy even when it comes to happiness, there are those who are clodhoppers from the start. In a strange way, they try their hardest, these blissful people, like elephants trying to stand on their heads.

Yet even better to be foolish when we're happy than when we're unhappy! Better to dance clumsily than to walk lamely! So learn my wisdom from me: "Every bad thing has two good sides."

So learn from me to leave behind the doldrums and all night-watchman's melancholy! Oh how sad these jesters still seem to me today! This today belongs to the rabble: so learn from me to leave behind this — today!

Make me like the wind that plunges down out of its mountain caves. It wants to dance to its own pipes, the oceans are trembling and skipping in time with its dancing feet.

The one who gives wings to donkeys, who milks lionesses: please honor this unruly good spirit, who comes like a storm-wind to all todays and to all rabble, —

— who is an enemy to thistleheads and ditherheads and to all small surly weeds, this wild brisk free storm-wind that blows sand in the eyes of all those people who have trouble seeing, who see things darkly through abscessed eyes:

— who hates dizzy rabble-dogs and all botched wispy breeds: for my sake, honor this spirit of all free spirits, this laughing storm that dances across oceans and miseries as if they were meadows.

Away, away now, you hunter's game and gang of misfits! Who are you really speaking about? Fly far away, you brisk roaring wind! Fly away like a cry and a rejoicing across wide oceans, until you find the isles of the blessed —

— greet my children on their islands, bring them the greetings of a neighbor of the sun, a neighbor of the snow, a neighbor of eagles, bring them their father's love as a greeting!

My children, my well-born brood, my new beautiful species: why do my children *hesitate* on their islands?

Wasn't it getting to be time and high time — then blow into their ears, you brisk storm-spirit — so that they finally will come to their father? Am I not waiting for my children as someone whose hair has grown white, like that of an old man?

Away, away, you unruly fair storm-wind! Plunge down out of your mountain caves into the ocean, make haste and bless my children before the evening comes —

bless them with my happiness, with this rose-garland happiness! Strew these roses down over their islands, like a question mark that asks: "Where did such happiness come from?"

— until they learn to ask: "Is our father still alive? What did you say, is our father Zarathustra still alive? Does our old father Zarathustra still love his children?"

Use my greatest happiness to entice my children to come to me! Lure them up to my faithful golden-brown father's yearning! Drizzle on them the honey of an endlessly lasting love from a father's heart!!

The wind blows, the wind blows, the moon shines, — oh my distant, distant children, why do you not abide here, with your father? The wind blows, there is not a cloud in the sky, the world sleeps. — Oh happiness! Oh happiness!

Yet no sooner had Zarathustra spoken these words, than his heart was deeply moved: for he noticed, as he looked down at his feet, that he was utterly alone. He had forgotten his guests — had his guests also forgotten him? "Where are you? Where are you?" Zarathustra called out into the night: but the night was silent. —

"Where are you? Where are you, my animals?" Zarathustra called out into the night once again. But even his animals remained silent — —

31 [65][176]
The Song of the Sorcerer.
On Science.
The Rose Speech.

31 [66]
Those who are happy are curious.

31 [67]
And if you call me your lord and master: then I want to let you know in rhyme what this master thinks of himself.

For this is what I once wrote above the door to my house, I mean above the entrance to this cave: — — — [177]

31 [68][178]
There is no greater misfortune on this earth than when the mightiest people on earth are not also ranked first among people. For then everything will go wrong and — — —

Yet if everything goes wrong, is it any wonder that the rabble seeks to be master? Then rabble-virtue says "behold, I alone am virtue!

Things like this happen from one day to the next: yet how this came to be and had to come to be — — —

31 [69]¹⁷⁹

    I want to speak G⟨erman⟩ and germanely with you

    Up to now, I haven't known what to do with you — Still, the best thing is that we are feasting together.

31 [70]¹⁸⁰

    the 2 kings
    the voluntary beggar
    the sorcerer
    the intellectually conscientious man
    the ugliest human being
    the Pope no longer in service
    the wanderer
    the noon⟨sleeper⟩

[32 = Z II 9. Winter 1884/85]

32 [1]
Tracing Moral Value Judgments Back to Their Roots.

32 [2]¹
He spoke for all of us, you redeemed us from disgust — this is one of the worst diseases in bad times like these

Zarathustra: what gift did you bring me — you yourselves can't know *what* you have just given me!

you are teaching how to breed a new nobility
you are teaching how to found colonies and to have contempt for huckster state politics
you care about the destiny of human beings
you are enabling morality to transcend itself (overcoming humans, not just "good and evil" awareness of sins)

Zarathustra's Speech on Superior Humans
you must bring to light the *advantages* of bad times like these.

32 [3]²
The Good Meal.
On Superior Humans.
The Sorcerer's Song.
On Science.
The Rose Speech.

32 [4]³

Concerning the "Ugliest Human"

Do not lose heart on account of human beings, oh my soul! Feast your eyes rather on all of their evil, on everything about them that is strange and terrible!

"Humans are evil" — this is what the greatest sages of all time said so as to comfort me. Oh, how the present day taught me to sigh: "What! Is even this true?"

"What? Can I no longer take comfort in this?" Said *my* faintheartedness with a sigh. But now this godliest of men comforted me.

32 [5]

Rabble, today this means: mishmash. In the rabble, everything is mixed up with everything else: scoundrels and saints and junkers⁴ and Jews and God and every animal from Noah's ark.⁵

And these women of today — aren't they pathetic, perfectly suited to the rabble? compliant, lusting, forgetful, compassionate — none of them are very far from being whores.⁶

— My friends, if you ever do say such things to your women, then add this in a proper and gracious manner: "For you alone, my darling, are the exception. And Zarathustra sends you greetings."

32 [6]⁷

You bad old sorcerer, this is the best and most honest thing that I admire about you: that you finally grew sick and tired of yourself and said it out loud "I am not great." It certainly took you long enough to reach the point where you are *this* honest.⁸

You fretful man, you fraud, you unredeemable man, for how many hours did your devil whisper to you: "first make them believe in you, speak, you are just the one who could redeem them, you are enough of a fraud to achieve this!"

32 [7]⁹

But now let me have this great playroom, my cave, to myself, and come outside! Here outside, cool down your hot arrogance and learn to be quietly happy.

The night looks clear, the moon is shining, there's not a cloud in the sky: ask me, ask yourselves, you odd people, whether it is worthwhile — to live!

Yet Zarathustra spoke the words that he had spoken once already, back when he affirmed life¹⁰ for eternity, and eternity for this selfsame and identical life: yet his voice had been transformed.

And all those who heard Zarathustra's question answered it in their hearts, yet no one said a word. And so they stood next to each other, silently holding each other's hands without saying a word and looking out. Then — — —

32 [8]¹¹

Homesickness without a Home. The Wanderer.

1 : thus, that I am not far from being the eternal Jew, except for the fact that I am neither eternal nor a Jew.

2 — whatever lives around me will soon make itself at home as well.¹²

3 — when the devil sheds his skin, his name also falls away: it, too, is skin.

4 — only those who know where they are going also know what wind is at *their* back

5 — he has lost his goal: alas, how he will then trivialize his loss and get over it!¹³

6 — he convinces them that they have lost their way — this flatterer! It flatters them that they are supposed to have a way at all!¹⁴

7 — that has been explained: now it doesn't concern me anymore. — Beware, you might become enlightened about too many things!

8 — even the most saintly people think: "I want to live as I wish — or I don't wish to live anymore!

9 — where can *I* be at home? I was searching for this for the longest time: this searching always hit home with me.

10 — I didn't want it before; so I have to really want it afterwards — I must therefore "make good" on everything

11 — now no one that I love — is left alive: how can I still live with myself!

12 — these cages and miserly souls[15] — how could they want to be free spirits! And anyone who has not committed every crime, like —[16]

13 — the substitute teachers and other blowflies[17]

14 — where gold jingles, where whores rule, where we can grab and attack only while wearing gloves[18]

15 — the people who are all too easily embarrassed, who have to be forced and chastised into doing what they would most like to do[19]

16 — their brains and private parts easily aroused, like the Jews and the Chinese[20]

17 — the kind of people who are convinced by sublime gestures, but who are made mistrustful by reasoned arguments

18 — how restless people feel safe even in prison! How imprisoned criminals sleep peacefully![21]

19 "watch out that you don't follow too closely on the heels of the truth: otherwise it might kick your head in!

20 "What? You call yourself a free spirit? Have you already committed every crime? broken your own admiring heart?

21 — dried-out sandy souls, dry riverbeds: in what sense — free spirits?[22]

22 — he strove for what is forbidden: this is the origin of all of his virtue.

23 — have you walked around amidst the most distant and coldest thoughts, like a ghost on winter roofs?

24 — whirling upward, driven here and there, restless: I have already slept on every surface, like dust I sat on every mirror, every windowpane

25 things are worse than you think: many people believed they were lying, and only then did they hit on the truth! —

26 — these ponderous anguished people whose conscience
makes them grunt: I am not like them

27 — what is Europe doing? — Oh this is a sick, bizarre little woman: we just have to let her throw tantrums, scream,
and break plates and tables, otherwise we will never be left
in peace:[23] a woman who wants whatever she loves to make
her suffer.

28 — more thoughtful times, more overanalyzed times than
our todays and yesterdays are

29 — oh, where did goodness and the faith of good people
go! Alas, where did the innocence of all of these noble lies go!

30 — the god that they once created for themselves out
of nothing — what a miracle! now he has come to mean
nothing to them

31 — hasty, like jumping spider monkeys

32 — a cold bath — do you want to go in there with your
head and heart? Oh, before you know it, you'll be standing
there like a red crab! (Zarathustra sees a fiery red person
coming toward him)

33 — to live between coffins and sawdust; I had no desire
to learn how to be a gravedigger

34 — "nothing is true! everything is permitted!"[24] I have
committed every crime: the most dangerous thoughts, the
most dangerous women

35 — there was a time when I devoted myself to thinking
about what is rare and enduring: but where can that be
found today! so I do not feel contempt for puny brief
moments of beauty!

36 — how little attraction knowledge would hold if there
weren't so much shame to be overcome on the way to
acquiring it —[25]

37 — those who know in this day and age, who teach: once
upon a time God wanted to become an animal — : God
himself as animal: behold, this is the human being![26]

38 — a free spirit, but a weak will; fluttering wings, but a
broken backbone

39 — soon they will be slighting each other, soon they will be fighting each other, these precious Fatherlanders²⁷

> 1, 9, 24, 2, 39, 13, 14
> 6, 5, 4, 35, 8, 37, 30
> 38, 11, 10
> 21, 32, 33, 23, 27, 16, 28
> 15, 36, 22, 20, 34, 7, 25, 3, 16, 26, 29
> 18, 12
> 19

The Good European

1, 9, 24, 2 (laughing about the *Fatherlanders*) people without a country, vagabonds 13, 14 pleasure seekers 8

6, 5, 4, 35 lacking goals, nothing can hold them in check 37, 30 38 weak-willed 11, 10

21, 32, 33 to the most powerful (most stimulating) thoughts, the coldest baths 23 habit:

27 *on the cutting edge*: this means *Europeanism*

16, 28 and peoples who are past their prime like the Jews

15, 36 (overcoming shame — — 22, 20 *crimes* of thought 34 "everything is permitted"²⁸

7, 25, 3, 16, 26, 29 filled with mockery about morality

18, 12 danger of trapping themselves in a cage

19 *tired of the intellect, disgusted by it*

32 [9]²⁹

Those Who Know and Those Who Are Intellectually Conscientious
— Someone who knows in this day and age, who asks: what is the human being, anyway? God himself as an animal? For it seems to me that once upon a time God wanted to become an animal.

— cold cool people, we don't want to believe they are capable of foolishness: we wrongly interpret their foolishness as cleverness gone wrong.

— at some point you learned to believe this without any arguments: how could I ever hope to overturn this for you by using arguments!

— isn't praise more intrusive than any blame? I even forgot how to praise, it lacks shame.

— those who know and those who are intellectually conscientious; how they, with gentle hands — *kill*!

— their memory says: "I did that," but their pride says: "you couldn't have done that": and remains adamant. In the end — their memory gives in.

— he has cold eyes, free of tears, each and every thing lies before him plucked naked and colorless, he suffers from his inability to lie and calls it "love of truth"!

— he stirs, looks around, runs his hand through his hair, and now he allows himself to be scolded as someone who knows! But being free of fever is still not "knowing."

— those delirious with fever see all things as ghosts, and those free of fever see them as empty shadows — and yet both use the same words.

— But you clever man, how could you act that way! That was stupid! — "It hasn't been easy for me either."

— in this day and age, having intelligence is not enough: we must also take control of our intelligence, "dare to be in control of it,"[30] this takes a lot of courage.

— there are also those whose corruption prevents them from acquiring knowledge because they are teachers: they take things seriously only for the sake of their students, including themselves.

— there they stand, the heavy granite cats, the values of ancient times: and you, oh Zarathustra, you want to topple them?

— their diction is a contradiction, their wit is a yes-but wit.

— those industrious, faithful people, for whom each day flows up evenly, like gleaming gold

— how a wanderer who dreams of distant things unexpectedly encounters a sleeping dog on a deserted street: both move toward each other like deadly enemies, startled to death. And yet! if truth be told, how close they are to stroking petting comforting each other: these two lonely ones!

— stubborn minds, cunning and petty

— give me a riddle to solve: your proofs are wearing down my intellect's hunger.

— you don't even feel that you are dreaming: oh, in such a state you are still far from waking up!

— my friend, virtue has nothing to do with "in order to" and "because" and "so that" it doesn't understand such petty phrases.

— full of deep mistrust, overgrown with the moss of solitude, a far-reaching will, a taciturn man, you enemy of all lustful people

— they are not burned at the stake from within, with green kindling, for what they believe: but rather because they can no longer find the courage to have these beliefs today

— clumsy as a corpse, dead in life, buried, hidden: he can no longer stand up, this cowering, lurking man: how could he ever — rise again!

— it is not enough that lightning does no more damage, it needs to learn to do my bidding.

— you wanted to be their light, but you have blinded them. It was your sun that gouged out their eyes.

— how was it that the truth triumphed for once? Perhaps a serious error came to its aid?

— here you are blind, for here is where your honesty ceases.

— they lie on their bellies in front of small round facts, they kiss the dust and the filth at their feet, they rejoice: "here, finally, is reality!"

32 [10][31]

The Voluntary Beggar.

Only then did I return to nature

— Are you one of those people who are excited about green vegetables, averse to all the joys of meat? preach sermons on the mount and philosophy for beloved cattle

— they are cold: that a bolt of lightning would strike their feed and their maws would learn to feed on fire!

— I grew weary of myself: and behold, only then did my happiness come to me, the happiness that had awaited me since the very beginning.

— they sit there with paws bound, these scratching cats, now they can't scratch, but they are giving me poisonous looks with their green eyes.

— many have already thrown themselves down from their heights. They were seduced by compassion for their inferiors: now they are lying there with broken limbs.

— what use was there in acting this way! I listened for an echo but I heard only praise.[32]

—[1] with thieves' eyes, no matter if they are already wallowing in wealth. And some of them I call rag-pickers and vultures.

—[1] I saw their long fingers at work, in the way they learned it from their fathers: then I preferred to draw the short straw.

—[1] leering eyes, bilious souls

—[1] Even brawling is preferable to these brokers! We should attack money and money changers with gloves on!

—[1] a small act of charity sparks outrage wherever the greatest act of charity is scarcely forgiven.

—[1] those of you who are super-wealthy, you drip like wide-bottomed bottles out of all-too-narrow necks: beware, bottles like these have already had their necks broken by impatience many times!

—[1] I was ashamed of wealth when I saw our wealthy people, I threw away what I had and, at the same time, I threw myself out into the desert.

2 — My esteemed little stranger, where were you waiting? Doesn't everyone haggle[33] today? they all can be bought, just not at any price: but if you do want to buy them, don't offer too little, otherwise you strengthen them in their virtue. Otherwise they will tell you No! and walk away swollen with pride, like incorruptible people — all these substitute teachers and paper-blowflies![34]

— miserly souls, huckster-souls: for when money jumps into the till, the soul of the huckster jumps in with it.

— "This is how I recognize people who are superabundant: they thank those who take from them" says Zarathustra.

—¹ prisoners of prosperity, whose thoughts rattle coldly like heavy chains.

—¹ they invented for themselves the holiest kind of boredom and the lust for Moon-days and workdays

— how a wanderer who dreams of distant things unexpectedly encounters a sleeping dog on a deserted street:

both move toward each other like deadly enemies, both startled to death: and yet, if truth be told: how close they were to stroking and petting each another, the two lonely ones!

— not based on that old sly piety that said "giving to the poor means lending to God. Be good bankers!"

— you love utility as a vehicle for your inclinations, but isn't the noise of its wheels unbearable to you? I love what is useless.

—¹ their women: compliant, lusting, forgetful: none of them are very far from being whores.

— I love silence, and those people love noise, that's why

— — —

32 [11]³⁵

On Superior Humans.

"So you are not going to become like little children"³⁶ — No! No! For the third time, no!

That's over with. Nor do we want to go to the kingdom of heaven at all.

We have become men, so we want the kingdom of earth.

(No! No! For the third time, no! What heavenly mumbo jumbo! Gong! We don't *want* to go to the kingdom of heaven: the kingdom of earth shall be ours!)

"you are being pushed up into the heights, up to where I live: the people may say "you are climbing." As I see it, you — *are being pushed around*!³⁷

— in an age where the satisfaction of the rabble rules, and where disgust has already become the hallmark of superior humans:

32 [12]³⁸

The Seven Solitudes.

And if someday I have to howl with wolves, then I'll do it well enough; and once in a while a wolf would say: "you howl better than we wolves do."

32 [13]³⁹

The Roundelay.

Yet when they had been standing this way for a long time and the secrecy of the night crept more and more deeply into their hearts, then something happened, the most astonishing thing that had happened on that long, astonishing day. First the ugliest human began to gurgle and snort anew: yet when he succeeded in forming words, one question emerged clearly and distinctly from his mouth, a question that brought about a change of heart in everyone who heard it.

My friends who are gathered here together, said the ugliest human, what do you think? For the first time I am satisfied with having lived my whole life — for the sake of this day.

And my having attested to this much is still far from being good enough for me. Living on this earth is worth it; one day spent with Zarathustra has taught me to love the earth.

"Was *that* — life? is how I want to speak to death. All right then! One more time! For Zarathustra's sake!" —

My friends, what do you think? Don't you want to say to death, along with me: "Was *that* — life? For Zarathustra's sake — all right then! One more time!" —

And you, our doctor and savior — let us, oh Zarathustra, go further with you into the future!

Thus spoke the ugliest human; but it wasn't long before midnight.

Then all of a sudden Zarathustra reached for the ugliest human's hand, held it in his own hands and, shaken, cried out with the voice of someone who has seen a precious gift and treasure fall unexpectedly from the sky:

"What? Is it really *you* saying this, my friend? Is *this* really your will? Is this how you want your entire, last, best, greatest will to be done?[40] All right then! Say it one more time!" — — —

And the ugliest human did as he was told: but as soon as the other superior humans heard his vow, they all at once became aware of their transformation and their convalescence and of the man who had bestowed this gift on them: then they sprang toward Zarathustra, thanking him, revering him, caressing him or kissing his hands, each according to his custom: so that some of them were laughing, some of them crying. But the old prophet danced with joy; and even if, as some think, he was filled with sweet wine back then, he was surely also even more filled with sweet life and had renounced all weariness. There are even those who say that the ass was dancing then; for they say that the ugliest human had earlier given it wine to drink instead of water, back when he prayed to the ass as his new god. Now this may have happened like this, or otherwise — and, truly, not everyone who tells the story of Zarathustra will believe it —: yet certainly the ugliest human would have been capable of such bad behavior.

But Zarathustra himself noticed how the prophet was dancing and pointed it out; then he turned around and tore himself away from the crowd of those who were loving and revering him, put his finger to his lips and ordered them to be silent. That darkest hour of the night is when Zarathustra began to sing the magnificent roundelay, and one after another, his guests joined in; but the ass, the eagle and the snake were listening, just as Zarathustra's cave was listening, and the night itself was listening. For this roundelay sounded like this:

Lift up your hearts, my brothers, high! higher! — but don't forget your legs either when you think of me! Lift your legs higher, too, you skillful dancers, and better still, even stand on your heads!

Hark! Hark! The depths of midnight are approaching!

Then the old prophet joined in: "There are animals who are heavy even when it comes to happiness, there are those who are clodhoppers from the start. In a strange way, they try their hardest, like an elephant trying to stand on its head.

Hark! Hark! The depths of midnight are approaching!"

Then the ugliest human joined in: "Better still to dance clumsily than to walk lamely, better to be foolish when we're happy than when we're unhappy. Yet this is Zarathustra's finest truth: even the worst thing has two good sides.

Hark! Hark! The depths of midnight are approaching!"

Then the old sorcerer joined in: "Now I have learned to leave behind misery and all night-watchman's melancholy! I want to act like the wind, which makes all heavens clear and all oceans roar: from now on I want to act like Zarathustra.

Hark! Hark! The depths of midnight are approaching!"

Then the king on the right joined in: "Stir me into the mix of all earthly tears and all human misery: I will always emerge on top again like oil on water. But I learned this from this man Zarathustra.

Hark! Hark! The depths of midnight are approaching!"

Then the king on the left joined in: "And if at times I must have a grudge against the earth: my malice will tear the stars out of the heavens and bring them down to the earth: this is the nature of all Zarathustra-revenge.

Hark! Hark! The depths of midnight are approaching!"

Then the good European joined in: "And even if there are moors and melancholy on earth and entire oceans of black slime: anyone who is light on his feet like Zarathustra still runs over slime, as quickly as over cleanly swept ice.

Hark! Hark! The depths of midnight are approaching!"

Then the voluntary beggar joined in: "Their stride reveals whether people are already on *their* way: look at Zarathustra go! But those who are closing in on their goals, they — are dancing!

Hark! Hark! The depths of midnight are approaching!"

Then the intellectually conscientious man joined in: "All good things approach their goals on crooked paths, they arch their backs like cats, inwardly they purr at their approaching happiness, all good things laugh.

Hark! Hark! The depths of midnight are approaching!"

Then the old Pope joined in: "Here on earth, what has been the greatest sin up to now? These were the words of the one who said: "Woe unto you that laugh here!"[41]

Hark! Hark! The depths of midnight are approaching!"

32 [14][42]

The Last Sin.

I.

But what happened then to Zarathustra himself? — Yes, who would like to guess what happened to him that night! — For he fell down when he saw the happiness of his superior humans, he fell down all at once like an oak tree that has endured many axe strokes for a long time — , heavily, suddenly, to the horror of just those people who had wanted to cut it. But the axe that struck down Zarathustra — this axe was called feeling *compassion*, feeling compassion for the *happiness* of these superior humans.

2.

The superior humans rushed over to where he lay on the ground, so that they could help him up again: but he was already jumping back up on his own, he pushed away all those

who were pressing around him and cried: "Away! Away! Away!"
"Let me out of here," he cried, so full of pain and so terribly
that the hearts of his friends stood still; and before even one
hand reached out to restrain him, he covered his head with his
cloak, ran out into the black night, and disappeared.

Then his friends stood there for a long while, numb and silent,
for they were strangers to these mountains, and at this hour no
one could have found his way, even for a hundred paces. For it
was getting close to midnight. And so, when they had no idea
how to help themselves and no idea what to do, they finally
stepped back again into Zarathustra's cave, even if it immediately
seemed sad and cold to them, and they spent the night right
there, with little sleep and many unpleasant thoughts and ghosts.

Yet it came to pass that, around the first light of early dawn,
the wanderer who called himself Zarathustra's shadow secretly
left his companions and kept watch in front of the cave for the
one who had been lost. And it wasn't long before he called into
the cave: "there comes Zarathustra!" Then they all cast away
their sleepiness and their unpleasant thoughts and jumped up
full of hope that the day was coming again. Yet as they kept an
eye out together — and even the ass had gone out with them
and was watching for Zarathustra — behold, there they spied
in the distance a strange spectacle. For Zarathustra was coming up the path, slowly, slowly: now and then he stopped and
looked back: but a mighty tawny animal was following him,
hesitating like Zarathustra himself, moving slowly and often
looking back. Yet whenever Zarathustra turned his head in its
direction, it moved forward more quickly for several paces, but
then it would hesitate again. What is happening down there?
the superior humans were asking themselves, and their hearts
were thumping; for they were worried that this mighty tawny
animal was a lion of the mountains. And behold, suddenly the
lion became aware of them: then he let out a wild roar and sprang
at them: so that all of them screamed with one voice and ran away
from him. And instantly Zarathustra was alone and was standing
in astonishment at the entrance to his cave. "What in the world

happened to me?" he said to his heart, while the strong lion pressed bashfully against his knees. "What cry of distress did I just hear!" But then his memories returned, and he grasped all at once everything that had happened. Here is the stone, he said, rejoicing, here is the stone on which I was sitting yesterday morning: that's when I heard the same cry. Oh you superior humans, it was definitely *your* cry of distress!

And it was my distress that the old prophet warned me about yesterday morning; he wanted to tempt me into my last sin, into compassion for *your* distress!

But your *happiness* was my danger — : compassion for your happiness, *that* — is what he did not figure out! Oh, to be sure, what these superior humans probably learned[43] from *me*!

So be it! they are gone — and I did *not* go with them: oh victory! oh happiness! This has turned out well for me!

But you, my animal and my emblem, you laughing lion, you stay here with me! Onward! Upward! You came to honor me, and at the right time, you are my third chosen animal!

Thus spoke Zarathustra to the lion, and he sat down on the rock where he had sat the day before, taking a deep breath — : but then he looked curiously into the heights — for he heard the piercing cry of his eagle above him.

My animals are returning, my two old chosen animals, cried Zarathustra and he rejoiced in his heart: they were supposed to find out if my children are on their way and have come to me. And truly, my children came, for the laughing lion came. Oh victory! Oh happiness!

32 [15][44]

The Sign.

Yet on the morning following this night Zarathustra sprang up from where he was lying, girded his loins and came out of his cave, glowing with happiness, like the morning sun rising up from behind dark mountains.

"They are still asleep, he cried, while *I* am awake — *these* are not the proper companions for me, these superior humans.

Humans who are superior to them must come, more spirited, freer, brighter — laughing lions must come to me: what
do I care about all this puny brief odd misery!

This is what I am now waiting for, this is what I am now
waiting for" — and as Zarathustra spoke in this way, he sat
down on the stone in front of his cave, deep in thought.

"Who shall rule the earth? thus he began again. Now! Certainly not *those* men over there — better still if I crush *those*
men with my hammer. Yet I myself am a hammer.

They will just barely survive on earth if they are made to feel
a lust for the earth, if they are addressed with inspiring words.
What! Upon this earth — just *to survive*? For the sake of the
earth I am ashamed of such talk.

I would much prefer to have wild evil animals around me
than these tame, failed people; I want to be that happy when I
once again see the wonders that are hatched by the hot sun —

— all the flourishing animals in their prime, of which the
earth itself is proud. Have human beings failed the earth so far?
So be it! Nevertheless, the lion flourished."

And once again Zarathustra descended into distant thoughts
and countries and into the silence that even gets out of the way
of our own hearts and has no witnesses.

32 [16]⁴⁵

The Honey Sacrifice.
The Cry of Distress.
Conversation with the Kings.
The Wanderer.
The Voluntary Beggar.
The Pope, No Longer in Service.
The Penitent of the Mind.
The Intellectually Conscientious Man
The Ugliest Human.
The Noontime Sleeper.
The Welcoming.
The Last Supper.

On Superior Humans.
The Sorcerer's Song.
On Science.
The Psalm After Dinner.
The Resurrected Man.
At Midnight.
The Wild Hunter.
The Laughing Lion.

32 [17][46]

The Good European.
What is German?
The Tartuffery of Good People.
Great Minds. Philosophers.
Artists and Con Artists.
Pessimists concerning the Intellect.
Mind and Property 310.
On the Dominion of Those Who Know 318
On the Art of Healing.

32 [18][47]

On Great Politics.
What is German?
Against the Concept of "Punishment."
On the Art of Healing.
Against Loving Thy Neighbor.
Great Intellects.
On the Greeks.
Christians and Saints.
The Tartuffery within Morality.
Against Our Upbringing.[48]
Herd-Morality.

32 [19][49]

Civil Service and Civil Servants.
Scholars — Misfits.

What can be learned from the Greeks
On the Superstitions of Philosophers.
The Good European (Socialism)
Godless, N. 125
Against Compassion and Loving Thy Neighbor

32 [20]⁵⁰

For the Benefit of the Nobility.
Against the Abolition of Slavery.
Against the *Socialists*, No. 235
On the Death of the State.
Morality as Herd-Instinct.
Great Men.
The Irrationality of Punishment.
What Liars Artists Are.
Against Pessimists and other — — —
Good People and the Spread of Stupidity.
The Value of Misinterpretation, No. 126
Subtle Obscurantism
What is German.
Misunderstanding Genius.

32 [21]⁵¹

A smell that has no name wafts upward from the depths, a
secret smell of eternity

Oh midnight! Oh eternity!

32 [22]⁵²

The Nihilistic Catastrophe:
Sign: prevalence of *compassion*
     intellectual fatigue and lack of discipline
     pleasure or *displeasure* — *everything* is reduced to this —

counter-movement against the glory *of war*
counter-movement against the establishment of borders and
     hostility between nations

"fraternity" . . .
religion has become useless, as long as it still speaks in fables
   and harsh phrases

Awe-inspiring reflection:
   as if at an old fortress

33 [1]¹

The Good Meal.

It was around the middle of this long Last Supper which had already begun in the afternoon: then someone said: "Listen to how the wind outside is howling and whistling! Who would like to be outside in the world now! It's good that we are sitting in Zarathustra's cave.

For, even if it is only a cave, it is still a good safe harbor for ships like us. How nice that we are here — in the harbor!"

As these words were spoken, no one replied, yet all of them looked at each other. Nevertheless, Zarathustra himself rose from his seat, examined his guests one after the other with amiable curiosity and finally said:

"I have my doubts about you, my new friends. You certainly do not look like people in despair. Who would have believed that not long ago, here in this cave, you cried out in distress!

It seems to me that you are not fit companions for each other, that you secretly feel contempt for each other² when you sit together? Maybe someone has to visit you who will make you laugh —

— an artful joyful clown, a dancer in his head and in his feet, a wind and a wild man,³ some old fool or other and Zarathustra — what do you think?"

At these words, the king on the right stood up and said: "Don't belittle your own name, oh Zarathustra! when you do this, you are ruining our reverence for you.

Look, we know very well *who* brought our cries of distress to an end! and we know the reason why our eyes and hearts are open in delight and our courage is becoming more courageous.

Oh Zarathustra, nothing that grows on earth brings more joy than a strong noble will: it is the earth's most beautiful flowering. An entire territory can be refreshed by a tree like that.

Someone who grows up like you, Zarathustra, I would compare to a pine tree: tall, silent, tough, alone, of the best, most flexible wood, majestic —

— in the end, though, reaching out with strong green branches for *his* realm, posing provocative questions to the wind and weather and to whatever makes its home in the heights,

— answering more forcefully, someone in command, someone who has enjoyed many victories: oh, who would not ascend high mountains in order to see such a flowering?

Even gloomy people, people who have failed, find refreshment here at your tree, oh Zarathustra, even restless people are made to feel secure, and have their hearts healed at the sight of you.

How marvelous it is that we first cried out in distress like this: then we *had to* go up to where we could see you! How grateful we are now to our disgust, to all the gathering storms, for teaching us to ask and to seek and to ascend, —

— for teaching us to pose a well-placed question, at a suitable height: "Is Zarathustra still alive, then? How is Zarathustra still living?"

Someone who asks good questions already has half the answer. And, truly, one very good answer is what we see here with our own eyes: Zarathustra is still alive, and more so than ever before, —

— Zarathustra the dancer, Zarathustra who is light on his feet, who is flapping his wings, who is ready to fly, who waves to all the birds, ready and willing, divinely light-hearted,

— Zarathustra the one who laughs, Zarathustra the silent one, not impatient, not an absolutist, someone who loves leaping and jumping sideways,

— who wears the crown of laughter, a rose-garland crown. For you yourself, oh Zarathustra, set this crown upon your own head, no one else today would be strong enough to do it!

And though you have already seen worse and bleaker things than anyone else who sees the darker side of things, and though no saint has ever endured your hells,

— and though you already wrapped yourself in new nights and already descended like icy dismal fog into new abysses: again and again, you finally stretched your tent of many colors above yourself,

— you spread your laughter over nights and hell and foggy chasms; and wherever your tall strong tree stands, there the heavens cannot be dark for long."

Yet here Zarathustra interrupted the king's speech, put his finger to the king's mouth and said: "Oh, these kings! —

— they know how to pay homage and how to use grand words: they themselves are used to it! But what shall become of my ears in the process!

In the process, my ears are growing small and smaller, don't you see? that is, they creep away from all grand pompous speeches.

And truly, you kings, you can topple the strongest men with such praise, no one should be toasted with a goblet of wine like that one. Other than *me*: for I defy every bit of praise, thanks to my nerves of steel[4] —

Thanks to my iron will: yet it demands difficult, exalted distant things from ⟨me⟩: praise and honor do not reach it.

And this is true: I did not become one of the desert saints, although I have lived in many deserts and desert wildernesses, I am not still standing there rigid, dull, stony, a pillar.

I resemble the tree that you had in mind, a tall strong tree, this is true: gnarled and crooked and with flexible hardness I stand above the ocean, a living lighthouse.

And, my new friends, I want to wave to you just as a tree like that would wave, with broad branches, strong-willed: come on up to me, I want to say, and gaze with me into these distant horizons!

33 [2]⁵
Regarding "One More Time!"

Then things happened one after the other, each one of which was stranger than the other.

— and although he was already gnashing his teeth and grimacing, compassion still overwhelmed him, like a thick cloud and stupor.

Over there — the eagle!   — Where am I!

He escapes.

Notes

The unpublished fragments from volumes 14 and 15 {*KSA* 10 and *KSA* 11, Notebooks 1–33} contain the indispensable and supplemental background material for the four parts of *Thus Spoke Zarathustra*. Reading the work and the unpublished notes side by side is facilitated by the commentary, which — in contrast to all other *KSA* commentaries — reproduces once again not only, in a narrow sense, the actual variants that were transmitted (*Pd*, *Sd*, *Pm*, *Pp*, *Fe*, *Se*) but also the unpublished texts that are most important for *Zarathustra*. The entire apparatus of texts and fragments allows us to draw many conclusions concerning N's creative activity at the time of *Zarathustra*. When N speaks of the four parts of his work as "creative products of a ten-day period" (cf. *EH* III Z4 {*CW* 9, 283}), this obviously does not apply to the appearance of the work's foundational ideas and their creative realization in the unpublished material, nor to the appearance of different parables, allegories, sayings, poetic ideas and framing narratives, individual characters, and so forth, but only to the actual preliminary drafts and revised versions of each part. N recorded notes in his notebooks constantly, almost daily (often during his walks); he then would copy them into larger notebooks (cf. N's letter to Peter Gast, {5 October} 1879 {*KGB* II:5, 450}, cited in the preliminary notes to the commentary to *HAH II* {*CW* 4, 434) without organizing them according to a particular scheme, nor with a particular arrangement in mind, nor by changing already existing outlines. When he then moved to the writing of a particular part of *Thus Spoke Zarathustra*, he was able to finish it so quickly because he had already done the preparation for it without knowing in advance how his work would find its literary realization. This final work phase is when the actual preliminary and final drafts of the respective parts of *Thus Spoke Zarathustra* would emerge. All of the notes that preceded this final phase and which have extensive connections to its form and content are being published as unpublished fragments and are reproduced in part in the commentary. As will be evident from the unpublished fragments, after completing each part of *Zarathustra*, N had differing plans for continuing his work that were subsequently abandoned. The same thing happened — up until autumn of 1888 — even after the completion of *Thus Spoke Zarathustra* (beginning of 1885).

{The preceding paragraph, translated by Paul S. Loeb and David F. Tinsley, is taken from the introduction to the commentary to *Thus Spoke Zarathustra* I–IV, *KSA* 14, 280. It also appears in their translation of *Z*, *CW* 7.}

The following symbols are used throughout the text and notes:

[ ]	Deletion by Nietzsche
| |	Addition by Nietzsche
{ }	Addition by the translator or editors
⟨ ⟩	Addition by the editors (Colli and Montinari)
[?]	Uncertain reading
— — —	Unfinished or incomplete sentence or thought
Italics	Underlined once by Nietzsche
Bold	Underlined twice or more by Nietzsche
NL	Books in Nietzsche's personal library

Variants and editions of Nietzsche's works are referred to by the following abbreviations:

CW	*The Complete Works of Friedrich Nietzsche*
KGB	*Briefwechsel: Kritische Gesamtausgabe*
KGW	*Werke: Kritische Gesamtausgabe*
KSA	*Werke: Kritische Studienausgabe*
Le	Twenty-volume 1894 Leipzig edition of Nietzsche's works (*Großoktav-Ausgabe*)
Pd	Preliminary draft
Pm	Printer's manuscript (clean final copy of handwritten MS)
Sd	Second draft
Se	Subsequent emendation
WP²	The Will to Power (= *Le* XV and XVI, 1911)

Titles of Nietzsche's works are referred to by the following abbreviations:

AC	*The Antichrist*
BGE	*Beyond Good and Evil*
BT	*The Birth of Tragedy*
D	*Dawn*
DD	*Dionysus Dithyrambs*
DS	*David Strauss the Confessor and the Writer*
EH	*Ecce Homo*
GM	*On the Genealogy of Morality*
HAH	*Human, All Too Human*
HL	*On the Utility and Liability of History for Life*
IM	*Idylls from Messina*
JS	*The Joyful Science*
JSA	*The Joyful Science, Appendix: Songs of Prince Vogelfrei*
JSP	*The Joyful Science, Prelude in German Rhymes*
MM	*Mixed Opinions and Maxims*
NCW	*Nietzsche Contra Wagner*
SE	*Schopenhauer as Educator*

TI	*Twilight of the Idols*
UO	*Unfashionable Observations*
WA	*The Case of Wagner*
WB	*Richard Wagner in Bayreuth*
WP	*The Will to Power*
WS	*The Wanderer and His Shadow*
Z	*Thus Spoke Zarathustra*

References to the following works will also appear in the notes:

| Flügel | Felix Flügel. *A Practical Dictionary of the English and German Languages in Two Parts / Praktisches Englisch-Deutsches und Deutsch-Englisches Wörterbuch in zwei Theilen.* Leipzig: Julius E. Richter; Hamburg: John Augustus Meissner, 1852. This is an expanded edition of his father Johann Gottfried Flügel's *A Complete Dictionary of the English and German and German and English Languages in Two Volumes/ Vollständige englisch-deutsche und deutsch-englische Wörterbuch in zwei Theilen*, first published in 1830. |
| Grimm | *Deutsches Wörterbuch von Jacob und Wilhelm Grimm.* 16 Bde. in 32 Teilbänden. Leipzig, 1854–1961. Quellenverzeichnis Leipzig 1971. Online version at http://www.woerterbuchnetz.de/DWB. |

[25 = W I 1. Spring 1884]

1. Cf. 25[2, 6, 227, 323]; 26[243, 259, 293, 298, 325, 465]; 27[58, 80, 82].

2. Cf. N to Peter Gast, 22 March 1884 {*KGB* III:1, 487}; (cf. Chronicle of N's life in *CW* 19).

3. Cf. *Z* IV "Conversation with the Kings"; 29[1]; 31[44, 61].

4. *"Paradise . . . swords."*] {Saying attributed to the Prophet Mohammed (cf. Muhammad al-Bukhari, *Sahih al-Bukhari*, 2818). Cf. Ralph Waldo Emerson, *Versuche* (*Essays*), trans. G. Fabricius (Hanover: Carl Meyer, 1858), 179. *NL*. Published in English as *The*

Collected Works of Ralph Waldo Emerson, vol. 2: *Essays: First Series* (Cambridge, MA: Belknap Press of Harvard University Press, 1979), 143, the epigraph of the chapter "Heroism."}

5. Cf. *Z* IV "The Song of Melancholy"; 31[31]; 28[14].

6. {Quoted from Anders Magnus Strinnholm, *Wikingszüge, Staatsverfassung und Sitten der alten Skandinavier* ("Viking expeditions, state constitution, and customs of the ancient Scandinavians"), trans. from Swedish by C. F. Frisch (Hamburg: Perthes, 1839), pt. 2, 270.}

7. Cf. *Z* IV "The Shadow"; 29[1]; 31[44]; 32[8].

8. Cf. the notes to 25[1].

9. *particular] diesmaligen*

10. *"Dans . . . corps."]* Cf. *BGE* 142; {the quote is from Astolphe de Custine, *Le monde comme il est* ("The world as it is"), 2 vols. (Paris: E. Renduel, 1835), 1:102: "In true love, it is the soul that envelops the body." Hereafter cited as "Custine, *Le monde*," followed by volume and page number.}

11. Only half {i.e., the first paragraph: "My friends . . . walk there.") of this published in *WP²* 57.

12. *to keep our heads above water] sich oben zu erhalten*

13. *la bêtise humaine]* "human stupidity" {N perhaps took this phrase from *Lettres de Gustave Flaubert à George Sand: Précédées d'une étude par Guy de Maupassant* ("Letters from Gustave Flaubert to George Sand: With an introduction by Guy de Maupassant") (Paris: Charpentier, 1884), xxviii, xxx, lxxv. *NL*.}

14. Cf. N to Peter Gast, 22 March 1884 {*KGB* III:1, 486–87}.

15. *as we know all too well] aus dem Grunde wissen*

16. *"fait-alisme"]* "fact-alism" {Underlined by N, who puns on the similar sound in French of this and "fatalism."}

17. Cf. *Z* IV "On Superior Humans" 9; {*CW* 14, 11[6];} 29[1]; 32[8].

18. {Cf. *WP²* 31.}

19. Cf. *Z* IV "The Shadow"; 29[1]; 31[44]; 32[8].

20. *"break out"]* {In English in the original.}

21. *We see . . . pieces)]* {Cf. Francis Galton, *Inquiries into Human Faculty and Its Development* (London: Macmillan and Co., 1883), 65, *NL*: "The criminal classes contain a considerable portion of

epileptics and other persons of instable, emotional temperament, subject to nervous explosions that burst out at intervals and relieve the system. The mad outbreaks of women in convict prisons is a most curious phenomenon. Some of them are apt from time to time to have a gradually increasing desire that at last becomes irresistible, to 'break out,' as it is technically called; that is, to smash and tear everything they can within reach, and to shriek, curse, and howl."}

22. {Cf. Galton, *Inquiries*, 64–65: "Now the ancestor of all this mischief, who was born about the year 1730, is described as having been a jolly companionable man, a hunter, and a fisher, averse to steady labour, but working hard and idling by turns, and who had numerous illegitimate children, whose issue has not been traced. He was, in fact, a somewhat good specimen of a half-savage, without any seriously criminal instincts. The girls were apparently attractive, marrying early and sometimes not badly; but the gipsy-like character of the race was unsuited to success in a civilised country. So the descendants went to the bad, and such hereditary moral weaknesses as they may have had, rose to the surface and worked their mischief without check. Cohabiting with criminals, and being extremely prolific, the result was the production of a stock exceeding 500 in number, of a prevalent criminal type."}

23. *in in⟨finitum⟩]* "into in⟨finity⟩"

24. *"admirable . . . audace!]* {Jules Michelet, *Le banquet: Papiers intimes* (Paris: Calmann Lévy, 1879), 15: "'admirable for tempering the strong.' Genoa is indeed the home of rough geniuses born to tame the ocean and dominate storms. On sea, on land, how many adventurous and wisely daring men!"}

25. N was reading at this time: Honoré de Balzac, *Correspondance 1819–1850,* in *Œuvres complètes* XXIV (Paris{: Calmann Lévy,} 1876; here N is quoting Balzac to Madame Hanska, 20 January 1838, 276–77{: {"}*St. Ronan's Well* the masterpiece and major work for detail and patience of finish. *Chronicles of the Canongate* for sentiment. *Ivanhoe* (by which I mean the first volume) as historical masterpiece. *The Antiquary* as poetry. *The Heart of Midlothian* for interest.{"} — "Compared to him, Lord Byron is nothing

or almost nothing." — "Scott will still be growing greater when Byron is forgotten." "Byron's brain never had any other imprint than that of his own personality, whereas the whole world posed before the creative genius of Scott and was, so to speak, reflected in it."}

26. Balzac to Madame Hanska, {1} October 1836, *Correspondance*, 241{: "I understand how Pascal's absolute continence and his immense labors have led him to constantly see an abyss at his side⟨s⟩" — }

27. *Notice . . . Lambert . . . "Il jettera . . . Nouvelles."]* Balzac to Laure Surville {Balzac's sister}, August 1832, *Correspondance*, 127–28{: Biographical note on *Louis Lambert . . .* "Perhaps, one day or another, it will propel science in new directions."}

28. *"un des . . . temps."*} Balzac to R. Colomb, 30 January 1846, *Correspondance*, 491{: "one of the most remarkable minds of this time."}

29. *madame Honesta]* Character from "Belphégor," short story by La Fontaine.

30. *"notre . . . léché."]* Balzac to R. Colomb, 30 January 1846, *Correspondance*, 492{: "our language is a sort of Madame Honesta, who finds nothing good other than that which is flawless, chiseled, licked."}

31. *"le livre . . . distingués."]* Balzac to R. Colomb, 30 January 1846, *Correspondance*, 492{: "the book of distinguished minds."}

32. *"je . . . s'échappe."]* Balzac to Madame Hanska, 4 March 1844, *Correspondance*, 400{: "I have no continuity of will. I make plans, I conceive books, but when it comes to execution, all escapes me."}

33. *Je fais . . . italiennes." . . . "Vous avez . . . l'Italie."]* Balzac to Stendhal, 6 April 1839, 329–30{: "I make a fresco and you made Italian statues." . . . "You explained the soul of Italy."}

34. *more literature idée than littérature imagée]* "more literature of ideas than of images"

35. Balzac to Astolphe de Custine, 10 February 1839, *Correspondance*, 321–22{: "à la Chamfort and in the spirit of Rivarol by the little broken sentence."}

36. *Scribe . . . absent!]* Balzac to Madame Hanska, 18 June 1838, *Correspondance*, 303.

37. {Cf. Galton, *Inquiries*, 67–68: "Another remarkable phase among the insane consists in strange views about their individuality. They think that their body is made of glass, or that their brains have literally disappeared, or that there are different persons inside them, or that they are somebody else, and so forth. It is said that this phase is most commonly associated with morbid disturbance of the alimentary organs. So in many religions fasting has been used as an agent for detaching the thoughts from the body and for inducing ecstasy. [. . .] In short, by enforcing celibacy, fasting, and solitude, they have done their best towards making men mad, and they have always largely succeeded in inducing morbid mental conditions among their followers."}

38. *"Profound . . . power." 1832.]* Balzac to Zulma Carraud, 1 June 1832, *Correspondance*, 109.

39. *"mes . . . aimé."]* Balzac to Laure Surville, 1821, *Correspondance*, 35: {"my only two immense desires, *to be famous and to be loved." être . . . aimé* underlined by N.}

40. {*WP²* 908.}

41. {Cf. *BGE* 197.}

42. *cozy manner]* Pantoffel-Manier {*Pantoffel* literally means "slipper" and has connotations here of the English ideal of comfort.}

43. *véritable goût]* "real taste"

44. *education]* Erziehung {N's use of this term throughout this volume indicates that his understanding of "education" goes well beyond formal schooling.}

45. *de Custine . . . voyages]* Astolphe de Custine, *Mémoires et voyages, ou lettres écrites à diverses époques, pendant des courses en Suisse, en Calabre, en Angleterre, et en Ecosse* {"Memoirs and travels, or letters written at various times, during tours in Switzerland, Calabria, England, and Scotland"}, 2 vols. (Paris{: A. Vezard,} 1830), hereafter cited as "Custine, *Mémoires*," followed by volume and page number; here N is quoting from vol. 1{: "I only aspire to powerful and serious affects"}.

46. Custine, *Mémoires*, 1:156{: "It is not out of vanity that the genius wants encouragement, it is out of modesty, out of self-defiance."}

47. Custine, *Mémoires*, 1:169–70{: "The man of genius senses, the man of talent recounts: but no one feels and speaks at the same

time. The truly unhappy man can only be silent: his silence is the effect and the very proof of his misfortune."}

48. Custine, *Mémoires*, 1:181{: "So many interests to humor, so many lies to be listened to with that air of a dupe, the first condition of social politeness, tire my mind without occupying it."}

49. Custine, *Mémoires*, 1:187{: "my friend, never allow yourself anything but follies that will give you great pleasure." "a crime, when you are impelled to it by a power which appears to you irresistible, disturbs the conscience less than a willful and conceited weakness."}

50. Custine, *Mémoires*, 1:223{: "the only perfect people are the ones you don't know."}

51. Custine, *Mémoires*, 1:225.

52. *Il . . . personnifiée.]* "He (Werner) is *Germany personified.*" {Custine is here referring to German poet and dramatist Zacharias Werner (1768–1823). N underlines *Allemagne personnifiée.*}

53. Custine, *Mémoires*, 1:248.

54. *René]* {Popular Romantic novella (1802) by French writer François-René de Chateaubriand (1768–1848).}

55. Custine, *Mémoires*, 1:273.

56. Custine, *Mémoires*, 1:332–33.

57. Custine, *Mémoires*, 2:163.

58. *But Catholicism . . . Plato!]* Written by N.

59. *"noblesse . . . ampoulé"]* "tragic nobility, this dignity, equality of style, our unnatural gestures, our bombastic song"

60. *"noblesse . . . ignoble.]* Custine, *Mémoires*, 2:256–57.

61. *subordinate to his point of view]* unter seinen Conceptions

62. *In Shakespeare . . . paroles."]* Custine, *Mémoires*, 2:261.

63. *les concetti . . . paroles."]* "the concepts, the research, the triviality, the abundance of words."

64. Custine, *Mémoires*, 2:276.

65. Custine, *Mémoires*, 2:292{: "some morose philosopher will perhaps end up daring to say *of modern freedom*, that it consists in the twin faculty of lying to others and of lying to oneself"; N underlines *de la liberté moderne.*}

66. Custine, *Mémoires*, 2:380.

67. *Décorateur]* "Designer"

68. *échappe . . . pinceau.]* "escapes this pen, which is never more than a paintbrush."

69. *l'expression . . . âme]* "the immediate expression of what is going on in his soul"

70. *il ne prend . . . dit]* "he is not himself involved enough in what he says"

71. *Rossini de la littérature]* "Rossini of literature"

72. *parce qu'il . . . lumière.]* "because he does not know how to side with the light."

73. *point de vue]* "point of view"

74. *des temps . . . vivons.]* "of the unscrupulous times in which we live."

75. *"pour avoir . . . faux."]* "for having managed to bring back, if not the feeling, *at least the fashion for the true in the century of the false.*" {N underlines *au moins . . . faux* and underlines *mode* twice.}

76. {Custine, *Mémoires,* 2:297.}

77. Custine, *Mémoires,* 2:291.

78. Custine, *Mémoires,* 2:272.

79. *on . . . fatigue]* "we made relaxation so painful, that it makes people love fatigue"

80. Custine, *Mémoires,* 2:251–52.

81. *un chant . . . tragiques.]* "a bombastic song very unfavorable to great tragic effects."

82. Custine, *Mémoires,* 2:252.

83. *fill in the blanks]* etwas rathen

84. Custine, *Mémoires,* 2:418.

85. *contre le positif]* "against the positive"

86. *élan vers l'idéal]* "drive toward the ideal"

87. Custine, *Mémoires,* 2:442–43.

88. *minutie; . . . puérilité]* "(excessive) thoroughness; the taste for elegance into puerility"

89. Custine, *Mémoires,* 2:448–49.

90. Custine, *Mémoires,* 2:464.

91. *"Les Anglais . . . opulens."]* "The English are opulent galley slaves."

92. Custine, *Mémoires,* 2:464.

93. *L'esprit . . . mais]* "Attention to detail, attention to the little things produces care, but"

94. *dans les arts]* "in the arts"

95. Custine, *Mémoires*, 2:466.

96. *L'esprit frondeur]* "Rebellious spirit"

97. Custine, *Mémoires*, 2:467.

98. *présumption]* "presumption"; "overconfidence" {N misspells French *présomption*.}

99. Custine, *Mémoires*, 2:467.

100. *par . . . parti]* "by pure *party* spirit" {N underlines *parti*.}

101. *soumission]* "submission"

102. *l'esprit de révolte]* "the spirit of revolt"

103. Custine, *Mémoires*, 2:474.

104. *suffrage universel, faits]* "universal suffrage, facts"

105. *sancti]* "holy ones"

106. *l'homme supérieur]* "superior humans"

107. {Excerpts from Custine, *Le monde*, 2:400–401.}

108. *"il souffre . . . vaincre.]* "he suffers, he succumbs instead of fighting and winning."

109. *l'attaque . . . source!]* "attack and defense would come from the same source!"

110. *puériles]* "childish"

111. {Cf. Custine, *Le monde*, 2:254–55.}

112. {Cf. Custine, *Le monde*, 2:6–7.}

113. {Cf. Custine, *Le monde*, 2:26.}

114. *il ne faudra . . . d'hypocrisie."]* {"it will not take less than an entire era of literary cynicism to shake off the habits of hypocrisy."}

115. {Custine, *Le monde*, 2:26–27.}

116. {Custine, *Le monde*, 2:30: "the exalted love of truth is the misanthropy of good hearts"}

117. {Custine, *Le monde*, 2:65–68.}

118. *The same génie . . . radoteur."]* "The same genius can be seen as *creator* or as *dotard.*" {N underlines *créateur* and *radoteur*.}

119. {Cf. Custine, *Le monde*, 2:209.}

120. *Luxe]* "Luxury"

121. {Cf. Custine, *Le monde*, 2:207.}

122. {Custine, *Le monde*, 2:222: " — the modern apostles, the philosophical authors, lie more than the priests whom they dethroned *without replacing them.*" {N underlines *sans les remplacer*.}

123. Arthur Schopenhauer, *Die Welt als Wille und Vorstellung*, vol. 2, ed. Julius Frauenstädt (Leipzig: F. A. Brockhaus, 1873), 495, 497. *NL.* {*The World as Will and Representation*, vol. 2, trans. and ed. Judith Norman, Alistair Welchman, and Christopher Janaway (Cambridge: Cambridge University Press, 2017), 450, 451.}

124. {Cf. Custine, *Le monde*, 2:221–22.}

125. {Custine, *Le monde*, 2:281–82: "The ordinary effect of despair is to restore energy to those who witness this moral sickness."}; N uses this thought in *Z* IV "The Welcoming."

126. {Custine, *Le monde*, 2:275–76.} Similar images in *Z* IV "The Song of Melancholy."

127. *women]* Frauen

128. *"pitiful mortals"]* {Cf. *Odyssey*, bk. 12, line 341.}

129. {*WP²* 1029.}

130. *Soul] Seele* {We use the conventional rendering. In N's time, the meaning was closer to "psyche." Cf. our Translators' Afterword, pp. 487–88.}

131. {Cf. Astolphe de Custine, *Ethel* (Brussels: Société Belge de Librairie, 1839), 2:41.}

132. *decoration] Decoration* {N uses the French term in place of the standard German *Verzierung* or *Schmuck*, imparting a nuance of the theater, of stagecraft.}

133. *moral] moral⟨ischen⟩* {We render Colli-Montinari's emendation of N's abbreviation of *moralischen* here without adding the brackets from the original text. See also 25[171, 254, 412, 437, 441, 483]; and Colli's Afterword, p. 470.}

134. *The "ugliest . . . better.]* Cf. *Z* IV "The Ugliest Human."

135. *billy goat] Bock* {Greek *tragos*, hence *tragodia* = "goat song."}

136. {The presentation of this fragment in *KSA* 11 is seriously misleading. We have rearranged the fragment section B) as it appears in W I 1, 132. It should also be noted that section A) follows section B) in N's notebook W I 1 on page 132.}

137. *L'école du document humain]* "The school of the human document" {N is summarizing the footnote in Edmond de Goncourt's preface to his novel *La Faustin* (Paris: Charpentier, 1882), ii.}

138. *romantisme]* "Romanticism"

139. {*WP²* 982.}

140. *parvenu-ism]* *Parvenu-thum* {N has the nouveau riche social climbers in mind.}

141. {Lucien Anatole Prévost-Paradol, *La France nouvelle* (Paris: Michel Lévy Frères, 1868), 296.}

142. {Prévost-Paradol, *La France nouvelle*, 297–301.}

143. {Cf. Luke 2:14.}

144. *honnet]* "decent"

145. *a noblesse]* *eine Noblesse* {"nobility"; N is using singular universals for all of these examples, meant to stand for an entire class or social group. Therefore we pluralize.}

146. *restaurateur . . . française]* "restorer of French liberty"

147. *le roi . . . faible]* "the king *too defiant, too weak*" {N underlines *trop défiant, trop faible*.}

148. *comme . . . premières]* "like *cowardice* its first concessions" {N underlines *lâcheté*.}

149. *la maladresse janséniste]* "Jansenist clumsiness"

150. *"red spectre"]* *rotes Gespenst* {Prévost-Paradol refers to the *spectre du socialism* ("spectre of socialism"; 301). The expressions *spectre rouge* and *fantôme rouge*, either of which would be translated into German as *rotes Gespenst*, were widely used in France at the time to refer to socialism. *Gespenst* is the term that Marx and Engels use in the opening sentence of the preamble to *The Communist Manifesto* to refer to communism.}

151. {Prévost-Paradol, *La France nouvelle*, 306–9.}

152. *cette . . . succès]* "this imperious thirst for success"

153. *la . . . (magnanimité)]* "greatness of soul (magnanimity)"

154. *à la . . . imprévue]* "at the height of unforeseen destiny"

155. *bonhomie bienveillante]* "benevolent bonhomie"

156. *ces rares relâchements]* "these rare releases"

157. *cette . . . indifférent.]* "this intermittent ease of an indifferent heart."

158. *désinteressée émotion]* "disinterested or selfless emotion"

159. *esprit . . . méridionale]* "badly cultivated mind, southern imagination"

160. *imbu . . . siens]* "imbued above all with monarchical fetishism, he dreams of purple, throne, and crown for his people"

161. *wherever there is cruelty]* wo Alles es Grausamkeit gibt {N underlines *wo Alles.*}

162. *Renée Mauperin]* Novel by Edmond and Jules de Goncourt (1864).

163. *For others to have]* Für andere

164. Cf. *EH* III WA2.

165. *J. Burckhardt . . . Pitti]* Cf. *Der Cicerone: Eine Anleitung zum Genuß der Kunstwerke Italiens* {"The *Cicerone*: A guide to art appreciation in Italy"}, 2nd ed., ed. A. v. Zahn (Leipzig{: E. A. Seeman,} 1869), 175, *NL*; cf. *CW* 13, 11[197] and corresponding note.

166. *Flaubert (Letters)]* Cf. Flaubert, *Lettres à George Sand*, note 13 above.

167. Cf. *BGE* 224.

168. {Cf. Hippolyte Taine, *Nouveaux essais de critique et d'histoire* ("New essays on criticism and history"), 3rd ed. (Paris: Hachette, 1880), 124–26.}

169. *commis]* "shopgirl"

170. *Taine]* In *Nouveaux essais de critique et d'histoire*, 107–8.

171. *l'orgueil, . . . calcul.]* "pride, rigidity of mind, obedient silliness, vanity, prejudice, calculation"

172. *substances infectes]* "infected material"

173. *la grandeur d'âme]* "greatness of soul" {Taine, in fact, writes "la grandeur d'idées" ("greatness of ideas").}

174. *la délicatesse d'âme]* "delicacy of soul"

175. {*La Princesse de Clèves* is a novel published anonymously in 1678, believed to be authored by Madame de La Fayette (1634–93).}

176. *psychotherapy]* Irren-Heilkunde {Healing methods involved in curing the insane.}

177. Cf. Hippolyte Taine, *Essais de critique et d'histoire*, 4th ed. (Paris{: Hachette,} 1882), 42; Taine references {François} Guizot, whose *Histoire de la révolution d'Angleterre* {"History of the English

revolution"} he is reviewing{: "this talent (philosophy of history) did not consist, *in the German way*, in the risky improvisation of sublime theories." N underlines *à l'allemande*}.

178. {*WP²* 958.}

179. *Theages]* 125e–126a.

180. {Hippolyte Taine, *Notes sur l'Angleterre* ("Notes on England") (Paris: Hachette, 1876), 352.}

181. *le moral de l'homme . . . sensibilité . . . désaccordée]* "human morality . . . sensibility . . . out of tune"

182. {Taine, *Notes sur l'Angleterre*, 355–56.}

183. Quotation from the Goncourt brothers' novel *Manette Salomon* (1867); information in the notes follows the 1889 edition: chap. XXXV, pp. 137–38{: "*Ingres*: the inventor in the 19th century of color photography for the reproduction of Peruginos and Raphaels. *Delacroix* is the antipole — image of the decadence of this time, waste, confusion, literature in painting, painting in literature, prose in verse, verse in prose, the passions, the nerves, the weaknesses of our time, the modern torment. Flashes of the sublime in all of this." N underlines *Ingres* and *Delacroix*.}

184. *Manette Salomon*, chap. XXXV, 138.

185. *foetus]* "fetus"

186. *après tout]* "after all"

187. *comme . . . incomplet]* "like any great unfinished"

188. *une agitation . . . fou]* "a shake of glasses, a crazy drawing"

189. *la boulette . . . désaccordé]* "the sculptor's dumpling, the modeling of triangles which is no longer the outline of the line of a body, but the expression, the thickness of the relief of its form — out of tune harmonist"

190. *la lie de Rubens]* "the dregs of Rubens"

191. *Manette Salomon*, chaps. XXXVI and LXV, 140–41 and 218–19.

192. *Manette Salomon*, chap. III, 13–16.

193. *peintres poètes]* "painters poets"

194. *un peintre de prose]* "a painter of *prose*" {N underlines *prose*.}

195. *ce grand . . . contemporanéité]* "that great scorned side of art: contemporaneity"

196. *le beau expressive]* "*expressive* beauty" {N underlines *expressive*.}

197. *comme . . . Raphaël]* "as savior of Raphael's beauty"

198. *Manette Salomon*, chap. LXXXIII, 266–67.

199. *making way for]* präsidieren

200. *A sequence . . . empire."]* Quotation from Ernest Renan, *Histoire des origines du Christianisme*, I: *La vie de Jésus* {*The History of the Origins of Christianity*, bk. I: *The Life of Jesus*} (Paris{: Michel Lévy Frères,} 1863), 47; N uses another edition; cf. *Z* IV "The Honey Sacrifice."

201. Renan, *Histoire*, 51–53.

202. Quoted in Renan, *Histoire*, 179; cf. *Z* IV "On Superior Humans" 16.

203. *"Be good bankers!"]* Quoted by means of Renan, *Histoire*, 180, who cites as his source Clement of Alexandria, *Stromata* I, 28; cf. 31[50]; 32[10].

204. Cf. 25[177].

205. Cf. Stendhal, *Rome, Naples et Florence* {"Rome, Naples, and Florence"}, Paris{: Michel Lévy Frères,} 1854, 30, *NL*: "La beauté n'est jamais, ce me semble, qu'une *promesse de bonheur*" {"Beauty, it seems to me, is only ever a *promise of happiness*"; N underlines *promesse de bonheur*}; cf. *GM* III 6.

206. Cf. *Z* IV "On Superior Humans" 16.

207. *camp followers]* Gesindel {We use the locution that refers to women who "accompanied" soldiers on campaigns.}

208. *Ego fatum]* "I am destiny"

209. {This quotation comes from Thucydides, *Geschichte des Peloponnesischen Kriegs* {*History of the Peloponnesian War*}, trans. Adolf Wahrmund, 2nd improved ed. (Stuttgart: Krais & Hoffmann, 1866), 117n201. *NL.*}

210. *person of power]* Cf. 25[117] and corresponding note.

211. {*WP²* 506.}

212. *"Il . . . lui."]* {Said of} Julien Sorel in {Stendhal's} *Le rouge et le noir* {*The Red and the Black*}{: "He is not afraid of being in bad taste."}; cf. N to Peter Gast, {9} December 1886 {*KGB* III:3, 289}.

213. *women]* Die Frau

214. {*WP²* 861.}

215. *suffrage universel]* "universal suffrage"

216. *rubbish]* Wirtschaft {A pejorative use of this term, preserved in modern German words like *Vetternwirtschaft* (nepotism).}

217. *secret personalities]* Hinterseelen

218. Cf. 25[152].

219. {*WP²* 94.}

220. *noblesse]* "nobility"

221. *Then . . . Stowe.]* Allusion to Harriet Beecher Stowe, *Uncle Tom's Cabin* (1852).

222. *désintéressement]* "disinterestedness"

223. *aegis] Aegide*; transcription uncertain.

224. *mesquin]* "mean"

225. *Stello]* Novel (1835) by Alfred de Vigny.

226. Cf. *BGE* 256; *WA* 7.

227. Cf. Emmanuel de Las Cases, *Mémorial de Sainte-Hélène* (Paris{: L'auteur,} 1823), 3:102–3. {Hereafter cited as *"Mémorial,"* followed by volume and page number.}

228. *Mémorial* 4:160{: "And then the restlessness of man is such that he needs this undefined and marvelous thing that it offers him."}

229. *Mémorial* 4:165{: "he said he was delighted, ecstatic at the purity, the sublimity and the beauty of such morality."}

230. *Mémorial* 3:240{: "I closed the chasm of anarchy and unraveled the chaos. I unearthed the revolution, ennobled the peoples and strengthened the kings. I have excited all emulations, rewarded all merits, and pushed the boundaries of glory. All this is indeed something!"}

231. *Mémorial* 3:104.

232. *cas pathologiques]* "pathological cases"

233. *Heinrich . . . Heilbronn]* N's source unknown; however, cf. Goethe's *Werke* (*Gedenkausgabe* {*der Werke, Briefe und Gespräche*), ed. Ernst Beutler (Zurich: Artemis, 1949}), 22:876: "After Goethe had read . . . Kleist's *Käthchen von Heilbronn*, he said: A wonderful mixture of sense and nonsense! The damned unnaturalness! And he threw it into the glowing fire of the oven with the words: I will not produce it, even if half of Weimar demands it." (E. W. Weber, date cannot be precisely determined.)

234. {Cf. Emile Montégut, *Poètes et artistes de l'Italie* (Paris: Hachette, 1881), 353–58.}

235. *inverted cripples]* Cf. *Z* II "On Redemption."

236. *committed all crimes]* Cf. *Z* IV "The Shadow"; 3[8]; {cf. 25[259, 484]; 29[51]; 32[8]}.

237. {*WP²* 938.}

238. *"l'amour, . . . souverain."] {Esprit du Mémorial de Ste. Hélène, par le Comte de Las Cases* (Paris: Boucher, 1823), 1:245: "love, according to Napoleon, the occupation of the idle man, the distraction of the warrior, the pitfall of the sovereign."}

239. *les Gaulois . . . vanité] {Memorial* 1:362: "the Gauls of yesteryear: the levity, the same fickleness and above all the same *vanity*." N underlines *vanité*.}

240. {Cf. *Memorial* 3:372–73.}

241. ἀρετή] *aretē* "virtue"

242. {Pluralized for gender neutrality.}

243. {*WP²* 67.}

244. *psyche] Seele*

245. {*WP²* 862.}

246. {This quote is from the work mentioned in 25[217]: Anders Magnus Strinnholm, *Wikingszüge, Staatsverfassung und Sitten der alten Skandinavier* ("Viking expeditions, state constitution and customs of the ancient Scandinavians"), trans. from Swedish by C. F. Frisch (Hamburg: Perthes, 1839), pt. 1, 216.}

247. *religiosi]* "religious people"

248. *engineers] Mechaniker* {Those engaged in an early form of theoretical study of physics and motion.}

249. Cf. 25[259]{, 25[212]. N wrote to Peter Gast on 22 March 1884 (*KGB* III:1, 487), inquiring whether there was a good library in Venice for German books; Gast responded on 25 March (*KGB* III:2, 428) that N might find things at the Münster lending library, and it is from there that N borrowed Strinnholm's book.}

250. {*WP²* 754.}

251. Cf. N to Malwida von Meysenbug, beginning of May 1884 {*KGB* III:1, 500–501} (through Elisabeth N).

252. *goose] Gans* {A traditional pejorative term for women, probably a reference to N's sister.}

253. *with the greatest empathy] Nachfühler*

254. *comfortism] Comfortismus*

255. {Cf. *WP²* 916.}

256. Cf. comments in the note to 25[1].

257. *selectionist] züchtende* {Here N is referring to his idea that eternal recurrence will act as a principle of artificial selection, in contrast to Darwin's principle of natural selection.}

258. *I want . . . thought.]* {Cf. *WP²* 1056.}

259. Concerning a new *Zarathustra* work (after *Z* III, which N considered to be the conclusion of his *Z* work); cf. 25[246, 247, 260, 306, 415, 523]; 26[222]; 27[71]; concerning the title of the new work, cf. 25[323].

260. *"Philosophy of the Future"]* As title or subtitle (often as "Prelude to a Philosophy of the Future," as in *BGE*) in 25[490, 500]; 26[426]; *CW* 16, 34[1]; 35[84]; 36[1, 6]; 40[45, 48]; 41[1].

261. *desert] Verdienst* {Standard philosophical term for praise or blame.}

262. {Cf. N to Franz Overbeck, 21 May 1884 (*KGB* III:1, 507): I am happy to make use of your expression "mystical separatists": I was just saying to Köselitz not long ago that there is no "German culture" and that there never has been — }

263. Cf. comments in the note to 25[237]; cf. *Z* IV "Conversation with the Kings."

264. Cf. comments in the note to 25[237]; some themes adopted for *Z* IV.

265. *Where . . . pity]* Cf. *Z* II "On Compassionate People"; cf. also the motto for *Z* IV.

266. Cf. 25[251].

267. Cf. comments in the note to 25[237].

268. *fatum]* "fate"; "destiny"

269. {N here mistakenly refers to August Friedrich Gfrörer, *Gustav Adolph, König von Schweden, und seine Zeit* ("Gustavus Adolphus, King of Sweden and his time") (Stuttgart: Rieger, 1837).}

270. {Walter Rogge, *Parlamentarische Größen*, I. *Die Conservativen*; II. *Die Demokraten* ("Great parliamentarians, I: The conservatives; II: The democrats") (Berlin: Hofmann, 1850, 1851). Rogge wrote these two books under the pseudonym "R. Walter," although he acknowledged the pseudonym in the foreword to the second volume.}

271. Cf. 25[248].

272. Cf. 31[61]; *Z* IV "On Superior Humans" 5.

273. Cf. *BGE* Preface.

274. Cf. 25[217]; some themes adopted for *GM*.

275. *Rée]* Cf. note to *CW* 14, 7[17]; {cf. 25[198, 484]; 29[51]; 32[8]}.

276. Cf. comments in the note to 25[237].

277. *bien public]* "public good" or "public property"

278. Cf. *Z* IV "No Longer in Service."

279. {*WP²* 757.}

280. Cf. comments in the note to 25[252].

281. {Cf. *TI* "Forays of an Untimely One" 16.}

282. Cf. 25[271, 272]; *Z* IV "Conversation with the Kings."

283. *supreme . . . tools.]* {*WP²* 998.}

284. Cf. 25[268].

285. Cf. 25[268]; 26[457].

286. *scape- and scrapegoat] Sünden- und Unfallsbock* {The latter term is N's coinage. We render it as "scrape" in the sense of accident.}

287. Refers to *Concerning the Future of Our Educational Institutions, WB, SE.*

288. Cf. Chronicle of N's life 1877 in *CW* 19.

289. Source unknown.

290. Refers to family conflicts during this time (Spring 1884); cf. Chronicle of N's life in *CW* 19.

291. Cf. *TI* "Forays of an Untimely One" 51; *EH* Foreword 4; cf. also N's letters from the spring of 1884 (following the completion of *Z* III).

292. {*WP²* 364.}

293. Cf. 25[305, 322, 331].

294. *esprit barroco]* "baroque spirit"

295. {Cf. Galton, *Inquiries* (note to 25[18]), 213: "There is an Oriental phrase, as I have been told, that the fear of the inevitable approach of death is a European malady."}

296. Cf. 26[293, 298]; 27[79, 80]; 29[40].

297. *death wish] Willen zum Todes*

298. {*WP²* 860.}

299. {*WP²* 595.}

300. *geese] Gänse* {Pejorative, misogynist metaphor usually applied to women who talk too much and know too little.}

301. Cf. *BGE* 11; N to Peter Gast, 7 March 1887 {*KGB* III:5, 41}.

302. *Tübingen Seminary] Tübinger Stift* {Founded by Duke Ulrich of Württemberg in 1536, the Tübingen Stift trained pastors and theologians to serve the Lutheran church. Some of the better-known seminarians included the astronomer Johannes Kepler, the poet Friedrich Hölderlin, the philosopher G. W. F. Hegel, the theologian David Friedrich Strauss, and the philologist August Pauly.}

303. Cf. *Z* IV "The Shadow"; {26[25];} 32[8]. {In *GM* III 24 (*CW* 8, 338), N refers to this maxim as the watchword of the Order of Assassins, an Islamic sect dating from the eleventh to the thirteenth century. Cf. Joseph von Hammer, *Die Geschichte der Assassinen, aus morgenländischen Quellen* ("The history of the Assassins, from Oriental sources") (Stuttgart: Cotta, 1818), 84.}

304. Cf. the note to 25[237].

305. Cf. the note to 25[237].

306. *limits of reason] vernünftige Grenze* {Here we have chosen to translate this as an allusion to the Kantian idea, but it could be translated as "rational limits."}

307. *tartarus stibiatus]* {Homeopathic remedy for treatment of loose cough.}

308. {*WP²* 614.}

309. *Lange, p 822]* Friedrich Albert Lange, *Geschichte des Materialismus* {*History of Materialism*}, ed. Hermann Cohen (Iserlohn{: Baedeker,} 1882), 4th printing (1887) in *NL*; concerning N and Lange, cf. Jörg Salaquarda, "Nietzsche und Lange," *Nietzsche-Studien* 7 (1978), esp. 239–40n20).

310. Cf. note to 25[237].

311. Cf. notes to 25[1] and 25[237].

312. *to project their image of the world] ihr Bild der Welt wiederstrahlen* {N could also mean "to project their image into the world."}

313. Cf. note to 25[237].

314. *lifespan of the stars] Dauer der Gestirne* {We use the English idiom. N's use of the neutral term *Dauer* is consistent with his rejection of all attempts to anthropomorphize stars or planets.}

315. *voluntas]* "will"

316. *Great human beings feel . . . before! —]* {Cf. *WP²* 964.}

317. *upstanding] rechtwinklig* {N has people in mind who are "proportional" in mind and body rather than people with moral rectitude.}

318. *woman] Frau*

319. Cf. *Z* IV "The Ugliest Human."

320. *cult of assassins]* Cf. *GM* III 24. {Cf. note to 25[304].}

321. {*WP²* 965.}

322. *The rights . . . them:]* {*WP²* 872.}

323. *The degeneration . . . cross!]* {*WP²* 874.}

324. {Cf. Romans 3:23.}

325. {*WP²* 870.}

326. *ruling types] die herrschenden Naturen* {See our Translators' Afterword, p. 487.}

327. *was not in their vocabulary] war nicht bei ihnen zu Hause*

328. *the rotten . . . commands]* {*WP²* 750.}

329. {*WP²* 940.}

330. μηδὲν ἄγαν] *mēden agan* "nothing in excess" {Inscription on the temple of Apollo at Delphi.}

331. ἐγκράτεια] *enkrateia* "power over oneself"

332. ἄσκησις] *askēsis* "exercise"; "training"; "practice"

333. Cf. note to 25[237].

334. {*WP²* 999.}

335. *important] großen*

336. *à peu près]* "approximately"

337. Cf. 25[401].

338. *cognitive mechanisms] Erkenntniß-Apparat*

339. *"Everything . . . mind"]* Emendation in *Le*: "Everything is mind"; "Everything thinks"

340. *"Everything . . . number"]* Emendation in *Le*: "Everything is number"; "Everything calculates"

341. Cf. 25[376].

342. *highest level of consciousness] oberstes Bewusstsein*

343. *of a mix-up and a dust-up] eines Durch- und Gegeneinanders*

344. *to give vent to our pain] seinem Schmerze Luft machen*

345. Cf. note to 25[237].

346. *escapism from reality] Weltflucht*

347. {Sébastien-Roch-Nicolas de Chamfort, *Pensées, maximes, anecdotes, dialogues: Précédés de l'histoire de Chamfort par P. J. Stahl*

(Paris: Michel Lévy Frères, n.d. {1860}), 40, NL: "The public!
The public! How many fools does it take to make an audience?"
N found this citation reading Paul Albert's "Essai sur Ducis" in
Albert's *Variétés morales et littéraires* (Paris: Hachette, 1879), 276.}

348. {Jean François Ducis, *Œuvres posthumes de J. F. Ducis*
(Paris: Nepveu, 1826), 366: "all our happiness is only more or less
consoled misfortune." N also found this citation in Albert's "Essai
sur Ducis," in *Variétés morales et littéraires*, 260.}

349. List of themes that were mentioned in earlier fragments.

350. *vae victis]* "woe to the vanquished"

351. — *a founder . . . more!]* {*WP²* 178.}

352. *find their way]* auf ihre große Bahn kommen

353. *Germanic tribesmen]* Germanen

354. Cf. *BGE* 233.

355. Cf. note to 25[318].

356. *more abstract]* höher

357. *superior human beings]* die hohen Menschen {Appears only
six times in N's oeuvre, as opposed to his common locution,
"superior humans" / *höhere Menschen*.}

358. *just one thing in mind]* ausschließlich Eins im Auge

359. {*WP²* 1046.}

360. *criticism he receives from his own conscience]* die Kritik vor
seinem Gewissen {The context indicates that N has Jesus's self-
criticism in mind.}

361. *better than good]* Übergefühl

362. *p. 261.]* of the Frauenstädt edition, vol. 4 (1874). *NL.*
{Arthur Schopenhauer, "On the Basis of Morals," in *The Two Fun-
damental Problems of Ethics*, trans. and ed. Christopher Janaway
(Cambridge: Cambridge University Press, 2009), 245.}

363. *l.c. 265.]* Cf. note to 25[441]. {Schopenhauer, "On the Basis
of Morals," 249; pluralized for gender neutrality.}

364. *most force at the end]* am meisten Schlußkraft

365. Cf. 25[237, 323]; 26[200, 221]; and corresponding footnotes.

366. *"Humans . . . overcome"]* Cf. *Z* I "Zarathustra's Preface"
3{; cf. *CW* 14, 3[1], 247; 4[165]; 24[16]; 11[8]; 18[43, 49, 56]; 21[6]}.

367. Cf. 25[237] and corresponding note.

368. Like 25[456].

369. *Sensorium commune]* {The part of the brain that was once thought to be the seat of sensation and feeling in the body.}

370. *temperaments] Charaktere*

371. *actions] facta* {In the sense of deeds here, rather than facts.}

372. *predatory instincts] Raubsucht*

373. {*WP²* 495.}

374. *the willing of power] Macht-wille*

375. Cf. *GM* I 5. {*bonus* = "good"; φαν = *fan*; *malus* = "bad"; μαν = *man*; *böse* = "evil"; *gut* = "good"; *man-lus* and *Manlius* are unknown, perhaps N experimenting with alternative etymologies.}

376. Cf. Goethe, *Maximen und Reflexionen* {Maxims and reflections}, 328{; *Sprüche in Prosa* ("Sayings in prose") (Berlin: Hempel, 1870), #287}.

377. Perhaps a commentary on Goethe, *Maximen und Reflexionen*, 313{; *Sprüche in Prosa*, #272}: ". . . It was the time that executed Socrates with poison . . . the times have always remained the same"?

378. Cf. Goethe, *Maximen und Reflexionen*, 332{; *Sprüche in Prosa*, #291}.

379. Cf. Goethe, *Maximen und Reflexionen*, 340{; *Sprüche in Prosa*, #299}; *BGE* 244.

380. Cf. Goethe, *Maximen und Reflexionen*, {371; *Sprüche in Prosa*, #330}.

381. Cf. Goethe, *Maximen und Reflexionen*, 316{; *Sprüche in Prosa*, #275}.

382. Quoted in Goethe, *Maximen und Reflexionen*, 228{; *Sprüche in Prosa*, #238}: "a man worthy of the highest praise that can be associated with valor."

383. Cf. Goethe, *Maximen und Reflexionen*, 186{; *Sprüche in Prosa*, #200}.

384. *Chi . . . falla]* Cf. Goethe, *Sprüche in Prosa*, note to #210{: "He who does nothing makes no mistakes"}.

385. Cf. Goethe, *Sprüche in Prosa*, note to #158{: "Great minds agree"}.

386. {Cf. 25[198, 259]; 29[51]; 32[8].}

387. *upper classes] Stände* {Includes the members of society in addition to the nobility.}

388. Cf. 25[451, 500, 504]; cf. also 25[489].

389. Cf. 25[237] and corresponding note.

390. *loses sight of itself]* sich selber vergisst

391. *he]* Richard Wagner

392. Cf. 25[490] and corresponding note; cf. also note to 25[238].

393. *Amor fati]* Cf. *JS* 276; *EH* "Why I Am So Clever" 10; *EH* III WA4; *NW* "Epilogue" 1.

394. Cf. 25[490].

395. {*WP²* 602.}

396. Cf. 25[304] and corresponding note.

397. Cf. *CW* 17, 7[12].

398. *of the contents of memory]* des Gedächtnis-Materials

399. *can . . . seas]* Cf. *JSA* "On to New Seas."

400. {Pietro Angelo Secchi (1818–78) was a Catholic priest and astronomer who directed the observatory at the Pontifical Gregorian University in Rome. N's source here might be P. Angelo Secchi, *Die Sterne: Grundzüge der Astronomie der Fixsterne* ("Stars: Basics of fixed-star astronomy") (Leipzig: F. A. Brockhaus, 1878); cf. 331–32.}

401. {Cf. Voltaire's satirical attack on Maupertuis in his *La diatribe du docteur akakia* (1752). Maupertuis mentions dissecting the skulls of Patagonian giants in his "Lettre sur le progrès des sciences," *Œuvres de Maupertuis* (Lyon: Bruyset, 1768), 2:386–88.}

402. Perhaps aimed at E. v. Hartmann; cf. 25[517].

403. *a mechanical account]* der Mechanik

404. *I'm the first one to see that this idea makes no sense]* Unverständliches erst in mir

405. Cf. 25[237] and corresponding note.

406. Cf. 26[390]; *CW* 16, 38[19]; *GM* Preface 3; *CW* 12, 28[7].

407. Cf. *CW* 16, 34[247].

[26 = W I 2. Summer–Autumn 1884]

1. Cf. *CW* 16, 34[29].

2. Cf. Paul de Lagarde, {*Ueber die gegenwärtige lage des deutschen Reichs. Ein bericht* ("On the present situation of the German Reich: A report") (Göttingen: Dieterich, 1876). *NL*.}

3. Cf. 28[53]{; cf. Luke 1:37}.

4. *"he allows . . . and unjust."]* {Cf. Matthew 5:45.}

5. Cf. 25[303]; 26[445, 412].

6. {*WP²* 854.}

7. *suffrage universel]* "universal suffrage"

8. Cf. 25[217, 259].

9. {*WP²* 497.}

10. {*WP²* 421.}

11. *cognitive mechanism]* *Erkenntniß-Apparat* {This could also be translated as a "mechanism of knowledge," which makes more evident the paradox that N has in mind.}

12. Refers to *WB.*

13. Cf. 25[304, 505].

14. *"Nothing . . . permitted."]* {Cf. Hammer, *Die Geschichte der Assassinen,* 84; see note to 25[304] above.}

15. Cf. 26[377]; *CW* 16, 35[49]; 41[2].

16. *Moira]* {In Greek mythology and religion, the incarnation of fate.}

17. {Cf. *TI* "The Four Great Errors" 4.}

18. *perspective]* *Seh-Winkel* {literally, "viewing angle"}

19. Cf. 25[490, 500].

20. Concerning 26[47].

21. {*WP²* 476.}

22. {Cf. *BGE* 4.}

23. *efficiency]* *Zweckmäßigkeit*

24. {*WP²* 503.}

25. *unintentional]* *Unzweckmäßige*

26. *Heraclitus:]* Cf. fragments 114, 28, 94, 80, 1, 2, 23 (Diels-Kranz).

27. *built and framed]* *gebaut und gezimmert* {In the sense of carpentry.}

28. Concerning 26[47, 48].

29. *The type . . . time.]* {*WP²* 987.}

30. Quote from the Frauenstädt edition (1873–74). *NL.* {Cf. Arthur Schopenhauer, *The Two Fundamental Problems of Ethics,* trans. and ed. Christopher Janaway (Cambridge: Cambridge University Press, 2009), 122.}

31. *ἐποχή]* *epochē* "suspension of judgment"

32. All quotes — including this one from Kant — from the Frauenstädt edition cited above.

33. {Cf. Schopenhauer, *The Two Fundamental Problems of Ethics*, 137.}

34. Like 26[84].

35. {Cf. Schopenhauer, *The Two Fundamental Problems of Ethics*, 139.}

36. ὅ, τι] "what"

37. διότι] "why"

38. *neminem laede, immo omnes quatum potes juva]* "harm no one, rather benefit everyone to the extent that you can"

39. {Cf. Schopenhauer, *The Two Fundamental Problems of Ethics*, 139–40. N also cites this sentence in *BGE* 186.}

40. *achievable] ausführbar* {KSA mistakenly has *ausführbar*, although this could be reproducing a misspelling by N in W I 2, 145.}

41. *There are . . . Kotzebue]* Cf. 26[96].

42. *nervus sympathicus]* "sympathetic nervous system"

43. *sensorium commune]* "seat of sensation"

44. {*WP²* 365.}

45. Cf. 26[85].

46. Cf. *Z* IV "On Superior Humans" 5.

47. {*WP²* 408.}

48. πολυτροπία] "versatility" {πολύτροπον is how Odysseus is introduced in the first line of Homer's *Odyssey*.}

49. {*WP²* 1043.}

50. *fortuitous coincidences] günstige Zufälle*

51. *If we could . . . aid.—]* {*WP²* 907.}

52. {*WP²* 259.}

53. {Here N uses the term *Mann*, so we did not adjust the English to reflect gender neutrality.}

54. {Cf. Aristotle, *Nicomachean Ethics*, 1124a6–9, 1125a3, 1124a13–15. Cf. Gustav Teichmüller, *Aristotelische Forschungen*, vol. 2: *Aristoteles Philosophie der Kunst* ("Aristotelian research, vol. 2: Aristotle's philosophy of art") (Halle: G. E. Barthel, 1867), 289.}

55. Cf. e.g., *Nicomachean Ethics*, 1177a1–5. {Cf. Teichmüller, *Aristoteles Philosophie der Kunst*, 182–83.}

56. *suffrage universel]* "universal suffrage"

57. {*WP²* 496.}

58. Cf. 26[131].

59. *causa efficiens]* "efficient cause" {i.e., that which is responsible for the change}

60. *causae finales]* "final causes" {i.e., the end or purpose, that for the sake of which something is done}

61. *causae efficientes]* "efficient causes"

62. {The verb is missing. N probably meant "imagine" or something related.}

63. {Cf. Georg Steinhart, *Evangelistarium* (Leipzig, 1588), 49; N most likely came across this line cited in Johannes Janssen, *Geschichte des deutschen Volkes seit dem Ausgang des Mittelalters*, vol. 3: *Die politisch-kirchliche Revolution der Fürsten und Städte und ihre Folgen für Volk und Reich bis zum sogenannten Augsburger Religionsfrieden von 1555* ("History of the German people since the end of the Middle Ages, vol. 3: The political and ecclesiastical revolution of the princes and cities and their consequences for people and empire up to the so-called Peace of Augsburg of 1555") (Freiburg im Breisgau: Herder, 1881), 702. Cf. 28[27].}

64. Cf. note to 26[128].

65. {*WP²* 498.}

66. From 1883 on, often-cited title before the publication of *BGE*; cf. 26[241, 297, 325].

67. *Extra-moral]* *außermoralischen*

68. Concerning 26[139].

69. *that will condense our experiences]* um *Erfahrungen zu ersparen*

70. *an autonomous reason]* eine *freie Vernunft*

71. {Cf. e.g., *Gorgias* 468a; *Meno* 77c; *Symposium* 204e; *Republic* 413a.}

72. *Plato]* {Cf. *Hyppias Minor* 367a ff.}

73. Cf. 26[47, 48, 160].

74. *as if under the weather]* wie unter *Wolken* {In N's wordplay with the idiomatic meaning of "unter"; the people are the weather.}

75. Cf. 25[6].

76. Cf. Schopenhauer, *Die Welt als Wille und Vorstellung*, 2:264? {The passage N might have in mind is unclear, but Schopenhauer

makes several remarks along these lines in *The World as Will and Representation*, vol. 2, chap. 19: "On the Primacy of the Will in Self-Consciousness."}

77. *farm] Landwirtschaft*

78. *compare an action with other actions] Vergleichung von Handlung mit anderen Handlungen*

79. {*WP²* 410.}

80. *method] Mittel*

81. *where . . . friends?]* Cf. *BGE* Aftersong.

82. {Cf. *Karl Semper, Die natürlichen Existenzbedingungen der Thiere* ("The natural conditions of existence of animals") (Leipzig: Brockhaus, 1880), 1:18–19, 236–37, 241–42; 2:218–19, 222–23, 253. *NL.*}

83. *Manfred]* By Lord Byron; cf. *EH* "Why I Am So Clever" 4.

84. *brotherly love] brüderlichen Liebe* {This is the only time this expression appears in any of N's writings other than in one letter to Erwin Rohde, 28 August 1877 (*KGB* II:5, 278).}

85. Cf. Paul Deussen, *Das System des Vedânta* (Leipzig{: Brockhaus,} 1883), 239, *NL* (henceforth cited as "*Vedanta*"). {*The System of the Vedânta*, trans. Charles Johnston (Chicago: Open Court, 1912).}

86. *Vedanta*, 303.

87. *Bidden and forbidden works] Gebotene und verbotene Werke*

88. *Vedanta*, 434–35.

89. *Vedanta*, 444.

90. *it] ihn* {In Deussen's text, the "it" here refers to Brahman, the principle of "ultimate reality"; cf. *Vedanta*, 434.}

91. *Vedanta*, 448.

92. *Rée]* Cf. note to *CW* 14, 7[17].

93. *beyond what is human] außermenschlichen*

94. *forms of government] Formen*

95. *against Rée]* Cf. note to 7[17] {*CW* 14, 655n22}.

96. Cf. 25[237] and corresponding note.

97. *Buddha]* Reference to Hermann Oldenberg, *Buddha: Sein Leben, seine Lehre, seine Gemeinde* (Berlin{: Wilhelm Hertz,} 1881), *NL*; source of the page numbers as well {*Buddha: His Life, His Doctrine, His Order*, trans. William Hoey (London: Williams and Norgate, 1882), 43–44, 45–46}.

98. Like 26[220].

99. {Ebion was the mythical founder of an apocryphal early Christian group known as the Ebionites, associated with ideals of poverty, adherence to the Beatitude of Poor in Spirit, and to the poverty of the Mosaic law that they strictly observed.}

100. Cf. 25[237] and corresponding note.

101. Like 26[222].

102. Cf. *GM* III 24. {Cf. also Hammer, *Die Geschichte der Assassinen*, 87, 123, 337 (see note to 25[304] above).}

103. *Deifying . . . priests.]* {Cf. *WP²* 145.}

104. *I have gained mastery over]* ich bin Herr geworden

105. {*WP²* 686.}

106. *Not . . . goal!]* {*WP²* 1001.}

107. *Dühring]* Reference to Dühring's autobiography, *Sache, Leben und Feinde* ("Things, life, and enemies"} (Karlsruhe{: Reuther,} 1882). *NL.*

108. Cf. *JSP.*

109. {*WP²* 615.}

110. Cf. N to Heinrich von Stein, 18 September 1884 {*KGB* III:1, 553} (see Chronicle of N's Life in *CW* 19).

111. {Allusion to the myth as told in Sophocles's *Philoctetes.*}

112. Cf. 26[241].

113. Concerning 26[239].

114. *the superior psychological state]* der . . . höhere Seelen-zustand

115. *skeptics out of weakness]* des Sceptikers der Schwäche

116. *Galiani]* Lettres à Madame d'Épinay ("Letters to Madame d'Épinay"); cf. note to *CW* 17, 9[107].

117. Cf. 25[1] and corresponding note.

118. *ruling structure for the earth]* Regierung der Erde

119. Cf. *BGE* 266. {The source of the Goethe quote is most likely Johannes Janssen, *Zeit- und Lebensbilder* ("Images of our life and times") (Freiburg im Breisgau: Herder, 1875), ii, where Janssen uses the Goethe quotation as the book's motto.}

120. Cf. Goethe, *Faust* II, line 11989; the same quotation {appears in slightly altered form} in *BGE* 286 and *TI* "Forays of an Untimely One" 46.

121. Reference to Johannes Janssen, *Geschichte des deutschen Volkes seit dem Ausgang des Mittelalters* ("History of the German people

since the end of the Middle Ages")}, 8 vols., the first four of which were published by 1885} (Freiburg{: Herder, 1878–94}); cf. N to Peter Gast, 5 October 1879 {*KGB* II:5, 451}; N to Overbeck, October 1882 {There is no letter to Overbeck in October in *KGB*; N does discuss Janssen's book in the letter to Overbeck of 10 November 1882 (*KGB* III:1, 275)} *GM* III 19; concerning D. F. Strauss, cf. *DS*.

122. Cf. 25[1] and corresponding note.

123. *I believe . . . actions!]* {*WP²* 1000.}

124. Concerning the work whose title varies between 25[1] and 26[259].

125. *according to the degree of power] nach der Seite der Kraft menge*

126. Cf. 25[1] and corresponding note; "Attempt at a Revaluation of All Values" later becomes the subtitle of the planned volume *WP*.

127. *ego]* "I"

128. {*WP²* 873.}

129. Cf. 25[237] and corresponding note.

130. Cf. 26[318]; the topic of "superior humans" is treated multiple times during this era until the writing of *Z* IV.

131. The fragments 26[273, 274, 275, 276, 277] are closely linked and explore the topic "will to power": they were all not included in the compilation by Elisabeth Förster-Nietzsche and Peter Gast.

132. *justice] Recht* {This could also be rendered as "right."}

133. *in praxi]* "in practice"

134. *v.] vide* {"see"}

135. *the brown binder] das braune Heft*

136. *otium]* "leisure"

137. {*WP²* 752.}

138. {*WP²* 1060.} Cf. 26[284]; 25[1] and corresponding note.

139. *concept of necessity] Nothwendigkeitsbegriff* {N underlines *Noth.*}

140. {*WP²* 1059.} Concerning 26[283].

141. *in case it is not prevented] falls nicht vorgebeugt wird*

142. *will to power] Wille . . . der Macht* {N uses the genitive here, literally "will of power," not his usual phrasing *Wille zur Macht.*}

143. *pro pudor]* "for shame"

144. Cf. note to 25[237]; some of the characters listed here appear in *Z* IV.

145. Cf. Montaigne, *Essais* ("Essays"), bk. 1, chap. XXIII. {The page reference is to vol. 1 of the 1753–54 German translation of the *Versuche* by Peter Coste (Leipzig: F. Lankischens Erben, 1753), 174–75, *NL*; in fact, N has lifted the passage from Eduard Reich, who cites it in *System der Hygiene*, 2 vols. (Leipzig: Fleischer, 1870–71), 1:188. *NL*.}

146. Cf. 26[297, 298].

147. Cf. 25[296] and corresponding note.

148. {*WP²* 609.}

149. Cf. 26[296, 302].

150. Cf. 26[295].

151. *obligation] Muß*

152. Cf. 26[139] and corresponding note; 26[292].

153. Cf. 26[293, 296]; 25[1] and corresponding note.

154. Cf. *CW* 16, 38[22]; 2[2].

155. *women] Frauen*

156. *Philosophers taken . . . human actions]* {Cf. *WP²* 407.}

157. *Boscovich]* Cf. *BGE* 12; 26[410, 432]; cf. *CW* 6, 15[21].

158. *et hoc genus omne]* "and all this sort of thing"

159. {*Mémorial de Sainte-Hélène* (1823), written by Emmanuel-Auguste-Dieudonné, Compte de Las Cases (aka Emmanuel de Las Cases), was a journal-memoir of the beginning of Napoleon's exile. Cf. note to 25[187] above.}

160. {Johann Peter Eckermann (1792–1854) was Goethe's private secretary for nine years and published an account of the conversations he had with Goethe about literature, philosophy, religion, and the events of the day, which N elsewhere calls "the best German book that exists" (*WS* 109).}

161. Cf. 26[51]; *CW* 16, 35[46].

162. *Laocoön-group] Laokoon-gruppe* {A Roman statue, excavated in 1506, showing the Trojan priest Laocoön and his sons being attacked by sea serpents, was the object of spirited debate among German literati and art historians in the eighteenth century, particularly in regard to the aesthetic possibilities of the plastic versus the literary arts. It was consistently identified with the depiction of agony and suffering.}

163. *intuitio mystica]* "mystical intuition"

164. {Cf. *BGE* 15.}

165. *circulus vitiosus*] "vicious circle" {Cf. *BGE* 56.}

166. {Cf. *BGE* 13.}

167. {Cf. Stendhal, *Correspondance inédite: Précedée d'une intro-duction par Prosper Mérimée* ("Unpublished correspondence: Pre-ceded with an introduction by Prosper Mérimée") (Paris: Michel Lévy Frères, 1855), 2:37, 73–74; cf. Hippolyte Taine, *Geschichte der englischen Literatur* ("History of English literature"), German edi-tion by L. Katscher und G. Gerth, vol. 3: *Die Neuzeit der englischen Literatur* ("The modern age of English literature") (Leipzig: Ernst Julius Günther Nachf., 1880), 136;} cf. *CW* 16, 34[8].

168. *Travels in France]* Stendhal, *Mémoires d'un touriste* ("Mem-oirs of a tourist") (Paris{: Lévy, 1877). *NL.*

169. Cf. *Z* IV; cf. 26[270] and corresponding note.

170. Cf. *CW* 16, 34[155]; 35[9]; the "shadow" in *Z* IV is also part of being "good Europeans."

171. Cf. *Z* IV "Conversation with the Kings."

172. Cf. 26[139] and corresponding note; in addition, cf. 25[1] and corresponding note.

173. *Hedone]* {Ancient Greek personification and goddess of pleasure.}

174. *deduced]* erschlossen

175. *Our becoming familiar with the causes of a thing]* Die Kennt-niß der Ursachen eines Dinges

176. *money people]* Geldmenschen

177. *buona . . . vuol bastone]* "both the good and bad woman want a big stick" Cf. *BGE* 147; {cf. Émile Gebhart, *Études méri-dionales*, vol. 1: *Les origines de la Renaissance en Italie* ("Southern studies, vol. 1: The origins of the Renaissance in Italy") (Paris: Hachette, 1879), 269. The quote from Sacchetti can be found in *Le novelle di Franco Sacchetti* ("The short stories of Franco Sacchetti") (Milan: Edoardo Sonzogno, 1874), 149.}

178. *hinc mihi . . . praesto est.]* "whatever holy joys I can partake of are available to me at any hour." {Gebhart, *Études méridionales*, 1:314.} {Translation from *Letters from Petrarch*, ed. and trans. Mor-ris Bishop (Bloomington: Indiana University Press, 1966), 165.}

179. *genuine philosophers]* *Philosophen selber*

180. *Pericles]* Cf. Thucydides, II, 41 {This quotation comes from Thucydides, *Geschichte des Peloponnesischen Kriegs*, 128.}; also quoted in *GM* I 11; cf. *HAH* 474; *CW* 12, 3[41]; 5[200].

181. *l'art pour l'art]* "art for art's sake"

182. *I will this]* *ich will* {Cf. Translators' Afterword in *CW* 14, 746–47.}

183. *those that are most evil]* *des Bösesten* {This could also be rendered as "that which is most evil."}

184. *the Good]* *das Gute* {Here it appears that N is referring to Plato's form of the Good.}

185. *niaiserie]* "nonsense"; "silliness"

186. *firmly establishing]* *die Feststellung* {N underlines only the first four letters.}

187. {*WP²* 755.}

188. *instinctive feelings]* *Triebgefühlen*

189. Cf. 25[237] and corresponding note; *Z* IV "The Welcoming."

190. Cf. 25[237] and corresponding note; N is referring to the "singing" of one of the Colossi of Memnon in the Theban necropolis in Egypt {located across the Nile from the modern city of Luxor}; cf. Tacitus, *Annals* 2.61.

191. *stimulant]* *stimulantia*

192. *magnum opus]* {Parts of Kant's *Opus Postumum*, his final work, were initially published in a number of installments in the *Altpreussische Monatsschrift* between 1882 and 1884.}

193. Cf. *CW* I, "On Truth and Lies in an Extra-Moral Sense" and "Exhortation to the Germans."

194. *pro memoria]* {Literally, "for memory," a reminder or memorandum; N composed "On Truth and Lies" in 1873, age 28.}

195. N's adversarial engagement with Kant is reflected in many fragments from this time; cf. among others 26[412, 461]; *CW* 16, 34[37, 79, 82, 116, 185]; 38[7]; cf. *BGE* 11.

196. {*WP²* 1053.}

197. *thought]* of the eternal recurrence of the same.

198. Cf. 26[31] and corresponding note.

199. {Wolf's Glen (*Wolfsschlucht*) is the most famous scene in Carl Maria von Weber's opera *Der Freischütz* (*The Marksman* or *The Freeshooter*); *Euryanthe* is another Weber opera.}

200. *opposite types]* *entgegengesetzte Rassen*

201. *utile . . . dulce] utile* = "useful"; *dulce* = "sweet" {Cf. *CW* 14, 4[59]; cf. Horace, *Ars poetica*, lines 343–44: "Omne tulit punctum qui miscuit utile dulci, lectorem delectando pariterque monendo." ("He wins every hand who mingles the useful with sweet, by delighting and instructing the reader at the same time.") These lines are annotated by N in his copy of *Des Q. Horatius Flaccus, Sämmtliche Werke: Zweiter Theil, Satiren und Episteln; Für den Schulgebrauch*, ed. Georg Theodor August Krüger (Leipzig: B. G. Teubner, 1853).}

202. Cf. *CW* 17, 4[2]; 10[159]; *CW* 18, 11[33]. {Cf. Stendhal, *Vie de Napoléon: Fragments* ("Life of Napoleon: Fragments") (Paris: Calmann-Lévy, 1876), xv: "an almost instinctive belief in me is that every powerful man lies, when he speaks, and even more so when he writes."

203. *At dinner . . . Dühring]* Highly probable that N is referring to a conversation with Heinrich von Stein, who visited him in Sils-Maria during the period 26–28 August 1884 (see Chronicle of N's life in *CW* 19).

204. Notes on a conversation; cf. note. to 26[382].

205. *instinct for reasons] Gründe-Instinkt*

206. *Désintéressement]* "Disinterestedness"

207. Cf. 25[525]; *CW* 16, 38[19]; *CW* 4, 28[7]; *GM* Preface 3.

208. {*WP²* 131.}

209. *Do you . . . swamp is?]* Cf. note. to 26[383].

210. *Bayreuther Blätter]* {Bayreuth-based journal founded in 1878 and dedicated to the discussion of Wagner's work.}

211. *Whatever the bird . . . tweet] Wie der Alte singt, so zwitschern die Jungen* {N is playing with the German saying "Wie die Alten sungen, so zwitschern die Jungen," for which there is no literal equivalent in English. This saying is usually translated as "Like father, like son."}

212. *Il faut être sec]* "You must be dry"

213. *Stendhal]* Cf. 26[396]. {Cf. Stendhal, *Correspondance inédite*, 2:87; see note to 26[314].}

214. *We should . . . mountains]* Cf. *Z* III "The Return Home."

215. *To be . . . ourselves]* Cf. *HAH* 323.

216. Cf. 26[394]; *CW* 16, 35[34].

217. *Pour être bon . . . ce qui est]* {Cf. Stendhal, *Correspondance inédite*, 2:87: "To be a good philosopher, you have to be dry, clear, and without illusion. A banker, who has made a fortune, *has part of the character required* to make discoveries in philosophy, that is, *to see clearly into what is*." N underlines *a une . . . caractère* and *voir . . . est*. N quotes this in *BGE* 39.}

218. *est-ce la recherche . . . sympathie?]* {Cf. Stendhal, *Correspondance inédite*, 2:85: "is it the search for pleasure, as Virgil says (each led on by their own longing {*Eclogues* 2.65}) Is it sympathy?" The Latin quote from Virgil appears on p. 86.}

219. *ou naît-il . . . au jeune poulet]* {Cf. Stendhal, *Correspondance inédite*, 2:86: "or does it start in the brain, like the idea of pecking wheat that comes to a young chicken."}

220. *Intellectual refinement]* Vergeistigung

221. Cf. *CW* 16, 43[3].

222. Cf. *CW* 17, 10[78].

223. Cf. 25[272]; 26[457].

224. *fraternity student]* Korpsstudent {*Korps* — an abbreviation of "*Korporation*" — student members of fraternal organizations formed in university cities prior to the Revolution of 1848, designated by Latin names and distinctive colors of dress, known for blind patriotism and anti-Semitism. Descendant organizations, known as *Verbindungen* ("fraternities"), still exist today in Germany, and membership has a political connotation of right-wing politics.}

225. Cf. *CW* 16, 38[6].

226. *Montaigne . . . Napoleon.]* {Cf. Paul Bourget, *Essais de psychologie contemporaine* ("Essays in contemporary psychology") (Paris: Lemerre, 1883), 224.}

227. Cf. *CW* 16, 38[5].

228. *in artibus et litteris]* "in arts and letters"

229. Cf. *CW* 18, 23[1].

230. Cf. 26[408].

231. Cf. *CW* 16, 34[201, 207]. {Much of this fragment is significantly reworked in *WP²* 972, providing a good example of how N's words were often significantly altered by Elisabeth Förster-Nietzsche and Heinrich Köselitz in the construction of *Der Wille zur Macht*.}

232. *factual knowledge]* Wissen

233. *revelation]* Eingebung

234. Cf. 26[406].

235. {*WP²* 995.}

236. *the world as humans see it]* die Menschen-Welt

237. *Boscovich]* Cf. note to 26[302].

238. Cf. note. to 26[375].

239. *Frederick . . . allemande]* Cf. 26[420].

240. *niaiserie allemande]* "German silliness"

241. *niaiserie . . . Goethe]* {Cf. Prosper Mérimée, *Lettres à une inconnue* ("Letters to a stranger"), 5th rev. ed. (Paris: Michel Lévy Frères, 1874), 1:332 (hereafter cited as "Mérimée" followed by the volume and page number).}

242. *Fichte . . . Church Fathers]* Cf. 25[303]; 26[8, 445]; *BGE* 11.

243. *contradictio in adjecto]* {Rhetorical term, borrowed from the Latin, describing a situation where the parts of an argument contradict each other.}

244. {Cf. Richard Wagner, the introduction to *Oper und Drama* ("Opera and drama"), in *Gesammelte Schriften und Dichtungen* ("Collected writings and poetry") (Leipzig: Fritzsch, 1872), 3:282. *NL.* Cf. also *JS* 368; *WA* 10, *CW* 9, 25; *NCW* "Where I Object," *CW* 9, 390.}

245. *amor dei]* "love of God"

246. *Teichmüller]* N read Gustav Teichmüller's *Die wirkliche und die scheinbare Welt* ("The real and the apparent world") {(Breslau: Koebner, 1882). Cf. p. 6, among several other examples, for his criticism of Spinoza.}

247. {*WP²* 127.}

248. {Cf. *Lettres de l'abbé Galiani à Madame d'Épinay* et al. (Paris: Charpentier, 1882): 20 July 1776, 1:235–36. *NL.*}

249. Cf. Mérimée 2:137.

250. *très supérieurs . . . la netteté.]* "very superior for precision and clarity"

251. Mérimée 2:21.

252. Mérimée 1:332; cf. 26[412] and variants of *BGE* 244.

253. *Après tout, . . . n'est triste.]* "After all, there are good times, and the memory of those good times is more pleasant than the memory of the bad ones is sad." Cf. Mérimée 1:317.

254. Mérimée 1:167.

255. Mérimée 1:79.

256. {*WP²* 976.}

257. Cf. 25[238].

258. Cf. *CW* 17, 10[69]. {Cf. *BGE* 28.}

259. *presto]* "quickness"

260. Citation?

261. Cf. 26[302]; *BGE* 12.

262. Cf. note to 26[383].

263. Cf. *HAH* II, 472.

264. *Il a la grâce . . . années]* "He has the grace of powerful young animals. — The admirable liveliness and strange energy of his tongue. He is like Lucretius for this virile youth. A young oak full of sap, made of hard wood and with the grace of the early years." Cf. X. Doudan, *Pensées et fragments {suivis des révolutions du goût}* ("Thoughts and fragments followed by revolutions of taste") (Paris{: Calmann Lévy,} 1881), 33. *NL.*

265. *cette race . . . et passionnée]* "this gentle, energetic, meditative and passionate race" {Cf. Ximénès Doudan, *Lettres* (Paris: Calmann Lévy, 1879), 3:361.}

266. *chantaient déjà, faute d'idées.]* "were already singing, for lack of ideas." {Cf. Doudan, *Lettres*, 3:330.}

267. *c'est un . . . pas à sentir]* "it's a noise in the ears and an indefinable little heartache that you don't like to feel." {Cf. Doudan, *Lettres*, 3:322.}

268. *Motu quiescunt . . . la volonté désennuie]* "Rest in motion . . . the will is diverting" {Cf. Doudan, *Lettres*, 3:164, 163.}

269. *Carcasse, . . . te mène]* "You tremble, carcass? You would tremble even more if you knew where I am taking you." Cf. the motto of *JS* Book 5 {Cf. Doudan, *Lettres*, 3:31}.

270. *c'est une . . . Cicéron.]* "he is a lovable and noble creature. The little upstart from Arpinum is quite simply the most beautiful result of all the long civilization that preceded him. I know nothing more honorable to human nature than the state of mind and spirit of Cicero." {Cf. Doudan, *Lettres*, 3:23.}

271. *l'habitude . . . dans l'inconnu]* "the habit of admiring the unintelligible instead of simply remaining in the unknown" {Cf. Doudan, *Lettres*, 3:24.}

272. *aucun de . . . dans le monde.]* "none of those imposing but shapeless ghosts which delighted Saint Anthony in the desert and Saint Ignatius of Loyola in society." {Cf. Doudan, *Lettres*, 3:24.}

273. *"il y a . . . Voltaire"]* "there is something of Cicero in Voltaire" {Cf. Doudan, *Lettres*, 3:24.}

274. *la raillerie . . . ensemble]* "sinister and tragic mockery — 'comedy and tragedy all together.'" Cf. Ximénès Doudan, *Mélanges et lettres* ("Compositions and letters") (Paris{: Calmann Lévy,} 1878), 2:586. *NL.*

275. *Provinciales]* {*Les provinciales* (*The Provincial Letters*), first published in 1657, were a series of eighteen letters written by Blaise Pascal under the pseudonym Louis de Montale, in defense of his friend Antoine Arnauld, a leader of the Jansenist group of Port-Royal.}

276. *On peut . . . contraste.]* "One can carry great sorrows there without suffering any contrast." Cf. Doudan, *Mélanges* 2:487.

277. Cf. 26[8].

278. *des bonbons . . . la liberté.]* "candy, which smells of infinity." "This dreamy, sweet, insinuating style, circling questions loosely, like little snakes. It is to the sounds of this music that we resign ourselves to having such fun with everything that we endure despotism while dreaming of freedom" Cf. Doudan, *Mélanges* 2:458–59; cf. *CW* 16, 38[5].

279. *mais que . . . de couleurs!]* "but how red, blue, green, orange, black, mother-of-pearl, opal, iris and purple! . . . it's a color merchant's shop. {. . .} Mirabeau senior: what a riot of colors!" Cf. Doudan, *Mélanges* 2:417.

280. {*WP²* 128.}

281. *training]* *Dressirbarkeit* {Meaning trainable in the sense that animals are trainable.}

282. {*WP²* 420.}

283. Cf. *CW* 16, 34[45]; 38[6].

284. *Flaubert . . . Emphasis]* {Cf. Mérimée 2:209.}

285. *On Rossini . . . people.]* {Cf. Mérimée 2:338.}

286. {Cf. Mérimée 2:350.}

287. *nivellement]* "leveling"

288. Cf. 25[272]; 26[402].

289. *Taine . . . Graindorge]* {Cf. Hippolyte Taine, *Notes sur Paris: Vie et opinions de M. Frédéric-Thomas Graindorge* (Paris: Hachette, 1867). Cf. N to Elisabeth Nietzsche, mid-March 1885 (KGB III:3, 25–26).}

290. μέμνησο ἀπιστεῖν] "remember not to trust" {Part of a line from the Greek comic playwright Epicharmus, quoted by Polybius and by Cicero in his *Letters to Atticus* (1.19); also attributed to Epicharmus in Lucian's *Hermotimus*, 47. Cf. *CW* 16, 34[196] and corresponding note.}

291. *acquiring and learning]* lernen und lernen

292. Cf. note to 26[375].

293. Cf. note to 26[375].

294. Cf. 25[1] and corresponding note.

295. *Adventavit . . . Mysterium]* "The ass arrived / beautiful and most mighty / *Mystery*" {N adds and underlines *Mysterium* to a Latin strophe quoted in Doudan, *Lettres* 3:92; it is also quoted in G. Christoph Lichtenberg, *Vermischte Schriften* ("Assorted writings") (Göttingen: Dieterich, 1867), 5:327. *NL*.} Cf. *BGE* 8 and corresponding note.

296. *Satis . . . nullus.]* "Few suffice for me, one suffices for me, none at all suffices for me." {Seneca, *Epistulae Morales ad Lucilium*, bk. 1, letter 7.} Cf. 26[139] and corresponding note; {cf. *CW* 16, 34[196]}.

297. Cf. *BGE* 9.

298. *appearance of a saint]* Heiligen-Larve {Here *Larve* could also be rendered as "mask."}

[27 = Z II 5a. Summer–Autumn 1884]

1. *of whatever is in command]* des Befehlenden

2. ἡδονή] hēdonē "delight"; "pleasure"

3. *well-being welfare]* Wohlbefinden Wohlfahrt {One of many examples of N's use of unpunctuated appositives.}

4. *Scholarly knowledge]* Wissenschaft {It would be misleading to render *Wissenschaft* here as "science" because its meaning includes all disciplines that are studied systematically. Cf. our Translators' Afterword, p. 488.}

5. *individual elements]* Individuen {Here N seems to be describing a process that is operating on a subpersonal level.}

6. Cf. 25[237] and corresponding note.

7. *because . . . expected] weil man in den allermeisten Fällen nur* will, *wenn der Erfolg* erwartet *werden kann*

8. *inevitability] Nothwendigkeit*

9. *Pleasure . . . felt.]* {Cf. *AC* 2.}

10. *and not in women either] und am Weibe auch nicht* {The allusion is to Shakespeare, *Hamlet* Act 2, Scene 2: Man delights not me; no, nor Woman neither; though by your smiling you seem to say so . . .}

11. {Cf. *BGE* 4.}

12. {Cf. Galton, *Inquiries*, 72.}

13. {Cf. Hyppolite Taine, *Geschichte der englischen Literatur* ("History of English literature"), 3 vols. (Leipzig{: Günther,} 1878–80), 3:95, where he slightly alters the following quote from Lord Byron's letter to John Murray (3 November 1821): "I am like the Tiger: if I miss the first spring, I go growling back to my Jungle again; but if I do hit, it is crushing." *NL.*}

14. *multiple interpretations] Zwei-Deutigkeit* {N underlines *Deutigkeit* both times.}

15. Cf. 25[1] and corresponding note.

16. {For N, chemistry is concerned with the inorganic, biology with the organic.}

17. Concerning 27[58].

18. *issue] Sache*

19. *substantival time] Sach-Zeit* {This is the only time this term shows up in N's corpus. We think it means projecting our grammar onto the reality of time and thinking of time as a kind of thing or substance. In the philosophy of time, this idea would refer to the contrast between substantival or absolute time, on the one hand, and relational time, on the other.}

20. Cf. 25[237] and corresponding note.

21. *psychological . . . physiological] seelische . . . leibliche*

22. Cf. 26[233] and corresponding note.

23. *"to bring . . . things" p. 49]* {N here quotes himself from the first edition of *Schopenhauer as Educator*, §4; cf. *CW* 2, 206, lines 27–28.}

24. Cf. 26[296] and corresponding note.

25. *mistaken choices] fehlerhafte Griffe* {*Griffe* refers here to a pianist hitting the wrong key.}

26. Taine, *Geschichte der englischen Literatur*{, 3, 47; cf. note 13 above.}

27. *spirit] Geist* {*Geist* is a notoriously difficult word to translate into English, as it can be justifiably rendered as "mind," "intellect," or "spirit." In English translations of Hegel, however, *Geist* is usually rendered as "spirit." For further discussion, see our Translators' Afterword in *CW* 14, 743.}

28. *their feelings of inadequacy, in and of themselves] ihr Ungenügen an sich* {Using *an sich* tells the reader that N has sympathy only for the feelings and not for the doctrine (and consciousness) of sinfulness that provokes such feelings in pious people.}

29. Cf. 25[1] and corresponding note.

30. Like 27[80].

31. *The New Kind of Truthful People] Die neuen Wahrhaftigen*

[28 = Poems and Poetic Fragments. Autumn 1884]

During the composition of the second and third parts of *Thus Spoke Zarathustra* (Summer 1883–beginning of 1884), a large number of turns of phrase, images, and similes written in verse can be documented, which N included in his notes without explanation. Only some of this found a place in *Z* II and *Z* III, while most of the poetry (that N didn't use) was recopied into new notebooks. In the autumn of 1884, N experimented with quite a few drafts of poems, sometimes using existing material, sometimes using some new compositions. He conceived a plan for publishing a collection of poetry, for which he hoped to find a publisher. All of these attempts were almost immediately abandoned in favor of completing the fourth part of *Thus Spoke Zarathustra*. The notebooks that contain N's poetic compositions include Z II 5, Z II 6, and Z II 7. We find in these notebooks titles for the planned collection of poetry, lists of poems, different kinds of outlines, a great many versions of particular poems, poetic fragments, and epigrams. In order to provide a clearer overview of these diverse materials, we provide the following list of poems that N composed during this period (or revised from already existing texts), poems

that he included in his publications from the years 1885–1887 —
after he decided not to publish a separate collection of poetry (the
numbering has been added by the editors):

  (1) The "Lament" of the sorcerer in *Z* IV "The Sorcerer" 1
  (2) The Song of Melancholy from the chapter of the same title
      in *Z* IV 3
  (3) Among Daughters of the Desert from the chapter of the
      same title in *Z* IV 2
  (4) Concluding verses to *BGE* 228
  (5) Concluding verses to *BGE* 256
  (6) From Lofty Mountains, poetic epilogue to *BGE*
  (7) Among Friends, poetic epilogue to *HAH* I
  (8) To Goethe, *JSA*
  (9) Poet's Calling, *JSA*
  (10) In the South, *JSA*
  (11) Pious Beppa, *JSA*
  (12) The Mysterious Bark, *JSA*
  (13) Declaration of Love, *JSA*
  (14) Song of a Theocritical Goatherd, *JSA*
  (15) "These Vacillating People," *JSA*
  (16) Fool in Despair, *JSA*
  (17) *Rimus remedium* {"Rhyme as remedy"}, *JSA*
  (18) "My Happiness!," *JSA*
  (19) On to New Seas, *JSA*
  (20) Sils-Maria, *JSA*
  (21) To the Mistral, *JSA*

Another group of poems and epigrams for which N had composed
final versions remained unpublished:

  (22) Dedicated to all those who create, = 28[1]
  (23) "Every hunchback . . . ," = 28[2]
  (24) Tree in Autumn, = 28[6]
  (25) Arthur Schopenhauer, = 28[11]
  (26) The Honey Sacrifice (cf. also *Z* IV), = 28[36]
  (27) To Hafiz, = 28[42]
  (28) "A very bashful woman . . . ," = 28[43]
  (29) "Those who can't laugh here . . . ," = 28[44]
  (30) While Looking at a Nightshirt, = 28[47]

(31) To Richard Wagner, = 28[48]
(32) To Spinoza, = 28[49]
(33) For False Friends, = 28[50]
(34) A Roman Exclamation, = 28[51]
(35) The "Real German," = 28[52]
(36) The New Testament, = 28[53]
(37) Riddle, = 28[54]
(38) The Hermit Speaks, = 28[55]
(39) Resolved, = 28[56]
(40) The Wanderer, = 28[58]
(41) A German November, = 28[59]
(42) At the Glacier, = 28[60]
(43) Yorick as a Gypsy, = 28[62]
(44) The Free Spirit, = 28[64]
(45) "It is you I love, grotto full of graves . . . ," = 28[65]
(46) "Courage, Friend Yorick! . . . ," = 28[66]
(47) "I envy industrious people . . . ," = 28[34]
(48) "Now all things will come to be mine . . . ," = 28[10]

Written in the autumn of 1884: (1)–(6), (8), (15), (17), (18), (21)–
(39), (44)–(48). Revisions of earlier versions: (7) from spring of
1882; (9)–(14), which originally appeared in *IM* (also from spring
of 1882); (16) from spring of 1882; (19) from autumn of 1882; (20)
from winter of 1882/83 (cf. the poem "Portofino," *CW* 14, 3[3]
{p. 92}); (40) from May of 1876; (41) from summer of 1877; (42)
from summer of 1877; (43) from spring of 1882.

During this time N drafted a large number of titles and early
versions of poems. Their significance becomes clear when we view
them in conjunction with the many poems either already completed or existing in draft form in the notebooks. Yet these poems
will remain completely meaningless as long as they are published in
the order they occur without providing any context (which is what
Erich F. Podach, *Ein Blick in Notizbücher Nietzsches* ("A look into
Nietzsche's notebooks") (Heidelberg{: Rothe}, 1963), has done).

The following titles and outlines are included in Z II 5, chronolog-
ically the first notebook that N used for his drafts and reworkings of
several poems: "Prince Vogelfrei / A Testament of Fools / Interlude /
Between two Serious Matters / By / Friedrich Nietzsche" — "Songs

for Dancing and Mockery. Mistral. ⟨21⟩ Psalm. ⟨3⟩ / Encounters with Ghosts. / From Seven Solitudes. Venice. ⟨18⟩ / Fools' Arrows."

In addition, Z II 5 contains several titles, each of which is followed by a more extensive list of poem titles: "The New Yorick. / How Yorick Became a Poet. ⟨9⟩ / Yorick in Venice. ⟨18⟩ / The Sick Poet. ⟨17⟩ / To the Mistral. ⟨21⟩ / November in the North. ⟨41⟩ / The Wanderer. ⟨40⟩ / Pious Juanita. ⟨11⟩ / The Nightly Mystery. ⟨12⟩ / The Goatherd. ⟨14⟩ / Yorick as a Gypsy. ⟨43⟩ / Angiolina. ⟨cf. *IM*⟩ / Yorick Below the Glaciers. ⟨42⟩ / In Staglieno. ⟨cf. *IM* and 43, respectively⟩ / Prince Vogelfrei. ⟨10⟩ / Among Daughters of the Desert. ⟨3⟩ / When the Light Grows Dim. ⟨2⟩ / The Albatross. ⟨13⟩ / Yorick as Columbus. ⟨19⟩."

Included under an additional title, we find fragments that N abandoned or made use of in different versions: "*Medusan Hymns. / The Eagle's Hatred.* ⟨= 28[14]⟩ / *To Evil People.* ⟨cf. 28[20] Loving the Evil People⟩ / *To Those Who Despair.* ⟨cf. 28[20] World-Weary People⟩ / *Get Away from Me!* (Time) ⟨cf. 28[23]: Beyond Time⟩ / *In Praise of Poverty.* ⟨= 28[25]⟩ / *The Agony of a Woman Giving Birth.* ⟨= 28[27]⟩ / *The Sun's Malice.* ⟨= 28[3]⟩."

The fragment "The Agony of a Woman Giving Birth" is one of the preliminary versions of the "Lament" of the sorcerer in *Z* IV. It is found on p. 69 of Notebook Z II 5, where the number "6" is included with it (in fact, "The Agony of a Woman Giving Birth" is the sixth of the Medusan Hymns; cf. 28[27].

After Z II 5, the very next notebook that N used for his poetic creations was Z II 7. Here we find the following title (Z II 7, 91): "*Mirror of Prophecy* / by Friedrich Nietzsche." The following list is found on the same page: "*Contra Wine* ⟨27⟩ / *The Honey Sacrifice* ⟨26⟩ / *Industriousness and Genius* ⟨47⟩ / *Music of the South* ⟨48⟩ / *To Schopenhauer* ⟨25⟩ / *Midnight Departure* / *Festival of Melancholy* ⟨perhaps this is the poem "To Melancholy" from July of 1871, composed in Gimmelwald; cf. *CW* 10, 15[1]⟩."

Additional titles with lists of poems are found at the end of Z II 7:

"Girl Songs / 1. *Among Songbirds.* Sicilian ⟨10⟩ / *Angiolina* / Angiolina is what they call me, etc. ⟨cf. *IM*⟩ / 3. Up on the Campo Santo. ⟨45⟩ / 4. Pious Beppa. ⟨11⟩ / 5. The Albatross. ⟨13⟩ / 6. The Goatherd. ⟨14⟩ / 7. The Nightly Mystery. ⟨12⟩ / On to New Seas.

⟨19⟩ / And One More Time! ⟨18⟩ / *Rimus remedium.* ⟨17⟩ / Fool in Despair. ⟨16⟩ / To These Uncertain Souls. ⟨15⟩ / To Goethe. ⟨8⟩ / Mistral. ⟨21⟩ / 15 Songs"

"*Ten Songs of a Hermit* / To the Mistral.* ⟨21⟩ / The Hermit's Longing.* ⟨6⟩ / Fool in Despair. ⟨16⟩ / Among Friends. Postlude. ⟨7⟩ / The Wanderer. ⟨40⟩ / Autumn. ⟨41⟩ / Sils-Maria. ⟨20⟩ / Yorick Below the Glaciers.* ⟨42⟩ / The New Columbus.* ⟨19⟩ / Venice.* ⟨18⟩ / Among Daughters of the Desert.* ⟨3⟩ What Poets Use to Comfort Themselves.* ⟨17⟩ / Bird Judgment. ⟨9⟩ / "Just a Fool! Just a Poet!"* ⟨2⟩ / The Weightiest Thought.* ⟨1⟩ / Left Alone "The Crows Call Out"* ⟨44⟩ / To Darwin's Disciples. ⟨49⟩ / While Looking at a Nightshirt. ⟨30⟩ / To R. Wagner. ⟨32⟩ / Certain Givers of Eulogies. ⟨15⟩ / Parsifal Music. ⟨5⟩ / Above the Front Door. ⟨cf. the motto of *JS*, 2nd ed.⟩ / To Hafiz. ⟨27⟩." ⟨The list was put together before the title was added; the titles marked with an asterisk make up the collection of poetry that N planned to call "Ten Songs of a Hermit."⟩

"*Homeless* / 1. Autumn ⟨41⟩ / 2. The Crows ⟨44⟩ / 3. No Way Back? ⟨cf. 28[61]⟩ / 4. A Wanderer Is Walking ⟨40⟩ / 5. Genoa. ⟨19⟩ / 6. Zarathustra. ⟨20⟩ / Yorick Below the Glaciers ⟨42⟩ / The Traveling Poet. ⟨possibly 43⟩ / To Certain Givers of Eulogies. ⟨15⟩."

"*Songs of a Hermit.* / 1. The Hermit's Longing. ⟨6⟩ / 2. In the Evening. ⟨2⟩ / 3. The Wanderer and His Shadow. ⟨= 28[61]⟩ / 4. In Venice. ⟨18⟩ / 5. The Weightiest Thought. ⟨1⟩ / 6. The Sick Poet. ⟨17⟩ / 7. Among Daughters of the Desert. ⟨3⟩ / 8. To the Mistral. ⟨21⟩."

In these same pages we find two titles similar to the title cited above on p. 440: "*Prince Vogelfrei.* / Interludes Between Two Serious Matters. / By / Friedrich Nietzsche." — "*Concerning Joyful Science*: / Fifth Book / *Prince Vogelfrei* / Interlude Between Two Serious Matters." The latter title is repeated in abbreviated form at the beginning of the third notebook, Z II 6, which N used for his poems during that time: "*Fifth Book / Prince Vogelfrei.*"

Z II 6 also includes the following titles: "*Just a Fool! Just a Poet! / Songs of a Modest Man*" — "*Majestic Songs*" — "*From Seven Solitudes* / A Book of Sayings and Songs / by / Friedrich Nietzsche" — "*Idyllic Maliciousness.*" — "*Songs and Sayings* / from / the *House of Vogelfrei*" — "*Songs* / of an Immodest Man."

One draft from Z II 6 should be seen as a variant of the titles on p. 441: "*Book of Fools* / Interludes / Between Two Serious Matters. / Songs of a Goatherd ⟨14⟩ / 1 — — — / 2 Oh *pia* {"pious"} Girl ⟨45⟩."

In addition, the following titles appear in Z II 6 with lists of poems:

"*From* / *Seven Solitudes*. / By / Friedrich Nietzsche. / The Wanderer ⟨40⟩ / The Fool ⟨2⟩ / The Sick Man ⟨17⟩ / The Sleepwalker ⟨Without Friends as Guides⟩ ⟨?⟩ / The Ghost (Genius) ⟨?⟩ / The Prophet ⟨?⟩ / The Scary Man ⟨?⟩."

"*The New Yorick*. / Songs / of a Sensitive Traveler. / By / Friedrich Nietzsche. / Rotund like a Fool ⟨?⟩ / The Sick Man ⟨17⟩ / Those Who Create ⟨cf. 28[27]⟩ / The Wanderer (Without a Home) ⟨40 and 44, respectively?⟩ / The (Ones Who Differ) Contemptuous Ones ⟨?⟩ / The Loneliness of Happiness ⟨possibly 18?⟩ / Without Friends ⟨possibly 6?⟩ / The Prophet ⟨?⟩ /."

"I. *The New Yorick*. Songs of a Sensitive Traveler. / II. *Fools' Arrows*. (with the motto: — — —) / III. *Prince Vogelfrei*. Or: The Good European. / Among Daughters of the Desert ⟨3⟩ / The New Poet ⟨?⟩ / The Wanderer and His Shadow ⟨28[61]⟩ / Dawn ⟨?⟩ / Girl Songs ⟨cf. p. 441⟩ / Songs of a Goatherd ⟨14⟩ / Winged Creatures. Albatross ⟨13⟩. Vogelfrei ⟨10⟩."

Most titles in this list do not refer to individual poems but rather to collections of poems, which is evident from the following lists that are also included in Notebook Z II 6.

"Contents / ⟨*1. The New Yorick*.⟩ / How Yorick became a Poet. ⟨9⟩ / Yorick in Venice. ⟨18⟩ / The Sick Poet. ⟨17⟩ / To the Mistral. ⟨21⟩ / A German November. ⟨41⟩ / The Wanderer. ⟨40⟩ / Pious Juanita. ⟨11⟩ / The Nightly Mystery. ⟨12⟩ / Yorick Below the Glaciers. ⟨42⟩ / Among Daughters of the Desert. ⟨3⟩."

"2. *Fools' Arrows*. / Yorick as Columbus. **In final form** ⟨19⟩ / Staglieno. ⟨45⟩ / To Certain Givers of Eulogies. ⟨15⟩ / Angiolina ⟨cf. *IM*⟩ / Beneath the Fig Leaves. ⟨?⟩ / Goatherd. ⟨14⟩ / Yorick as a Gypsy. ⟨43⟩ / Sils-Maria. ⟨20⟩ / To Goethe. ⟨8⟩ / To Spinoza. ⟨32 ⟩ / To Richard Wagner. ⟨31⟩ / The Albatross. ⟨13⟩."

"3. *Among Friends* / Epilogue. ⟨7⟩."

"*The Poet.* / How Yorick ⟨Became⟩ a Poet. ⟨9⟩ / The Sick Poet. ⟨17⟩ / A Toast. ⟨27⟩ / Over There the Gallows. ⟨43⟩ / Venice. ⟨18⟩ / Song of the Sun. ⟨2⟩."

"*The Wanderer and His Shadow.* / 1 A Wanderer Is Walking — ⟨40⟩ / 2 This Is Autumn — ⟨41⟩ / 3 The Crows Call Out — ⟨44⟩ / 4 Who Will Keep Me Warm — ⟨1⟩ / 5 No Way Back? — ⟨28[61]⟩ / 6 At Midday, When — ⟨42⟩ / 7 Oh in the Midst of Life — ⟨6⟩"

"*The New Poet.* / 1 Not Long Ago, When I — ⟨9⟩ / 2 The Sick Poet — ⟨17⟩ / 3 Over There the Gallows — ⟨43⟩ / The Alehouse, That I {Built} for Myself — ⟨27⟩ / 5 The Doves of San Marco —⟨18⟩ / 6 The Sun's Malice ⟨2⟩ / 7 Sils-Maria ⟨20⟩"

"*Dawn.* / I Want to Go — in That Direction ⟨19⟩"

(The collection "The New Poet" consists of the very same poems as "The Poet" and in the same order as well, albeit with the addition of the poem "Sils-Maria.")

Notebook Z II 6 also contains the following brief list without a unifying title: "To Goethe. ⟨8⟩ / To Spinoza. ⟨32⟩ / To R. Wagner. ⟨31⟩ / To Schopenhauer ⟨25⟩."

Notebook N VI 9 contains a series of titles for the collection of poems that N was planning. N used this notebook, which includes preliminary drafts for the fourth part of *Thus Spoke Zarathustra*, from the autumn of 1884 through the winter of 1884/85: "*Book of Fools.* / Interludes / Between Two Serious Matters. / By / Friedrich Nietzsche." — "*From the Seventh Solitude* / Songs of Zarathustra" — *Songs of the Heights.* / Dedicated to All People of the Future / by / Zarathustra" — "*The New Yorick.* / Songs / of a Sensitive Traveler." — *Dionysus* / or: The Holy Orgies." — "*Dionysus.* / Songs of a Prophet. / By / Friedrich Nietzsche." — "*Songs of the Heights.* / Dedicated to All People of the Future. / By / Friedrich Nietzsche." — "*Songs of the Heights.* / Dedicated to All People of the Future / and Performed. / By / a Prophet."

Fragment 29[8] at the end (Notebook N VI 9) provides a transition to *Z* IV in much the same way: "4. Zarathustra. These are the songs of Zarathustra, which he performed for himself, so as to make his final solitude endurable: — — — ." The editors of the *Le* used this fragment as the "epigraph" to *DD*, but this is inaccurate, because (1) this text dates from the year 1884 (and not 1888, the year of *DD*; (2) it was intended for *Z* IV; cf. the beginning of the commentary to *Z* IV {in *CW* 7}. Finally, we have two versions of a list from the year 1884, organized by theme, one in Z II 5, the other in Z II 7 ⟨cf. 28[32, 33]⟩. It is impossible to determine whether there exist actual poems that N wrote to match the titles that appear in the lists. If this were the case, we would have to assume that some manuscripts have been lost, which does not seem possible for this period of N's work. It is more probable that N decided not to pursue his work on the themes contained in the list.

We have already said that N abandoned plans to publish his poems in a separate edition; he used a substantial portion of the material that he collected in the autumn of 1884 in subsequent publications: *Z* IV (1885), *BGE* (1886), *HAH* I (1886), *JSA* (1887). That he was considering publishing a collection containing only poetry is evident in the draft of a letter to Julius Rodenberg, publisher of the *Deutsche Rundschau*. This draft is included in Z II 7, 92 {November/December 1884; cf. *KGB* III/1, 567}: " — Finally, I don't even know if your 'Rundschau' has ever published poetry. Yet the current situation — that [I myself am] Friedrich Nietzsche himself is asking a magazine to print something that I have written — this is such a violation of all of my principles that even someone like you can make an exception in this case — an exception that I am confident in assuming will be to the benefit and advantage of your magazine [my friends tell me that it is the foremost German magazine] So please, most distinguished sir [if you want to please me], say yes! in response to this letter, and include your proposal in regard to compensation. My address follows: — — — " Whether N actually sent such a letter to Rodenberg is still not known.

1. Cf. *JSP* "To Goethe."

2. Cf. the concluding verses of Goethe's *Faust*. {N's playful but pointed reworking of the concluding verses in Goethe's *Faust* II: "All that is transitory / Is only a symbol; / What seems unachievable; / Here is seen done: / What is indescribable, / Here becomes fact; / The Eternal-Feminine / Lifts us up" (12104–111).}

3. Cf. N's letter to Resa von Schirnhofer, end of November 1884 {*KGB* III:1, 564}.

4. *charges interest like a Jew] treibt Juden-Schacher* {N repurposes the anti-Semitic slur *Juden-Schacher treiben*, identified even in Flügel (1852), 814, as a vulgar euphemism for usury, in order to target Christian hypocrisy.}

5. Verses to *Z* IV "The Song of Melancholy."

6. Cf. *DD* "Among Daughters of the Desert," {*CW* 9, 326–39}.

7. *dragon's teeth of the desert]* {A reference to the sowing of dragon's teeth by Cadmus and Jason in Greek mythology, from which soldiers sprout out of the ground to battle the hero.}

8. *-iving] -eiben* {N omitted the beginning consonants of what is probably the infinitive of a verb. We use the gerund ending in English for the equivalent.}

9. Allusion to Richard Wagner; cf. *BGE* 256; 28[48].

10. Cf. *Z* IV "The Sorcerer" 1.

11. *Now . . . mountain]* {N's reversal of Horace's *Ars poetica* (*Art of Poetry*), 139: "Parturient montes, nascetur ridiculus mus." ("The mountains are in labor, a ridiculous mouse will be brought forth."). Cf. 28[42].}

12. Cf. 28[9, 20].

13. Only some excerpts were published in *Le* VIII, 371, 454; perhaps dedicated to Peter Gast?

14. Cf. 28[9, 34, 27].

15. Cf. 28[3].

16. Cf. *Z* IV "The Song of Melancholy."

17. Cf. 28[25].

18. *the lust for Moon-days and workdays] die Begierde nach Mond- und Werkeltagen* {N's ridicule of monastic life includes a punning reference to "Mondays" as "mooning days," which, when paired with "workdays," caricatures the Benedictine ideal of *ora et labora* ("prayer and work"); cf. 29[1]; 31[45]; 32[10].}

19. Cf. *CW* 18, 20[140].

20. Cf. *Z* IV "The Song of Melancholy" and "On Superior Humans." {Cf. 29[1].}

21. Cf. *Z* IV "The Song of Melancholy."

22. Collection of earlier sayings about the theme "World-Weary People"; see also *Z* IV "The Shadow."

23. Cf. 31[44, 45]; 32[8]; *Z* IV "The Shadow"

24. *conscientious . . . conscience] Gewissenhafte . . . Gewissen*

25. Collection of earlier sayings and phrases; previously entitled: "Time"; see also *Z* IV "The Sorcerer" 1; "The Shadow"; "On Superior Humans" 9.

26. Cf. 28[15].

27. Initial drafts of *BGE* "Aftersong."

28. *Leaves . . . rain]* The passage concludes with: 7. When the Light Grows Dim; cf. p. 441 of the introduction to Group 28 above. {Cf. Janssen, *Geschichte des deutschen Volkes seit dem Ausgang des Mittetalters*, 3:702; cf. 26[129] and corresponding note.}

29. Cf. *Z* IV "On Superior Humans" 17.

30. Concerning Zarathustra's cave. {Cf. 28[9].}

31. Cf. *BGE* "Aftersong."

32. Regarding this list of titles, cf. p. 445 of the introduction to Group 28 above}.

33. Cf. 28[10]?

34. *Greeks] Griechen* {N means here the ancient Greeks.}

35. Cf. *BGE* 228.

36. Cf. *Z* IV "The Honey Sacrifice."

37. Cf. N's plan {on p. 441 of the introduction to Group 28 above}.

38. Cf. N's plan {on p. 441 of the introduction to Group 28 above}.

39. *Calina]* Wind of Provence.

40. Cf. 28[7, 48].

41. Cf. 28[32] and the accompanying notes.

42. Cf. *CW* 18, 20[94].

43. Cf. *Z* IV "The Honey Sacrifice."

44. Cf. *Z* IV "The Sorcerer" 1.

45. Cf. *Z* IV "The Sorcerer" 1.

46. Previous titles: "*Vanitas Vanitatum*" ("Vanity of vanities") (Z II 5); "Fools' Toasts"; from "Fools' Sobriety"; from "A Toast" (Z II 6).

47. Cf. *BGE* 228.

48. Previous titles: "*Majestas Genii*" and "Anti-Darwin."

49. *majestatem Genii]* "the majesty of genius"

50. Cf. *BGE* 228.

51. Cf. *BGE* 256; 28[7].

52. *amor dei]* "love of God"

53. *Babst]* {An archaic way of spelling the word *Pabst*, meaning the Pope, mirroring the archaic spelling *teutsch* as opposed to N's contemporary spelling *deutsch*. These playful verses are commenting on the political struggles between Bismarck and the papacy.}

54. Previous titles: "The Bard Speaks" and "Yorick Among the Germans."

55. *Ô peuple des meilleurs Tartuffes]* "O people with the best Tartuffes"

56. *possessed by the devil]* *der ist besessen* {"by the devil" added to make N's meaning clear.}

57. Composed in July 1876 on the occasion of Erwin Rohde's engagement; cf. N's letter to Rohde, 18 July 1876 {*KGB* II:5, 177}; *CW* 12, 17[31].

58. *wayfarer] Wandersmann* {as opposed to *Wanderer* ("wanderer").}

59. Composed in Rosenlauibad, in the summer of 1877; cf. *CW* 12, 22[93].

60. Composed in Rosenlauibad, in the summer of 1877; cf. *CW* 12, 22[94].

61. Cf. *CW* 14, 1[105] {pp. 26–27}.

62. See also 28[67]; previous title: "Among Enemies"; from "To My Enemies."

63. *Yorick]* {Character borrowed from one of N's favorite writers, Anglo-Irish novelist Laurence Sterne (1713–68).}

64. Cf. *JSP*; *CW* 14, 1[15, 101] {pp. 6, 25}; 3[1] Motto {p. 32}; 3[4] {p. 93}; composed in the summer of 1882.

65. *Friend] Freundin* {The poetic "I" is addressing a woman.}

66. Previous titles: "To Hermits," "Notes from the Winter Desert," "A Late Fall in Germany," "Compassion Here and There."

67. *Le* VIII 352 erroneously gives this poem the title *Pia, caritatevole, amorosissima* ("Pious one, charitable, most filled with love"); cf. *Idylls from Messina* {where a poem with this title appears. N found this inscription on a girl's tombstone near Genoa}.

68. The number "2" at the beginning supports the conjecture that this poem was meant as a continuation of the poem that eventually became the "Lament" of the sorcerer in *Z* IV "The Sorcerer."

69. *spleen]* {N uses the English term.}

70. Inversion of a passage from Hebrews 12:6.

71. Cf. 28[62].

[29 = N VI 9. Autumn 1884 – Beginning of 1885]

1. Collection of sayings and parables; cf. 31[44, 45, 48, 49, 50]; 32[8, 9, 10]; used for the following chapters of *Z* IV: "The Shadow," "The Song of Melancholy," "On Superior Humans," "The Welcoming," "The Leech," "The Honey Sacrifice."

2. Cf. 28[23].

3. Cf. 28[53].

4. Cf. 25[4].

5. Cf. 25[3].

6. *How criminals . . . babies!]* {Cf. Galton, *Inquiries*, 61. *NL*.}

7. Cf. *CW* 18, 20[158].

8. Cf. *CW* 18, 20[159]; cf. 28[22].

9. Cf. 28[22].

10. Cf. 28[23].

11. Cf. 28[22].

12. Cf. 28[16].

13. Cf. 28[15, 25].

14. Cf. 28[18]; *CW* 18, 20[140].

15. Cf. 28[9].

16. Cf. 28[22].

17. Cf. *CW* 18, 20[89].

18. Cf. 28[9, 20].

19. Cf. 28[22].

20. — *clumsy . . . awry]* {Cf. note to 27[52] above.}

21. Cf. 28[34]; *CW* 18, 20[94].

22. Cf. 28[39].

23. Cf. 28[19].

24. Cf. *CW* 18, 20[90].

25. Cf. *CW* 18, 20[91].

26. Hermann Paul, *Grundprinzipien der Sprachwissenschaft* ("Fundamental principles of linguistics") ({Halle: Niemeyer,} 1880).

27. *readers] Vorleser* {Given his poor eyesight, N made frequent use of people who read aloud to him. This might be the meaning here.}

28. Heinrich von Stein had visited N in Sils-Maria from 26 to 28 August 1884.

29. *of my]* {Not in the German text, but the context indicates that it is N's mission.}

30. Cf. 26[270].

31. *against gods] gegen den Gott* {We are reading this as a masculine universal. Cf. our Translators' Afterword in *CW* 14, 730–32.}

32. N is referring here to the idea of the eternal return of the same.

33. Cf. *Z* IV "On Superior Humans."

34. *ultimate] letzte* {This could also be rendered as "final."}

35. Erroneously used as the epigraph to *DD* in the *Le* VIII; cf. pp. 444–45 of the introduction to Group 28 above.

36. Cf. 31[50]; part of N's plans for *Z* before the writing of *Z* IV.

37. Part of N's plans for *Z* before the writing of *Z* IV.

38. Cf. 31[50], used in *Z* IV: "The Cry of Distress," "The Welcoming," "On Superior Humans," "At Noon," "The Honey Sacrifice."

39. Outline for a *Z* draft, cf. 29[13, 14].

40. Regarding the above outline, cf. 29[12].

41. *give wings to donkeys]* Cf. *Z* IV, "On Superior Humans."

42. *Silence once the clouds have cleared]* Cf. *Z* IV "The Honey Sacrifice."

43. This draft already includes several characters from the final version of *Z* IV.

44. Perhaps this refers to #4 of 29[12].

45. Outline for a *Z* project (cf. 19[12]) which preceded the writing of *Z* IV.

46. Later used in "Conversation with the Kings" from *Z* IV.

47. Cf. note to 29[15].

48. Cf. note to 29[15].

49. Cf. 29[14] and corresponding note.

50. Cf. 29[14] and corresponding note.

51. Cf. 29[14] and corresponding note.

52. Cf. 29[14] and corresponding note.

53. *goes to meet] geht . . . entgegen* {N does not include the dative object.}

54. Cf. 29[14] and corresponding note.

55. Cf. 29[14] and corresponding note; cf. also 29[23].

56. Cf. 29[14] and corresponding note; cf. also 31[4, 10].

57. Cf. 29[14] and corresponding note; cf. 29[23, 30].

58. Draft for a continuation of a fourth part preceding the actual composition of *Z* IV.

59. *Ennoblement — nobility for sale] Veredelung — Veradelung* {N coined the latter term as a playful pun on *Veredelung*.

60. Cf. 32[44, 8]; *CW* 18, 20[139].

61. Cf. 29[14] and corresponding note.

62. Cf. 27[79]; 26[293].

63. *power is evil]* Cf. *WB* 11, *CW* 2, 330, line 27.

64. Cf. *Z* IV "On Superior Humans."

65. Cf. 29[43]; 31[41, 61].

66. Cf. *Z* IV "The Welcoming."

67. Regarding *Z* IV "The Sorcerer."

68. Cf. 31[30].

69. Cf. *Z* IV "The Sign."

70. Cf. 29[46] and corresponding note.

71. Cf. *Z* IV "No Longer in Service," "The Festival of the Ass," "The Voluntary Beggar," "The Leech."

72. Cf. *CW* 18, 20[102].

73. Cf. *CW* 18, 20[157].

74. Cf. 31[36]; for the chapter "On Superior Humans" in *Z* IV.

75. Cf. *CW* 18, 20[138].

76. Cf. *Z* IV "The Shadow."

77. Cf. 29[51], notes for a conversation with the "superior humans."

78. Cf. *CW* 18, 20[155].

79. Cf. *Z* IV "The Cry of Distress," "The Sign."

80. Cf. *Z* IV "The Sleepwalker Song."

81. Cf. 29[1]; 31[45]; cf. also *Z* IV "On Superior Humans."

82. Draft previous to the composition of *Z* IV.

83. Cf. *Z* IV "The Honey Sacrifice," "Conversation with the Kings"; cf. 31[35].

84. *months] Monde* {literally, moons.}

85. Cf. *CW* 18, 20[99].

86. In regard to the first part of this outline, cf. 31[30]; cf. also 29[47].

87. {Cf. Sergej Ouwaroff [Uvarov], *Nonnos von Panopolis der Dichter: Ein Beitrag zur Geschichte der griechischen Poesie* ("Nonnos by Panopolis the poet: A contribution to the history of Greek poetry") (St. Petersburg: Alexander Pluchart, 1817).}

88. {Charles} Letourneau, *Physiologie des passions* ("Physiology of the passions") (Paris{: Baillière,} 1868). *NL.*

89. *biblioth⟨èque⟩ des sciences contemporaines]* "libra⟨ry⟩ of contemporary sciences"

90. Henri-Frédéric Amiel, Swiss writer; the *Fragments d'un journal intime* ("Fragments of an intimate diary") were published in two volumes in 1883–84; {vol. 2 (Geneva: H. Georg, 1884)}; cf. *CW* 17, 10[121].

91. {Horace de Viel-Castel, *Mémoires sur le règne de Napoléon III (1851–1864)*, vol. 1: *1851* ("Memoirs during the reign of Napoleon III, vol. 1: 1851") (Paris: Chez tous les Libraires, 1883).}

92. {Jean-Marie} Guyau, *Esquisse d'une morale sans obligation ni sanction* ("Outline of a morality without obligation or sanction") (Paris{: Alcan,} 1885). *NL;* acquired 28 October 1884.

93. {Julius} Wellhausen, *Skizzen und Vorarbeiten* ("Sketches and preliminary works"), pt. 1: *Abriß der Geschichte Israels und Juda's*; pt. 2: *Lieder der Hudailiten* (pt. 1: "Condensed history of Israel and Juda"; pt. 2: "Songs of the Hudailites") (Berlin{: Georg Reimer,} 1884). *NL.*

94. Adolf Schöll, *Goethe in Hauptzügen seines Lebens and Wirkens* ("Significant aspects of Goethe's life and influence") ({Berlin: Hertz,} 1882). *NL.*

95. Adolf Schöll, *Gesammelte Aufsätze zur klassischen Litteratur alter and neuer Zeit* ("Collected essays on the classical literature of antiquity and of more recent times") (Berlin{: Hertz,} 1884). *NL.*

96. {Cf. Hippolyte Taine, *Voyage en Italie* ("Journeys in Italy"), vol. 2: *Florence et Venise* ("Florence and Venice"), 5th ed. (Paris: Hachette, 1884), 304n: "Voyez les peintures du carnaval par Tiepolo, les mémoires de Gozzi, Goldoni, Casanova, le voyage du président De Brosses, et surtoit les quatre volumes allemande de Maier, 1795" ("See the paintings of Carnival by Tiepolo, the Memoirs of Gozzi,

Goldoni, Casanova, the travels of President De Brosses, and especially the four German volumes by Maier, 1795").}

[30 = Z II 5, 83. Z II 7b. Z II 6b. Autumn 1884–Beginning of 1885]

1. *the great realist]* Otto von Bismarck.

2. Part of the outline in 29[12]? Cf. also 31[30].

3. Cf. *Z* IV "The Shadow."

4. Final listing of the characters that appear in *Z* IV.

5. *the good European]* I.e., the shadow.

6. Cf. *Z* IV "The Last Supper," "The Welcoming."

7. *welcomings] Begrüssungen* {A pluralization of the chapter title in *Z* IV.}

8. *Last Supper] das Abendmahl* {An allusion to the Last Supper that Jesus celebrates with his disciples on the evening before the crucifixion.}

9. Possibly refers to the chapter "Among Daughters of the Desert."

10. There is no such song in *Z* IV; cf. 31[63].

11. Cf. *Z* IV "The Sorcerer."

12. *Enchanter] Bezauberer* {As opposed to the "sorcerer" (*Zauberer*) of the chapter title.}

13. Cf. *Z* IV "At Noon."

14. Cf. *CW* 18, 20[33].

15. *gathering storm] schwere Luft* {A paraphrase of N's metaphor drawn from sailing parlance.}

16. Cf. 31[39]; *BGE* 90.

17. Cf. *DD* "The Sun Is Sinking"; cf. also 31[38].

18. Cf. 31[36].

19. Cf. 31[51].

20. *stay awake] mich auswachen* {N's wordplay is between *sich ausschlafen*, "to sleep in," and *sich auswachen*, "to stay awake."}

21. Cf. *BGE* 11.

22. *vis soporifica]* "soporific power" {N here misquotes Molière's *Le malade imaginaire* (*The Imaginary Invalid*), Act III, third interlude; he subsequently corrected the Molière quote (to *virtus dormitiva*) when he developed this fragment in *BGE* 11. Cf. Andreas Urs Sommer's excellent commentary on this note in his *Kommentar zu Nietzsches Jenseits von Gut und Böse* (Berlin: de Gruyter, 2016), 140–42.}

23. Cf. *CW* 16, 34[194, 213].

24. Notes for the chapter "On Superior Humans" in *Z* IV.

25. Cf. N's notes for *BT*: *CW* 16, 34[4, 17].

26. *aussi trop allemand]* "also too German"

27. Refers to Wagner's "Open Letter" in the *Norddeutsche Allge-meine Zeitung* from 23 June 1872.

[31 = Z II 8. Winter 1884/85]

1. Early draft of *Z* IV.

2. Cf. 29[66] (regarding the continuation and expansion of *Z*); cf. 31[19, 27].

3. Cf. 31[10, 30]; 29[31].

4. Said to the sorcerer (= poet) in *Z* IV.

5. Not included in *Z* IV.

6. Not included in *Z* IV.

7. *they will either exist or they won't] sein oder nicht sein* {"to be or not to be"; here N quotes the famous line from the Schlegel-Tieck translation of Shakespeare's *Hamlet* but completely devoid of Hamlet's uncertainty, hence the different wording.}

8. Early draft of the "prophet" material for the chapter "The Cry of Distress" from *Z* IV, previous to the final version; cf. 31[9].

9. *"birds of a feather"] gleich und gleich* {Cf. the German idiom: *gleich und gleich gesellt sich gern* = "birds of a feather flock together."}

10. *in summa]* "in summary"

11. Cf. 31[8]; 29[14].

12. Draft of *Z* IV; list of characters.

13. Cf. *Z* IV "The Shadow."

14. Not included in *Z* IV.

15. Cf. *Z* IV "The Leech."

16. Will be combined with "The Sorcerer" in *Z* IV.

17. Cf. *Z* IV "The Voluntary Beggar."

18. Will be combined with "The Sorcerer" in *Z* IV.

19. Not included in *Z* IV.

20. *12 good people . . . me."]* Not included in *Z* IV.

21. I.e., the announcement of the thought of the eternal return of the same; cf. 31[4]; 29[31].

22. Preliminary draft of *Z* IV.

23. Cf. 31[4].

24. Concerning the conclusion to *Z* IV.

25. *now no one . . . alive]* Cf. *Z* IV "The Shadow."

26. Cf. *Z* IV "On Superior Humans."

27. Concerning *Z* IV "The Sign"; cf. *Z* IV "The Welcoming"; cf. also 31[21, 22].

28. Concerning the draft in 31[11].

29. Concerning the draft in 31[11].

30. Concerning the conclusion to *Z* IV as per the draft in 31[11].

31. Cf. 31[3, 27].

32. Cf. *Z* IV "The Sign"; 31[21].

33. Cf. 31[16].

34. Concerning the "laughing lion," cf. 31[14, 21, 22].

35. Cf. 31[33, 36].

36. Concerning the chapter "The Shadow" in *Z* IV.

37. Concerning the chapter "On Superior Humans" in *Z* IV.

38. Cf. 31[3, 19].

39. Cf. 29[66].

40. Prose version of "The Song of Melancholy" in *Z* IV. {Cf. *DD* "Just a Fool! Just a Poet!," in *CW* 9, 318–25.}

41. Prose version of the lament of the sorcerer; cf. *Z* IV "The Sorcerer" 1.

42. *my thought] Gedanke* {We added the possessive pronoun to avoid ambiguity.}

43. Collection of sayings and parables; cf. 29[11]; 31[24]; used for *Z* IV "On Superior Humans," "Conversation with the Kings," "The Voluntary Beggar," "The Sorcerer," "The Awakening," "At Noon."

44. Collection of sayings and parables; used in *Z* IV "The Cry of Distress," On Superior Humans," "The Welcoming," "The Honey Sacrifice."

45. Cf. 32[9]; *CW* 18, 20[135].

46. Cf. 31[62].

47. Cf. 32[10]; *CW* 18, 20[98].

48. Collection of sayings and parables; cf. 29[64]; used in *Z* IV "Conversation with the Kings," "On Superior Humans," "The Honey Sacrifice."

49. Cf. *BGE* 132; 29[56].

50. Cf. 32[7].

51. Cf. 32[10]; *CW* 18, 20[2].

52. Cf. 29[64]; *CW* 18, 20[99].

53. Cf. 31[36]; *BGE* 99.

54. Collection of sayings and parables; cf. 29[56]; 31[24, 33, 35].

55. Cf. 30[9]; *Z* IV "At Noon."

56. Cf. 32[9].

57. Cf. *BGE* 99.

58. Cf. *CW* 18, 20[108].

59. Cf. *Z* IV "On Superior Humans."

60. Cf. *Z* IV "The Ugliest Human."

61. Cf. *Z* IV "Conversation with the Kings."

62. Collection of sayings and parables; used in *Z* IV "On Superior Humans."

63. Cf. *DD* "Among Birds of Prey."

64. Cf. *CW* 18, 20[11]; *DD* "On the Poverty of the Richest Man."

65. Cf. *CW* 18, 20[138].

66. Cf. *Z* IV "The Voluntary Beggar."

67. Cf. 31[38]; *CW* 18, 20[15].

68. Collection of sayings and parables; used in *Z* IV "The Shadow," "On Superior Humans"; cf. 32[8].

69. Cf. 31[37]; *CW* 18, 20[15].

70. Cf. 30[9]; *DD* "The Sun Is Sinking."

71. Cf. *CW* 18, 20[20].

72. Cf. *Z* IV "The Voluntary Beggar"; 32[10].

73. Cf. 32[10]; *CW* 18, 20[26].

74. Cf. *BGE*, 129; 31[46].

75. Collection of sayings and parables; used in *Z* IV "The Sorcerer," "The Shadow," "At Noon."

76. Cf. 32[8]; *CW* 18, 20[31].

77. Cf. 30[9]; 32[9]; *CW* 18, 20[33].

78. *has been explained] klärte sich auf* {N's wordplay is between *sich aufklären*, a matter being "cleared up," and *aufgeklärt sein*, "to be enlightened."}

79. Cf. *BGE* 90; 30[9].

80. Cf. 31[61].

81. Cf. *DD* "Fame and Eternity."

82. Cf. *CW* 18, 20[104].

83. Cf. *DD* "Among Birds of Prey"; *CW* 18, 20[33].

84. Collection of sayings and parables; used in *Z* IV "The Shadow," "The Voluntary Beggar," "The Last Supper."

85. {Perhaps a reference to Goethe's "Requiem dem frohesten Mann des Jahrhunderts, *dem Fürsten von Ligne*" ("Requiem for the happiest man of the century, *the Prince of Ligne*"); cf. Goethe, *Sämmtliche Werke in vierzig Bänden* (Stuttgart: J. G. Cotta, 1856), 6:16–20. *NL.* Goethe wrote this cantata in 1815 for the Belgian military officer and man of letters Charles-Joseph Lamoral (1735–1814).}

86. *Even brawling is preferable to brokers!] Lieber noch Händel als Händler!* {We have changed how we translated this phrase in *CW* 14, 506, 558.}

87. Cf. *CW* 18, 20[35].

88. Cf. 31[61]; *DD* "Fame and Eternity."

89. Collection of sayings and parables, used in *Z* IV "The Shadow."

90. Cf. 31[61].

91. Cf. *CW* 18, 20[37].

92. Cf. 32[9]; *CW* 18, 20[95].

93. Cf. 31[61]; *CW* 18, 20[38].

94. Cf. 32[8].

95. *souls] Herzen*

96. Cf. 31[61]; 32[8].

97. Cf. 31[61]; 32[8].

98. Cf. 32[9]; *CW* 18, 20[137].

99. Collection of sayings and parables, used in *Z* IV "On Superior Humans."

100. *yoke is light]* {Here N parodies Matthew 11:30.}

101. *Emerson]* Cf. Emerson, *Versuche*, 283. *NL.* {Although *KSA* 14 points the reader to Emerson's *Versuche*, there is no connection on p. 283 (from Emerson's chapter "The Poet") to these two sentences.}

102. {Cf. Matthew 7:23.}

103. *blowflies] Schmeißfliegen* {Their larvae are maggots.} Cf. 31[61]; 32[8, 10]; *CW* 18, 20[101].

104. Cf. 32[10]; *CW* 18, 20[42]; paraphrase of the "familiar quotation" from the time of the Reformation: *Sobald das Geld im Kasten klingt, / Die Seele aus dem Fegefeuer springt* {"As soon as money in the register rings, / The soul out of purgatory springs"} (Hans Sachs speaking about Johann Tetzel).

105. Cf. 32[8].

106. Cf. 31[61]; 32[10]; *DD* "Fame and Eternity."

107. Collection of sayings and parables, used in *Z* IV "On Superior Humans," "The Ugliest Human," "The Honey Sacrifice."

108. Cf. 29[59]; *CW* 18, 20[153].

109. Cf. *Z* III "On Old and New Tablets {4}."

110. Cf. *CW* 18, 20[45].

111. Cf. 31[61]; 32[8].

112. Cf. *Z* IV "At Noon."

113. Collection of sayings and parables, used in *Z* IV "The Shadow," "On Superior Humans"; cf. 29[1] and corresponding note.

114. {Cf. *EH* "Foreword" 3 (*CW* 9, 213), where N cites Ovid's "Nitimur in vetitum" — "We strive for what is forbidden" — from *Amores* III, 4, 17.}

115. Cf. 32[10].

116. Cf. *CW* 18, 20[78].

117. Cf. 31[61].

118. Cf. 29[38]; 32[8]; *CW* 18, 20[139].

119. {Cf. Galton, *Inquiries*, 61.}

120. Collection of sayings and parables, used in *Z* IV "The Shadow"; cf. 29[1].

121. *completely at home] zu Heim- und Hause*

122. Cf. 31[47].

123. Cf. *BGE* 129; 31[38].

124. Concerning the chapter "The Sorcerer" in *Z* IV; cf. 31[45].

125. Collection of sayings and parables, used in *Z* IV "The Shadow," "The Welcoming"; cf. 29[1] and corresponding notes.

126. {Cf. Galton, *Inquiries*, 65.}

127. Collection of sayings and similes, used in *Z* IV "The Leech," "The Shadow"; cf. 29[1] and corresponding notes.

128. — *clumsy . . . awry]* {Cf. note to 27[52] above.}

129. Collection of sayings and parables, used in *Z* IV "On Superior Humans," "The Shadow," "At Noon"; cf. 29[1] and corresponding notes.

130. Cf. 29[9].

131. *lending to God]* das ist Gott leihen {Cf. Proverbs 19:17.}

132. Collection of sayings and parables, used in *Z* IV "On Superior Humans," "The Shadow."

133. Cf. 32[8]; *Z* IV "On Superior Humans."

134. {Cf. Hammer, *Die Geschichte der Assassinen*, 84; see note to 25[304] above.}

135. Cf. 32[9]; *CW* 18, 20[92].

136. *destroy their sense of fairness]* ihr billiges Herz zerbrechen

137. Cf. *Z* IV "The Song of Melancholy."

138. Cf. 30[9].

139. *hazar]* "thousand" {Old Persian term.} Cf. *Z* IV "The Honey Sacrifice."

140. Cf. 32[9]; *CW* 18, 20[93].

141. Collection of sayings and parables, used in *Z* IV "On Superior Humans," "The Festival of the Ass."

142. Cf. *BGE* 65.

143. Cf. *BGE* 174.

144. Cf. *BGE* 63.

145. Cf. *TI* "What the Germans Lack" 1, {*CW* 9, 81}; 32[9].

146. Collection of sayings and parables, used in *Z* IV "On Superior Humans."

147. Cf. *BGE* 68.

148. Cf. *BGE* 69.

149. Collection of sayings and parables, used in *Z* IV "On Superior Humans," "The Welcoming," "The Honey Sacrifice"; cf. 31[55, 62].

150. Cf. *BGE* 101.

151. Concerning the chapter "The Welcoming" in *Z* IV; cf. 31[54, 62].

152. Concerning the chapter "Conversation with the Kings" in *Z* IV.

153. Concerning the conclusion to *Z* IV as N had originally conceived it.

154. Cf. *Z* IV "The Welcoming."

155. Cf. 31[61, 64].

156. Cf. 31[61]; *CW* 18, 20[97].

157. Concerning the chapter "Conversation with the Kings"; also used for the chapters "On Superior Humans," "The Voluntary Beggar" in *Z* IV.

158. Cf. 31[41]; *CW* 18, 20[38].

159. Cf. 31[40]; *CW* 18, 20[36]; *DD* "Fame and Eternity."

160. Cf. 31[59, 64].

161. Cf. 31[60].

162. Cf. 31[39].

163. Cf. 31[34].

164. Cf. 31[41, 35]; 32[8].

165. Cf. 31[41].

166. Cf. 31[42]; 32[10]; *DD* "Fame and Eternity."

167. Cf. 31[42]; 32[8, 10]; *CW* 18, 20[101].

168. Cf. 31[43]; 32[8].

169. Cf. 31[44]; 29[1].

170. Cf. 31[44].

171. A variant of the chapter "The Welcoming" in *Z* IV; cf. 31[54, 55].

172. Cf. 30[7]; 31[65].

173. A variant of the conclusion to *Z* IV, used in large part eventually for the chapter "On Superior Humans"; cf. also 31[59, 61]; 33[2].

174. *silent about the truth*] *Wahr-schweiger* {As opposed to *Wahr-sager*, "prophet."}

175. *wailing . . . teeth*] {Cf. Matthew 13:42.}

176. Cf. 30[7]; 31[63].

177. Complete when the motto of the second edition of *JS* is added: This house is my own and here I dwell, / I've never aped nothing from no one / And — laugh at each master, mark me well, / Who at himself has not poked fun.

178. Concerning *Z* IV "Conversation with the Kings."

179. Concerning *Z* IV "The Welcoming."

180. List of characters in *Z* IV; cf. 29[24, 39]; 30[4]; 31[10].

[32 = Z II 9. Winter 1884/85]

1. Concerning *Z* IV "The Welcoming."

2. Cf. 30[7]; 31[63, 65].

3. Concerning *Z* IV "The Ugliest Human," also used in the chapter "On Superior Humans."

4. *junkers] Junker* {Often associated in N's time with the provincial and conservative attitudes of members of the Prussian landed aristocracy.}

5. Cf. *Z* IV "Conversation with the Kings."

6. Cf. *Z* IV "The Voluntary Beggar."

7. Concerning *Z* IV "The Sorcerer."

8. Cf. *Z* IV "The Sorcerer."

9. Draft for the conclusion of *Z* IV; cf. also 31[35].

10. *affirmed life] dem Leben sein Jawort gab*

11. Collection of sayings and parables for the chapter "The Shadow" in *Z* IV, also used in the chapter "On Superior Humans"; cf. the collections 31[48, 49, 50, 51]; 29[1] and corresponding notes.

12. Cf. 29[56]; 31[37]; *CW* 18, 20[138].

13. *trivialize his loss and get over it] seinen Verlust verscherzen und verschmerzen*

14. Cf. 31[39]; *CW* 18, 20[31].

15. *souls] Herzen*

16. Cf. 31[41, 61].

17. Cf. 31[42, 61]; 32[10]; *CW* 18, 20[101].

18. Cf. 31[42].

19. Cf. 31[43, 61].

20. Cf. 28[23]; 29[1]; 31[44].

21. {Cf. Galton, *Inquiries*, 61.}

22. Cf. 29[38]; 31[44]; *CW* 18, 20[139].

23. {Cf. Galton, *Inquiries*, 65.}

24. *"nothing . . . permitted!"]* {Cf. Hammer, *Die Geschichte der Assassinen*, 84; see note to 25[304] above.}

25. Cf. *BGE* 65.

26. Cf. *BGE* 101.

27. *Fatherlanders] Vaterländer* {We render N's neologism with one of our own.}

28. {Cf. note 24 above.}

29. Used only to a limited extent for the chapter "The Leech" in *Z* IV; cf. the chapters "On Superior Humans," "The Festival of the Ass," and fragments 31[53, 51, 50, 48, 43, 41]; 30[9]; 31[39, 36, 34]; 29[1] and corresponding notes; in addition, cf. *BGE* 101, 170, 69, 68, 63, as well as the fragments from *CW* 18, 20[92, 93].

30. *"dare to be in control of it,"] sich Geist "herausnehmen,"* {Cf. 31[52].}

31. Collection of sayings and parables for *Z* IV "The Voluntary Beggar," also used in the chapter "The Leech"; in addition, cf. fragments 31[34, 35, 36, 38, 40, 42, 44, 45, 50]; 29[1, 64]; also see *CW* 18, 20[98, 100, 42]; and *BGE* 99 and 174.

32. {For no obvious reason, N placed a small superscripted number 1 immediately following the dash for several of the following lines. Colli and Montinari chose to include this in their edition, and we include it as well.}

33. *haggle] Schacher treiben* {This has anti-Semitic connotations of usury.}

34. *paper-blowflies] Papier-Schmeißfliegen* {N uses "blowflies" elsewhere as a derogatory term for journalists.} Cf. 31[61, 42]; *CW* 18, 20[101].

35. Concerning *Z* IV "On Superior Humans."

36. {Cf. Matthew 18:3.}

37. *As I . . . around] Ihr seid mir — Gedrückte* {N's wordplay is between *drücken*, "to push," and *Gedrückte*, people who are feeling pressured or oppressed by their situation.} Cf. 31[40]; *CW* 18, 20[35].

38. Cf. 29[53]; *CW* 18, 20[102].

39. Cf. Z IV "The Sleepwalker Song," "On Superior Humans."

40. {Cf. Matthew 26:39.}

41. {Cf. Luke 6:25.}

42. Cf. *Z* IV "The Sign"; cf. 29[60].

43. *learned] erriethen* {N uses the same word in the previous clause, but we adjusted the English to accommodate "from me."}

44. A variant of the chapter "The Sign" in *Z* IV.

45. Draft of *Z* IV.

46. Concerning a subsequent revision of *HAH* (summer of 1885).

47. Cf. note to 32[17].

48. *Upbringing] Erziehung* {This could also be rendered as "Education."}

49. Cf. note to 32[17].

50. Cf. note to 32[17].

51. Notes for the conclusion of *Z* IV.

52. Draft for *WP*, written at the beginning of 1888; cf. *CW* 16, 34[19]; *CW* 18, 13[5]. {At the bottom of the page in *KSA* 11, the following footnote was inserted: "Created at the beginning of 1888."}

[33 = Z II 10. Winter 1884/85]

1. Variant of the chapter "The Welcoming" in *Z* IV.

2. *secretly feel contempt for each other] ihr macht einander das Herz unwirsch*

3. *wild man] Wildfang* {Cf. Grimm 24, 2233.}

4. *my nerves of steel] Dank meiner ehernen Stirn*

5. Variant of the conclusion of *Z* IV; cf. 32[14].

Afterword to the Unpublished Fragments from Spring through Winter 1884/85

Giorgio Colli

The Unpublished Fragments from
Spring through Autumn 1884
(Groups 25–27)

The unpublished fragments from the year 1884 occupy the period between the writing of the third part and the writing of the fourth part of *Thus Spoke Zarathustra*; they have their origin in a more relaxed state of mind and are the reflection of an interlude between two outpourings of creativity. Nietzsche turns inward, almost as if he wants to examine the path he had followed; he ponders old and new ideas without feeling a need to bring them to an immediate and decisive conclusion; his mind is receptive, and he occupies himself with a wide range of sources that leave traces in his notes. A serene flow of thought is his response, a sober alternative to the preceding periods of excitement, in which a tangle of images and symbols works itself out within more peaceful, unhurried language and cool-headed deliberation. Several persistent problems do emerge in the course of this integration of the abstract and the intuitive, of discursiveness with lightning-quick inspiration, when earlier intimations take on a complexity that demands new formulations. The theme of chance is just one of the more interesting examples that emerge from these developments.

In *Thus Spoke Zarathustra* the motifs of play and chance
are fused with the character of the protagonist with remarkable passion, even as Nietzsche's emphasis on the contrasting
motive of necessity, which has its origin in years of devotion
to science, also continues — indeed, is interwoven with the
former motif in remarkable fashion. Nietzsche does not find
it easy to make necessity characteristic of the literary figure
Zarathustra, and even so there is more often talk of necessity
in *Thus Spoke Zarathustra* than there is of chance; the praise
of necessity is also a way of trying to bring the motive of play
back into the mix. In this period of thoughtfulness, in which
powerful affects accumulate, chance now clearly resurfaces
and sometimes seeks a confrontation with necessity — something that is only natural otherwise. An entire series of fragments is concerned with this theme, in the attempt to weave
chance into the web of concepts that underlie Nietzsche's
entire undertaking in this period and provide discursive documentation of the essential role that this chance plays among
the differing perspectives. Thus we read, concerning the formation of organisms: "For in the final analysis humans are
also, to be sure, a multiplicity of existences: they have created
for themselves these organs in common, like blood circulation, concentration of the senses, stomach etc. not for these
purposes, but rather as random formations which had the
advantage of making the survival of the whole possible, are
better developed and have survived" (26[157]). And in regard
to knowledge, the structure of the intellect, we read: "perhaps
this *actual* condition of existence is merely *coincidental* and
perhaps in no way necessary. Our cognitive mechanism not
set up for gaining 'knowledge'" (26[127]). The same argumentation is extended to the area of behavior: "In *every action,
no matter how consciously purposeful,* the sum of coincidental
non-purposeful factors, whose purpose we're not conscious
of, outweighs everything else completely" (25[127]). In apply-
ing this argumentation to the discipline of history, this point
of view led Nietzsche to the following assertion: "It is not at

all advisable to search for necessities within history regarding ends and means! The irrationality of coincidence is the rule!" (25[166]) — a perspective that turns up again even in present-day historical judgments: "The enormous mass of randomness contradiction disharmony idiocy in the world of humans today is a premonition of the future" (26[228]). And in regard to the makeup of outstanding individuals: "'Chance' — in great minds that are replete with conceptions and possibilities, and are, as it were, replete with a play of forms, out of all this a process of selecting and integrating from what was selected earlier" (26[53]). In particular, the element of chance is identified by Nietzsche in great individuals who possess knowledge, in sages: "The wisest people would be *the ones richest in contradictions*, who at the same time have organs for sensing all kinds of people: and, in between, their great moments of *grandiose harmony* — the magnificence of *chance* even within us! (26[119]). Celebrations of chance are found in Nietzsche even in the years preceding *Zarathustra*, but now he succeeds in bringing together all of his perspectives within this fundamental valuation. Several of the passages that I have cited already reference the antithesis between chance and necessity, something that nevertheless does not appear in *Zarathustra*. Necessity as an incubator is reflected in the emergence of Nietzsche's predominant thought at this time, the thought of eternal recurrence. Nietzsche moves away from this in the fragments of 1884. He actually says in conjunction with the theme of eternal recurrence: "To prove the tremendously *coincidental* character of all combinations: it follows *from this* that *every* human action has an *unlimited huge* effect on everything to come" (25[158]). And the "elimination of the concept of necessity" is prominently listed among the things that are needed "in order to *bear* the thought of recurrence" (26[283]). Play, that which can be identified as the intuitive side of chance, is celebrated alongside chance: "In the sense that the world is a divine game and beyond good and evil — I have Vedanta philos⟨ophy⟩ and Heraclitus as predecessors" (26[193]).

Moral speculation moves analogously to this. Nietzsche
seeks within the area of human behavior a prominent feature, a
constant that can be grasped. And one result of this search can
perhaps be rediscovered in the unpublished fragments of 1884
— in conjunction with the theme of hypocrisy. Nietzsche's psychology often falls back upon this concept, as is well known,
but here it is put at the center of decisive connections, in each
case in a revealing context. "The characteristic trait of a great
human being was profound insight into the *moral hypocrisy* of
everyone" (26[98]). Even in this case we take part in the discursive elaboration of moments that have already been intuitively
experienced: Zarathustra's words continually refer to human
hypocrisy. Here in these fragments Nietzsche outlines a theoretical generalization: "I have looked around, but up to now
I have seen no greater danger for all acquisition of knowledge
than moral hypocrisy: or, to leave absolutely no doubt, that
hypocrisy which is called morality" (26[188]), and immediately
afterward, he notes the title: "Morality as Hypocrisy" (26[189]).
Several bullet points[1] then additionally follow under this title:
"[. . .] On *dissimulation* in the presence of "equals" as the origin of herd-morality. Fear. Wanting to understand each other.
To present ourselves as equal. *Becoming equal* [. . .] A hypocrisy
that is still ubiquitous [. . .] Morality as costume and jewelry,
as a *disguise* for people with shameworthy natures" (27[42]).
And from a broader perspective: "[. . .] the herd, juxtaposed
with the ideal herd-animal (*equal*) — those who are powerful, juxtaposed with those *tools* that are the most worshipful,
most useful (slave-like) 'unequal' (this results in hypocrisy two
times over)" (27[42]). A bit later Nietzsche attempts another
formulation: "Morality considered in relation to dissimulation (equating things), cunning and hypocrisy ('*not* revealing
ourselves') — as a falsification of emotional expression (self-
control) in order to provoke a misunderstanding" (27[56]). It

    1. {The bullet points to which Colli refers are in fact included in 27[42],
where there is no mention of "Morality as Hypocrisy."}

is notable here that even self-control is seen to have its roots in hypocrisy.

With this, the examination of behavioral patterns is extended even to people with "superior natures." And in fact Nietzsche is especially engaged at this time, inwardly, with the fourth part of *Zarathustra*, the writing of which he will undertake soon after this and the central theme of which will be "superior humans." Philosophers and scientists are foregrounded: "the Greeks: conceal their agonal affect, drape themselves in virtue as 'the happiest ones,' and as the most virtuous ones (hypocrisy on two counts) [. . .] Leibniz Kant Hegel Schopenhauer, their German dual natures. Spinoza and the revenge-seeking affect, the hypocrisy of overcoming the affects. The hypocrisy of 'pure science,' of 'knowledge for the sake of knowledge'" (26[285]). And the hypocrisy of the philosophers finds expression not only in their attitudes but also in their doctrines: "On the dishonesty of philosophers, *to derive* something that they believe to be good and true from the start (tartuffery e.g., Kant practical reason)" (27[76]). Analogous observations are made about science as well. "*Science* is a *dangerous* thing: and before we are taken to task for some other reason, this has nothing to do with its 'value.'" The popularity of science is a mistake: "[. . .] this has to do with the fact that science has always been practiced with *moral tartuffery*. This is what I want to put an end to" (25[309]).

The emphasis on the theme of hypocrisy is broadened, finally, as is normally the case with Nietzsche, to include the discipline of history. " — the '*transformation*' of a person through a dominant idea is the original phenomenon on which Christianity is built; it sees 'a miracle' in this. [. . .] I don't believe for an instant that a person suddenly becomes a *superior more valuable* person; a Christian is for me a completely normal person with a few other phrases and value judgments. *In the long run*, certainly, these words and works do have an effect and perhaps create a type: *the Christians as the most mendacious kind of people*" (25[499]). And when Nietzsche moves closer to the present, this is what he says: "The profound *mendacity* is European. Whoever wants to have a large-scale effect on Europeans has up to now required moral tartuffery (e.g., the first Napoleon in his proclamations, recently R. Wagner through his music of attitudes" (25[254]). This is true, however, not only for those who want to have an extremely broad effect: "Yet in the main I believe that mendacity in moral matters is a part of the character of this democratic age. The kind of age, that is, which has appropriated the great lie 'human equality' as its campaign slogan, is shallow, in a hurry, and intent upon the illusion that people are doing well" (26[364]).

What can be done against hypocrisy? Transform it into deliberate lies, Nietzsche says. The point is to "to make the entire actions of princes and statesmen into an *intentional lie*, to rob them of good conscience, and to once again **drive the unconscious tartuffery out of the bodies of European people**" (25[294]).

In all this we have a rough summary of Nietzsche's views in this year 1884, in which chance appears to him as the principle of things and hypocrisy as the principle of morality. These two principles can even be unified inasmuch as that which Nietzsche is now calling chance is transformed during his final phase into the principle of lying as the universal root of humankind and every kind of organic life. In truth, hypocrisy is one aspect of lying, the aspect that works to pervert things and which for that reason must be rejected, just as every human endeavor, from art to science, is a lie, a deception, in which morality constitutes the perverting aspect of the lie. Through hypocrisy we feign something that wins approval and conceal beneath it something that provokes disapproval. In a game, when we lie, we feign something for no reason, creatively, while when we act hypocritically, approval and disapproval have their foundation in a judgment of the herd, and therefore become ossified. This is why this kind of lie is not creative, not original, has no roots in nature, but rather merely reinforces an already existing judgment.

On the other hand, in the unpublished fragments of 1884, the urge to theorize has been bridled, relegated into the background, not so much in favor of "actions" as in favor of "being." Nietzsche seems to be more interested in life than he is in thought. And parallel to this, in the case of a philosopher, he finds the person, the person's vital characteristics, more interesting than the doctrines. In this sense, not only the negative sides of philosophers come under scrutiny but also their positive sides. The same interest will be evident, too, in the unpublished fragments of the following years, as well as in the fourth part of *Zarathustra*, where it is treated in a context that extends from philosophers to "superior humans." Concerning philosophers as fully realized individuals, as superior human types, Nietzsche writes in 1884: "Why philosophers *rarely* succeed: their makeup includes characteristics that normally drive people to ruin" (26[425]). And elsewhere he says more specifically: "A magnificent intellect is the effect of an abundance of moral qualities e.g., courage, force of will, fairness, seriousness — but at the same time also of much πολυτροπία {"versatility"}, deception, transformation, experience with opposites, mischief, audacity, malice, unruliness" (26[101]). Additional prerequisites are to fly beyond ourselves, a vital immediacy: "We must be capable of powerful feelings of admiration and be able to creep lovingly into the heart of many matters: otherwise we are not fit to be philosophers. Cold gray eyes do not know the value of things; cold gray minds do not know how to weigh things" (26[451]).

If philosophers are everything that Nietzsche says they are, then they cease to be humans with discursive knowledge; Nietzsche speaks of "contradictions between life and the initial functions of coming to 'know.' The more knowable something is, the further it is from being, the more it is a *concept*" (26[70]). Or better still, discursive knowledge is degraded to the point of being a preliminary phase: "[. . .] the new feeling of power: the mystical condition, and the brightest, bravest rationality as a way to get there" (26[241]). It should be noted that Nietzsche does not speak of "knowledge" but rather of a "state," of a mystical state, thus of being, not of knowing (in contrast to the era of the *Birth of Tragedy*, where "knowing" was above all the Dionysian intuition of the world's suffering). Aside from this, the importance of recognizing the mystical state as the epitome of philosophical existence cannot be stressed enough: "Actual purpose of all philosophizing, the *intuitio mystica*" (26[308]). This realization is evident only in this period; elsewhere the word "mysticism" has negative connotations in Nietzsche's works. Recalling his own experiences is what changes his attitude, recalling his intuition of eternal recurrence. It is through this, or through something, that he then makes the connection even to the mysticism of Spinoza: "The fact that something like Spinoza's *amor dei* could be *experienced* again is *his* great event [. . .] What a blessing that the most precious things are there for a second time! — Philosophers all! These are people who have experienced something *extraordinary*" (26[416]).

But reflecting on this kind of experience leads him back to the ancient Greeks: "'I will this' is superior to 'thou shalt' (heroes); 'I am' is superior to 'I will this' (the Greek gods)" (25[351]). Seeing things in this light even causes Nietzsche to temper his usual animus for Plato — yes, he falls into admiration: "Plato is worth more than his philosophy! Our instincts are better than their conceptual expressions" (26[355]). And further: "Ecstasy differs in the case of a pious sublime noble person like Plato — and in the case of camel drivers who are smoking hashish" (26[312]). That's why it is probably the case that the anti-systematic polemical motif in this period has a mystical rather than a skeptical origin: "All philosophical systems have been *overcome*; the Greeks shine more brightly than ever, particularly the Greeks before Socrates" (26[43]).

The Unpublished Fragments from Autumn 1884
through {Winter 1884/85}
(Groups 28–33)

The first group of these unpublished fragments, created
during the autumn of 1884 and the subsequent winter (28–33),
consists of poetic drafts and preparatory material for the fourth
part of *Zarathustra*. This initially includes an extensive group
of poems and poetic fragments (28), mostly traditional in their
use of poetic form, but which even so constitute an important
source concerning Nietzsche's early work on the fourth part
of *Thus Spoke Zarathustra*. At this point, during the autumn of
1884, Nietzsche was considering publishing a volume containing only poetry. Yet this was also a time when he was "tempted"
to devote himself entirely to poetry, a temptation which was
then overcome, in a literal sense, by the composition of the
fourth part of *Zarathustra*. The extremely extensive preparatory
material that follows (29–33) consists of brief poetically formulated images, outlines, and collections of maxims and parables
that were still in need of expansion and classification, as well
as preliminary, though already coherently constructed, drafts
of individual chapters. These fragments are of great interest
from a literary standpoint — indeed, not only for studying
how Nietzsche's style develops in his greatest work but also —
in the case of passages that were not used for the final version
of *Thus Spoke Zarathustra* — considered on their own terms.[2]

2. {The remainder of Giogio Colli's Afterword in *KSA* 11, which discusses
groups 34–40, written from spring through autumn 1885, is translated by
Adrian Del Caro in the volume in which the translation of those notes appear:
CW 16, 465–71.}

Translators' Afterword

Paul S. Loeb and David F. Tinsley

The fragments and notes contained in this volume, which Nietzsche wrote shortly before and during his composition of the fourth part of *Thus Spoke Zarathustra* (*Z*), cover the period from January 1884 through April 1885. Building on the Afterword from our previous volume (*CW* 14, 717–97, and esp. 723–47), we begin with an introduction to our philosophy of translation. We then focus in our Glossary on global translation decisions that are specific to the material in this volume (although there is some overlap) and that could not be addressed briefly in the Notes. Next, we provide a biographical sketch of this fourteen-month period in Nietzsche's life. We conclude with a brief overview of what Nietzsche was reading, an introduction to the poetry he wrote during this period, and, finally, an analysis of the unifying philosophical concept of superior humans that is presented in the notebooks in this volume and in the fourth part of *Z*.

Our Approach to Translation

Our goal in translating this second volume of unpublished notes remains the same: not only to find the most accurate English equivalent for each word or turn of phrase, but also to capture the style and spirit of what Nietzsche was trying to say, as he might have formulated it in English.

We are assuming that readers interested in the unpublished notes will be consulting both of our volumes; we therefore recommend that they begin by reading our Translators' Afterword to *CW* 14, where we introduce our philosophy of translation, give examples of how we deal with significant semantic and syntactical differences between German and English, and explore briefly not only the challenges that every translator of Nietzsche encounters but also those challenges specific to translating notebooks full of unpublished material.[1] We also recommend that our readers consult the "Glossary of Standardized Terms" in both volumes,[2] where we explain our translation choices for important terms that occur throughout the notebooks, such as where we render *Geist* as "mind" or "intellect" and where we render it as "spirit"; why we don't translate the simple but significant phrase *ich will* as "I will"; and how we respond to the semantic differences between Nietzsche's time and modern German when it comes to the words for "woman" (*das Weib* vs. *die Frau*). Most of our Translators' Afterword in the previous volume is devoted to detailed philological and philosophical arguments in support of our decision to render Nietzsche's key term *Übermensch* with the English plural "superhumans."[3]

Our remarks on translation in the Translators' Afterword to *CW* 14 were anchored in specific comparisons of grammatical structures and syntactical features that are distinctive to German and English and were thereby intended to demonstrate our general approach. We provide a complementary perspective in this volume; we begin with a general description of our principles and methods, and then define our approach against what have become conventional methods used by many translators. To begin, the most distinctive feature of *CW* 14 and 15 is that they are collaborative, integrating the linguistic insights of a philosopher and Nietzsche specialist with those of a Germanist and cultural historian. Of course, such collaboration

1. Cf. *CW* 14, 723–36.
2. Cf. *CW* 14, 738–47, and pages 483–88 below.
3. Cf. *CW* 14, 748–97.

happens at every level even when translators work alone; they consult earlier translations, they run difficult passages by other translators, and they solicit feedback from different native speakers on semantic nuances. But the difference is that the translation of Nietzsche's notes in these two volumes emerged, at every level, through the interaction of two scholars with different backgrounds and, not infrequently, differing opinions, not only on the meaning of Nietzsche's German but also on the best way of rendering it in English.

Translation is as old as language itself, but the methods developed in the Western European tradition go back to the earliest sources of vernacular writing, many of which were translations of scripture from the original Latin for missionary purposes. Such foundational principles of translation find their clearest illustration in interlinear translations of scripture. As an example, we provide the first verse from Mark 10:14, to which Nietzsche provides a sardonic response in 32[11] of this volume:

3708[e]	1161[e]	3588[e]	2424[e]	23[e]	2532[e]	2036[e]	846[e]	863[e]
Idôn	de	ho	Iêsous	êganaktêsen	kai	eipen	autois	Aphete
14 Ἰδὼν	δὲ ,	ὁ	Ἰησοῦς	ἠγανάκηοεν	καὶ	εἶπεν	αὐτοῖς ,	Ἄφετε
Having seen	*now*	*-*	*Jesus*	*was indignant*	*and*	*said*	*to them*	*Permit*
V-APA-NMS	Conj	Art-NMS	N-NMS	V-AIA-3S	Conj	V-AIA-3S	PPro-DM3P	V-AMA-2P

The original Greek is in the middle in the largest font. A transliteration (phonetic transcription) of the Greek is in a smaller font above the original, and an English translation is in a smaller font below it. The numbers at the very top are links to James Strong's concordance, with information about usage and variant meanings of each numbered term. The acronyms at the very bottom designate the part of speech of each element and its relation to the elements around it.

If we look closely at how Mark's Greek is rendered in English, we recognize several principles of translation which are still in common use today: (1) The presentation of the English and of the accompanying apparatus is designed for any level of fluency; it does not assume knowledge of the Greek alphabet.

(2) The original Greek has been divided into individual parts of speech; the choice of English word is based on this division of the original language, as well as on the equivalent English part of speech: each noun is rendered as a noun; each adjective as an adjective. (3) The syntax of the English is also determined by the syntax of the original Greek. Mark begins with the aorist form *eidon* of the Greek verb *horaó*; the translator begins with an English participial construction that is the closest equivalent; the order of English elements follows the structure of the Greek sentence. In general, when taking this approach, the accuracy of the translation is determined not only by how it renders the original but also by how exactly it *mirrors* the original. An implicit measure of the appropriateness of the translation is therefore how readily the reader can link each English word or phrase in the translation to the appropriate word or phrase in the original Greek.

The virtues of this approach are undeniable. The English rendering of the Greek is accurate according to each of the principles we just enumerated. The reader has a precise rendering of what Mark is saying. The reader knows at every moment which Greek word is being rendered and how the different elements fit together. And through Strong's concordance or other online or print resources, the reader can seek out alternative translations for each element. But one obvious fact remains: When we read the entire verse, "Having seen now, Jesus was indignant and said to them, 'Permit the little children to come to me, not do hinder them,'" the translation is not English. This is because the language of an interlinear-based translation finds its primary value in its function *as a conduit* to the original; it is not meant to stand alone. Of course, the translator would not leave the English in this form; she would modify the interlinear "gloss" into grammatical phrasing suitable for her intended readers, whether of King James's time ("But when Jesus saw it, he was much displeased, and said unto them, Suffer the little children to come unto me, and forbid them not: for of such is the kingdom of God"); or of the present ("But when Jesus saw this, he was indignant and said to them, 'Let the little children come to me; do not stop them; for it is to such as these that the kingdom of God belongs'" [New Revised Standard Version]); or even in the colloquial twentieth-century American English of Eugene Peterson: "But Jesus was irate and let them know it: 'Don't push these children away. Don't ever get between them and me. These children are at the very center of life in the kingdom'"[4]

Two global assumptions shaped our response to the challenges of translating Nietzsche's nineteenth-century German into twenty-first-century American English. First, the readers of *CW* 14 and 15 do not necessarily have access to the original German. Thus, our English phrasing has to convey what Nietzsche was trying to say without reference to the original, beyond occasional clarifications that we provide in the notes. We therefore made our translation choices with the assumption that the English text had to function more autonomously than in the interlinear contexts discussed above; we viewed the English not as a conduit to or a gloss on the original but as a *reasonable equivalent* of the original. Second, when we say that our goal is "to capture the style and spirit of what Nietzsche was trying to say, as he might have formulated it in English," we are acknowledging that translating a master of rhetoric and repartee like Nietzsche can actually demand *more* than phrase-by-phrase accuracy. In hundreds of hours of collaborative sessions, we continually posed the following questions: We know what the German means, but is this how we would convey it in English? Does the sentence flow as well as Nietzsche's German does? If Nietzsche uses wordplay, as he so often does, how do we render it into English without sacrificing too much of the wit that we see in his German? If the fragment in question concludes with a dash followed by a punchline, is it possible to find English phrasing that can do the same thing?

We strongly agree that every element in Nietzsche's German must be accounted for in the English version, but we do

4. Eugene H. Peterson, *The Message: The Bible in Contemporary Language* (Colorado Springs, CO: NavPress, 2018).

not always follow the second interlinear-based principle listed
above, namely, that each element of the German must be rendered in the same order by the equivalent part of speech. This
can be easily demonstrated by looking at how we translated two
of Nietzsche's titles. Fragment 31[65] includes the title *Von der
Wissenschaft*, composed of the dative preposition *von* followed
by the dative form of the feminine article *die* and the object
of the preposition *Wissenschaft*. Working from the second
interlinear-based principle, a translator would render this combination as "On the Science," which is accurate in its rendering
of each element and also grammatical. But when we looked
at the English phrasing during our final stage of revisions, we
agreed that Nietzsche does not have a particular application
of science in mind but rather science in general. We decided
that the more appropriate phrasing would be "On Science,"
which is not what Nietzsche says literally but reflects the phrasing that a philosopher would choose for a section on science
in general.[5] The subtitle to 29[40] provides another example
from this volume. The one-to-one approach works perfectly for
Nietzsche's title, "The New Enlightenment." But the subtitle
reads *Eine Vorbereitung zu . . .* , with the object of the preposition *zu* being here "the Philosophy of Eternal Recurrence." The
German literally reads "A Preparation having to do with." Of
course this isn't English. A philosopher wouldn't say "a preparation" in this context. When we reviewed other nominal render-
ings for *Vorbereitung*, we could not settle on a noun equivalent
that a philosopher would use. After much debate, we chose a
paraphrase — "Laying the Groundwork for" — which conveys
what Nietzsche was saying in a style more appropriate to philosophical discourse.

This paraphrase is an egregious violation of another assumption that underlies the "one-to-one" principle: no element
should ever be introduced into the English that is not actually

5. Whether N's use of the term *Wissenschaft* means "natural science" here or
"any academic discipline that requires a systematic approach and standardized
methods of analysis" is another question. See our Glossary below.

present in the German. Nietzsche does not use the noun *Grundlage* or *Fundament*, so neither should the translator. We agree that paraphrases should be used sparingly — this is a judgment call — but we based our decisions not only on the meaning of individual elements in Nietzsche's German but also on whether the English reads as well as the German does. Most other examples that we cite in the Translators' Afterword to *CW* 14 arise from the fact that German is more highly inflected than English, which is why a one-to-one rendering can introduce ambiguities that are not present in the original. For example, pronouns designating things or objects are gendered as *er*, *sie*, or *es* in German, which allows a German reader to determine easily what the noun antecedent is in a preceding passage. But the English equivalent is "it" for all three genders, thus severing the connection. This is why we sometimes substitute the noun for the German pronoun in our English rendering, so that the English reader does not encounter ambiguities that do not exist in the text that the German reader encounters.[6]

We often chose not to follow the third interlinear-based principle cited above, that the word order of the English sentence must mirror the word order of Nietzsche's original.[7] Rules governing word order in German dependent clauses make exact mirroring impossible. The elaborate extended adjectival constructions in Nietzsche's German can only be rendered reasonably in English by relative clauses. Finally, the inflection of nouns and pronouns in German affords the writer much greater flexibility in ordering the subject and objects. A noun subject can begin an utterance, follow the conjugated verb, or even follow the conjugated verb *and* a pronoun object; its position varies according to the emphasis that the author chooses to impart. Since English subjects and objects are not inflected, the English reader relies on word order to identify who is doing what for whom. Fragment 27[21] illustrates our approach to several of the above issues:

6. Cf. *CW* 14, 726–28.
7. Cf. *CW* 14, 727–78.

| Also: zu jeder *Lust* und *Unlust* ist *Denken* nöthig (ob es schon nicht zum Bewußtsein kommt) und sofern Gegenhandlungen dadurch veranlaßt werden, auch *Wille*. | Thus: *thinking* is required for each occurrence of *pleasure and displeasure* (whether it reaches consciousness or not) and, insofar as countermovements are initiated as a result of the process, the *will* is required as well. |

We moved "thinking" to the beginning of the first clause in order to make its function as the subject clear, added "of the process" to simulate the referential function of *dadurch* — it references the entire preceding clause — and repeated the verb at the end to make the existence of the parallel subject clear to English readers, something that the nominative inflection of *Wille* makes clear to German readers without any additional elements. Our addenda thus do not add elements that are not present; they merely seek to provide for readers of the English text the same clarity that inflection does for the readers of the original German.

Our goal was never to "modernize" what Nietzsche wrote, as Peterson did in his contemporary version of the Bible; instead, we sought English phrasing appropriate to each context. The range of rhetoric in Nietzsche's unpublished notes posed a considerable challenge. Translating Nietzsche's brief critiques of Kant's thing-in-itself or English utilitarianism required philosophical vocabulary and discourse; the many aphorisms written in the style of a Montaigne or a Goethe had us seeking out phrasing that could convey Nietzsche's rhetorical skill and sharp wit. Nietzsche's cutting asides about the shortcomings of his contemporaries, especially his fellow Germans, demanded a style more appropriate to today's Twitterverse, whereas the notes that Nietzsche takes on his readings of French authors could be rendered in more straightforward prose. The vivid imagery of Nietzsche's poetry dictated still another approach, and whenever Zarathustra speaks, the style and the cadence of the language had to change in order to communicate his unique style, the roots of which Nietzsche found in the biblical language of Luther. Our final step was always to read each sentence aloud. Hearing the English not only enabled us to make tiny adjustments in phrasing and word order to achieve the most appropriate cadence for each sentence, it also helped us to simulate the reading and writing dynamics that Nietzsche's failing eyesight had compelled him to adopt during this period of his life. His apprehension of his own writing during these years was based on how it sounded, not on how it read.

A Glossary of Standardized Terms

In the glossary that follows, we discuss our translation choices for additional terms that are more prevalent in our second volume. As a convenience to our readers, we also include brief definitions of the terms from the Glossary for *CW* 14.[8]

Aufgabe — Nietzsche uses this term in two contexts. When he has "a piece of work" or "an obligation" in mind, we translate it as "task." The English word "task" also retains the nuance of "a matter of considerable difficulty," but when Nietzsche has in mind his life goal of transforming the European cultural and moral landscape or Zarathustra's goal of initiating the self-overcoming of humankind, we render it as "mission."

aufheben — "abolish," "lift," "set aside," "repeal"; *sich aufheben* = "nullify themselves"; *Selbst-Aufhebung* = "self-abolishing."

Bildner (der) — sculptor; *Götzenbildner* = "idol-makers."

Empfindung (die) — "feeling," "perception"; "sensation" in Kantian contexts.

---

8. See *CW* 14, 738–47, for more detailed explanations of the translation choices that are merely listed here.

Entwicklung (die) — When Nietzsche uses this term in connection with organic life, he sometimes (as in 26[80]) means the *development* of parts or structures (as in embryology or morphology) and sometimes (as in 26[388]) *evolution* (as in natural history). Our decision on the appropriate translation is determined by the context.

erkennen / Erkenntnis (die) / Erkennender(r) — "know" / "knowledge" / "those who know."

erlösen / Erlösung (die) — "redeem" / "redemption."

Feuerhund (der) / Höllenhund (der) — "hound of fire" / "hound of hell."

Freigeist (der) — "free spirit(s)" or "free thinker(s)," depending on whether N approaches them positively or negatively.

Frau (die) / Weib (das) / Weibchen (das) — "woman" / "woman," except in the misogynist sense, where we render it as "female" / "little woman."

Geist (der) — "mind" or "intellect" where cognitive or intellectual connotations are emphasized, "spirit" where affective nuances are also in play. See also our comments in the next entry.

Gewissenhafte des Geistes (der) — Recent translations of *Z* follow Walter Kaufmann in rendering this term as "conscientious of spirit." However, in the passages included in this volume, Nietzsche means good habits of mind (such as honesty and rigor) and scrupulous attention to methodology (cf. 28[22]; 29[51, 58]; 30[4]; 31[70]; 32[9, 13, 16]). So, in line with our decision to render *Geist* as "intellect" in such contexts, we have rendered this term as "intellectually conscientious." This rendering also avoids the ambiguity inherent in Kaufmann's translation, as possibly meaning "governed by conscience or principles" — as in, for example, the idea of a conscientious judge who is not influenced by personal prejudice.

Gemüth (das) — "(the faculty of) feeling and perception" vs. *Geist* = "mind."

Gleichniss / Gleichniß (das) — "symbol" in allusions to Goethe's *Faust*, "parable," "simile," or "analogy," depending on the context.

hart / Härte (die) — "hard" for things or objects, "hard-hearted" for people / "hardness" for things or objects, "hard-heartedness" for people.

höhere Mensch (der) — This term is not used by Nietzsche in parts I–III of *Z*, only in part IV, but it is connected to his discussion of great (versus puny) humans in the earlier parts of *Z*. Following Nietzsche's citation in 25[71] of Paul Bourget's French term *homme supérieur*, and keeping in mind Nietzsche's own gender-neutral term *Mensch* (instead of *Mann*), we have chosen to translate this term as "superior humans" (even in the case of those fictional superior individuals who are all males in part IV). Other translators (except for Graham Parkes) have followed Walter Kaufmann in rendering this term as "the higher man," but we don't think this choice accurately conveys Nietzsche's meaning or corresponds to typical English usage. In 27[16, 37] and 31[27] Nietzsche contrasts this term with *der niedere Mensch*, which we have translated as "inferior humans" (and not, as with Kaufmann and others, "lower"). See also 25[343] where Nietzsche uses the contrasting loan word, *der inferiore Mensch*. Sometimes (25[198, 211, 222]) Nietzsche will also write of the contrast between those with superior and inferior natures. (See also *CW* 14, 744–45, and the conclusion to this Afterword.)

kleine Menschen — "puny people."

klug / Klugheit (die) — "clever" or "prudent" / "cleverness" or "prudence," depending on the context.

Kraft (die) — "force," occasionally "power" or "strength" if the context demands it, although we usually render *Macht* (*die*) as "power."

Lebendige (das) — The issue is how to render the terms that Nietzsche uses for both senses of life: *das Leben* vs. *das Lebendige*. Because most readers would assume that "the living" refers only to people, we translate *das Leben* as "life" and *das Lebendige* (literally, "that which is alive") as "living things."

Mitleid (das) — This is a central term for Nietzsche, especially with reference to his critique of Schopenhauer and to the narrative and philosophical themes of *Z* IV. Although most translators of *Z* have followed Walter Kaufmann in rendering this term as "pity," we have chosen the Latinate term "compassion" so as to render Nietzsche's literalistic and Schopenhauerian understanding of this term as a kind of "suffering-with." Other possible translations are "sympathy" and "commiseration."[9] See also 32[14], where Zarathustra realizes that he was wrong to feel compassion or to rejoice along with superior humans.

Nächste (der) / Nächstenliebe (die) — "neighbor" / "loving thy neighbor."

Naturen (pl.) — The challenge is how to render the meaning "the particular combinations of qualities belonging to a person" when Nietzsche uses it in the plural. We typically do not use the unmodified plural "natures" in this way. Whenever Nietzsche uses it unmodified, we avoid ambiguity by rendering

---

9. For further discussion, see Christopher Janaway, "Zarathustra's Response to Schopenhauer," forthcoming in *Nietzsche's "Thus Spoke Zarathustra": A Critical Guide*, ed. Keith Ansell-Pearson and Paul S. Loeb (Cambridge: Cambridge University Press, 2021).

it with paraphrases such as "temperaments." When an attributive is present or when the context is clear, we render it as "natures," as in "slavish natures."

Notschrei (der) — We have translated -*schrei* as "cry" in order to render Nietzsche's depiction of the feeling of urgent despair and self-loathing that is experienced by the superior humans who are visiting Zarathustra. And we have chosen to translate *Not-* as "distress" instead of "need" in order to follow Nietzsche's narrative suggestion that there is an objective source for this feeling in the failure and inadequacy of these superior humans.

reich / Reichtum (das) — We differentiate between the conventional meaning of *reich* ("wealthy / rich / wealth"), which Nietzsche views negatively (as in 31[40]), and Nietzsche's broader notion of overflowing prosperity or abundance ("prosperous / abundant / prosperity") found in exceptional individuals, which he portrays positively (as in 31[48]).

Seele (die) — This term had multiple meanings in Nietzsche's time, as did its English cognate, "soul." Our nineteenth-century sources cite "soul," "mind," or "heart," or when used rhetorically as a *pars pro toto*, "person." Nietzsche seldom uses the biblical triad of "body, mind, spirit/soul" except to dismiss it (25[7]), but he does make ubiquitous use of *Seele* in the sense of "the inner person" (Kant) or "our true self, the core of our being" (Wieland).[10] There was an emerging meaning of *Seele* as "psyche," at least in a proto-Freudian sense; in Nietzsche's time the term *Seelenkunde* was a synonym for "psychology." This is what Nietzsche most likely means when he speaks of the soul in 25[96] as "a multitude of affects." After much discussion we decided to follow most *Z*-translators and render *Seele* as "soul" in all contexts, even if the word-field for "soul" is becoming

10. Cf. Grimm, https://www.woerterbuchnetz.de/DWB?lemid=S23665.

increasingly concentrated in American English usage around
religious contexts.

Selbstsucht (die) / Herrschsucht (die) — "selfishness" /
"imperiousness."

sollen/wollen — *du sollt* = "thou shalt" / *ich will* = "I will
this."

Tafel (die) — "tablet" in biblical contexts, "code" in the context of moral philosophy.

Wissenschaft (die) — In the twenty-first century, the meaning
of the English word "science" has become synonymous with
"natural science," whereas the meaning of the German word
Wissenschaft includes any academic discipline that requires a
systematic approach and standardized methods of analysis,
hence the variants *Naturwissenschaft* ("natural science[s]"),
Geisteswissenschaft ("humanities"), and *Sozialwissenschaft*
("social science[s]"). When Nietzsche uses this term in his
preliminary drafts of *Z* IV, he usually has "natural science" in
mind, so we translate *Wissenschaft* as science and adjust our
rendering when he intends the broader meaning.

Zufall (der) — "chance" for the phenomenon, "coincidence"
or "accident" for an individual instance.

Nietzsche's Life, January 1884–April 1885: A Biographical Sketch[11]

Unique among the unpublished fragments of the *Zarathustra* period in its autobiographical focus and unsparing honesty, the fourth fragment of Notebook 29 will serve here as a snapshot of Nietzsche's life during this period. Written in the late autumn of 1884, 29[4] consists of a list of assets, accomplishments, and needs — philosophical, financial, and personal — that Nietzsche compiled while taking stock of his life and prospects during the closing months of what had been a productive and promising year.[12] In April he had published the third part of his self-described masterpiece *Zarathustra*.[13] He had devoted the late spring and summer to extensive note-taking and commentary for an uncompleted "masterwork," in addition to preliminary drafts for what would be published two years later as *Beyond Good and Evil* (Notebooks 25–27). In September and October he engaged in a brief but intensive foray into poetry. Shortly before writing this note, he had abruptly abandoned plans to publish this poetry and would immediately set to work on the "fourth and final" part of *Z* (Notebooks 29–33).

29[4] begins with a list of services that Nietzsche thinks he will need in order to continue his work.

> I lack 1) a cook[14]
>   2) musicians

11. For our brief biography, we draw upon the *Chronik zu Nietzsches Leben* ("Chronicle of Nietzsche's life") (*KSA* 15 / *CW* 19); Curt Paul Janz, *Friedrich Nietzsche: Biographie in drei Bänden* ("FN: Biography in three volumes"), (Leipzig: Zweitausendeins, 1999), esp. 2:247–390 (hereafter, "Janz" followed by vol. and page no.); Curtis Cate, *Friedrich Nietzsche* (New York: Overlook Press, 2002); and William H. Schaberg, *The Nietzsche Canon: A Publication History and Bibliography* (Chicago: University of Chicago Press, 1996).

12. Three other autobiographical fragments look back on Nietzsche's life: 25[9]; 25[285]; and 26[372].

13. Cf. Janz 2:238–39. For a contrary view to Janz, that Nietzsche had always intended his book to have four parts, see Paul S. Loeb, *The Death of Nietzsche's Zarathustra* (Cambridge: Cambridge University Press, 2010), 86–95.

14. The German word *Köchin* indicates that Nietzsche would prefer a woman for this.

3) readers
4) a kind of master of ceremonies

"If only I weren't so poor!" he exclaimed in a letter to his close friend from Basel, Franz Overbeck. "At the least I would like to have a slave, such as the poorest Greek philosopher had! I am too blind to do almost everything."[15] Nietzsche was well aware that the wages required would far exceed his limited financial resources, but he was growing increasingly concerned about his declining health. The sensitivity to light and humidity, the debilitating headaches and the bouts of nausea and vomiting had continued, sometimes forcing him to take to his bed for days at a time in response to travel or to unseasonable weather. His frustration was mounting at the restrictions that his declining eyesight imposed on his daily routine. "Traveling alone — is for a blind man like me almost the equivalent of cruelty to animals," he complained in the same letter to Overbeck. His failing eyesight made dining in hotels or restaurants embarrassing at best; he started restricting his diet to dishes that he could prepare himself in his rooms. He had to rely on Köselitz to decipher his notes and to revise his manuscripts for publication, and his mother and various friends and acquaintances were called upon to serve as lectors of sources he wished to study.[16] In the absence of recordings, Nietzsche needed access to musicians in order to experience the musical trends that he hoped to nurture as alternatives to Wagner. With "master of ceremonies," Nietzsche might have had in mind someone who could take on the social requirements of interaction with townspeople and academics at institutions such as the University

15. Letter to Franz Overbeck, 12 February 1884 (*KGB* III:1, 477–78); cited in Janz 2:264–65.
16. When circumstances demanded it, Nietzsche even hired strangers to read for him, but there are also many periods where no assistance can be documented. See Thomas H. Brobjer, *Nietzsche's Philosophical Context: An Intellectual Biography* (Champaign: University of Illinois Press, 2008), 29.

of Basel, an experience that had "completely exhausted" him
during a brief visit in July 1884.[17]

All of these concerns, as real as they were, serve to conceal
an even greater fear, to which Nietzsche gives voice during this
period. Plagued by insomnia caused by a moving kaleidoscope
of shapes and images whenever he closed his eyes, Nietzsche had
described these sensations to Resa von Schirnhofer during her
visit in Sils-Maria in the middle of August and then confided
the following: "Don't you think that this condition might be
a symptom of the onset of insanity? My father died of a brain
disorder." As Schirnhofer recalls the powerful impression that
Nietzsche's anxiety and candor made on her, she writes that it
was like meeting a Nietzsche she had never seen before.[18] It could
well be that Nietzsche's profound insight into human psychology and his sensitivity to his own condition afforded him at least
an inkling of the fate that would befall him just a few years later.

In the next part of fragment 29[4], Nietzsche reviews the
status of the mission upon which he had embarked during
the early months of 1884:

Probability of success: like a pyramid. The vast framework of
    my life. Utilizing failures
As my first success: Köselitz (my *taste*) — as my second
    (*moral* effect) Stein.

Nietzsche felt that he was on the brink of a monumental breakthrough: "[I]t is possible that, for the first time, a thought has
occurred me that will create a great divide in the history of
humanity [. . .] Yet I am still **far** from being able to give it
voice and to communicate it properly. If it is true, or rather, if
it is believed to be true, then everything will change, everything

17. Letter to Franz Overbeck, 12 July 1884 (*KGB* III:1, 511).
18. Resa von Schirnhofer, "Vom Menschen Nietzsche" ("On Nietzsche as
a person"), *Zeitschrift für philosophische Forschung* ("Journal of philosophical
research") 22, no. 2 (1968): 250–60; no. 3 (1968): 441–58, here 443–44. Quoted
in Janz 2:319.

will be turned on its head, and all values that have existed up to now will lose their value."[19] At the same time, Nietzsche had no illusions concerning the enormity of the challenge that remained — "the hardest work, demanding the greatest self-sacrifice, that a mortal man can ask of himself"[20] — both of *communicating* his "weightiest thought" and of *creating* the kind of European cultural impact that might eventually per-suade the leading minds of his time to abandon the entrenched values of compassion and selflessness. His optimism restored by the praise of *Z* I he received from his lifelong friend Erwin Rohde, as well as from close acquaintances such as Köselitz and the historian Jacob Burckhardt, Nietzsche spoke several times during these months of founding "a small, extremely accom-plished community devoted to the belief in *gaya scienza*,"[21] a seaside "colony" where he would be surrounded by "congenial" — with this phrase Nietzsche meant "suitable" — disciples with whom he could discuss his ideas and discourse on his "weightiest thought." In Heinrich von Stein, the young Wag-nerian who had just communicated his interest in being men-tored by Nietzsche, the "father of Zarathustra" thought that he recognized a kindred spirit and future disciple, who, he hoped, would soon join him in philosophical fellowship. Other poten-tial disciples included Köselitz, the literary historian and hote-lier Paul Lanzky, doctoral students Meta von Salis and Resa von Schirnhofer, and the translator and mediator of Schopenhauer in England, Helen Zimmern, among others.[22]

19. Letter to Franz Overbeck, 8 March 1884 (*KGB* III:1, 485); cf. *KSA* 15, 139 (*CW* 19).
20. Letter to Malwida von Meysenbug, late March 1884 (*KGB* III:1, 489). Cf. Cate, *Friedrich Nietzsche*, 449.
21. E.g., in his letter to Heinrich Köselitz, 9 February 1884 (*KGB* III:1, 524–25). Cf. Janz 2:335–36.
22. Janz 2:335. See also Cate, *Friedrich Nietzsche*, 446–59. Brief mentions in a few letters indicate that Nietzsche had not yet abandoned the hope that Paul Rée and Lou Salomé might join the group, despite the catastrophic rela-tionship with Salomé that had cost him his friendship with Rée and damaged his reputation. Cf. Janz 2:141–52; Cate, *Friedrich Nietzsche*, 382–91; and our Translators' Afterword to *CW* 14, 719.

Köselitz receives special mention here in conjunction with Nietzsche's phrase "my *taste*" not because of his indispensable role as Nietzsche's lector and scribe but because Nietzsche saw in him a composer who could spearhead a movement of more cosmopolitan music in the style of Bizet's *Carmen*, with the goal of eventually challenging the hegemony of Wagner's cultural legacy.[23] It was Nietzsche who had bestowed upon Köselitz what he thought was a more fitting name for a composer: Peter Gast.[24] It was Nietzsche who recognized that Köselitz would never be able to establish himself in Italy; and it was Nietzsche who, after Köselitz was unable to find support in Dresden for staging the opera that Nietzsche had retitled "The Lion of Venice," arranged with the conductor of the Zurich symphony, Friedrich Hegar, for Köselitz to come to Zurich at the end of October to rehearse in person. Hegar then invited Köselitz to conduct a performance of the overture on December 7, which was well received despite Hegar's concerns about orchestration. Nietzsche's hope that Köselitz would establish himself in Zurich would soon be crushed by two developments:[25] in November Nietzsche had sent his dance song "To the Mistral" to Köselitz and urged him to set it to music; after three months Köselitz confessed that he had been unable to do anything with it. Then Nietzsche would learn in March from Overbeck that Köselitz had given up on Zurich and returned to Venice. Even these disappointments were not enough to make Nietzsche abandon his musical ambitions. His comments in this fragment, which were formulated between Köselitz's rehearsals and the successful premiere of his overture, still resonate with enthusiasm and hope.

What Nietzsche meant by linking Heinrich von Stein to "*moral* effect" (*moralischer Effekt*) remains unclear, especially

23. N writes to Köselitz on 19 February 1883 (*KGB* III:1, 334): "Now different things are possible, e.g., that we will once again be sitting in the 'Temple of Bayreuth' in order to hear you"; quoted in Janz 2:173; cf. also Janz 2:282–87.

24. Cf. Robin Small, "Peter Gast," *Journal of Nietzsche Studies* 32 (2006): 62–67.

25. Janz 2:364–66.

as to whether he has in mind Stein as the origin or the object of this effect when he includes him among his successes. Nevertheless, it is instructive to recall how much of their interaction took place in the shadow of Richard Wagner, whose death on 13 February 1883 had left a huge lacuna in both of their lives. Stein had made a name for himself in Bayreuth as the tutor of Wagner's son Siegfried, after moving from the study of theology and then natural science in order to dedicate himself to music as the most valid means of transmitting what he considered to be Wagner's essential vision. In addition to the many interests and philosophers that Nietzsche and Stein had in common, among them Schopenhauer and Spinoza, Nietzsche writes to Overbeck of "someone new who is suited to me and has an instinctual respect for me," of a "splendid specimen of a human being and of a man" who is forthright enough to tell Nietzsche that he understood "no more than twelve sentences" of Z, yet who is "enough of a poet" to have learned the third part of Nietzsche's "The Other Dance Song" from Z III by heart, and most important, who "had promised on his own accord to join me in Nice as soon as his father is no longer with us."[26] The playful correspondence between master and future disciple revolves around the city of Bayreuth as Troy and around an emblematic figure, Philoctetes, the exiled archer from the Sophoclean tragedy, "without whose arrows Troy will never be conquered."[27] Even though the parallels between Achilles/ Wagner and Philoctetes/Nietzsche do not hold up consistently, there can be no doubt that Nietzsche wished to lure Stein into discipleship, at least in part, through the possibility that Nietzsche might return from "exile" to Bayreuth, where the "arrows" of his philosophy would bring about the fall of Troy, which for Stein meant the triumph of Wagner's worldview. In fact, for Nietzsche, the emblematic figure of Philoctetes was a stand-in for the emblematic figure of Napoleon, who in Nietzsche's view

26. Letter to Overbeck, 14 September 1884 (*KGB* III:1, 531); cf. Janz 2:325–36; different excerpts from the letter are cited in Janz 2:331.

27. Cf. 26[237]; Janz 2:333–35.

was an extraordinary outsider who not only conquered the Old World but also imposed his values on it. Thus the fall of Troy in Nietzsche's hidden Napoleon analogy stands for Nietzsche's victory *over* Wagner and for the triumph of Nietzsche's preferred musical style and of the extra-moral "revaluation of all values."

In the third part of 29[4], subtitled "Finances," Nietzsche mentions three names: Overbeck, Naumburg, and Schmeitzner, which correspond to the sources of Nietzsche's modest income, the status of which was the cause of considerable anxiety at this stage of Nietzsche's life. Nietzsche's friend and former colleague Franz Overbeck had been the principal contact for his financial arrangements with the University of Basel. The pension that Nietzsche received in 1879 following his retirement for health reasons was due to run out in June 1885. A serious economic downturn also made it unlikely that additional support would be forthcoming from the state. Nevertheless, on 28 March, Overbeck gave Nietzsche the welcome news that at least 2,000 francs would be made available from private pension funds for the next three years, with an additional 500 francs coming on the first of July. This meant that Nietzsche could look forward to a brief period of financial stability, and it is from these funds that Nietzsche would finance the private printing of *Z* IV and would also fulfill a promise he had made to his mother: the purchase of a headstone for the grave of his father.

Nietzsche includes the reference to Naumburg, where his mother and sister still resided, under the rubric "Finances" because, in addition to his pension from the University of Basel, Nietzsche had received a significant inheritance from his paternal grandmother from which the interest payments were administered by his sister Elisabeth.[28] Their relationship was fraught.

28. Cf. Daniel Blue, *The Making of Friedrich Nietzsche: The Quest for Identity, 1844–1869* (Cambridge: Cambridge University Press, 2019), 74–75, 296. It remains to be documented just how much of the principal of Nietzsche's inheritance was left by 1884–85. We are indebted to Daniel Blue for providing a more accurate picture of Nietzsche's financial resources than is available in the standard biographies, as well as for helpful feedback on this Afterword.

We see in *CW* 14 how Nietzsche had been devastated by the announcement of Elisabeth's engagement to the Prussian super-patriot and anti-Semite Bernhard Förster,[29] and he was profoundly embarrassed by the pernicious campaign that Elisabeth continued to wage against Paul Rée and Lou Salome.[30] Attempts by their mother and by Nietzsche himself to get Elisabeth to renounce her engagement fell on deaf ears. Nietzsche was deeply offended by the anti-Semitism of her recent letters, and there were financial repercussions because Elisabeth had apparently asked him for money to help finance Förster's plans to found a colony in Paraguay after the two were married.[31] Nietzsche had cut off all communication with Elisabeth for several months, beginning in February 1884. When his mother asked him to come to Naumburg to try and reconcile, Nietzsche would only agree to meet Elisabeth "halfway" in Zurich in September of the same year. There the two did meet briefly and achieved a superficial reconciliation only because Nietzsche expected that the Försters' relocation to Paraguay would mean the severing of all regular contact between him and his sister.[32]

Nietzsche's stand against anti-Semitism would also ruin his professional relationship with the publisher of all of his previous works, Ernst Schmeitzner. Nietzsche's financial grievances had nothing to do with Schmeitzner's refusal to pay Nietzsche for his publications, as Elisabeth would falsely claim, but rather was focused on recovering the sum of around 5,000 francs, drawn from Nietzsche's pensions, which he had given to Schmeitzner to invest on his behalf. Schmeitzner refused to produce the money because he didn't have it. He had neglected his publishing business in favor of fundraising for anti-Semitic causes.[33] The Schmeitzner affair took a decisive turn at the beginning of 1885 when Nietzsche engaged his uncle, Bernhard

29. Cf. Janz 2:261–65, on the break with Elisabeth.
30. Janz 2:263.
31. Schaberg, *The Nietzsche Canon*, 110.
32. Janz 2:337.
33. Schaberg, *The Nietzsche Canon*, 94–95.

Dächsel, to pursue the matter in court.[34] Nietzsche's concerns went beyond the implications for his financial future: he was afraid that Schmeitzner's devotion to anti-Semitism would sabotage his reputation as a philosopher, and furthermore, that Schmeitzner's animosity would result in his books languishing in storage. After a number of setbacks, including Schmeitzner reneging on agreements and Dächsel falling ill, the financial dispute would finally be settled in late October 1885, only after Schmeitzner's father intervened and agreed to take responsibility for Schmeitzner's debt. Nietzsche's other concerns remained. He grew increasingly doubtful that Schmeitzner would succeed in selling Nietzsche's recent publications to another publisher, and already in November we see Nietzsche dispatching Elisabeth to Leipzig in search of a replacement, armed with the promise that additional parts of *Z* would be forthcoming.[35]

The seemingly significant heading of 29[4], "What have we *achieved*?," is devoted to a seemingly insignificant topic: Nietzsche's places of residence. A bit more background is required in order to grasp the importance of this connection.

What have we *achieved*? **what have we established?**
1) My *places of residence*
    a) to Engadin I owe   *life*,
                               Zarathustra
    b) to Nice I owe the *ending* of Zarathustra
    c) both places fit my task well: Nice as cosmopolitan,
       Sils as high up in the mountains
(*Both* should contribute to the *impression* I leave. —)
Fundamentally: *not* to live in Germany, because of my European mission.

34. For a detailed account of Nietzsche's dispute with Schmeitzner, see Schaberg, *The Nietzsche Canon*, 94–119; Janz 2:355–56; and Adrian Del Caro's discussion of the dispute and its resolution in his Translator's Afterword to *CW* 16, 488–94.

35. Cf. 25[323] and 26[464], where the prospective title, *Noon and Eternity*, is explicitly linked to Nietzsche's "weightiest thought" of eternal recurrence; and 29[66] and 31[30], where it is linked to *Z* IV. Cf. Schaberg, *The Nietzsche Canon*, 101–2.

— *not* around universities —
— my predecessors: Schopenhauer and Richard Wagner
  are still viable European movements.
Perhaps some kind of teaching activity possible in *both* places.

After almost four years of searching for congenial climates,
Nietzsche had found two places where he could work productively: he spent the summers in his "cave," a dark room in the
back second story of the Durisch family home in the mountain village Sils-Maria in the Engadin region of southeastern
Switzerland and the winters in his recently discovered refuge of
Nice on the French Riviera, where the weather and especially
the lower humidity agreed with him. During the period covered by this volume, exceptions to this pattern included visits
to Köselitz in Venice, brief stays with his friends the Overbecks
in Basel, and two trips to Zurich. We also see from Nietzsche's
notes here, and from his letters, that he associated certain
places with philosophical discoveries, with specific stages
of the works that he composed, and, in a larger sense, with
a particular mindset or goal. For example, in *CW* 14 we see
how Nietzsche came to associate Genoa, and his own mission,
with the emblematic figure Columbus as a courageous captain
steering his vessel through the unknown depths and currents of
uncharted seas. In similar fashion, Nietzsche associates Engadin,
and more specifically, the mountain heights around Sils-Maria,
with his own creation, the emblematic figure Zarathustra, who
from his cave atop mountain peaks discovers a doctrine that
will change the world and human beings forever. Sils-Maria
is also the place near where the "weightiest thought" of eternal recurrence had first occurred to him. Nice serves as the
cosmopolitan counterpoint to Sils-Maria in Nietzsche's pan-
theon of places. Germany is far too provincial to be considered;
universities are too bureaucratic and too subservient to traditional morality. Nietzsche still dreams of founding a movement
based in joyful science which will transcend the influence of
Schopenhauer and even of Wagner. The "teaching activity" to

which he refers in this section would not have involved any sort of official position; his published views on Christianity and also his temperament precluded such employment. He had in mind an exclusive oceanside counterpart to Plato's Academy or to the Garden of Epicurus, where he would be teaching a select group of future disciples.

Nietzsche concludes this many-faceted fragment with a wistful look into his immediate future.

> What remains to be invented *in the immediate future*?
> Concealment. Restorative places. Calming techniques.

Nietzsche hopes for concealment, for a respite in places where the climate agrees with him, for developing techniques and practices that will allow him to remain calm as he turns to the composition of the fourth part of *Z* and to the continuation of his great mission.

As we have seen, more than a few clouds had appeared on Nietzsche's horizon of hope. He had already been disappointed by the few reactions he received to *Z* II and *Z* III: the enthusiastic responses of Köselitz, Rohde, and Burkhardt to the unconventional style and images of *Z* I had been transformed into frustration and bewilderment at the greater obscurity and more radical pronouncements of Zarathustra in *Z* II and especially in *Z* III. Sales of the *Zarathustra* volumes were almost nonexistent.[36] Even more devastating was the bombshell of a "dark" response that Nietzsche received from Heinrich von Stein to the encouraging verses he had sent him at the end of November. Stein made no further mention of joining Nietzsche's small community and invited Nietzsche to join him instead in his work on the Wagner encyclopedia. In just a few sentences the young man whom Nietzsche saw as his most promising future disciple revealed himself to be completely unsuited for the mission that Nietzsche had in mind. And as we have seen,

36. Schaberg, *The Nietzsche Canon*, 100.

Nietzsche's hopes for Köselitz's future as a composer in Zurich would experience yet another setback in March.

Despite these disappointments, the winter months in Nice were surprisingly productive. The last five notebooks of this volume (29–33) contain outlines, chapter titles, and drafts of entire scenes for the fourth part of *Z*, which Nietzsche would finish and show to Köselitz on February 14. Nietzsche also completed substantial revisions to *The Joyful Science* and assembled reams of notes in preparation for his anticipated "major work," as well as for *Beyond Good and Evil*. A private printing of forty-five copies of part IV had been undertaken by C. G. Naumann at the end of April, and Nietzsche arranged to send copies to a select group of nine friends and acquaintances, accompanied by a stern warning not to allow anyone else to see them.[37] The list of people who did *not* receive copies says even more about the controversial content and style of *Z* IV than the list of those who did: it included Erwin Rohde and Jacob Burckhardt, both of whom had enthusiastically responded to *Z* I; Malwida von Meysenbug, whose circle of feminist disciples in Rome had been both a model for Nietzsche and a source of contacts; and even more tellingly, none of the young men and women whom he saw as future disciples. All of them had been among the early recipients of the first three parts of *Z*.

A final event of personal significance loomed large in the early months of 1885: Elisabeth's wedding to Bernhard Förster, set for May 22 in Naumburg. Following the September "reconciliation," Nietzsche had done his best to keep things civil. He arranged to send a generous wedding gift via Overbeck, but he did not journey north for the ceremony. Nietzsche's mood at this time was the polar opposite of the energy and optimism that we sense in 29[4]. Nevertheless, the unsparing self-portrait that he sketches in a letter to Elisabeth before her wedding can still stand as a suitably conclusive epitaph to this phase of Nietzsche's life:

37. Schaberg, *The Nietzsche Canon*, 104–9, provides the most complete and convincing documentation of how many copies were printed and who the recipients were.

Until now, from the time I was a toddler, I have not found
anyone with whom I could share the same needs that I have
on my heart and conscience. This forces me, even today,
to present myself as a socially acceptable kind of person.
My watchword has always been that it is possible to prosper only among people with similar sensibilities [. . .];
my misfortune has been that I have never had any such
person. My existence at the university was the exhaustive
attempt to fit in to a mendacious milieu; developing a relationship with Wagner involved the same situation, only
in the opposite direction [. . .] The feeling that there is
something distant and foreign within me, that words have
a different meaning coming out of my mouth than they do
coming from the mouths of others [. . .] is still the most
sophisticated level of "understanding" that I have discovered up to now. Everything that I have written up to this
point is mere foreground; things only begin working for
me at the point [where words end] and my dashes begin.[38]

Nietzsche's Notes on Secondary Sources[39]

Whereas Nietzsche's notes and commentary in the period
covered by our previous volume reflect his return to key
philosophical sources such as Schopenhauer, Emerson, and
Dühring, the first two notebooks of this volume contain
extensive notes that Nietzsche took in French[40] and German
on French authors such as Balzac, as well as on the memoirist

38. Letter to Elisabeth Nietzsche, 20 May 1885 (*KGB* III:3, 52–53); cited in
Janz 2:388–89.

39. For essential studies of the principal sources that Nietzsche cites, quotes,
or paraphrases in his works, see Brobjer, *Nietzsche's Philosophical Context*; and
Robin Small, *Nietzsche in Context* (Aldershot, UK: Ashgate, 2001).

40. We owe a considerable debt of gratitude to Alan D. Schrift, the editor of
the Stanford edition of Nietzsche's *Complete Works*, for translating the French passages in this volume as well as for providing helpful explanatory notes. The English
phrasing is entirely his work. Thanks also to Rudolf Beer for helpful consultation
on the French passages during the early years of our work on this volume.

and travel writer Astolphe de Custine and the politician and writer Ximénes Doudan. As with Nietzsche's ability to work independently despite his blindness, there are contradictory accounts regarding his proficiency in French. Paul Lanzky, who had studied Romance languages in Zurich, Pisa, and Rome, and who was Nietzsche's lector of Stendhal in January of 1884 in Nice, says of Nietzsche: "[H]e was almost blind, his French was bad, he scarcely knew a word of Italian."[41] During Resa von Schirnhofer's Easter visit with Nietzsche in Nice in 1884, this doctoral student in philosophy who had spent a year in Paris was impressed by Nietzsche's recommended readings from French literature and culture; Stendhal and the French classical dramatists assumed special prominence in their wide-ranging conversations, among other French authors.[42] It would be no exaggeration to say that Nietzsche's experiences during the first six months of 1884 consisted, at least to some degree, in viewing European culture through a French lens.

Honoré de Balzac *(25[24–34])*

At the beginning of 1884, Nietzsche was reading Balzac's letters, from which he notes a series of observations about continental authors, including Stendhal and Scott, as well as on asceticism as it relates to productivity.

Astolphe de Custine *(25[41–100])*

Most of the quotes in this section come from Custine's "Memoirs and Travels," a two-volume account of his travels in Switzerland, Italy, England, and Scotland. Nietzsche felt a kinship with Custine, based on their youthful aspirations, and finds much to reflect upon in Custine regarding the nature of genius, what we would today call cultural criticism of English and German values, and above all, regarding Custine's caustic critique of the moral hypocrisy of modernity. The ideals of equal

41. Janz 2:250–54, here 251.
42. Janz 2:274–78, includes a comprehensive list, with biographical data, of the works that Schirnhofer reports discussing with Nietzsche during her visit.

rights and universal suffrage appear in Nietzsche's notes here, as in *CW* 14, as signs of "*slavish* sensibility" (25[70]). Shakespeare and Walter Scott are dismissed as flawed and inferior, whereas Nietzsche's "pinnacles of honesty" include "Machiavelli, Jesuitism, Montaigne, [and] La Rochefoucauld" (25[74]).

Hippolyte Taine

Taine's eclectic opinions on European cultural phenomena are a persistent presence in Notebooks 25 and 26, for example, on English landscape painting (25[138, 139]) and German historiography (25[133]; 26[424]).

Johann Wolfgang von Goethe *(25[473–80])*

Goethe provides a crucial presence in many of Nietzsche's cultural and aesthetic observations. When Nietzsche notes that Goethe's Faust and Byron's Manfred were models for Balzac (25[28]), it takes us back to the poetic invention of extraordinary individuals that we discussed in *CW* 14 in the context of superhumans.[43] Nietzsche also sees Goethe as having discovered his "Hellenistic spirit" in Italy as Nietzsche would do (25[162]), as living and embodying the kind of "noble isolation" to which Nietzsche aspires (25[175]), and finally, he names Goethe as one of his true "ancestors," along with Heraclitus, Empedocles, and Spinoza (25[454]). The concentration of reflections cited above consists of quotations from Goethe's *Maxims and Reflections*, which were a model for Nietzsche's aphoristic writing in both form and content.

Paul Deussen *(26[193– 200])*

The German Indologist's writings were the most important source for Nietzsche's continued studies in Brahmanism and Vedanta philosophy during this period.

43. *CW* 14, 769–72.

Stendhal (Henri Beyle) *(26[394–98])*

Stendhal, whom Nietzsche calls "a man after his own heart," was the first French author that Nietzsche mentioned in his conversations with Resa von Schirnhofer in Nice. In these fragments Nietzsche takes note of Stendhal's comments about the proper mindset of the philosopher.

Prosper Mérimée *(26[418–23])*

Mérimée, like Taine, is another source of sharp-witted observations about European cultural phenomena.

Ximénès Doudan *(26[435–47])*

Nietzsche's source here is Doudan's *Thoughts and Fragments*, from which Nietzsche notes any number of opinions about authors from Cicero to Montaigne to Renan.

If we were to contrast the focus of the first two notebooks with similarly eclectic material in *CW* 14, we would note the shift in focus from philosophy and science to philosophy and culture. If one principle could be said to dominate Nietzsche's perspective in the first two notebooks, it would be cosmopolitanism, arising in his multifaceted and critical exploration of aesthetic and cultural influences that transcend national (and nationalist) notions of literature, music, and culture. As Nietzsche observes, "to view Europe as a center of culture: nationalist folly should not make us blind to the fact that *a continuing mutual dependence is already in existence in the more cultured regions*. France and German philosophy. R. Wagner of 1830–50 and Paris. Goethe and Greece. Everything is striving for a *synthesis of the European past within the most highly developed intellectual types*" (25[112]).

Nietzsche's Poetry

Nietzsche's correspondence and unpublished notes from this period more than corroborate Philip Grundlehner's claim that

"Nietzsche believed poetry to be a vital and inseparable part
of his production as a philosopher."[44] This is especially clear in
Nietzsche's exuberant response to his childhood friend Erwin
Rohde's praise of *Z*I. Rohde writes: "I believe that using this new
format — which is indeed capable of many variations and transformations — is helping you find a format all your own. Even
your language is only now achieving its most mellifluous tones
[. . .]"[45] Nietzsche replies: "By the way, I have remained a *poet*
within the furthest boundaries that the concept allows, even if I
may have *thoroughly oppressed* myself with the complete opposite
of poetic activity." In the same letter Nietzsche gives voice to
the dizzying height of his aspirations: "With this *Z*⟨*arathustra*⟩
I pride myself on having brought the German language to perfection. After *Luther* and *Goethe*, one more step remained," and
"my style is a *dance*; a play of symmetries of every kind, and
at the same time it leaps beyond those symmetries and renders
them ridiculous. This extends even into my choice of vowels."[46]

When Nietzsche introduces Resa von Schirnhofer to his
weightiest thought of eternal recurrence, he does so through
the poetry of Zarathustra.[47] He first asks her to read aloud to
him "The Night Song" and later "The Dance Song" from *Z* II.
When he asks her to read "The Other Dance Song" from *Z*
III, he is not satisfied with the quality of her voice and immediate recites the verses of the bell tolling midnight as he feels
they should resound. He then chooses this moment to begin
discussions of eternal recurrence, which he conducts in a whis-
pered tone. Schirnhofer recalls that she was disconcerted, "not
so much by the idea, but by the way it was communicated,"
but we include the scene here as an example of how much
importance Nietzsche placed on the experience of poetry as
the most effective accompaniment to his most cherished and

44. Philip Grundlehner, *The Poetry of Friedrich Nietzsche* (Oxford: Oxford
University Press, 1986), xiv.
    45. Rohde to N, 22 December 1883 (*KGB* III:2, 412); cited in Janz 2:259.
    46. N to Rohde, 22 February 1884 (*KGB* III:1, 479); cited in Janz 2:260.
    47. Quoted from Schirnhofer's memoirs in Janz 2:278–80.

challenging ideas. Poetry and philosophy work in concert. Lest our readers see the above scene as Nietzsche assigning a particular role to poetry only in his interactions with women, when Nietzsche begins to suspect that the young Wagnerian, Heinrich von Stein, is wavering in his decision to be mentored by Nietzsche, he sends Stein the poem "The Hermit's Longing" with the concluding verses "Ready day and night, I await friends / *New* friends! Come! It's time! It's time!"[48]

For Nietzsche, *Z* itself was poetry, but poetry from an unmistakable source. In a series of three fragments in Notebook 25, he stresses the importance of Luther's Bible translation for shaping the cadences and rhythms that will best resonate with his intended audience: "Playing with the most diverse meters and occasionally unmetrical verse is the right thing: the freedom that we have achieved already in music through R⟨ichard⟩W⟨agner⟩! we can certainly take this for our poetry! In the final analysis: it is the only kind of poetry that speaks strongly to our hearts! — Thanks to Luther!" (25[172]). He then identifies the language of Luther as the basis for the "new German poetry" that he is inventing in the writing of *Z*: "Making things classical, the rhyme scheme[49] — is all wrong and does not speak profoundly enough to us: not even Wagner's alliteration!" (25[173]). Characteristically, Nietzsche prefers diversity in meter and structure to alliteration, the dominant poetic form of the oldest Germanic oral formulaic verse, found in works such as *The Lay of Hildebrand* and *Beowulf*, which Wagner adapted as a signature device.

Space does not permit detailed analysis and interpretation of all of the verses collected in this part of our volume, but readers will be rewarded with witty and poignant phrases that Nietzsche would continue to revise in 29[1] and in the

48. N to Stein, end of November 1884 (*KGB* III:1, 564–67); cited in Janz 2:367–69.

49. Nietzsche rejects any sustained rhyme schemes as unsophisticated, and although he praises the adaptations of classical verse forms by August von Platen and Friedrich Hölderlin, especially of the ode, he finds them too restrictive.

notebooks that follow. They will find poems addressed to Spinoza and Wagner, companion pieces of Nietzsche's verses to Goethe in *Joyful Science*, along with a poem of praise to the Persian poet Hafiz. They will also encounter a treasure trove of ridicule regarding the behavior and pretensions of the Germans, stunning nature poetry such as "At the Glacier" (28[60]) and "A German November" (28[59]), and an evocation of refuge and exile titled "Farewell" (28[64]). There is also a further adaptation of the philosopher-as-Columbus motif, where Columbus-Yorick turns his vessel toward eternity.

We have already noted how the inclusion of poems in the appendix to *Joyful Science* and in the notebooks of *CW* 14 signaled Nietzsche's return to writing poetry after a five-year hiatus, and specifically how Nietzsche used poetry in *CW* 14 to explore the emblematic figure of the philosopher as Columbus.[50] Poetry has a more significant presence in *CW* 15, where a collection of nearly seventy poems and verses provides a transition from prolific, extremely wide-ranging notes and commentary (25–27) to a series of notebooks (29–33) consisting of aphorisms and preliminary drafts of scenes for the fourth part of *Z*. Nietzsche spent almost two months during the autumn of 1884 revising drafts of verses and composing new ones. Poetry was his focus before he took up the *Zarathustra* material again in the winter of 1884–85,[51] poetry not as a diversion, but rather as an essential means of giving voice to his ideas.

Nietzsche's Philosophical Concept of Superior Humans

As Giorgi Colli notes in his Afterword, the central theme of the preparatory notes included in this volume is the concept of superior humans that is the basis of *Z* IV. This is true even in the collection of fragments that Nietzsche wrote before he

50. Cf. *CW* 14, 737.

51. For a thorough analysis of Nietzsche's poetic compositions and plans during this time, see the introduction to Nietzsche's poetry in the Notes, 438–45.

started writing *Z* IV in Notebook 29.[52] Here we offer a brief discussion of his treatment of this concept, concentrating first of all on his distinction between superior and inferior humans; second, on his view of the ultimate goal pursued by superior humans; third, on his distinction between successful and failed superior humans; and finally, on his profiles of failed superior humans. This final section is the longest because this is where Nietzsche spent most of his creative thought and energy. We will argue that all of these profiles were directly inspired by actual historical figures who were active in nineteenth-century Europe.

Superior and Inferior Humans

Nietzsche had discussed great human beings in his works prior to *Z*, especially, for example, in his early essay on Schopenhauer, and there is plenty of debate about this concept in the secondary literature.[53] But everything changes with his introduction of the doctrine of will to power in *Z*, and now he quite simply defines greatness in humans as consisting in power, that is, in the ability to control, dominate, and command other human beings (*Z* II "On Self-Overcoming").[54] Human beings who

52. For example, in Notebook 25, Fragments 9, 13, 71, 99, 110, 137, 140, 155, 157, 174–75, 183, 187, 198–99, 211, 216, 221, 243, 245–47, 259, 261, 270, 273, 278, 283, 307, 309, 317, 328, 335, 342–45, 348–55, 382, 405, 435, 450–52, 459, 462, 491; in Notebook 26, Fragments 75, 93, 122, 172–73, 202, 234, 238, 243, 256, 258, 289, 318–19, 342, 344, 346, 355, 357, 360, 366, 392, 407, 409, 425, 462; and in Notebook 27, Fragments 10–11, 16, 23, 40, 43, 58–60, 67, 74, 79–80.

53. See, e.g., the debate started by James Conant's essay "Nietzsche's Perfectionism: A Reading of Schopenhauer as Educator," in *Nietzsche's Postmoralism*, ed. Richard Schacht (Cambridge: Cambridge University Press, 2001), 181–257.

54. The best example of this crucial change can be found in *JS* 301, where Nietzsche claims that the superior humans who call themselves "contemplatives" are distinguished from inferior humans on the basis of their *vis creativa*, that is, their power (*Kraft*) to create the world of valuations that is studied and translated into the everyday by the inferior humans. In *Z* II "On Self-Overcoming," Nietzsche makes the same claim, but this time he adds his new idea that the valuations created by the wisest humans are expressions of their dominating will to power which are issued as commands to be obeyed by those who are not wise, that is, the people (*das Volk*).

have this ability to rule over most others he now calls "superior" (*höher*) and those in the majority who cannot help but obey he now calls "inferior" (*nieder, inferior*) (25[335]; 26[344]; 27[23]; *Z* IV "On Superior Humans" 3).[55] For this reason, he also defines superior humans as having an overwhelming inclination to rule over inferior humans to the full extent of their ability to do so (*Z* III "On the Three Evils"), and he criticizes them if they fall short in this motivation or in its realization.[56]

Certainly this definition captures Nietzsche's great admiration for some of the most famous political and military leaders in Western history, such as Pericles, Caesar, and Napoleon. But it doesn't seem to capture most of the other ways in which scholars have come to think of Nietzsche's distinction between superior and inferior human beings. They usually think that he draws this distinction in terms of loftier concerns, as, for example, with his triad of the philosopher-artist-saint exemplars in that early essay on Schopenhauer — as opposed to other more ordinary types of human beings. Or they think that he draws it in terms of the creative ambition and genius that have produced the finest cultural achievements of humankind, such as the ancient Greek Parthenon, or the Copernican revolution, or Beethoven's symphonies — as opposed to the complacency

---

55. Please see our Glossary entry on these terms. Nietzsche had used these German terms frequently prior to writing *Z*, so it is noteworthy that he doesn't use them at all in the first three parts of *Z*, opting instead to draw a distinction between great (*grosse*) and puny (*kleine*) humans (cf. *Z* III "The Convalescent" 2). This change in formulation, and even his basic idea for *Z* IV, seem to have been strongly influenced by his contemporaneous reading (25[71]) of the novelist and critic Paul Bourget's discussion of the *homme supérieur* in his *Essays in Contemporary Psychology* (Paris: Lemerre, 1883) and *New Essays in Contemporary Psychology* (Paris: Lemerre, 1885). See Benedetta Zavatta, "Laughter as Weapon: Parody and Satire in *Thus Spoke Zarathustra*," forthcoming in Ansell-Pearson and Loeb, *Nietzsche's "Thus Spoke Zarathustra."*

56. For Nietzsche, this is a philosophical definition because it is a normative definition and all value judgments have their ultimate source in a philosophical legislation of values (26[407]; *CW* 16, 38[13]; *BGE* 211). Insofar as this distinction is unique to his own philosophy, he would say that it is part of his own value legislation.

and mediocrity of sheep-like "last humans." Or they think that he has in mind great-souled humans, that is, those superbly healthy, well-rounded, and complete humans with a rich and complex set of conflicting yet unified drives, just as he portrays himself in *Ecce Homo* — as opposed to those sickly and fragmentary humans with rudimentary and limited psychological makeups. Or they think that he has in mind free-spirited, life-affirming noble elites such as Goethe who disdain morality and egalitarian ideals and are always in a process of self-overcoming — as opposed to the base and plebeian masses who are content to live a long time, conform, and stagnate (27[17]).

These are all legitimate interpretations of Nietzsche's distinction between superior and inferior humans. However, as the notes in this volume make clear, at the time of writing *Z* he has come to understand all of them in terms of his monistic theory of will to power. Philosophers, he writes, are the most powerful of all superior humans; their power lies in their ability to create new values and ideals that serve as background commands and laws for all inferior humans: "*Order of rank*: those who *determine* values and guide the will of millennia, by guiding the most superior types, are *the most superior humans*" (25[355]; cf. also 25[307, 450–52]; 26[75, 407]).[57] Philosophers (or "sages") are even the natural rulers of all other types of superior humans, including those who are artists (*CW* 14, 4[268]; 26[238]; *GM* III 5) and those who are religious ("saints") (*BGE* 61–62) — as seen, for example, in the enormous influence of Schopenhauer's values and ideals on Wagner and Tolstoy. But even considered as autonomous agents, the artistic types of superior humans are driven to find reflections of their own power in their works of art (25[307]; *TI* "Forays" 9), and the religious types seek to wield power over their sickly followers (*GM* III 15). As for the great-souled superior humans, Nietzsche

57. See Paul S. Loeb, "Genuine Philosophers, Value-Creation, and Will to Power: An Exegesis of Nietzsche's *Beyond Good and Evil* §211," in *Nietzsche's Metaphilosophy: The Nature, Method and Aims of Philosophy*, ed. Paul S. Loeb and Matthew Meyer (Cambridge: Cambridge University Press, 2019), 83–105.

thinks that all drives are simply embodied forces, which means that well-rounded humans who embody an array of powerful, diverse, and highly organized forces are able to rule over all fragmentary humans who have only weak, minimal, and disorganized forces at their disposal:

> Unlike animals, humans have conceived and nurtured within themselves an abundance of *conflicting* drives and impulses: by means of this synthesis they rule the earth [. . .] The most superior human beings would have the greatest multiplicity of drives, and also the comparatively strongest drives that can still be tolerated. In fact: wherever the human plant is strong, we find instincts that are powerfully working *against* each other (e.g., Shakespeare), yet constrained. (27[59]; cf. also 27[11, 16])

In Nietzsche's view, superior humans certainly gravitate toward aristocratic and elitist ideals and configurations, but this is only because they know that these are the best means of maximizing their own power and the overall power of any sociopolitical structure they inhabit (25[382]; *BGE* 257–59). Superior humans disdain morality and egalitarian ideals because these restrict and diminish their power (26[173]; 27[80]); but on the other hand, they engage in continual self-overcoming because this is the very best means of enhancing and expanding their power (*Z* II "On Self-Overcoming"). They are free-spirited, both cognitively and affectively, because their power will not allow itself to be fettered in any way. Their worldview is one of total life-affirmation because this conveys the exultation they feel when contemplating their own overflowing power (*TI* "Forays" 49). And they display noble virtues such as courage and generosity because these are simply manifestations of this feeling of overflowing power (*Z* I "On the Virtue of Gift-Giving").

Scholars who find Nietzsche's new formulation of this distinction somewhat extreme or unfamiliar should keep in mind that his new doctrine of will to power, as introduced for the first time in *Z*, is part of his project of naturalizing humans and placing them on a par with other animals and living creatures (*JS* 109; *BGE* 230). According to Nietzsche, all living creatures, humans included, strive to control and dominate everything around them as much as possible, and this means that everything they do is an extension of this striving (*Z* II "On Self-Overcoming"). So, for example, when Nietzsche says that great philosophers like Plato (26[355, 357]) are the most superior humans because they influence all other humans through their created values and ideals, he means that this influence is a kind of commanding and legislating that allows them to control and dominate others. Or when he says that great artists like Michelangelo or Beethoven accomplish their best creative work when they are seeking to project into it their feeling of overwhelming power, he means by this their feeling of being able to control and dominate others (and that this is actually achieved through the response to their art). Both these points can seem strange if we are interpreting Nietzsche's talk of control and domination in political terms, as perhaps requiring some kind of physical force. But as the outline above makes clear, this would be the wrong way to understand what Nietzsche means, since he categorizes political and military domination as just one kind of will to power, and likewise, superior humans who strive for this particular kind of domination as just one type of superior human. Indeed, one of his frequent complaints about the German Reich is that the superior humans who were its founders and rulers sacrificed German intellectual, artistic, and cultural power for the sake of enhanced political and military power (cf. *TI* "Germans" 1, 4). Again, this complaint should not be interpreted as expressing Nietzsche's self-reflecting preference for intellectual and cultural accomplishments over military and political accomplishments. Instead, given his considered view that the former (especially in philosophy) unleash far more power than the latter, this complaint expresses nothing other than his preference for more power rather than less. For example, he claims, the control exerted by Plato's philosophy has been far more inward-reaching and has extended to far more people over a far longer time period than anything Pericles could have imagined:

> — in all circumstances, *princes* are ranked second: the *truly superior people* rule for millennia and are unable to take an interest in contemporary things. The princes are their *tools* or sly dogs who *volunteer* to be tools.
>
> To elevate the image of the most superior sage *above* the image of the prince (as a tool of the sage). (25[354]; cf. also 25[270])

The Goal of Superior Humans

The most interesting aspect of Nietzsche's concept of superior humans (*höhere Menschen*) is his claim that they are motivated by their will to power to want to facilitate the self-overcoming of humankind and the creation of superhumans (*der Übermensch*):

> *What can be made out of humans*: this is what matters to superior human beings. The breadth of their vision (25[435])

> *the destiny of humankind lies in its most superior type achieving success.* (26[75])

> Not "humankind," but rather *superhumans* are the goal! (26[232])

This claim has been overlooked in the secondary literature because most scholars have tended to assimilate Nietzsche's concept of superhumans to his concept of superior humans.[58] But the notes in this volume, as well as *Z* IV, present a sharp distinction between these two concepts and offer the following reasoning for this claim. Superior humans are the most

58. As we explained in our Translators' Afterword to *CW* 14, 748–97.

powerful humans, and indeed, despite being a tiny minority, embody within themselves most of the enormous power that is distributed throughout the human species. What this means is that their continual process of individual self-overcoming, which is driven by their individual will to power, also represents most of the self-overcoming that is performed by the human species as a whole (27[9]). The problem for superior humans arises when they attain their maximum power and are unable to attain any more. Instead of resting content with this achievement, their insatiable will to power drives them to want still more power, but this time by striving to create something beyond themselves that is capable of attaining more power than they are:

greatest increase in the humans' awareness of their power as the ones who are creating superhumans. (26[283])

What is superior is the *will to create* above and beyond ourselves, by means of ourselves, and even if this should be by means of our own downfall. (26[346])

Designating superior humans as those who create. Organization of the superior humans, education of *those who will rule* in the future as theme of Zarathustra 3. Your superpower must find joy in itself, in ruling and shaping things. "Not only humans, but *also superhumans, return eternally!*" (27[23])

In concrete terms, this means initiating a process of selective breeding that enables them to become the ancestors of a new species that is far more powerful than the human species (25[211], 27[60]).[59] According to Nietzsche, when enough

59. Through choice of not just lineage but also place, climate, diet, lifestyle, etc., as in *CW* 14:15[4]. Cf. Hugo Drochon, *Nietzsche's Great Politics* (Princeton, NJ: Princeton University Press, 2016), 169–70. See also 25[211] for Nietzsche's suggestion that the thought of eternal recurrence will be an element in the process of selective breeding.

superior humans are driven by their maximized will to power to contribute to this long-term collective and creative task, humankind will have overcome itself and superhumans will come into existence.

Given that the ultimate goal of superior humans is to create superhumans, why haven't they already done so? Why does Nietzsche say that superhumans have never yet existed (*Z* II "On Priests"), despite his view that so many superior humans with maximized will to power have prevailed throughout history? His main answer, in these notes and in *Z*, is that superior humans have been confused about their ultimate goal. Instead of trying to create superhumans on this earth, they have pinned their hopes on extraterrestrial and supernatural fantasies. They have always had the correct instinct, but this instinct has been diverted and perverted into religious and metaphysical speculation.

> Our contempt for h⟨umans⟩ drove us beyond the stars. Religion, metaphysics, as symptom of a desire to create superhumans. (*CW* 14, 4[214])

> — their *displeasure* with human beings misled the Brahmins, Plato etc. into striving for a *divine* form of existence *beyond what is human* — beyond space, time, multiplicity etc. (26[203])

> I think that all metaphysical and religious ways of thinking are the result of dissatisfaction *with humans*, the result of the drive for a superior, superhuman future — except that humans *themselves* wanted to flee into the hereafter: rather than build a future. *A misunderstanding of those who have superior natures, who suffer on account of the ugly image presented by humans.* (27[74])

> God and the hereafter as mistaken choices of the creative urge (27[79])

This is why Nietzsche depicts Zarathustra as teaching the superior humans that they can indeed create superhumans now that all gods are dead. They should want to rule the kingdom of earth, not hope to enter the kingdom of heaven (32[11]). And this is why he has Zarathustra implore his disciples to stop looking beyond the stars and remain faithful to the earth (*Z* I "Zarathustra's Preface" 3–4); to avoid fleeing into the hereafter and instead build the future; to reject the impossible task of creating divine beings and choose instead the humanly conceivable task of re-creating themselves into fathers and forefathers of the superhumans (*Z* II "Upon the Blessed Isles").

Successful and Failed Superior Humans

There are two ways, then, in which Nietzsche thinks superior humans can fail to live up to their true natures. First, they can somehow lack the desire to rule over inferior humans, or supposing that they do have this appropriate desire, they can simply fail in their efforts to fulfill this desire. In either case, since the struggle between superior and inferior humans is a zero-sum game (25[174, 343–44], *BGE* 228), their abdication of their ruling responsibility leads them to act on behalf of inferior humans instead of superior humans. This means that they act to resist, suppress, and decrease the overall power of humankind. Second, superior humans can become so disgusted with humankind and suffer so much as a result that they waste their creative energies on fantasized alternatives instead of concentrating on their true goal of building an earthly superhuman future (29[8], 29[52]). In *Z*, Nietzsche presents his protagonist as a superior human being who does not fail in either of these ways. Zarathustra confesses to his stillest hour that he doubts whether he has the lion's voice for commanding the self-overcoming of humankind, but in the end he does find this voice.[60] And Zarathustra admits that he himself used to dabble in religion and metaphysics when he

60. Loeb, *Death of Nietzsche's Zarathustra*, 166–67. Cf. also 26[407] and *CW* 16, 38[13].

was younger (*Z* I "On the Hinterworldly").[61] But the start of the narrative shows him casually remarking on the fact that God has died and then, right after that, announcing that the time has come for humankind to overcome itself and create the superhumans (*Z* I "Zarathustra's Preface" 2–3). Zarathustra is therefore Nietzsche's representation of a completely successful superior human with a maximized will to power who, for the first time in history, inspires others like him to join him in pursuing their true vocation of building a superhuman future (31[2]).

Thus, what is especially striking about the fourth part of *Z*, and about the preparatory notes in this volume, is that in these texts Nietzsche focuses most of his attention on his idea of superior humans who are failures in both of the senses just mentioned (*Z* IV "On Superior Humans" 14–15, 20; 31[2]):

> *The Cry of Distress of Superior Humans?*
> Yes, of those who have failed — (26[289])

Considered collectively, the superior humans depicted in this material have all evaded their responsibility to rule and are all described as the last remnants of God (*Z* IV "The Welcoming"). What this means is that in effect they have become servants of the herd and deserters from the earth. Because they have not lived up to their true nature and have lost faith in themselves, they are filled with self-loathing, and this leads them to seek Zarathustra with their cry of distress. Since they represent the most powerful members of humankind, who give meaning to the earth and guide its future (33[1]), their plight is the actual cause of the nihilistic spirit that troubles the age in which they live. Accordingly, and in order to address this cause directly, Zarathustra takes it upon himself to teach these superior humans about their true natures and their true vocation. He teaches them that they are supposed to rule

---

61. Here, and in this chapter of *Z*, Nietzsche appears to allude to his own ideas in his first book, *BT*: "My youthful misunderstanding: I had not yet entirely freed myself from metaphysics — but the deepest need for an *alternative image of humans*" (27[78]).

over inferior humans and that their resulting maximized will to power should lead them to want to use their ruling position for the sake of creating the superhumans as the new meaning of the earth (Z IV "On Superior Humans" 2; Z I "Zarathustra's Preface" 3). His teaching seems at first to have the desired effect, but then the superior humans are collectively scared away by the impending arrival of Zarathustra's returning disciples, and he realizes that he was wrong to feel any compassion for their distress (Z IV "The Sign") or any rejoicing along with their convalescent happiness (32[14]). The isolated and failed superior humans will not be able to heal the despair that is enveloping the world. This is something that can only be accomplished by Zarathustra and those returning disciples he has been collectively training, like a father with his children (31[64]), to become the new rulers of the earth and the first ancestors of the superhumans (29[21, 25]; 31[2]).

Profiles in Failure

Arthur Schopenhauer, Friedrich Wilhelm IV and Wilhelm I, Charles Darwin, Richard Wagner, Pope Pius IX, David Friedrich Strauss, Leo Tolstoy, and Lord Byron — these are the nine famous historical figures from the nineteenth century that Nietzsche depicts as failed superior humans in the order in which they appear in Z IV. Or at least this is a reasonable hypothesis about their identities based on the notes collected in this volume and the clues that Nietzsche includes in his profiles of the superior humans he labels as the prophet, the two kings on the left and the right, the intellectually conscientious human, the sorcerer, the pope who is no longer in service, the ugliest human, the voluntary beggar, and the wanderer who calls himself Zarathustra's shadow.[62]

62. For some very different hypotheses, see Francesca Cauchi, *Zarathustra Contra Zarathustra* (Aldershot, UK: Ashgate, 1998); and Weaver Santaniello, *Zarathustra's Last Supper: Nietzsche's Eight Higher Humans* (Aldershot, UK: Ashgate, 2005).

It is true that Nietzsche doesn't explicitly reveal any of these identities in any of the many lists he compiles in his preparatory notes. But he does indicate that he wants us to guess these identities when he reintroduces the prophet from *Z* II who is obviously a representation of his engagement with Schopenhauer's pessimistic philosophy.[63] He also indicates this with his transparent depiction of Wagner in the guise of the sorcerer who has extraordinary musical and acting skills (26[377]) — something confirmed by the fact that he calls Wagner an "old sorcerer" (*alte Zauberer*) in his later *WA* ("Postcript"). Most tellingly, there is the following preparatory note in which Nietzsche sketches the method he will use for writing about the failed superior humans in the text that will become the fourth part of *Z*:

> Zarathustra 1 all sorts of superior humans and their distress and decline (individual examples e.g., Dühring, destroyed by isolation) — in general the *fate of superior humans* at present, how they seem *doomed to die out*: it comes to Zarathustra's attention like a great cry for help. He is approached by all kinds of insane degeneration (e.g., nihilism) in those with superior natures. (27[23])

Here Nietzsche explains that he will offer individual examples of failed superior humans who are distressed, and he cites as one such example the name of an actual historical figure, Eugen Dühring. This example is especially interesting because he had already alluded to Dühring, and to his home city of Berlin, in the *Z* III chapter that depicts Zarathustra's encounter, at the gate of the big city, with a foaming fool who is called "Zarathustra's ape" (*Z* III "On Passing By"). Moreover, in his various lists of possible superior humans that he was considering in his notes, Nietzsche twice mentions "the fool from the big city" (29[14, 24]). We can therefore suppose that at one

---

63. See Christopher Janaway, "Zarathustra's Response to Schopenhauer," regarding the nuances of this representation.

point Nietzsche was thinking about depicting a failed superior human with this label who was inspired by the real person Dühring, and that this was going to be the same method
he would be using for his entire final grouping of superior
humans.[64] Since Schopenhauer, Wagner, and Dühring all lived
in nineteenth-century Europe, we can further suppose that
this final grouping includes only figures who lived in this time
and place. This constraint immediately rules out many of the
guesses that have been offered by scholars, such as Buddha,
Socrates, and Jesus.

Turning now to our hypothesis, we can begin with the
prophet and the sorcerer that we have just mentioned. Both
of these are prominent superior humans in the narrative of Z
IV. This is because the prophet, besides already having been
the subject of a chapter in Z II, is the one who first speaks to
Zarathustra in order to seduce and tempt him into feeling compassion for the distress, as well as rejoicing for the convalescent
happiness (32[14]), of all the superior humans who are about to
arrive (Z IV "The Cry of Distress," "The Sign"). After that, the
sorcerer (*Zauberer*) (also called "the enchanter" (*Bezauberer*)
in 31[39], and "the fool," and "the poet" in 31[31]) is the one
who imitates Zarathustra and who actively seeks to lure the
assembled superior humans into again feeling the melancholy
and sadness that Zarathustra had just been dispelling. In the
preparatory notes in this volume, Nietzsche frequently pairs
these two superior humans together and presents them as allies
in order to convey the extent of Schopenhauer's philosophical
influence on Wagner's art. According to Nietzsche, both these
historical figures were failed superior humans because both of
them rejected hierarchy and diverted their creative urge for the
superhumans into the beyond. Schopenhauer did this by seeking the unity of all things in a world behind the appearances,
a unity that he then converted into an egalitarian bond among

64. Fragment 30[4] contains this final grouping with the minor variants
that the two kings are listed separately and the wanderer-shadow is called "the
good European."

all humans that justifies compassion as the ideal basis of all human relations. He also denied the possibility that humans can create anything new, thereby nullifying his own urge to create the superhumans (*Z* II "The Prophet," "On Redemption"). According to Nietzsche, Wagner followed Schopenhauer's philosophical lead in these ideas. In addition, and in keeping with one of his designations as "the poet" (31[31]), Wagner fantasized about superhumans living in the clouds who followed his own earlier revolutionary ideals and gave up all of their ruling power (*Z* II "On Poets"). Although both these historical figures were atheists, Nietzsche thinks that they were actually among the last remnants of the Christian God because they submitted to the Christian worldview (cf. 25[416]; 26[377]; 28[48]) and therefore took sides with inferior humans against their own nature and their own kind.

The next most prominent superior human in the narrative of *Z* IV is the ugliest human. He claims to have murdered God; his shame, suffering, and self-loathing cause Zarathustra to feel more compassion for him than for any of the other superior humans. It is he who initiates the superior humans' cheerful and childish worship of the ass as a resuscitated God; who leads the superior humans in affirming eternal recurrence; and who announces on behalf of all of the assembled superior humans that Zarathustra has helped them to recover from the distress they were feeling before they met him. Additionally, the place where Zarathustra first meets the ugliest human reminds him of the place where he experienced his decisive struggle with the serpent-monster in *Z* III ("On the Vision and the Riddle").[65]

As Greg Whitlock has suggested, Nietzsche's most important clue regarding this character's identity is the ugliest human's confession that he has murdered God and that this has caused him to be persecuted and pitied. This should be seen as an allusion to David Friedrich Strauss's scholarly effort to demythologize the historical person of Jesus in his controversial book *The*

65. See Loeb, *Death of Nietzsche's Zarathustra*, 230–31.

Life of Jesus.[66] But there is also Nietzsche's narrative suggestion that this character, who is always gurgling and snorting, is incapable of using language properly, which is an allusion to his own vicious criticism of Strauss's writing skills in the lengthy second part of his early essay on Strauss (*DS* 9–12).[67] Moreover, Nietzsche writes that this ugliest human made his appearance tolerable by adorning himself with a historical sense (31[10]). According to Nietzsche, Strauss was a failed superior human and one of the last remnants of God because he did not actually give up his theistic fantasies, only the idea that Jesus was divine.[68] These fantasies, which diverted Strauss from his true goal of creating superhumans, were the result of his feeling repulsed by his own ugliness and by the ugliness of humanity in general. Also, when Nietzsche depicts this outcast human as harboring deep guilt and shame for having vengefully "murdered" (not just killed) the omniscient witnessing God, he is conveying his view (as expressed at length in his *DS* essay) that Strauss was still deeply committed to Christian morality and hence to the interests of the inferior humans rather than to those of his own kind.[69]

The intellectually conscientious human and the wanderer who calls himself Zarathustra's shadow (also called "the good European" in 29[51], 31[10]) are the next two most prominent superior humans, because each of them makes a presentation

66. See Greg Whitlock, *Returning to Sils-Maria: A Commentary to Nietzsche's "Also Sprach Zarathustra"* (New York: Peter Lang, 1990), 10, 272, and esp. 287n63, where Whitlock notes that the original title of the combined "The Awakening" and "The Festival of the Ass" chapters was "The Old and the New Faith," a reference to the Strauss book that Nietzsche criticized in *DS*.

67. See Loeb, *Death of Nietzsche's Zarathustra*, 229n40.

68. In *TI* ("Germans" 2), Nietzsche praises Strauss as "our first German freethinker" (presumably on account of his first book about Jesus), but speculates that his alcoholism caused him to degenerate into the author of a beer-house gospel and "new faith" (referring to the title of Strauss's last book). For more discussion regarding the question of Strauss's faith, see Frederick C. Beiser, *David Friedrich Strauss, Father of Unbelief: An Intellectual Biography* (Oxford: Oxford University Press, 2020).

69. See Loeb, *Death of Nietzsche's Zarathustra*, 229.

during Zarathustra's last supper with the superior humans. However, these two superior humans could not be more different from each other. The former is a scientist who devotes himself to honest, rigorous, and inexorable inquiry, even if his subject is nothing grander than the brain of a leech and even if he needs to give his own blood in order to gain knowledge. According to this superior human's speech at the last supper, which excoriates the sorcerer for his deceptive artistry, all humans are driven by an ancient primitive fear to seek the security and certainty of truth and scientific knowledge. By contrast, the wanderer who has been shadowing Zarathustra is a restless free spirit and adventurer (27[40]) who has always chosen the path of least certainty and lived by the creed of the oriental order of the Assassins, "Nothing is true, everything is permitted." As a consequence, however, he is now without any goal and without any home, and he has become emaciated and outdated, always in danger of being tempted and imprisoned by some strict belief or severe delusion. In his song at the last supper, he inhabits his role as a doubt-ridden nihilistic European and recounts his journey through oriental landscapes of fresh air, blue skies, and palm trees where he became ever more consumed by his lustful fantasies of oriental dancing girls. This song is framed at the start and at the end by what he imagines would be the sanctimonious outrage of the Europeans he has left behind.

Once again, Nietzsche leaves some clear clues as to the identity of the figures that inspired these two profiles. In the case of the intellectually conscientious human, these include his feeling most at home in the wilderness and the pride he takes in his unrivaled mastery of this realm, his intense study of a seemingly minor biological organism, his self-sacrificing pursuit of scientific knowledge, his monomaniacal drive toward specialized and exhaustive research, and his idea that knowledge and science have their evolutionary origins in the prehistoric human fear of wild animals. These details all point to the most famous scientist of Nietzsche's time, Charles Darwin, who published his first scientific paper on the eggs of marine leeches, then spent eight years of his life studying barnacles, and concluded his career with a very popular book that generated a lot of controversy with its speculation about the intelligence of earthworms (which belong to the phylum Annelida, which includes leeches).[70] Darwin's self-sacrificing devotion to his scientific studies — for example, in his study of the role that fear played in the evolution of humans[71] — was legendary and cost him much in his personal life. Also, when the intellectually conscientious human admiringly quotes Zarathustra's idea that intellect is the life that cruelly cuts into life itself, this aptly captures Darwin's anxiety that his discoveries would fatally injure the pride that humans took in themselves and their accomplishments.

From Nietzsche's perspective, however, Darwin was a failed superior human. This is because his theory of natural selection, with its emphasis on environmentally adaptive fitness, left no room for the distinction between superior and inferior humans, much less for the idea that the former should rule over the latter. In addition, Nietzsche believed that Darwin's thinking revolved around a conception of humans as herd-animals ("last humans") instead of envisioning humans as possible ancestors to the superhumans. These two points against Darwin are captured in this note:

70. Charles Darwin, *The Formation of Vegetable Mould Through the Action of Worms, with Observations on Their Habits* (London: John Murray, 1881). Nietzsche might have had the following passage in mind: "With respect to the small size of the cerebral ganglia, we should remember what a mass of inherited knowledge, with some power of adapting means to an end, is crowded into the minute brain of a worker-ant" (58).

71. Cf. Charles Darwin, *The Descent of Man, and Selection in Relation to Sex* (London: John Murray, 1871), and *The Expression of the Emotions in Humans and Animals* (New York: D. Appleton, 1872). Darwin's evolutionary theories, like the one in the speech about fear, were the most important influence for Nietzsche's one-time philosophical companion, Paul Rée, which is why in *CW* 14 (782) we noted Rée as the possible inspiration for Nietzsche's depiction of the intellectually conscientious human. But Nietzsche did not think that Rée was a superior human (cf. 25[259]; 26[202]; and *CW* 14, 7[37]; 17[49]), so the real inspiration had to be Darwin himself.

Hail to you, you upright English
Hail to your Darwin, if only he understood
You as well as he does his animals!

You English have no trouble
Raising your Darwin high, even if he understood
Nothing more than cattle-breeding.

Yet — to put him *on the same level as Goethe*
Means a crime against majesty
Majestatem genii! (28[46])

It is a little more difficult to see why Nietzsche thinks that Darwin, who was at best agnostic about theism, belongs among the last remnants of the Christian God. Nietzsche himself suggests this difficulty when he has Zarathustra especially rebuke the intellectually conscientious human for his prayerful worship of the ass. But here it helps to look ahead a little to Nietzsche's later account of "these people who are unconditional about one thing, their claim to intellectual cleanliness [. . .] these last idealists of knowledge, in whom alone today the intellectual conscience dwells and became incarnate" (*GM* III 24). These people, he writes, are not really as free-thinking as they believe because their unconditional faith in truth and their metaphysical faith in science are actually the remnants of the thousand-year-old Christian belief that God is the truth and the truth is divine.

As for the wanderer and shadow, who is also called "the good European" (29[51], 31[10]), these clues include Nietzsche's allusions to Lord Byron's Romantic poetry, his identification with Europe (not just England), his love of nature and his famous wandering travels in eastern Europe and Turkey, his claim to doubt everything and believe in nothing, his rebellion against European social mores, and his scandalous libertine exploits. In the wanderer's song, Nietzsche twice uses the name "Dudu" to refer to the dancing girls, which is an allusion to the odalisque

Dudù in Byron's *Don Juan* (*CW* 9, 628n6). He also includes in this song the image of a dancing girl who is missing a little leg (*Beinchen*), perhaps a veiled allusion to Byron's famously malformed right foot.[72] Although Byron was an atheist who spurned conventional morality, his embrace of the French Revolution and his militant stance against all forms of authority were enough to convince Nietzsche that he had abdicated his responsibility to rule over inferior humans. Again, it is difficult to see why Nietzsche would count Byron among the last remnants of God, especially since the wanderer-shadow subscribes to the motto that nothing is true and hence doesn't share what Nietzsche thinks is Darwin's unconditional faith in truth (*GM* III 24). Byron, it would seem, was a genuine free spirit in Nietzsche's estimation. However, Zarathustra's remark that the shadow's idolatrous worship of the ass resembles his wicked worship of the dancing girls suggests that in Nietzsche's view Byron's lustful fantasies were themselves a kind of enslaving idolatry that diverted him from his true goal of creating the superhumans. This suggestion is supported by Nietzsche's later inclusion of Byron among a group of superior humans who were great poets. These sensual men, he writes, pretended to be stars while actually they were lost in the mud and in love with it, desperately needing the devotional compassion of women (*BGE* 269).

The next two superior humans to consider are the two kings, and here a couple of difficulties arise right away. First, how can Nietzsche claim that they failed to rule when they are by definition rulers? And second, the fact that there are two of them, one on the left and one on the right, seems to preclude the idea that Nietzsche had any specific historical figures in mind. Indeed, most scholars have deemed his characterizations of the

72. Benita Eisler, *Byron: Child of Passion, Fool of Fame* (New York: Vintage, 2000), 13. In this song, Nietzsche also uses the name "Suleika," which is an allusion to the female protagonist in Goethe's collection of poems *West-Eastern Divan* (1819) (*CW* 9, 628n7), thus suggesting that Goethe was another European Romantic poet with fantasies about women from the exotic Orient.

two kings as too vague to have been inspired by any actual persons. The answers to both these questions require a closer look at the text of the chapter of *Z* IV entitled "Conversation with the Kings," along with Nietzsche's preparatory notes for this chapter. In the first place, it is a crucial part of Nietzsche's description that the two kings are driving before them a single ass burdened with wine. Zarathustra finds this peculiar, and the kings agree that it is. Right after this, the two kings, who at one point speak with one voice,[73] proceed to berate the kingdom of the rabble over which they rule and from which they have just escaped in order to seek out Zarathustra. Nietzsche's point here, which he had already made in the earlier *Z* II chapter on famous sages, is that these kings do not rule over inferior humans but are rather ruled by them. The rabble they serve are symbolized by the malevolent wine-carrying ass, and this is why the ass is leading them and not the other way around. The kings know that they are only pretending to fulfill their role as superior humans, and it is this deception that disgusts them and fills them with self-loathing. At one point, the king on the right says that the peasant today is actually the best and that the peasant-type should be the ruler in the kingdom of the rabble. Here we see Nietzsche including a thought from his preparatory notes that makes a direct reference to Otto von Bismarck, the Prussian statesman who became the first chancellor of Germany during Nietzsche's lifetime:

Peasants as the most common species of noblesse: because they are most dependent upon themselves. Peasant blood is still the *best blood* in Germany: e.g., Luther Niebuhr Bismarck

73. This is why Weaver Santaniello, in *Zarathustra's Last Supper*, says that she regards Zarathustra's encounter with the "*two* kings" as "one" higher human (4n1). In *CW* 14 (782), we made the same mistake in identifying only Napoleon in place of the two kings. This was also a mistake because Nietzsche regards Napoleon as a *successful* superior human (even if still human, all-too-human).

Where is there a noble family whose blood is not tainted
by venereal disease and degeneracy?

Bismarck a slave. Just look at the faces of the Germans
(it is understandable that Napoleon was astonished when
he met the author of Werther and encountered a *man*!):
anyone having a drop of blood overflowing with manliness
left the country: as for the pitiful populace that remained,
the people with servant's souls experienced an improvement from abroad, particularly through *slave blood.*

The nobility of Brandenburg and the Prussian nobility
in general (and the peasants of certain northern German
regions) currently possess the *most manly* natures in Germany.

That the *manliest men* rule is the order of things.
(25[268], cf. also 29[14], where Nietzsche writes: "the king
[the statesman "peasant"])

In these passages, then, Nietzsche is alluding to the relationship between Kaiser Wilhelm I and his governing chancellor,
of which the Kaiser famously said: "It isn't easy being emperor
under such a chancellor."[74] Nietzsche's depiction of the king on
the right is thus inspired by the Kaiser, which means that the
question about the identity of the king on the left is immediately resolved once we note that during the last supper he says
that he and his "brother" (who both speak German) have taken
care of the wine. The older brother of the Kaiser was Friedrich
Wilhelm IV, who served as the king of Prussia until he died, at
which time his brother took the throne. They were both sons of
Friedrich Wilhelm III, and they both served as kings of Prussia during Nietzsche's lifetime (in 1840–61 and 1861–88, respectively). It must have given Nietzsche great satisfaction to include
this hidden reference to his namesake Friedrich Wilhelm IV. As
for the ass that symbolizes the rabble (and perhaps also its ruling representative, Bismarck), the two kings are grateful to see
that Zarathustra thinks they should be leading the ass:

74. "Es ist nicht leicht, unter einem solchen Kanzler Kaiser zu sein." Lud-
wig Bamberger, *Bismarck Posthumus* (Berlin: Harmonie, 1899), 8.

> The superior human, you know, should also be the most superior ruler on earth. / There is no harder misfortune in all human destiny than when the powerful of the earth are not also the first humans. Then everything becomes false and crooked and monstrous. (*Z* IV "Conversation with the Kings")

In his later writings, however, Nietzsche launches some of his harshest invective against the Hohenzollern dynasty to which all these Prussian kings belonged, and especially against what he called the "Christian Reich" that was ruled by the Kaiser and his devout Pietist chancellor (26[335]).[75] This explains Nietzsche's claim that even these two kings should be counted among the remnants of God who remained busy fantasizing about extraterrestrial improvements instead of creating the superhumans on earth.

Finally, the last two superior humans are obviously remnants of God because they are both devout Christians. One of these is the voluntary beggar, a fairly transparent depiction of Leo Tolstoy. Like Wagner and Nietzsche, Tolstoy was deeply influenced by Schopenhauer. Late in life, after suffering an existential crisis, he decided to emulate Jesus and gave his land and his wealth to the peasants who worked for him. He also became a pacifist and a vegetarian, which helps to explain Nietzsche's amusing picture of the peaceful man living among the cows (also Nietzsche's symbol for the bovine human herd; cf. 25[343]) and preaching to them while subsisting on a diet of honey, grains, and water. The other devout Christian is the pope who is no longer in service (*ausser Dienst*) because his God has died. Nietzsche's point here is that the Christian faith has become untenable even for the kind of superior human who becomes the leader of the Roman Catholic Church. This pope, in accordance with his priestly nature, thinks that he rules as a shepherd over the inferior humans who populate his

75. Cf. Drochon, *Nietzsche's Great Politics*, 153–79.

flock, but in reality he is a servant of this herd and hence a failed superior human. Moreover, even after having retired from this service, the pope remains fixated on his memories of the fantasized divinity instead of turning his attention to his true goal of creating the superhumans. However, the clues Nietzsche leaves about the historical figure who inspired this depiction are rather sparse. Here we need to keep in mind Nietzsche's focus on famous figures in the nineteenth century and also our claim that his depiction of the two kings was in fact inspired by two actual kings of Prussia. Since there were only two actual popes reigning during Nietzsche's lifetime, and since the depicted pope is no longer in service and calls himself the last pope, perhaps Nietzsche is playing with the word *letzte* and has in mind the very consequential Pope Pius IX, who served from 1846 to 1878 (which means that he was the previous pope at the time Nietzsche was writing *Z*).[76] This pope's name would explain why Nietzsche constantly emphasizes piety whenever he mentions the pope. For example, the wanderer calls him "the good pious pope" (*der gute fromme Papst*); and the pope asks Zarathustra to forgive an old pious pope's heart (*einen alten frommen Papst-Herzen*). Nietzsche actually uses the word *fromm* (and its variants) thirteen times in connection with the pope. Since this is the only German word for "pious" and there is no Latinate cognate, we can assume that Nietzsche would expect his readers to understand the allusion.[77]

76. Perhaps Nietzsche also had in mind the fact that Pope Pius IX was the very last pope to rule as a king over the Papal States. Cf. David I. Kertzer, *The Pope Who Would Be King: The Exile of Pius IX and the Emergence of Modern Europe* (New York: Random House, 2018).

77. Building on a guess by Nietzsche's biographer, Curt Paul Janz, Weaver Santaniello, in *Zarathustra's Last Supper* (40–42, 68), concentrates on Nietzsche's description of the Pope's physical appearance as a tall, half-blind old man dressed in black with a gaunt, pale face and beautiful long hands. She argues that this description bears a strong resemblance to the famous pianist and composer Franz Liszt, who was Cosima Wagner's father and who devoted the last thirty years of his life to the Catholic faith. But this argument fails to explain why Nietzsche would want to depict Liszt, who was famous for his

Conclusion

Most scholars who have studied the fourth part of Z have concluded that Nietzsche's depictions of the superior humans are not meant to identify or criticize any actual historical figures. Instead, they agree, these depictions are supposed to be composite illustrations of various idealized types, or perhaps personifications of various general tendencies and mindsets, or even recollections of various psychological aspects and phases of development in Nietzsche himself (or in his alter ego Zarathustra).[78] Our overview of the preparatory notes collected in this volume, as read in conjunction with the fourth part of Z, suggests a quite different conclusion. In these texts Nietzsche is taking stock of what were then regarded as the most talented, influential, and celebrated men of nineteenth-century Europe. His survey ranges across many different nations, including Germany, England, Italy, and Russia, as well as over many different aspects of human civilization, including science; philosophy, religion, and theology; art and culture; and politics, diplomacy, and the military. Nietzsche's conclusion is quite concrete and specific, namely, that all the following individual men from his era were indeed superior and destined to rule over inferior humans but had all failed to do so: the inventor of pessimistic philosophy (Schopenhauer), the Prussian monarchs who unified Germany (King Friedrich Wilhelm IV, Kaiser Wilhelm I), the greatest biological scientist of the age (Darwin), one of the most original and influential musicians of the century (Wagner), one of the heads of the Catholic Church

music, as the Pope. It's true that Nietzsche calls the Pope a "Church Father" and also later uses this term in relation to Liszt (WA "Epilogue"). But the context of this later remark is a sarcastic pairing of Wagner and Liszt as two "clowns" who don't know the first thing about Christianity: "If Wagner was a Christian, well then, Liszt was perhaps a Church Father!" This contempt for Liszt's religiosity does not sit well with his extended description of the Pope's genuine religiosity. For a different interpretation of the Pope's one eye as an allusion to the Cyclops in Euripides's satyr play, see Loeb, Death of Nietzsche's Zarathustra, 95.

78. See Zavatta, "Laughter as Weapon."

in the nineteenth-century (Pope Pius IX), the most powerful
critic of the founding document of Christianity (Strauss), one
of the most accomplished novelists of the century (Tolstoy),
and one of the most famous poets and personalities of his time
(Byron). According to Nietzsche's analysis in the notes included
in this volume and in the fourth part of *Z* that was composed
alongside them, these superior humans failed because superior
types fail more easily (26[75, 425], 29[7]) and because each of
them was inadequate in some particular respect: "In any place
where that which is superior is not that which is most powerful, something is lacking precisely in that which is superior: it is
only a fragment and a mere shadow" (*CW* 14 7[24]). However,
the root cause of their failures was the same for all of them,
namely, the inescapable and continuing influence of a dying
Christian faith and especially the overwhelming political rise
and dominance of the masses: "*There is no longer any faith in
philosophers*, not even among scholars; this is the skepticism
of a **democratic** age which *rejects* superior kinds of humans.
Our century's psychology is essentially oriented *against* people with superior natures" (26[342]). In Nietzsche's view, the
principal outcome of this collective failure among the best and
brightest men of his age was a pervasive and devastating European nihilism that would soon engulf the rest of the world.
In order to find relief, consolation, and inspiration, Nietzsche
looked to the few men in his time who were not just superior
but also successful in their superiority: for example, Beethoven,
Emerson, Stendhal, and especially Goethe and Napoleon. But
in the end he decided that it was up to him, and no one else,
to rescue not just Europe but the whole world, by envisioning
a far more successful superior man in a later and stronger age
who would outshine all these historical figures (25[405]). His
name would be "Zarathustra" and his mission as a ruler of the
earth would be to guide humankind into a pivotal moment of
self-overcoming that would ensure the emergence of a far more
powerful new species.

Index of Persons

Vigny, Alfred, comte de (1797–1863), French poet and author of the novel *Stello* (1835), 413n225

Virgil (Publius Vergilius Maro) (70–19 BCE), Roman poet, best known for his national epic, the *Aeneid*, 235, 432n218

Voltaire, pen name of François-Marie Arouet (1694–1778), French Enlightenment philosopher and writer, 55–56, 159, 234, 237, 248, 421n401, 435n273

Wagner, Cosima (1837–1930), Richard Wagner's wife, daughter of Franz Liszt, 530n77

Wagner, Richard (1813–83), German late Romantic operatic composer, dramatist, and theorist, 34, 40, 42, 50, 53–54, 56, 68, 72, 107–8, 129, 138–41, 143, 145, 183, 216, 223, 225, 230, 232, 234, 236, 238, 240, 242, 250, 253, 289–90, 295, 311, 330, 410n164, 421n391, 421n393, 431n210, 433n244, 440, 442, 444, 446n9, 454n27, 470, 490, 494–95, 498–99, 501, 504, 506–7, 510, 518–21, 529–31n77

Wagner, Siegfried (1869–1930), German composer and conductor, son of Richard Wagner, 494

Wahrmund, Adolf (1827–1913), German orientalist and anti-Semite, 412n209

Weber, Carl Maria von (1786–1826), German composer of the operas *Der Freischütz* and *Euryanthe*, 430n199

Weber, Ernst Wilhelm (1796–1865), German pedagogue and philologist, 413n233

Wellhausen, Julius (1844–1918), German biblical scholar and orientalist, 326, 452n93

Werner, Zacharius (1768–1823), German poet, dramatist, and preacher, 16, 405n52

Werther, protagonist of Goethe's epistolary novel *The Sorrows of Young Werther* (1774), 70

Wieland, Christoph Martin (1733–1813), German poet and novelist, 487

Wilhelm I (1797–1888), German emperor (1871–88) and king of Prussia (1861–88), 518, 528–31

Winckelmann, Johann (1717–68), German classical archaeologist and art historian, 47, 139

Yorick, character in several of Laurence Sterne's novels, 302–3, 305, 440–44, 448n54, 507

Zarathustra (Zoroaster), fictional prophet-hero of N's *Thus Spoke Zarathustra*, 44, 66–67, 72, 74, 77, 83, 85, 93, 108, 119–20, 134, 170, 190, 194, 198, 203, 235, 260–61, 271, 309, 313–25, 327–29, 332–35, 337–38, 340, 343, 345, 348, 350, 354–55, 358, 361–66, 368–69, 371–73, 375, 377, 380–87, 391–93, 447n30, 466, 468, 486, 499, 516–32, 519n63

Zimmern, Helen (1846–1934), translator and popularizer of Schopenhauer in Britain, and acquaintance of N, 492

Zöllner, Johann Karl Friedrich (1834–82), German astronomer and physicist, 78

Subject Index

Future, 68, 73, 79, 191, 271, 314, 324; caring for future of humankind, 321; decisions for, 105; hound of hell called, 353; lawgiver of, 238–40; philosophers of, 245; philosophy of, 127, 130; science and, 40; superior, superhuman, 272; value judgments and, 200

Gauls, 237

Genius, 17, 57, 214, 243, 273, 319–20, 333, 336, 389; abolition of, 13; actor as essence of, 24; blathering about, 113; critique of, 104; Custine and, 15, 404nn46–47; journalistic, 14; rule and, 69; suffering of, 6

Genoa, 11, 248, 303, 402n24; commentary on, 498

Germans, 47, 74, 192, 220–21, 227, 229, 232, 235–36, 244, 247, 281, 289–90, 294, 296, 304–5, 310; dual natures, 208; European culture and, 35; faces of, 70; Germanic tribes, 243–44; lyric poets, 214; migration of, 109; moral mendacity and, 21; more shallow, 276; mystics, 248; philistinism, 253; philosophers, 248, 330; phony German-ness, 225; profundity, 330; Romanticism, 231; ruining us, 253; as rulers, 33; sensibility, 125; skepticism and, 37, 109; slave-like, 116; Slavs and, 219; as stragglers, 37

Germany, 241, 250–51; barbarism of, 33; Christianity and, 231; commentary on, 512; culture in, 64, 331, 415n262; Germanic customs and chastity, 227; "Germany, Germany above everything," 66–67; lack of respect for, 199; music and German culture, 139; not to live in, 311; peasant blood in, 70; the Reich, 67, 208, 219, 231, 237

Gifts, 120, 371, 382

Goal(s), 6, 41, 204, 384; crooked paths toward, 347; English, 192; happiness as, 52, 89, 221–22; intellectual refinement as, 235–36; lacking, 376; lost, 373; of moralists, 31; superhumans as, 192

God, 41, 44, 77, 79, 90–91, 124, 131, 137, 141, 245, 273, 283, 296–97, 304–9, 315, 318, 336, 372; adultery of, 137, 296, 307, 352; aftereffects of the ancient God, 232; as animal, 359, 375–76; becoming one with, 215; belief in, 178, 182; casting away idea of, 239; commentary on, 521–22, 525; creating, 355, 375; on the cross, 75, 90; death of, 323, 351; desire of, 285, 353; as devil, 197; devil keeps distant from, 347, 354; dialogue with, 216; dispensability of, 104; equality before, 90; existence without, 29; as first cause, 187; frailty of, 115; God-murderer, 350; goodness of, 123; of goodness or justice, 117; humans feeling themselves to be, 43; inferior people looking up to, 339; instrument of, 25; intentions in history, 38; Jews measuring selves against, 115–16; lending to, 356, 380; of love, 75, 135, 358–59; loving, 252, 359; mystics and, 248; no God, 71, 76; refuted, 80; as spirit, 322; "thou shalt" and, 239; Trinity, 233–34; as tyrant, 47; will of, 215

Gods, 41, 124, 283, 315; Aristotle and, 10; barbarian, 93; belief in, 58, 119; commands of, 199; creating, 30, 222, as first cause, 187; Greek, 93; guest gods, 287; humans viewed as, 341; mask of, 277; overpowering, 214; perceived differently in antiquity, 88; song of an unknown god, 313; unknown, 342–43; visible, 100

The Complete Works of Friedrich Nietzsche

IN NINETEEN VOLUMES

Library of Congress Cataloging-in-Publication Data

Names: Nietzsche, Friedrich Wilhelm, 1844–1900, author. | Loeb, Paul S.,
    translator, writer of afterword. | Tinsley, David Fletcher, translator, writer
    of afterword. | Nietzsche, Friedrich Wilhelm, 1844–1900. Works. English.
    1995 ; v. 15.
Title: Unpublished fragments from the period of Thus spoke Zarathustra :
    (spring 1884-winter 1884/85) / Friedrich Nietzsche ; translated, with an
    afterword, by Paul S. Loeb and David F. Tinsley.
Description: Stanford, California : Stanford University Press, 2022. | Series:
    The complete works of Friedrich Nietzsche ; volume 15 | "Translated from
    Friedrich Nietzsche, Samtliche Werke: Kritische Studienausgabe, ed.
    Giorgio Colli and Mazzino Montinari, in 15 vols. This book corresponds
    to Vol. 11, pp. 9–422 and Vol. 14, pp. 698–723." | Includes bibliographical
    references and indexes.
Identifiers: LCCN 2021049969 | ISBN 9780804728881 (cloth) | ISBN
    9781503629707 (paperback)
Subjects: LCSH: Nietzsche, Friedrich Wilhelm, 1844–1900—Notebooks,
    sketchbooks, etc. | Philosophy, German—19th century.
Classification: LCC B3312.E5 L64 2022 | DDC 193—dc23/eng/20211104
LC record available at https://lccn.loc.gov/2021049969

Printed and bound by CPI Group (UK) Ltd, Croydon, CR0 4YY

22/06/2023

03229463-0001